The Concept of Causality in the Lvov-Warsaw School

Poznań Studies in the Philosophy of the Sciences and the Humanities

Founding Editor
Leszek Nowak (1943–2009)

Editor-in-Chief
Katarzyna Paprzycka-Hausman (*University of Warsaw*)

Editors
Tomasz Bigaj (*University of Warsaw*) – Krzysztof Brzechczyn (*Adam Mickiewicz University*) – Jerzy Brzeziński (*Adam Mickiewicz University*) – Krzysztof Łastowski (*Adam Mickiewicz University*) – Joanna Odrowąż-Sypniewska (*University of Warsaw*) – Piotr Przybysz (*Adam Mickiewicz University*) – Mieszko Tałasiewicz (*University of Warsaw*) – Krzysztof Wójtowicz (*University of Warsaw*)

Advisory Committee

VOLUME 121

Polish Analytical Philosophy

Editor-in-Chief
Jacek Juliusz Jadacki (*Professor Emeritus, University of Warsaw*)

Editors
Jacek Paśniczek (*Professor, Maria Curie- Skłodowska University, Lublin*) – Jan Woleński (*Professor Emeritus, Jagiellonian University, Kraków*) – Ryszard Wójcicki (*Professor Emeritus, Polish Academy of Sciences*)

VOLUME XIV

The titles published in this series are listed at brill.com/*paph*

The Concept of Causality in the Lvov-Warsaw School

The Legacy of Jan Łukasiewicz

Edited by

Jacek J. Jadacki and Edward M. Świderski

BRILL

LEIDEN | BOSTON

 NARODOWE CENTRUM NAUKI The volume was prepared as part of the project 2016/ 23/ b/ hs1/ 00684 "Kazimierz Twardowski's place in Polish culture and European philosophy", financed by the National Science Centre (Poland).

Cover illustration: A bust of Jan Łukasiewicz by Alfons Karny (1938). Photo by Jacek J. Jadacki (2017). We thank the Podlasie Museum in Białystok (Poland) for its kind permission to use it on the cover of this publication.

The Library of Congress Cataloging-in-Publication Data is available online at https://catalog.loc.gov
LC record available at https://lccn.loc.gov/2022035335

Typeface for the Latin, Greek, and Cyrillic scripts: "Brill". See and download: brill.com/brill-typeface.

ISSN 1389-6768
ISBN 978-90-04-51551-2 (hardback)
ISBN 978-90-04-52224-4 (e-book)

This book is printed on acid-free paper and produced in a sustainable manner.

Contents

PART 1
Jan Łukasiewicz: Analysis and Construction of the Concept of Cause

PART 2
Resonance of Łukasiewicz's "Analysis" in the First Half of the Twentieth Century in Poland

PART 3
The Concept of Causality in Poland Many Years Hence

Notes on Contributors of Part III

Anna Brożek, prof.
Faculty of Philosophy, University of Warsaw / Poland
E-mail: abrozek@uw.edu.pl
ORCID: 0000-0003-1807-7631

Tomasz Bigaj, prof.
Faculty of Philosophy, University of Warsaw / Poland
E-mail: t.f.bigaj@uw.edu.pl
ORCID: 0000-0002-8121-9789

Bartosz Brożek, prof.
Faculty of Law and Administration, Jagiellonian University, Cracow / Poland
E-mail: bartosz.brozek@uj.edu.pl
ORCID: 0000-0002-4324-6700

Bartłomiej Kucharzyk, dr.
Faculty of Law and Administration, Jagiellonian University, Cracow / Poland
E-mail: bartek.kucharzyk@uj.edu.pl
ORCID: 0000-0002-6703-7962

Marcin Tkaczyk, prof.
Faculty of Philosophy, Catholic University of Lublin / Poland
E-mail: marcin.tkaczyk@kul.pl
ORCID: 0000-0003-038-7072

Preface

1

The central text of this volume, comprising the first part, is the classic dissertation of Jan Łukasiewicz (1878–1956) "Analysis and Construction of the Concept of Cause" (1906). Łukasiewicz, a doctoral student (1902) of the founder of the Lvov-Warsaw School, Kazimierz Twardowski, is known in the world primarily as the creator of many-valued logic and Polish logical notation, as well as for his ground-breaking research on classical sentence calculus.

Łukasiewicz's dissertation is the central text because it contains the first analysis in the history of Polish analytic thought of conceptual analysis itself. In addition, Łukasiewicz presents a clear and exact concept[1] of an abstract object Finally, in this text he constructed the concept of cause: for decades, Łukasiewicz's construction was a direct or indirect reference point for all texts on causality created within the Lvov-Warsaw School. The prosaic reason why Łukasiewicz's dissertation did not become such a reference point for texts on causality within other currents of Euro-American analytic philosophy is that until the publication of this volume it was only available in Polish.

One of the many advantages of this dissertation is that it was "constructed" so perfectly that most likely only its author could summarize its results in a way that reflects their excellent "composition".

Fortunately, when it comes to key results, viz., those regarding the concept of cause, the author himself summarized them at the end of the dissertation. There is nothing better than to quote his own summary:

> The purpose of this work has been to give a logical analysis and construction of the concept of cause, thus, to discover the features of the abstract object called cause and to examine the relations obtaining between them. It has not been about constructing some ideal abstract object, but only creating a real concept whose scope includes concrete, real causes.
>
> Using an *inductive* method, I determined, first of all, when it is that we signify some concrete objects by the expression "cause". It turned out

---

1 The Polish term "pojęcie" has two equivalents in English: "concept" and "notion" (comp. Latin "conceptus" and "notio"). However, the English terms "concept" and "notion" are not differentiated in any consistent way. Therefore, the editor decided to translate "pojęcie" everywhere as "concept".

that we use this word only for objects which are correlative in relation to an effect and which stand to an effect in *a necessary relation* such that an object that is a cause necessarily *brings about* an object that is an effect. Having compared various instances of causal relations I then showed that *an effect does not necessarily have to bring about a cause,* and for terminological reasons I excluded from the concept of cause such instances of necessary relations in which both members necessarily imply one another. Having again compared concrete examples of causal relations, I came to the conclusion that they do not involve any special *temporal relation* that would require us to define a cause either as an object simultaneous with the effect or one preceding it. I also showed, on the basis of concrete examples, that a causal relation does not have to occur between nothing else but *changes.*

In examining these features using a *deductive* method, I proved in particular that a causal relation involves another necessary relation running in the opposite direction, which states that the non-occurrence *of an effect necessarily brings about the* non-occurrence *of a cause;* this is also how I showed that the non-occurrence of a cause is not necessarily connected with the non-occurrence of an effect. Using the deductive method, I discriminated further features of the causal relation: *irreversibility* and *transitivity.* The concepts of *direct* and *indirect* causes are connected with the latter. In examining members of causal relations, I showed that they are *relations of having a certain feature by a given object.*

Throughout this study, I had occasion to consider theories I find mistaken. Thus, I attempted to show the falsity of the *substantial* and *empiricist* theory of causality, the falsity of the view that a causal relation can be reduced to the relation of *reason and consequence,* and that a cause must be an *antecedent* or occur *simultaneously* with the effect. Finally, I tried to justify the claim that the terms "efficient" and "cognitive" causes, "complete" and "partial" causes, should no longer be used.

While discussing the necessary relation that connects a cause and an effect, I defined the concept of *necessity,* and I pointed out similar relations of reason and consequence and other nameless unnamed relations of the same kind among abstract objects, calling them all connections of *simple dependence* and distinguished them from connections of *complex dependence.*

ŁUKASIEWICZ 1906: 54–55

2

Twardowski's doctoral student (1904), Marian Borowski (1879–1938), the author of the dissertation "Criticism of the Concept of Causal Connection", opens the second part of the volume.

Borowski begins his considerations by emphasizing the one-sidedness of the traditional understanding of causality. The thing is that the formula:

$\bigwedge x \bigwedge y$ {y is the cause of $x \leftrightarrow [(y$ has existed $\rightarrow$ it is necessary for x to exist)]}.

must be traditionally supplemented by the proviso that:

$\bigwedge x \bigwedge y$ {y is the cause of $x \leftrightarrow \sim [(x$ has existed $\rightarrow$ it is necessary that y has existed)]}.

Borowski believes that this proviso is erroneous, because it suggests that the effect connects with its cause in a "completely random" way; meanwhile, in practice, we sometimes reasonably conclude "from the effect to a cause".

According to Borowski, therefore, the cause of the occurrence of a certain y – more precisely: the proper cause of the occurrence of a certain y – should be considered only as a sufficient and necessary condition for this y:

$\bigwedge x \bigwedge y$ [y is the proper cause of $x \leftrightarrow_{def}$ it is necessary that (y has existed $\leftrightarrow x$ will exist)].

In addition, if we have a cause-and-effect chain of the type:

... z is the cause of $y \wedge y$ is the reason of z.

it is only y, so the direct cause (not z or some previous links of this chain) can be considered the proper cause of x.

In his opinion, the "one-sided" interpretation of a causal relation is due to the inaccurate characterization of what is considered to be the cause of something and what is thought to be the effect of something; usually the characterization of cause is "too broad and too sketchy", and that of the effect "too narrow and too detailed". The point is that the variables x and y, occurring in causal formulas, actually run over entire complexes of phenomena and should be represented in these formulas by the sequences of these phenomena: $x_1, x_2,$ ... x_n – and respectively: $y_1, y_2,$ ... y_n. Then it would come to light that those who accept the admissibility of a "one-sided" interpretation of a causal relation, as an illustration of the fact that the same thing may have different causes, indicate situations in which only one element of such sequences is included – e.g., x_k and y_k. Meanwhile, "the total effects of poisoning, shooting a person, etc., are always different"; they are complexes that admittedly have the same part, "namely the death of a given individual – whereas the rest of the elements are different"; similarly, in poisoning, shooting, etc., there is some common element, if all these complexes are in fact the cause of the complex involving death.

Progress in science lies in the fact that research on causal relations tends to isolate from cause-complexes and effect-complexes those elements that can be rightly considered to be causes and effects assigned to them in one-to-one way.

One consequence of this concept of causality is that the principle of causality, stating (in simplified terms):

$\bigwedge x \bigvee y$ (y is the cause of x).

is equivalent to the principle of "effectivity":

$\bigwedge x \bigvee y$ (x is the cause of y).

3

The question Zygmunt Zawirski (1882–1948) answered in his dissertation "Causality and the Functional Relation" (1910), written under the direction of Twardowski and with reference to both Łukasiewicz and Borowski, presented below, reads: Can the concept of causality be reduced to the concept of function in a mathematical sense (or similar to it)?

From among various senses of the term "function", Zawirski distinguishes the mathematical one. In this sense (limited to the functional relation of two quantities): "the variable quantity y is called "the function of another variable quantity x" in the interval from $x = a$ to $x = b$ if each value of x in this interval is assigned one or more values y according to a certain law ... given in the form of an equation". The mathematical concept of functional relation can be extended to any measurable physical objects; in that case, we speak of a real function.

A functional relation – both mathematical and real – is mutually necessary, and thus symmetric and transitive. This is not the case with a causal relation, which, although transitive, is asymmetric (viz., unidirectional).

Proponents of the reduction of the cause-and-effect relation to a functional relation maintain that in the world we are in fact dealing with real functional relations (mutual and simultaneous), and the idea that it is not the case comes from inaccurate (including non-metric, qualitative) analysis of factual (or metric, quantitative) relations between phenomena.

Zawirski considers this justification of reductionism to be insufficient, because there are cases in which the necessity of a causal relation is mutual, but there are also probably more numerous cases in which, as should be recognized, this necessity is unilateral. In addition, an important element of a causal relation is its temporal nature, particularly the precedence of the cause relative to the effect, and this nature is not captured by the functional relation. Zawirski also does not accept the following reasoning:

Since:

$\bigwedge x \bigwedge y$ {the occurrence of y is the cause of the occurrence of $x \leftrightarrow [(y$ occurs in moment $t_1 \to x$ occurs in moment $t_2) \wedge$ moment t_1 is later than moment $t_2]$}.

so:

$\bigwedge x \bigwedge y$ {the non-occurrence of x is the cause of the non-occurrence of $y \leftrightarrow [\sim (y$ occurs at moment $t_1) \to \sim (x$ occurs at $t_2)] \wedge$ moment t_1 is later than moment $t_2]$}.

The existence of the dependence referred to in the conclusion would mean that there are causes (here: non-occurrence of x) that are later than their effects (here: non-occurrence of y). To avoid such a non-intuitive consequence, it must be assumed that negative states of affairs cannot be considered the cause of anything (in the strict sense of the term "cause").

Zawirski's final answer to the question about the reducibility of the concept of causality to the concept of function is a negative answer, and its simplified justification is as follows: "In order for the concept of a function to be applied to the real course of phenomena, it suffices to state that changes in one quantity are combined with changes in the second quantity. Which of them, however, is really dependent and which is truly independent, that is completely neutral for the application of the concept of function." Ergo: a causal relation cannot be fully grasped in terms of a functional relation.

4

The dissertation by Tadeusz Czeżowski (1889–1981), "How Did the Problem of Causality Arise?" (1933), likewise directed by Twardowski (1914), belongs to the history of philosophy, but the discussion there of the problem of causality in ancient Greek philosophy is preceded by an examination of various meanings of the word "cause" already present in philosophical considerations at that time. Namely, the word has the following meanings:

The cause of that $p =_{\text{def}}$:

(a)   a sentence which results in a sentence stating that p (viz., the logical reason for the sentence 'p');

(b)   the phenomenon preceding that p, which conditions that p (viz., the sufficient condition that p);

(c)   an object which, by acting on an object x, caused that p (viz., the causative agent that p);

(d)   what that p intends (viz., the goal of that p).
        And further, the cause of $x =_{\text{def}}$:
(e)   what x is made of (viz., the matter of x);
(f)   what from within a given object x "impelled" object x, more precisely its
        matter, to be x (viz., the essence of x);
(g)   the first link of the transformation chain whose last link is x (viz., the
        co-origin of elements of x);
(h)   a mental category used for the mental grasp of the "place" of that p
        in the "chaos" of real phenomena (viz., the term locating that p in the
        mental image of the world).

In ancient Greek philosophy, the earliest was the problem of the cause-co-origin of the real world, considered among others by Thales, Anaximander, Anaximenes – with Heraclitus and Parmenides (and later Zeno of Elea and Gorgias) denying that such a thing as a co-cause of what fills the real world and, consequently, would ensure its "unity", exists at all. Then Empedocles and Anaxagoras – and in a more mature form Leucippus and Democritus – raised the problem of the cause-matter of real objects. Plato provided a new approach to cause: he was interested in the causes-goals of what is happening in the real world. Plato situated them in ideas (in an ideal world): every real object is namely a "reflection" of the idea to which it is subordinated.

The first philosopher who was fully aware of the ambiguity of the word "cause" was Aristotle; he distinguished *expressis verbis* five concepts of the cause: (a) and (c)-(f), where he identified the cause-essence of x with the form of x. Aristotle was also the first to formulate the "double" principle of causality: everything that really exists has cause-matter and cause-essence (viz., form). Later philosophers, including Epicurus, took an indeterministic position, which implied a rejection of causalism. Others, and in particular the Stoics, e.g., Zeno of Kition and Chrysippus, were in favor of determinism or generalized causalism; they also recognized that the causes are substances, i.e., entities composed of cause-matter and cause-essence (form), which act as efficient causes. We also owe to the Stoics a clear condition put on the causes that they be prior to their effects.

Reflections on the problems of causality were paradoxical for Skeptics, with Sextus Empiricus at the forefront, trying to show that no acting – which would be the basis of causal relations – is logically possible, and the cause is only a useful mental category. According to Czeżowski, this view would be revived centuries later by David Hume whereby the basic understanding of "cause" is a cause-condition.

5

Józef M. Bocheński (1902–1995) was not a doctoral student of Twardowski or any of Twardowski's students. Thanks to his many years of scholarly contact with Łukasiewicz and a group of Łukasiewicz's Warsaw collaborators he was "tuned in" completely to the ideals of the Lvov-Warsaw School. His dissertation, "The Problem of Causality in the Neo-scholastics" (1935), presented below, shows clearly the mark of the school.

The paper contains a review of positions concerning the concept of cause and the principle of causality based on texts from the turn of the 1920s and 1930s in the circle of neo-scholastics. As these positions can also be found outside this circle, the paper has a general historical value.

In the said circle, the so-called dynamic definition of "cause" is accepted:

$\bigwedge x \bigwedge y$ {y is the cause of $y \leftrightarrow_{\text{def}} [(y$ occurs $\rightarrow x$ occurs$) \wedge y$ really affects the existence of x]}.

In turn, the principle of causality takes the form:

$\bigwedge x$ [(x exists $\wedge x$ is a relative object)$\rightarrow \bigvee y$ ($y \neq x \wedge y$ is the cause of x)].

The starting point for the definition of "relative object" is the principle of sufficient reason:

$\bigwedge x$ [x exists $\rightarrow \bigvee y$ (y is the reason of the existence of x)].

The reason can be internal (when $y = x$) or external (when $y \neq x$). One can say that an object having an internal reason of its existence exists "by itself"; such an object is absolute. While:

$\bigwedge x$ {x is a relative object $\leftrightarrow_{\text{def}} \bigvee y$ [($y \neq x$) $\wedge y$ is the reason of the existence of x]}.

Besides, this is not the only concept of relative object. According to the second understanding of "relative object":

$\bigwedge x$ ⟨x is a relative object $\leftrightarrow_{\text{def}} \bigvee t_1 \bigvee t_2$ {t_1 is earlier than $t_2 \wedge [\sim (x$ existis in $t_1) \wedge (x$ exists in $t_2)]$}⟩.

In the third understanding, a relative object is, in simplified terms, a change.

Le us note, by the way, that the above formulas have two primary concepts (undefined) as parts: y is the reason of x and y really affects the existence of x.

In neo-scholastics circle, all real objects are considered relative (usually in the first sense).

The principle of causality is justified in various ways: inductively, phenomenologically, deductively, or analytically. The principle of causality is justified inductively by those who rely on the fact that in the real world objects other than relative objects have not yet been encountered – by way of external experience. Those who rely on internal experience, justify the fact that the principle of causality is true by means of "substantial insight" into the idea of the relative object. In turn, the deductive justification is based on recognizing the principle of causality as resulting from the principle of sufficient reason. Finally, analytical justification is referred to by those according to whom conceptual analysis leads to the conclusion that the concept of the relative object such that it has no external cause would be an internally contradictory concept.

6

A set of classic texts on the problem of causality, originating within the Lvov-Warsaw School, closes with "The Negative Concept of Causality" (1938) by Mieczysław Kreutz (1893–1971), another of Twardowski's doctoral students (1924). In this short, but rather intricate paper, Kreutz suggests reinterpreting the concept of cause in such a way as to avoid difficulties arising from the problem of justifying causal laws.

Causal laws have the following general form:

$\bigwedge x \bigwedge y\, [(y$ is $P \wedge x$ is $Q) \to y$ is the cause of $x]$.

On the other hand, according to the traditional understanding of "cause":

$\bigwedge x \bigwedge y\, \{y$ is the cause of $x \leftrightarrow_{\text{def}} [(y$ has existed $\to$ it is necessary for x to exist$)]\}$.

Since the definiens of the above definition contains the concept of necessity, no causal law can receive empirical sanction, because nothing happening in the future can have such a sanction, and causal laws claim the right to hold in relation to future phenomena as well.

The reinterpretation proposed by Kreutz concerns two matters.

First, according to Kreutz, elements of the domain of the relation of being-cause are contacts (resp. collisions) of two bodies, say bodies a and b; while elements of the counter-domain of this relation are changes in both contiguous (resp. colliding) bodies, and thus – in our case, a simultaneous change in body x and in body y.

Secondly, according to Kreutz, the contact of bodies a and b is considered to be the cause of, say, change$_A$ of a and change$_B$ of b on the basis that no combination of states of a and b following their contact, not including change$_A$ of a and change$_B$ of b, would be possible.

Schematically, then, Kreutz's proposition can be summarized as follows. Let's assume that:

$\bigwedge x \bigwedge y\, (\sim$ change$_A$ of x occurs $\vee \sim$ change$_B$ of y occurs$) \to (x$ and y are in state $S)$.

Then:

$\bigwedge x \bigwedge y\, \{x$ contacts/collides with $y \to [$contact/collision of x with y causes change$_A$ of x and/or change$_B$ of $y \leftrightarrow \sim \langle\rangle\, (x$ and y are in state $S)]\}$.

Kreutz believes that the impossibility referred to in the above formula is asserted by establishing that these states, the combination of which is impossible, are contradictory. It should be noted that the term "contradiction" is used here in an unorthodox way, because from the examples given by Kreutz, one can see that he only means that the respective states cannot coexist. Let us add that the fact of impossibility of coexistence is always stated on the basis of a law – and usually other than the principle of (non-)contradiction, as Kreutz thought; whereas the necessity of regularity specified in such an extra-logical law is exposed to charges similar to those that concern causal laws.

7

The three authors of the texts in the third part of the book can be considered representatives of the newer generation of the Lvov-Warsaw School. Jacek Jadacki (1946-), the author of these words, studied under Twardowski's scientific "grandchildren"; Tomasz Bigaj (1964-) and Anna Brożek (1980-) were long-time participants of Jadacki's seminars, and the latter also wrote a dissertation under his supervision (2006).

From outside the School circle are: Marcin Tkaczyk (1975-) and Bartosz Brożek (1977-) with Bartłomiej Kucharzyk (1984-). Tkaczyk, however, devoted his master thesis (2001) to Bocheński, and the promoter of his doctorate (2005) was the outstanding Lublin logician, Stanisław Kiczuk; anyone who knows even a little about the history of the recent Polish logic knows that nothing happened therein without the seal of approval of logicians under the sign of Twardowski's School. Bartosz Brożek was a graduate student (2001) and doctoral student (2007) of Stanisław Wszołek, a metaphysician and philosopher of religion, practicing his disciplines in a manner similar to that of Bocheński. Incidentally, Wszołek was also a promoter of Anna Brożek's master thesis (2003), while Kucharzyk was Bartosz Brożek's doctoral student (2019).

Hence, we can say that both Tkaczyk and Bartosz Brożek (with Kucharzyk) are clearly related to the Lvov-Warsaw School. This is evident in their arguments about causality.

8

Anna Brożek's text, "Łukasiewicz on Analysis of Concepts", is the reconstruction and development of Łukasiewicz's general views on conceptual analysis contained in his dissertation presented below, probably the first in such an extensive and deep manner in analytic philosophy.

Łukasiewicz held the function of conceptual analysis in philosophy in high esteem; he believed that it must precede all philosophical research, and in particular the determination of the logical value of sentences that report the results of such research. It was a logical (not psychological) analysis in the sense that it concerned concepts understood logically and was carried out using logical tools. The logical concept, e.g., the concept of A, can be represented by the connotation of the name 'A' or a sequence – in particular a conjunction or an alternative – of properties of designata of name 'A' forming the essence of these designata (without prejudging whether these objects can be identified).

Therefore, the analysis of a concept can be treated as a procedure supposed to establish the essence of the designata of the expression understood in this way, to which a given concept is assigned. The result of this procedure is the definition of that expression.

The analytical procedure must have its database: what we base our decision on, that we consider these and not other properties as components of the connotation of a given expression. It can be an object database (certain subsets of the denotation of a defined expression), a linguistic database (certain sets of contexts in which this expression occurs – existing definitions not excluded), or a mixed (subject-linguistic) database. It is extremely important that the choice of database be deliberate and explicitly specified.

In case the analysis cannot be carried out for fundamental reasons (e.g. when the appropriate denotation is non-predicative) or the results of the conceptual analysis turned out to be unsatisfactory for one reason or another, it must be supplemented either with the reconstruction of the analyzed concept (and, as a result, a new definition must be formulated), or even with the construction of new concept which would replace the "imperfect" one (when, for example, we want to construct the connotation of properties belonging to a predetermined set).

Łukasiewicz also attends to one especially important issue, viz., the case when we decide to construct a new concept – be it a real concept (i.e., one to which real designates correspond) or an ideal concept (i.e., one to which such designations do not correspond). There is only one condition imposed on the construction of ideal concepts: that they do not contain incompatible properties, i.e., those which cannot coexist.

In addition to presenting – and, where necessary, supplementing – Łukasiewicz's concept of conceptual analysis and showing the place of this concept against the background of other concepts appealed to in the Lvov-Warsaw School, Anna Brozek added various critical remarks. One of these concerns the relation, unexplained by Łukasiewicz himself, between the real properties taken into account when analyzing the objects belonging to the object database and the properties included in the analyzed or constructed concept itself. The point is that the simplest solution, namely that the latter properties are "ordinary", real properties, leads to paradoxical consequences.

9

Tomasz Bigaj's text "On the Causal Role of Limit Properties in Physics" is his voice in the discussion on the ontic status of derivative – and thus limit – physical properties, such as instantaneous velocities and accelerations. He considers, in particular, the question whether such properties can participate in cause-and-effect relations.

Bigaj answers that question is the affirmative.

Let us consider, for example, the second law of dynamics, according to which – to recall – the acceleration given at some point to a body of a given mass by a given (unbalanced) force is directly proportional to this force and inversely proportional to the mass of that body at the moment. This principle can be interpreted in terms of causality. The acceleration of an object at a given time, on the other hand, can be seen as a partial cause of its later velocity. It is a partial cause, because the value of velocity is determined not only by the initial acceleration, but also by the initial velocity and the values of acceleration in the intervening moments.

We note, by the way, that the cause-and-effect relation is understood here broadly – as a kind of determination of "effect" by its "cause". Similarly, the cause-and-effect relation is broadly understood when interpreting the causal relation between derivative properties in the example of a bathtub filled with water which on the one hand leaks from the bathtub through a hole in the bottom and on the other is supplemented with an inflow of water from an external source.

According to the author, to deal with the reservations that some put forward regarding the possibility of causal interpretation of similar situations, the appropriate definition of the concept of limit properties has to include derivative properties. And this is exactly the very subtle clarification the author provides.

10

Bartosz Brożek and Bartłomiej Kucharzyk, in the text "Causality in Law", start from the observation that the importance of the concept of cause in law comes primarily from the fact that it is an indispensable element of statements assigning criminal or civil responsibility to people. Generally speaking, someone is responsible for some situation only when that person stands in a certain cause-and-effect relationship with this situation. More specifically, the law is interested in the actions of given persons when: (a) this action – or failure to act – is essentially the intentional (conscious) act of these persons such that they are the perpetrators of that act; (b) the act is "unlawful"; (c) the act is the cause of some undesirable state of affairs considered a criminal offense or when it causes damage to someone.

In the situation described, there are two causal relations: one mental, linking intent with deed, the other physical, linking deed with a punishable state of affairs. At the same time, the first connection, the mental one, has a teleological character, i.e., the goal of the act is to be a specific state of affairs; while the second, physical connection, connects the deed with the realized state of affairs in such a way that this act is considered to be the cause of this state of affairs, since this state is the "expected" state, and considered as well as a necessary condition of this state. Since it is admitted that a given act may have a whole class of effects, the agents are responsible for only some, viz., the "standard" ("proximate") elements of this class. The criteria of "standardness" ("proximity", "non-randomness") are usually intuitive and refer to unspecified "common sense", "life experience of the man in the street", or possibly equally unspecified "rationality" or "scientific knowledge".

The authors of the paper believe that both concepts of causality used in law – the concept of mental cause and the concept of physical cause – "grow out" of the everyday ideas of causality, and do not come from science, in particular physics or philosophy.

As for the everyday concept of mental causality, the main methodological problem attending this concept concerns its genesis. Two positions clash here. According to one position, which on our own responsibility we could call "generalizational", people have "latent" knowledge about the relation between the mental life of individuals and their behavior; supporters of this position differ as to whether it is innate ("natural", "universal") or acquired ("cultural") knowledge. According to the second position, "simulational" (let us add that it has a long tradition in Polish philosophy, reaching back at least to the considerations of Tadeusz Kotarbiński in the 1920s), we simply transfer motivations observed in ourselves to other people.

11

The concept of causality is one of the key concepts in theology – more precisely: in classical Catholic theology – because: (a) the term "causality" is used to define many other theological concepts; (b) the detection of cause-and-effect relations is an important procedure leading to theological theses, including those concerning God. Both the creation of the world and miracles in this world, as well as, for example, prophecy and revelation can be considered – and are considered – in terms of causality.

The trouble is that – this is opinio communis – the term "causality" (including derivative terms) suffers from notorious ambiguity. According to Marcin Tkaczyk, this is ambiguity of a special type: the point is that the individual concepts that are assigned to this term are semantically related to each other, in such a way, however, that there is no property that would be common to all these concepts. Their kinship of these related concepts can be set out in the form of a sequence ordered by means of the relation of being-earlier, and this sequence has a beginning, i.e., there is an "oldest" concept in it.

In the text "Cause and Effect Relationships in Theology", the author considers the oldest ("intuitive") concept of cause-and-effect relation to be the everyday inductive generalization of some facts, such that we are inclined to consider ourselves the "cause" of the opening of an umbrella, but we don't have a similar tendency to consider ourselves the "cause" of the rain from which this open umbrella is to protect us. The second ("natural") concept of causation arises under the influence of the observation that the "cause" (but in a slightly different sense than before, because in the absence of a purposive parameter) of the rain in question is the clouds. Both the intuitive and natural concept of causality refer to ostensive manipulation. They initiate the aforementioned series of concepts, some of which are treated as metaphorical, and some are attached to new terms (e.g., instead of "x is the cause of y" we begin to say: "x calls forth y", "x creates y" etc.).

Detailed analyses of theological "situations" lead the author to the conclusion that all the above-mentioned acts – such as (to recall) the creation of the world, performing miracles, prophecies or revelation – are described in theology by means of concepts that evolved from the initial concepts of cause: intuitive or natural. An interesting case is the so-called instrumental causality (constructed by Saint Thomas Aquinas), which is a crossing sui generis between these two initial concepts.

Tkaczyk – not without regret – states that research on these problems, initiated by students of Łukasiewicz, belonging to the Cracow Circle (above all Jan Salamucha), was interrupted for many decades, and the analysis of problem stated in the title of his article must be started as if ab ovo.

12

My text "The Problem of Causality" functions also as a kind of conclusion and a clamp connecting the texts preceding it.

It is a banal fact that the term "cause" is ubiquitous in life and science. It is therefore surprising how usually clumsy general-dictionary and even "professional" definitions of "cause" and derivative terms are. There is therefore an urgent need to formulate satisfactory definitions of these terms. My proposal for the definition of "cause" in full form is as follows:

$\bigwedge x \bigwedge y \bigwedge t \bigwedge t' \bigwedge m \bigwedge m' \bigwedge o$

⟨(the fact) that x at period t on area m under circumstances o acts in way K on y is the *cause* of (the fact) that y at period t' on area m' changes in way L

$\underset{\text{def}}{\leftrightarrow}$

$\{[(x$ at period t on area m under circumstances o acts in way K on $y \wedge y$ at period t' on/at area m' changes in way $L)$

$\wedge$

$\bigwedge x \bigwedge y \bigwedge \mathbf{t} \bigwedge t' \bigwedge \mathbf{m} \bigwedge m' \bigwedge o$ (x at period $\mathbf{t}$ on area $\mathbf{m}$ under circumstances o acts in way K on $y \rightarrow y$ at period t' on/at area m' changes in way $L)\}\rangle$.

In this formula: variables $x, y, \mathbf{x}$, and $\mathbf{y}$ represent any individuals, variables o and $\mathbf{o}$ any circumstances, variables $t, t', \mathbf{t}$, and t' any periods (of time), and variables $m, m', \mathbf{m}$, and m' any areas (of space); letters K and L symbolize specific types of (processes of) acting-on and changes respectively.

To put it simply: the acting of object x on object y is the cause that y changes when: x acts on y and y changes, and whenever something like x acts on something like y, so often something like y changes.

Against the background of the proposed definition, I am considering, among others: (a) traditional counterarguments aimed at the existence of cause-effect relations, (b) the issue of necessity as a component of the concept of causality, (c) the concept of acting and the circumstances of its occurrence, (d) the nature of change and (e) the principle of causality.

In addition, I sketch how the reconstructed concept of causality relates to the concepts belonging to the "semantic nest" of this concept and thus to the concepts of motivation (in psychology), agency (in praxiology), and the act of creation (in the arts and in Catholicism).

And so (prescinding from generalizations) we have:

(The fact) that the (excited) willingness of x with strength s_1 (from the volitional center of x) aimed at achieving goal c, in conditions w (including, among others, a belief or a sense of x about the reachability of goal c by x through action d), acts on the manipulation apparatus of x – it is the *motive* of the change in the manipulation apparatus of x, which consists in x performing action d.

In turn:

x is in the circumstances o the *perpetrator* of (the fact) that y changes in way $L \leftrightarrow_{\text{def}}$ ((the fact) that x in circumstances o acts in way K on y is the cause (the fact) that y changes in way L).

On the other hand, when it comes to the concept of the act of creation closer analysis shows that on the basis of assumptions adopted in the theory of art and theology, they cannot be reconstructed with the proposed concept of cause-and-effect relations.

13

No modifications were made to the classic texts of the first and second parts of this volume – in particular, neither terminological peculiarities (e.g. in Łukasiewicz's text, the term "object" in the context "object occurs" was preserved, although in the original Polish as well as in the English translation such a combination of words does not sound good), individual neologisms (like Avenarius's "idiosyndems" or "multiponibles"), nor, for example, atypical punctuation (e.g. the material supposition is not marked with quotation marks if it is not present in the original). References to non-English works were also preserved, even if there are presently English translations of them. However, the bibliographic description and the reference system have been unified. All footnotes come from the authors of the individual texts unless they bear initials of the volume editors [JJ&ES] or of the translators [ZG or SW].

14

The initiator of the publication of this volume and sponsor of the translations included in the first and second parts of it is Mieszko Tałasiewicz, the dean of the Faculty of Philosophy and Sociology at the University of Warsaw – and my former graduate (1995) and PhD student (1999).

On behalf of both of editors – and on behalf of the authors of the third part of the book – I would like to thank him for that.

Jacek J. Jadacki
Warsaw, 2020–2021

Figures

PART 1

Jan Łukasiewicz:
Analysis and Construction of the Concept of Cause

Arceo psychologiam.
Analiza i konstrukcja pojęcia przyczyny.
Przegląd Filozoficzny vol. IX (1906), f. II, pp. 105–179

..
.

Analysis and Construction of the Concept of Cause

Jan Łukasiewicz

1

1   *Introduction*

Whoever wants to address any question concerning the "problem of causality" needs to know what a cause means; otherwise, he acts against the rules of a scientific method and exposes himself to errors. Whoever claims, for instance, that every phenomenon has a cause but does not know what a cause is exactly acts like a beginning mathematician who proves that every function has a derivative but does not know what a derivative is exactly.

To know what a cause is, one needs to analyze this concept thoroughly. Although many scholars have tried to accomplish this significant task, I claim, and the following considerations perhaps justify this conviction of mine, that none of these attempts conforms to due requirements of logic. The aim of this dissertation is therefore to carry out anew these basic studies and *provide logical analysis and construction of the concept of cause.*

2   *Concepts are Abstract Objects*

What does it mean to give a logical analysis of a concept? Before I answer this question, I should first specify what I understand by a concept.

Each expression of speech that has some meaning of its own, or each combination of expressions that means something but does not form a sentence, indicates either some *concrete* object existing in the world around us, or some *abstract* object that is not really out there. Expressions such as: the author of *Pan Tadeusz* [Sir Thaddeus], the painting "Holy Virgin who shelters our Bright Częstochowa" indicate real concrete objects; expressions such as: a man in general, a circle in general, indicate unreal abstract objects. Thus, by concepts I understand meanings of such expressions that do not indicate concrete objects, in other words, *by concepts I understand abstract objects.*

What these abstract objects are I cannot specify; I can only point at them, in the same way that I can only point at objects red in color, but I cannot specify the color red itself. I can say though what they are not. For, as I would like to emphasize, by concepts, that is, by abstract objects, I do not understand psychic acts that are formed when we think about some concept, nor any spiritual "images" that can be given to us in an internal experience. What convinces me of this view are the following considerations. Whoever claims, for instance, that a geometrical circle is a closed curve does not make a claim about some psychic act or about some intangible, imitative image of a drawn circle which maybe appears now in his consciousness, but about some unreal object for which this real mental image is a symbol just like the expression "circle". Whoever makes claims about some mental act or about some imitative image and studies their peculiarities[1] is doing psychology; whoever makes claims about a circle and studies peculiarities of a circle is doing geometry. Thousands of people can think about a circle, thousands of presented objects are formed that start at a given time, last shorter or longer, and may significantly differ one from another. A circle as an abstract object is always one and the same and it does not exist in time nor in space, nor in any man's mind.

I do not doubt that nowadays only few will agree with the last sentence. Thus, I would like to show, in at least a few words, the logical error that caused this old, the only correct, "Platonic" view on the nature of concepts to disappear almost completely in modern philosophy.

To present something to oneself is an ambiguous expression. Whoever presents to himself, for instance, a skeleton of Casimir the Great, lying in Wawel, has in their consciousness, along with an act of presenting, as accepted by some, usually as well some imitative or creative image of the skeleton. Maybe they depict in their thought the figure of the king in Wyspiański's famous stained-glass. We call this internal image recreated in thought an object of presentation;[2] it is this "something" that this man presents to himself in a given moment. However, this image refers to a material thing closed in a sarcophagus; it signifies the real and true skeleton of king Casimir; and about this latter, material object we also say that this man presents it to himself. Therefore, we have two distinct objects of presentation: a spiritual image and the real skeleton. Thus, the expression "to present to oneself the skeleton of the king Casimir" means in one case: to have a spiritual image in thought, in another: to think about the real object signified by this image. We may call the internal image the *presented* object and what it refers to the *signified* object. A presented object is always some concrete object of a spiritual state – according to some, it is simply some spiritual state which appears in an internal experience, at times

---

1   Łukasiewicz used three Polish words to signify attributes: "cecha", "własność" and "właściwość". In this text, these words are translated respectively as: "feature", "property" and "peculiarity". [JJ & ES].
2   The Polish term "przedstawienie" (comp. German "Vorstellung") is translated here as "presentation". [JJ&ES].

moving in thought in a lackluster and unclear manner, but then appearing vividly and distinctly, lasting for a while, changing and disappearing; the signified object is in this case the king's skeleton closed in a sarcophagus, covered in faded purple, with a crown on the skull and a scepter on the crossbones, resting in peace in Wawel's cellar. There are some other expressions characterized by the same ambiguity that "to present something to oneself" is such as "to paint a landscape" means to paint a painting, to paint fields and meadows that this painting is to present.

This ambiguity appears also when we apply the expression "to present something to oneself" not to concrete objects but to abstract objects, e.g., a geometrical circle in general. Thus, to present to oneself a circle in general means either to have an image of a circle in thought – to which are connected, as some hold, certain presented judgments[3] – or to think about the object signified by this image. The *logical error* that philosophers usually make is that they fail to distinguish between a presented object and a signified object. In this case too, the presented object is something that appears in an internal experience, a certain *immanent* object that is studied by psychology; however, the signified object in this case is something abstract and *transcendent:* it is a concept of the circle or simply a circle in general the properties of which are studied by geometry. Whoever does not see this difference confuses the two objects and believes that a concept exists in an internal experience as some spiritual image. This is how a theory is formed which, resorting to medieval terminology, might be called *conceptualism,* and which is as mistaken as *nominalism* for which general concepts are just words. Man in general, circle in general, cause in general are neither objects of internal experience nor words; *universalia neque sunt conceptus, neque nomina.* I rehearsed the arguments above using the example of a circle; be that as it may, whoever has grasped the difference between presented and signified objects will immediately see that these considerations are correct.

That conceptualism is nowadays so widely accepted is due to the general direction of modern philosophy. Ever since in the first half of the 17th century philosophy renounced, along with Descartes, an already deteriorating scholasticism it has stood and continues to develop to this day under the sign of psychology. Psychological studies and analyses are certainly very valuable and significant, and they have greatly widened our intellectual horizon. However, I do not hesitate to claim that due to the central and dominant place of

---

3   Polish term "sąd" (comp. German: "Urteil") is translated here consequently as "judgment".
    [JJ&ES].

psychology in philosophical studies we long ago lost the sense and understanding of true philosophy. Logic had to give way to psychology of cognition;
metaphysics, the old, good metaphysics, as understood by Aristotle and the
scholastics, that is, the study of beings, in so far as they are beings (περὶ τοῦ
ὄντος ᾗ ὄν), was moved aside by the theory of cognition and various kinds of
"criticisms"; ethics understood as a normative study about how man should
act is being replaced by more and more psychological analyses of feelings and
ethical dispositions. We have to realize once and for all that psychology, just
as physics or physiology, is not a philosophical science at all; and that logic,
ethics, aesthetics, metaphysics have as much in common with psychology, as
do, e.g., arithmetic or geometry. In order to defend this ideal and to acquire for
it not only a generous justification, among other "points of view", but gracious
recognition in the philosophical world, it is not enough to fight with arguments concerning the totality of this controversy; it also needs to be shown, via
methodically carried out monographs in logic, ethics, aesthetics, or metaphysics, that these disciplines concern vast fields of questions so far either ineptly
studied or not at all, having nothing to do with psychology, and can be solved
independently of psychology by means of a strict scientific method. I consider
this work a monograph of this kind.

As I aim to give a logical analysis of the concept of cause, I will not therefore
investigate what I present to myself, that is, what happens or appears in my
consciousness when I think about a cause, or what someone else presents to
himself while doing so – for that would be a psychological analysis that I am
not concerned with; instead, I will try to specify what the word "cause" *signifies*;
I will try, in other words, to study the *abstract object* that is the meaning of the
word cause.

3   *Analysis of Abstract Objects*

In view of these considerations, it is not difficult to say what it means to give a
logical analysis of a concept, that is – as we now know – some abstract object.
Any object, concrete or abstract, has some properties or features. The features
of a man include "alive", "rational" ...; the features of a circle – "curved", "closed"
... Features of different objects never form some chaotic collection, but an
ordered whole, thanks to being connected to one another by various relations.
Among relations that can connect the features of an object, the most important for us are necessary relations. Thus, we take it for instance, that between
the features of a man "alive" and "rational" there is some necessary relation, as
we suppose that where there is no living organism *nor can* there exist the life
of mind.

With respect to the necessary relations within which features of an object can stand, we normally distinguish two categories: we call *consecutive* those features of an object that result with necessity from its other features, and we call *constitutive* those features from which the former consecutively *result*. A consecutive feature of a circle, for instance, is "equality of all its diameters", because this feature results with necessity from a constitutive feature of a circle: "equal distance of all points of the circumference from the middle".

To give a logical analysis of some concept, that is, of some abstract object, means finding all its features and examining the relations among them, with a particular attention to the necessary relations, that is, singling out the constitutive and consecutive features. To give a logical analysis of the concept of cause means therefore finding all features of the abstract object called a cause and examining the relations among them while at the same time indicating the constitutive and consecutive peculiarities of this concept.

Having defined the task that I want to accomplish in this manner, I cannot deny that there I have a doubt whether it can be solved at all. In particular, there are two difficulties, ἀπορίαι, that must be taken into account.

First of all, it is very doubtful whether one can discriminate all the features of some object. For every object has not only its own features, which are *absolute*, but it also acquires some new features, which we call *relative,* due to its relations with other objects. Thus, for instance, a circle, besides its absolute features "permanent curvature", "equal distance of all the points of the circuit from the middle", and so on, also has many relative features, such as with a given circumference it it always encloses an area larger than any other geometrical figure of the same circumference. The number of relative features of a given object is indefinite, because every object can be connected by some relation with every other object. Therefore, it is impossible to list all the features of a given object; in any case, there are features that do not require a clear identification, such as, for example, that a cause differs from a circle. By openly admitting that I will not be able to discriminate all the features of the concept of cause, perhaps I can avoid the objection that I have not satisfactorily fulfilled envisaged.

The second difficulty is, however, bigger and more serious. Whoever wants to analyze something needs to have some object of analysis. When a chemist wants to examine the chemical composition of calcium carbonate, he needs to have a sample of this substance in front of him; and when a psychologist wants to study the inner state that appears when someone represents a concept to himself, he needs to have this psychic state in front of him. Calcium carbonate can be found in nature and a psychic state can be brought about in oneself. Abstract objects, however, do not exist in the real sense, like pieces of calcium; it is only the human mind that creates them. Some have a given meaning, like, e.g., the concept of circle in geometry; thus, whoever wishes to analyze a circle knows what they are to analyze. But other abstract objects are not specified like this, the concept of cause being one of them.

In our everyday life, we use the expression "cause" very often, and we normally know what to call a cause and what not; however, we usually are not aware *why*, that is, due to what features do we call some things and not other things causes. Hence, we always speak of some cause or other, but a cause *in general*, as an abstract object, is in our life only an empty sound. In science, this term is used to signify some *concept*; however, in this case, there is another difficulty, for different scientists determine this concept differently. Each of them creates therefore a different abstract object which he signifies with the same word. Thus, whoever wishes to analyze the concept of cause encounters a serious problem. What is it that he is to analyze? Certain concrete objects that we call causes in our everyday language, or abstract objects created by this or that scientist?

There is, it seems to me, only one way around this difficulty. We need to accept that there is no pregiven abstract object called cause that we could analyze, and that such an object has to be yet *created*. And to create, that is, to construct, some abstract object, is to find certain features, consider which can be combined and which removed, and by this means arrive at a whole set of features connected by relations constituting the very object in question. While constructing the scientific concept of cause, following the method that I describe in the next section, I will be also able to give all the features that constitute the content of this concept, that is, I will be able to carry out its analysis. This is how the two tasks are brought together: *the analysis and the construction* of the concept of cause.

4 *Construction of Abstract Objects*

Abstract objects, that is, those wholes consisting of various features connected by relations, are constructed by the human mind when we seek either to grasp scientifically given experiences or to create systems of truths regardless of experience and reality. Therefore, in view of the purpose for which a man creates these objects, we can distinguish between two large groups among them.

It is mainly mathematicians and logicians who deal with objects belonging to one of these groups. When, for instance, a mathematician talks about a number e, or about a four-dimensional figure, when a logician forms the concept of reason and consequence or of contradictory objects, he does not care whether in the actually existing world there are any concrete objects which correspond to these abstract objects. No one doubts that there is no four-dimensional figure or a contradictory object, such as, e.g., "wooden iron"; however, a mathematician calculates the dimensions of that abstract figure, and a logician examines the features even of contradictory objects. Such abstract objects that the human mind creates regardless of whether something corresponds to them in reality or not, and, thus, which are not intended to cover concrete objects, may be called *ideal* abstract objects.

A physicist, chemist, biologist, psychologist, sociologist ... deal not only with concrete, particular objects, such as an instance of a ball rolling on a sloping gutter, a certain piece of calcium carbonate, a specimen of a nerve cell under a microscope, successive changes of afterimages in a given man's consciousness, the workers' strike in Łódź in 1892 – but also with abstract objects, that is, concepts [such as] acceleration of heavy bodies, a neuron in general, an afterimage in general, a strike in general. Each of these scientists, while creating concepts of acceleration of gravity, calcium carbonate, a neuron, an afterimage or strike, seeks, however, to construct abstract objects such that some concrete objects fall under them. A chemist, for instance, certainly does not want even to hear about a "calcium carbonate" that besides having one atom of calcium, one atom of carbonate, and three atoms of oxygen, includes also two atoms of hydrogen; for in all likelihood in reality there are no combinations of chemical composition of H_2CaCO_3. Such abstract objects that the mind creates *with regard to* reality, that is, which are supposed to cover some concrete objects, we may call abstract objects with *real* meaning or simply real abstract objects.

All abstract objects that we construct for one of these goals must meet certain conditions if they are to be scientific concepts. An essential condition that all scientific concepts, both real and ideal, must meet is that *they cannot have contrary or contradictory features*, that is, features that necessarily exclude one another. It follows from this condition that all scientific concepts must be unambiguous, that is, they have to have some strictly defined features. For if at some time we assign some features to an object and then different features at a later another time, we create an object that contains a contradiction. Unambiguity is therefore a consecutive feature of scientific concepts because it follows with necessity from another feature which we can simply call the feature of *non-contradiction*. "A geometrical circle" or "calcium carbonate" are, for instance, scientific concepts; but "integer π" is not, because the features "integer" and "irrational" exclude one another. Words signifying scientific concepts are called *terms*.

The feature of non-contradiction is sufficient when it comes to scientific ideal objects. However, real abstract objects, if they are to be scientific concepts, must also be *consistent with reality*, thus, they have to have such features that we either discover or at least surmise about the corresponding concrete objects. This is why we cannot, for instance, add two atoms of hydrogen to the chemical composition of calcium carbonate, because so construed the concept would not be consistent with the calcium carbonate that we find in nature.

From this difference between real and ideal concepts it follows that a different method should be used when it comes to constructing real concepts and when ideal concepts are to be created. When a mathematician wants to define the features of a four-dimensional figure he does not need to, nor can he, appeal to experience; but when a chemist wants to examine the composition of calcium carbonate he cannot, like a medieval monk, lock himself in a cellar and sink deep into his deliberations but instead needs to observe closely the concrete objects that he calls calcium carbonates, weigh and heat them, examine their behavior within other chemical combinations, and so on. It is only when he has collected sufficient experimental material that he can define the features of calcium carbonate in general, again comparing the abstract object created in this way with the corresponding concrete objects. Thus, to create some real concept one needs to employ the *inductive method*.

In constructing the concept of cause, I intend to create such an abstract object that covers all concrete and real causes, the existence of which we accept either in external world or in the world of spiritual[4] phenomena; and I do not mean some ideal object, such as a four-dimensional figure, to which perhaps nothing corresponds in reality. Thus, since I conceive a cause as some *real* abstract object, then I can follow only one path to create it – the inductive method. Just like a chemist who has to examine particular, concrete pieces or solutions of calcium carbonate in order to define the concept of this chemical composition, a metaphysician has to examine the features of particular, concrete causes in order to create the concept of cause. In science, as well as in our everyday lives, there are plenty of cases in which we call certain phenomena or events causes. Thus, we say, e.g., that a flow of electric current through a thin platinum wire is the cause of this wire's heating, the heating of a body is the cause of this body's dilation, stabbing someone's heart with a dagger

---

4   Łukasiewicz distinguishes three predicates: "duchowy" ("spiritual"), "psychiczny" ("psychic") and "umysłowy" ("mental"). [JJ&ES].

is the cause for this man's death, political turmoil or war is the cause of the decrease in financial securities, and so forth. Comparing all these examples we can, thanks to *the method of agreement*, arrive at their *common* features and thanks to *the method of difference* distinguish among these common features certain *characteristic* features that are inherent only for causes. In this way, employing the inductive method makes it possible to discriminate the features of the concept of cause.

However, neither in this nor in any other inductive research can we stop here. The features gleaned by means of the inductive method are but material that requires scientific elaboration. This involves defining the exact meaning of the features that have been uncovered, examining their consecutive features, indicating the relations among them and checking whether some contrary or inconsistent features have not slipped into the content of the concept. In such investigations, we will no longer be able to use the inductive method but will need the *deductive method*. All this labour is simplified insofar as others, by these or similar means, have already tried to discover certain features of the concept of cause; but it needs to be checked whether they have not made mistakes in their research.

By use of the method sketched above, I want to create a non-contradictory, unambiguous, scientific concept of cause consistent with reality. Perhaps this concept will appear as slightly different from usual definitions of a cause found in logic textbooks or works of metaphysics; perhaps it will not even be always consistent with what our everyday speech names as a cause in a more or less shaky and imprecise way. In case of such inconsistency, I will not be able to provide any remedy. It would simply require *breaking the habit* of calling a cause something that does not fall under the concept of cause, just as one needs to break the habit of calling carbonic acid the compound symbolized by CO_2, which is not an acid, but an acid anhydride.

I have reached the end of these introductory considerations which I by no means consider to be an insignificant part of the study. For not only do they provide me with a weapon and an instrument for proceeding in the investigations that follow; they can also instruct the reader about what to pay attention to in *methodically* conducted works of this kind. A work lacking in scientific method is not a scientific work at all but merely fantasizing about science. I would like this to be remembered not only by dilettantes who feel entitled to address philosophical questions, but also true philosophers who too often proclaim with emphasis far-reaching metaphysical views, such as, e.g., that everything in the world has some cause or that the principle of causality is some innate form of cognition, but because they have no clue what a cause is they do not satisfy the simplest rules of scientific method.

2

5   *Correlation of Cause and Effect*

If we compare carefully the examples listed in the previous section, such as that a flow of electric current is a cause for the heating of the platinum wire, or that a war or political turmoil is a cause for the decrease in financial securities, we will notice that we never call *a cause* some object *taken by itself,* but we give it this name because of some other object that is its *effect.* The words "a cause" and "an effect" signify therefore two members of a relation called a *causal* relation, just as the words "a husband" and "a wife" signify two members of a relation called a relation of marriage. Just as we call a man a husband because of a woman who is his wife, and we call a woman a wife because of a man who is her husband, we call some object a cause because of another object that is its effect, and we call some object an effect because of another object that is its cause. Any pair of concepts that stand to one another like the concepts of husband and wife or cause and effect we call *correlated* concepts.

The first feature of the concept of cause obtained by means of the method of agreement is therefore a *correlation with respect to the effect.* This feature is included in all concrete examples of causes regardless of what otherwise someone understands by a cause, and it may be a criterion for finding further features of the concept of cause. For with respect to this feature whatever turns out to be contrary or contradictory will have to be definitely excluded from the content of this concept. Having defined a cause as an object that is correlative with respect to an effect, I can therefore say that *each cause has to have some effect, and each effect has to have some cause.* These claims, which are certain *ex definitione*, should not be confused with the principle of causality stating that every *phenomenon* has to have some cause, and which is not certain as it stands but requires justification.

Given this feature of the concept of cause, further examination concerning the analysis and construction of this concept may be divided into two parts. First, it needs to be examined what kind of relation connects a cause and an effect; second, it needs to be defined what kind of objects can be causes in this relation. In order to clarify how these investigations differ and are connected, the following remarks will perhaps suffice.

Let us signify an object that is a cause with letter A, an object that is an effect with letter B, and the causal relation between them with letter r (*relatio*). From whole ArB, we need to define A. Object A has some features $a_1, a_2, a_3, ...$, regardless of whether or not it is connected with object B by relation r. These features can be either absolute or relative. Because of relation r, which connects these two objects, A acquires some new features $w_1, w_2, w_3, ...$, that are, of course, only relative features. Thus, a man acquires the relative feature of being a husband when he enters into the relation of matrimony. Now, the first part of the task that I intend to accomplish is to identify these relative features $w_1, w_2, w_3, ...$, as it is precisely because of these that we call object A a cause. Then, however, we need to examine also other features of this object to see whether there are some necessary relations between them and the relative features that result from the causal relation. For it may be that not every object can be a cause, just as not every man can be a husband but only a mature and physically healthy man. Thus, the second part of the task consists in examining these other features that object A has to have in order to be a cause. For completeness, I will also discuss, in the same way, the object that is an effect, although only in a short sketch.

In this chapter I turn to the first part of the work and, first and foremost, criticize existing views on the essence of the causal relation.

6   The Causal Relation Is Not a Relation of Activity

When comparing particular cases of what we call causal relations, some scholars, such as Sigwart, came to believe that a common feature of these instances is some sort of acting or bringing-about. If a man moves some weight, if water pours down on a heavy mill wheel, if a cannonball breaks through the steel plating of a dreadnought, if electric current heats a thin platinum wire, these are cases of acting in some way and bringing about changes in the environment which are precisely effects of the activity. That is why we call a man the cause of the weight's movement, water the cause of the mill wheel's turning, the cannonball the cause of the break in the dreadnought's plating, and the electric current the cause of the platinum wire's heating. Therefore, it is always some person, a thing or, in general, some *acting substance* that is a cause, and some *change*, brought about in some other thing or substance that is the effect. A relative feature w_1, because of which we call some object a cause, is thus, according to this view, the feature of "acting" that results from the relation of acting, and a causal relation is precisely this relation of "acting".[5]

---

5   Sigwart's views on the essence of a causal relation are included in his great work [Sigwart 1879a]. In the second volume of this work, on p. 137, Sigwart claims in particular that whoever wants to define the concept of cause, needs to consider the concept of acting, and he continues as follows: "Hier lässt sich zunächst Dreierlei aufstellen. *Zuerst*, dass dasjenige,

Thus, the answer that we receive to the question of what this relation of activity and the feature of "acting" that results from it actually are is usually very insufficient. Sigwart describes a characteristic feature of activity as "the passing over of the activity of one thing into the sphere of another".[6] It is a figurative, not scientific, way of speaking, and it obfuscates rather than clarifies the meaning of this concept. If that is the only way this concept could be "made accessible", it would seem that it cannot be defined at all, much as simple sensual qualities, e.g., the color red, cannot be defined. That a concept of activity is not primitive but can be reduced to primitive elements may be shown in the following way.

Comparing different cases in which we talk about activity shows that we apply this concept above all to a *man*. A man acts *physically* when he lifts or carries weights, when he hauls wheelbarrows or digs trenches, hammers marble or iron, bends something and breaks it or binds it and straightens it: in short, when he overcomes, in any way, some physical resistance with his muscular strength; a man acts *spiritually* when he teaches or convinces others, invokes in them feelings or resolutions, hardens weak characters and transforms distorted ones: when, in general, he overcomes and conquers laziness and stupidity, and spiritual inertia. What do all these instances of activity have in common? Let us look at quite concrete examples. A laborer moves a heavy block of stone on a wagon in order to push it to the road, he leans forward, bends down his head, puts his hands on the stone, flexes and tightens his muscles – the stone moves

---

was wirkt, ursprünglich immer ein *Ding* ist (eine *Ur-Sache*), und dass im eigentlichen Sinne nur von solchen konkreten, einzeln existierenden Dingen ein Wirken ausgesagt wird, wie denn die Verba, welche ein Wirken ausdrücken, zuletzt überall ein solches konkretes Subjekt verlangen; *zum zweiten*, dass das Wirken, wo es am deutlichsten und unabweisbarsten uns entgegenzutreten scheint, ein in bestimmter Zeit eintretendes, momentanes oder eine Zeitstrecke hindurch dauerndes, auf ein anderes Ding gerichtetes Thun ist; *zum dritten*, dass das, was gewirkt wird, eine bestimmte *Veränderung* dieses zweiten Dinges ist, und das sich das Wirken in dem Hervorbringen dieser Veränderung, in der Verwirklichung des Effects vollendet." Translation [Sigwart 1879b: 95]: "Here we may note three points: *First*, that which takes effect is originally always a thing (according to Sigwart *Ur-Sache* literally means "a pre-thing"), and properly peaking, efficient action can only be predicated on concrete things with a particular existence; indeed, those verbs which express efficient action must always have such a concrete subject. *Secondly*, efficient action, where we seem to find it most clearly and indisputably, is action which occurs at a definite time, is instantaneous or persists for a space of time and is directed towards some other thing. *Thirdly*, that which is effected is a definite *change* of this second thing, and the action finds its fulfilment in just this production of change, in the realization of the *effect*." I use the formulation given in this paragraph as a background for assessing the substantial theory of causality.

6   [Sigwart 1879b: 96]. Literally: "das Hineingreifen der Tätigkeit eines Dings in die Sphäre eines andern" [Sigwart 1879a: vol. II, 139].

and falls. Some *movements* of a torso, arms, head are occurring here as well as some physiological changes in nerves and muscles that we experience as pressure or *muscular effort*. With this effort, which is usually followed by *weariness*, the laborer overcomes the stone's *resistance*. Or: a philosopher argues with a naturalist from a materialist school that he has no right to make categorical claims about philosophy, which he does not understand, nor more than he can criticize the theory of elliptic functions or the historical-comparative grammar of Romance languages since he does not have a clue about mathematics or linguistics. Let us suppose that after a longer discussion the naturalist is convinced. In this case too, *movements* of the arguer's vocal chords, of his larynx, tongue, hands and head are occurring, but also some *intellectual effort* in choosing the right arguments and examples to defeat the opponent's reasoning and overcome his *resistance*. This intellectual activity too, just like physical activity, is followed by *weariness*. Therefore, when applied to a man the expression "to act" means *calling forth movements and making an effort, either physically or mentally, in order to overcome some resistance.*

Among these factors, the most significant is this *effort* with which we overcome resistance and which is followed by weariness; for in instances of intellectual activity movements are apparently something secondary and need not occur, as when, for example, a man acts on himself and tries to reach a decision that he finds appropriate albeit difficult to meet. As for physical activity, this effort is a certain muscular sensation resulting from the contraction or tightness of the muscles, and resistance is the feature of bodies that is the cause of a weaker or stronger effort; finally, weariness seems to be nothing else but a modified state of a muscular sensation arising after a lengthy effort, just as when looking for some time at a sheet of white paper a greyish cloudiness arises covering the paper and changing the optical impression. In cases of intellectual activity, instead of muscular sensations other spiritual states emerge that are not well studied as of now, which we describe as an exertion of will or a focus of attention or, in general, as an intellectual effort. Resistance, either of one's own thoughts or of someone else's spiritual states, as well as intellectual weariness, remain, it seems, in the same relation with respect to an intellectual effort as physical resistance or muscular weariness with respect to physical effort. In any case, the *expressions "effort and weariness" signify psychic states possessed by beings endowed with spiritual life, and the concept of resistance remains strictly connected with the concept of these states.*

We apply these expressions and concepts not only to other organic beings who may not have such a developed spiritual life, but also to inanimate objects. Thus, we say about water that it makes an effort to move a heavy mill wheel and overcome its resistance, but it does not exhaust itself as ever more fresh waves flow; a cannonball cuts through the air, penetrates the steel plate of the dread-nought, explodes, and spatters into thousands of pieces crushing everything around, until its fragments roll helplessly on the deck as though exhausted; an electric current forces its way through a thin platinum wire, pushing aside its particles, heating and thicking it, and with its intensity overcoming the resistance of the conductor, until, weakened, it finally returns to the battery. All these expressions: intensity, resistance, fresh, exhausted, helpless, weakened, to penetrate, to force a way, to push (there is some effort in it) have reasonable sense only when we apply them to a living and sentient human. Water *does not feel* resistance, a cannonball *does not experience* effort, an electric current *does not become weary*. However, these, not other factors that we ascribe to animate beings are the proper features of the concept of activity; for where there is no effort and overcoming resistance there is no activity. Thus, when we say that water *acts* or that an electric current *acts*, we use this word in a figurative and *anthropomorphic* way, not scientifically. Animism is a view of primitives people, young children and poets; there is no room for it in science and it should be removed.

It follows from these considerations that whoever defines a cause as some acting object should restrict the scope of the concrete objects that fall under the concept of cause to living organic beings. To put it properly and scientifically, one should say on this view that only a man, a horse, an ox, etc. can be a cause, because these beings have nerves and muscles and some spiritual life, and so they can experience an effort and overcome resistance. There could be no causes in inanimate nature, because the "activity" of a thing is neither making an effort nor overcoming resistance. When water falls on a mill wheel there is only falling followed by, or rather – as we shall soon see – that must be followed by the wheel's movement, but because we have to expend some effort to move the wheel, and we experience its resistance, it appears to us that the same happens with water.

It follows from this reasoning that the relation of activity is not a causal relation, and an acting substance is not a cause. *For there are many examples of the occurrence of causal relations albeit absent activity.* Perhaps not everyone will accept the validity of these arguments, as they will claim that to act means something other than making an effort to overcome resistance. If so, they should define exactly the meaning in which they want to use this word; and if they maintain that this word signifies some primitive element that cannot be specified more closely, they should point at instances of such primitive activity, just as you can point at red objects, and, using concrete examples, they should prove beyond doubt that activity includes something other than, e.g., relations of necessary succession, just as by using concrete examples you can show beyond doubt the difference between the colors red and green. Appealing to some indefinite feeling or defining the concept of activity as unclearly as Sigwart did is unacceptable in science.

In addition to the above argument, which relies on the analysis of the meaning of the expression "to act", there are other arguments to prove that the view under discussion is mistaken. Thus, on that view, only some acting *substance* can be a cause, so, e.g., a man, water, a cannonball, an electric current (as some "fluid"), etc. However, it is not difficult to show that to treat a thing or a person, substances in general, as causes is inaccurate at best. If a laborer only stares at the block, he is supposed to move but does not set to work, if water stands still in a carafe on a table and a cannonball is stuck motionless in the barrel of a cannon, if an electric current found a quicker way and carefully skips the uncomfortable passage through the thin platinum wire, then these are not the causes of the stone's movement, the mill wheel's turning, the dreadnought's walls breaking, the platinum's heating. It is the laborer's *effort,* the water's *falling,* the balls' *penetrating* the steel plate, the current's *flowing* through the wire, thus, what we correctly or not call *acting*, that are the actual causes of these changes. *And if acting is a cause, it cannot be this tie that joins a cause and an effect, because acting does not act, just as walking does not walk.*

The third argument is even more convincing as it is deductive: A cause cannot be identified with an acting substance; for how often do we speak of instances of *inefficient* acting? A man who would move a rock face reaching to the sky, however hard he tries and strains, would not "do" anything. Someone might say that even in this case some small changes occur in the structure of the rock's particles, and so there would be some effect; I don't deny this, but I can think without contradiction that there would be no changes at all. Thus, there was an acting object, there was acting, but no *change was brought about,* so there was no effect. When there is a cause, however, there must be an effect; from this it follows that an acting object and a cause are not one and the same thing.

It seems to me that this argument is conclusive. The concept of cause as an acting substance cannot be maintained, as it contains contradictory features. *For one may claim, without contradiction, that there is an acting substance but no effect, but one may not claim, without contradiction, that there is a cause but no effect.* At the same time, we see from this how useful the deductive method is in these studies. On the strength of the already acquired feature "correlative with respect to an effect", one may claim without hesitation that the feature "acting" cannot be the relative feature of objects due to which we call them causes.

I do not doubt that there are also other arguments that could show just as well the flaws in the view I am arguing against. For all false judgments have this particular feature that they can be attacked from various angles, while true judgments very often show a surprising connection with truths that were discovered in a completely different way and for completely different purposes.

I thought it was appropriate to discuss this stubbornly persisting *substantive* theory of causality more broadly, as I find it not only mistaken, but also damaging, because "activity" combined with "force" and "substance" leads to a metaphysical view of the world which, although it may withstand the bullets fired by "the theory of cognition", it will not be able to defend itself against logical principles of scientific investigation. The *empiricist* view acquired its right to great scientific merit by removing the concepts of substance and activity from metaphysics; and it is perhaps the main significance of David Hume that he was the first to show the error of the claim that we perceive not only that by its action a cause brings about an effect, but also how it achieves this.[7]

7   *The Causal Relation Is Not a Relation of Constant Succession*

Although English philosophers, who normally admire the empiricist orientation, which, by the way, has a lot in common with psychologism, exclude the concepts of substance and activity from the causal relation, considering them to be metaphysical speculations, they do not create anything new in place of these concepts since being given to empiricism and psychologism they cannot, despite the sharpness and clarity of their thinking, access philosophical questions from the proper angle. Hume describes a cause as *"an object followed*

---

7   Hume carried out his classical studies of a causal relation twice, in his main work: [Hume 1739–1740], part III, ch. XIV (Of the Idea of Necessary Connexion), and, in a slightly changed form, in [Hume 1748], ch. VII of the same title. Insofar as I agree with Hume that we never perceive the *necessity* that connects a cause and an effect, nor the *acting* of a cause, I find completely mistaken both his definition of a cause, which I discuss in the next section, and his view on necessary relations. That Hume was stuck deep in psychologism, the characteristic mark of almost all modern philosophy, is shown, for instance, by a paragraph from the cited chapter of [Hume 1739–1740: 460], where Hume maintains that a necessity occurring between the equality of a product of 2×2 and a number 4, or between the equality of a sum of the three angles of a triangle and 180 degrees, is due solely to the *mind's activity* with which we consider and compare these ideas. It takes, to put it cautiously, great logical sluggishness not to notice that such a view leads to complete *subjectivism* in mathematics and hence to *skepticism* which consequently should not admit even the law of non-contradiction. When Hume considers where the idea of force may come from, he admits in a note to chapter VIII of [Hume 1748: 56] that the concept of physical effort falls in significant part under this colloquial and imprecise idea of force that we brought into being. I intend to carry out this thought with respect to the concept of acting.

by another; with all objects similar to the first being followed by objects similar to the second".[8] John Stuart Mill says that a cause is an "unchangeable and absolute *antecedent*", where by "absolute *antecedents*" he understands such phenomena which are constantly followed by other phenomena, regardless of the behavior of any other objects.[9] Both these views are sometimes summarized with a short, but not very precise expression: *a cause is a constant antecedent and an effect is a constant consequent*. Thus, e.g., the flow of an electric current is the cause of the heating of the platinum wire, for on every occasion when the current flows, the heating of the wire occurs. A causal relation is therefore, according to these scholars, a relation of *constant succession*, and the relative feature w_1 due to which we call an object a cause is the feature "constantly preceding".

In these expressions we can distinguish two factors: a relation of "temporal" succession and a relation of "constant" succession. A significant majority of scholars agree that there is some relation of temporal succession between a cause and an effect. Whether this view is correct we will see later; here let us only point out that virtually all philosophers agree that the relation of temporal succession is not the essence of the causal relation. What is *post hoc* doe not have to be *propter hoc*. The feature "preceding" cannot therefore be the relative feature w_1 in question which characterizes some object as a cause.

Hume and Mill are perfectly aware of this; that is why they supplement their definitions with another factor – the constancy of succession. But even superficial consideration shows that this correction does not at all change the relation of some concrete cause to its concrete, individual effect. That *always*, on each occasion when an electric current flows a platinum wire is heated, does not mean that in a *single* case where these two phenomena occur their relation would be *different* from there not being a constant succession between

---

8   In the original work, this expression is formulated as follows: (a) [Hume 1739–1740: 465]: "We define a cause to be an object precedent and contiguous to another, and where all objects resembling the former are placed in like relations of precedence and contiguity to those objects, that resemble the latter." [...] (b) [Hume 1748: 63]: "We may define a cause to be an object followed by another, and where all the objects similar to the first are followed by objects similar to the second."

9   [Mill 1843: vol. III, ch. IV, §6]: "We may define, therefore, the cause of a phenomenon to be the antecedent, or the concurrence of antecedents, on which it is invariably and *unconditionally* consequent." [...] To the concept of "unconditional consequence" Mill relates the concept of necessity; the way he understands it is, however, mistaken and, as an empiricist, he does not show much predilection in favor of this concept. For we can read in the same paragraph 6: "If there be any meaning which confessedly belongs to the term necessity, it is *unconditionalness*. That, which is necessary, that, which *must* be, means that, which will be, whatever supposition we may make in regard to all other things" [...].

them. From this it follows immediately that neither can the feature "constantly preceding" which, when applied to individual, concrete cases, means nothing more than simply "preceding", be this relative feature of objects due to which we call them causes.

Hume senses this objection, since he admits himself that "there is nothing in a number of instances, different from every single instance, which is supposed to be exactly similar", and he tries to omit this difficulty with a certain psychological ploy. That is, he says that the mind's attitude is different in regard to cases of constant succession than in regard to other events that do not follow one another, and that in cases of constant succession the mind "is carried by habit, upon the appearance of one event, to expect its usual attendant, and to believe, that it will exist" [Hume 1748: §122]. For example, someone who has often seen that one billiard ball's hitting another is followed by the second ball's movement has become *used* to expect this latter event as soon as the former occurs. On the basis of this psychological analysis, Hume gives a second definition of cause: a cause is *"an object that is followed by another and whose appearance always conveys the thought to that other"*.[10]

---

10   Hume formulates the psychological "pendants" of the definitions cited in note 8 as follows: (a) [Hume 1739–1740: 465]: "We define a cause to be an object precedent and contiguous to another, and so united with it in the imagination, that the idea of the one determines the mind to form the idea of the other, and the impression of the one to form a more lively idea of the other." [...] (b) [Hume 1748: 63]: [We may define a cause to be] "an object, followed by another, and whose appearance always conveys the thought to that other". [...] The section in *Enquiry* in which both definitions of a cause formulated by Hume can be found is so characteristic for the whole empiricist standpoint of this great, after all, philosopher that I do not hesitate to quote it in here *in extenso*: [...] "And what stronger instance can be produced of the surprising ignorance and weakness of the understanding than the present? For surely, if there be any relation among objects, which it imports to us to know perfectly, it is that of cause and effect. On this are founded all our reasonings concerning matter of fact or existence. By means of it alone we attain any assurance concerning objects, which are removed from the present testimony of our memory and senses. The only immediate utility of all sciences, is to teach us how to control and regulate future events by their causes. Our thoughts and enquiries are, therefore, every moment, employed about this relation: Yet so imperfect are the ideas which we form concerning it, that it is impossible to give any just definition of cause, except what is drawn from something extraneous and foreign to it. Similar objects are always conjoined with similar. Of this we have experience. Suitably to this experience, therefore, we may define a cause to be *an object, followed by another, and where all the objects similar to the first are followed by objects similar to the second.* Or, in other words, *where, if the first object had not been, the second never had existed.* The appearance of a cause always conveys the mind, by a customary transition, to the idea of the effect. Of this also we have experience. We may, therefore, suitably to this experience, form another definition of cause, and call it, *an object followed by another, and whose appearance always conveys the thought to*

It does not require much to show that this view is false; pointing out two things will suffice. First, one can indicate plenty of cases that involve the features listed by Hume but in which there are no causal relations. Suppose that someone has a chiming clock in his bedroom, and he always hears when waking at 6 a.m., after the clock has struck the hour, a bugle-call from a nearby church tower. Over the course of many years he became used to this, and whenever he hears the clock striking that hour he thinks of the bugle-call, expecting it will follow. Thus, we have in this case "an object that is followed by another and which appearance always leads our thought to this other object"; but the striking of the clock in this man's bedroom is not the cause of the bugle-call in the tower. Second, there are objects that we call causes which do not have the features listed by Hume. Whoever knows nothing about the features of selenium and stands in front of a microphone which can be connected to electricity only via a bar of selenium plugged into a conductor, will certainly not think that if a ray of light hits selenium there will be a crackle in the microphone. However, it is the ray of light hitting the selenium that definitely is the cause, even if only an indirect one of the crackle in the microphone, because it has been shown that selenium illuminated conducts electricity much more efficiently than in the dark. Therefore, Hume's psychological ploy cannot be maintained.

Moreover, the same arguments that I used here can be raised also against non-psychological definitions of cause formulated by Hume and Mill. I give them here not because I believe that the objection raised above ("constantly preceding" in any particular case means simply "preceding") is not sufficient to undermine this thesis, but because it is precisely these arguments that are most often brought forth and apparently have considearable impact. Thus, first, one might point to instances of constant succession in which causal relations do not occur. In our latitude day constantly succeeds, within a certain number of hours, night, and night constantly succeeds day; however, no one would want to claim that a day is the cause of a night or that a night is the

---

that other. But though both these definitions be drawn from circumstances foreign to the cause, we cannot remedy this inconvenience, or attain any more perfect definition, which may point out that circumstance in the cause which gives it a connexion with its effect. We have no idea of this connexion; nor even any distinct notion what it is we desire to know, when we endeavour at a conception of it. We say, for instance, that the vibration of this string is the cause of this particular sound. But what do we mean by that affirmation? We either mean, that *this vibration is followed by this sound, and that all similar vibrations have been followed by similar sounds.* Or, *that this vibration is followed by this sound, and that, upon the appearance of one, the mind anticipates the senses, and forms immediately an idea of the other.* We may consider the relation of cause and effect in either of these two lights; but beyond these, we have no idea of it."

cause of a day. Wherever the Polish language is heard, the words of the prayer "Mother Cordial" are constantly followed by words "People's Protectress"; the former pair of words is not, however, the cause of the latter pair. Second, one might bring forth, or at least think of, cases in which a causal relation occurs but constant succession is lacking, as the objects connected thereby existed only once. A group of asteroids, that could have been formed – as astronomers suppose – as a result of the disintegration of a huge planet, circulates between Mars and Jupiter; this cosmic catastrophe, if it happened at all, certainly had some cause, even though it happened maybe only once in our solar system. Therefore, the concepts of constant succession and causal relation do not overlap but criss-cross. Hume's opponent, Reid, was already aware of that; the same argument was made as well by Meinong.[11]

The empiricist theory of causality is correct only insofar as it shows that we do not perceive any tie that would bind a cause and an effect. But to infer from this that we cannot accept any tie of this kind or even that there simply is no connection in the world among phenomena other than temporal succession is at least as mistaken as claiming that the tie connecting a cause and an effect is some undefined relation of activity. Pure empiricism, which in the form of *empiriocriticism* has so many followers even in Poland unfortunately, is a theory that not only cannot be consistently sustained, it cannot even answer to the right requirements of scientific investigation.

8   *The Casual Relation Is a Necessary Relation*

Proponents of both the substantial and the empiricist theory of causality normally sense quite well where the essence of causal relations lies; but because they cannot define this singular factor properly and explain its meaning to themselves, they either negate it completely, in the case of empiricists, or reduce it to substance and activity, in the case of the substantivists. This proper factor of causal connections is some *necessary relation*.

If we think carefully over why we do not call day the cause of night, even though it constantly precedes night, it turns out that we do not recognize any necessary relation between day and night. The phenomenon of nocturnal

11   Reid held that a causal relation cannot be understood as a relation of constant succession, because if it were, night would turn to be the cause of day, and day of night. Faced with this correct objection, Mill adds the feature of "unconditionality" to his definition of a cause (see [Mill 1843: vol. III, ch. IV, §6]). Alexius Meinong, a professor at the University of Graz, gave a first sketch of the general theory of relations in his work [Meinong 1882]. There are many accurate thoughts in this work, although it is written from a psychologistic point of view. The relevant notes are on pp. 123 and 124.

darkening is not a necessary consequence of diurnal brightness but an effect of the earth's rotation around its axis which causes the solar rays to strike one place on earth after another; and if we consider why we call the diurnal rotation of the the *cause* of night, we will see that we do this because we take there to be some *necessary* relation between the turning of the earth's luminescent hemisphere away from the sun and the places on this hemisphere that are becoming darker. The same happens in every other instance of the causal relation. We call an electric current's flowing through a thin platinum wire the cause of the heating of this wire, because we suppose that the wire *has* to heat up if an electric current flows through it; we call water's falling on a heavy mill wheel the cause of the wheel's turning, because we suppose that when water falls on the wheel, it *has* to turn; we call stabbing some man's heart with a dagger the cause of his death, because we suppose that when someone has their heart stabbed, they *cannot* live; we call a war or political turmoil the cause of the decrease in value of financial securities, because we suppose that in the face of these events the value of securities *has* to lower. If we assumed that these events and phenomena that we define as causes and effects are not connected necessarily but only *randomly* follow one after another, we would not be able to formulate any general law nor predict the future; the entire scientific and practical value of the concept of cause lie precisely in this necessary relation. Thus, on this view, which is shared, among others by Meinong and Höfler[12] and many other scholars, a causal relation is a *necessary relation*, and the relative feature w_1, due to which we call some object a cause, is the feature *"entailing or bringing-about with necessity"*.

In the next chapter, I will exhaustively answer the question about what this necessity is that connects a cause and an effect. Here I would like to address certain misunderstandings that many readers might have entertained and that perhaps could prejudice further studies in this direction.

Having defined a cause as an object necessarily entailing or bringing about some other object – where by the word "bringing-about" I obviously do not understand an activity – I omit the objection that I raised against defining a

---

12   [Meinong 1882: 124]. Alois Höfler, a professor at the University of Czech Prague, co-authored, together with Meinong, one of the best logic textbooks [Höfler 1890] the only flaw of which is that it is written from a psychologistic point of view. However, this psychologism does not, in principle, negatively affect the results of the logical studies in this book, because Höfler is an exceptionally clear and a scholastically – in the positive sense of this word – trained thinker. Formally, the section concerning a cause, which can be found on pp. 63–68 of this book, is excellently constructed. I consider it my duty to bring Polish readers' attention to such excellent works, because not only in Poland, but also abroad, they are not sufficiently recognized.

cause as an acting object, namely that this definition contains a contradiction due to the correlation of cause and effect. For necessarily if there is an object that *brings about*, then necessarily there *must* be some other object brought about that is the effect of the former. Were there no object brought about, we could not say that some other object brought it about *with necessity*. Thus, the features "bringing about" and "necessarily brought about" indeed are correlative features, and they result from the necessary relation connecting a cause and an effect.

Therefore, if by this reasoning I do not encounter any objection that would immediately, on the spot so to say, banish my theory, I still have to take into account another, incomparably more serious, difficulty of the following kind.

I noted in §4 that "in constructing the concept of cause, I intend to create an abstract object that covers all concrete and real causes, the existence of which we accept either in the external world or in the world of spiritual phenomena; and I do not mean some ideal object, such as a four-dimensional figure, to which perhaps nothing corresponds in reality".

Now, someone might object that what I am doing is exactly the opposite, because I include in the concept of cause a feature that concrete and real causes lack. Already Hume proved, with extremely sharp and accurate arguments, that just as we do not perceive an activity connecting a cause and an effect, we do not perceive any necessary tie between them either. Hence, can it be maintained that the concept of cause as an object that necessarily brings about some other object is a real concept?

My answer to this question is positive. For that we do not perceive this feature in concrete objects called causes does not mean that these objects lack it. A chemist calls gold a chemical element, even though no one as of now has *seen*, or with some other senses *perceived*, that gold is not composed of some other simpler elements; and there is a serious doubt whether it could ever be possible to visualize the elementary character of gold.

However, no one has a right to object to chemistry that the concept of gold that it creates is, like the concept of a four-dimensional figure, a merely ideal abstract object scope of which does not include concrete pieces of gold. On the basis of numerous and repeatedly confirmed experiences we are *justified* in supposing with high probability that gold cannot be chemically decomposed, and our concept of gold would turn out to be ideal only if someone managed to find facts that are inconsistent with the features that contemporary chemistry ascribes to gold.

The same right that chemistry and physics and all the other empirical sciences are correct to invoke, which allows them to ascribe to concrete objects such features that, although they cannot be directly established, can be assumed with high probability to exist on the basis of facts established, is a right that belongs to metaphysics. Thus, we can ascribe to concrete causes some mark of necessity, even though we do not perceive it, if only our assumption can be, in some fashion, justified by some other facts.

However, to reach such a proof, it is not sufficient to appeal solely to the fact that, consciously or not, in science as in life, despite numerous contrary theories, we only speak of causes when we recognize some necessary relation. The only way in which we can justify this assumption is, just as with any other hypothesis, by examining the consequences to which it leads and compare these consequences with the behavior of real objects and phenomena. And in order to acquire these consequences, we must first carefully analyze both the *concept of necessity* and the *features* of this necessary relation connecting a cause and an effect. I expect to show in the next chapter that this is a domain of investigation so far ignored. Modern philosophy had an open mind to only those aspects of the problem of causality that were related either to the theory of cognition, this weird creature of psychologism, or to the modern, distorted concept of metaphysics; logico-metaphysical investigations in the old style, modeled on Aristotle, were almost unknown. That is why it is not strange that, so long as it was in thrall to an imprecise and sketchy concept of cause, philosophy could not properly solve any question concerning this problem of utmost significance for all our knowledge.

3

9   *Properties of the Necessary Relation that Connects a Cause and an Effect*

In the previous chapter I showed, using the method of agreement, that in every causal relation we acknowledge the existence of some necessary relation that connects a cause and an effect. This is, of course, only an assumption, since we do not perceive necessary relations in nature; in order to justify this assumption, we need to show that its consequences are consistent with facts and allow the prediction of new facts. However, first and foremost, before turning to this task, I will examine the properties of this necessary relation that is said to occur between a cause and an effect, and I will give a definition of the concept of necessity.

In order to, first, solve the former of these tasks, I will use a symbolic representation that is used to considerable effect in the mathematical sciences. Consider two objects P_1 and P_2; let P_1 signify, e.g., electric current, and P_2 – a platinum wire. Let us call the features of these objects the *flowing* of electric current through a platinum wire and the *heating* of the wire, c_1 and c_2, respectively. The flow of electric current is the cause, and the wire's heating is the effect. When P_1 has c_1 (when electric current is flowing through the wire), we suppose that P_2 *must* have c_2 (that the wire must be heating); between the having of c_1 by P_1 and the having of c_2 by P_2 we thus accept the existence of some necessary relation. If having c_1 by P_1 we simply signify by letter p_1 and having c_2 by P_2 – p_2, we can express symbolically this necessary relation by putting these two letters together p_1p_2; symbol p_1p_2 means therefore that when P_1 has c_1, P_2 must have c_2. We assume that there is the same necessary relation in every other instance of a causal relation, the only difference being that P_1 and P_2, as well as c_1 and c_2, stand for different objects and features.

There is another necessary relation that coexists with relation p_1p_2, a relation that runs in the opposite direction. If P_2 *must* have c_2 when P_1 has c_1, then obviously P_1 *cannot* have c_1 when P_2 does not have c_2; if P_1 had c_1 and P_2 did not have c_2, there would appear to be a contradiction. If by n_1 we understand non-having c_1 by P_1, and by n_2 non-having c_2 by P_2, we can signify symbolically this latter necessary relation as n_2n_1; symbol n_2n_1 means therefore that when P_2 does not have c_2, P_1 cannot have c_1. When we suppose, for example, that the flowing of the electric current entails with necessity the heating of the platinum wire, we have to assume also that when the wire is not heating, the electric current cannot be flowing through it. Based on these considerations, we may lay down the following rule: *the occurrence of a cause entails with necessity the occurrence of an effect, and the non-occurrence of an effect entails with necessity the non- occurrence of a cause.*

Whereas we do suppose that the flowing of electric current brings about with necessity the heating of the platinum wire, we do not assume that, conversely, the heating of the wire entails with necessity the flowing of electric current. It is the same in many other cases: water's falling on a wheel mill brings about with necessity the wheel's movement, but, conversely, the wheel's turning is not necessarily connected with water's falling; stabbing a man's heart with a dagger necessarily entails this man's death, but, conversely, a man's death does not necessarily imply stabbing with a dagger; war or political turmoil necessarily influence a decrease in financial securities, but, conversely, the decrease in the value of securities is not necessarily connected with war or political turmoil. Thus, the simple relation of necessity, which by analogy to the previous cases may be signified by p_2p_1, does not figure among causal relations; that is, when P_2 has c_2, P_1 does not have to have c_1. It follows from this that relation n_1n_2, which necessarily coexists with relation p_2p_1, as can be shown in the same way in which I previously showed the coexistence of relations p_1p_2 and n_2n_1, does not figure among such cases either. There are, indeed, instances of causal relations where in addition to relations p_1p_2 and

$n_2 n_1$, there are also relations $p_2 p_1$ and $n_1 n_2$. Thus, e.g., if we heat or cool two soldered pieces of bismuth and stibnite, electric current must appear in these metals (Seebeck); and conversely, if electric current appears in two soldered pieces of bismuth and stibnite, the soldered joints must heat or cool (Peltier). Thus, in this case there is a (supposed) necessary relation consisting of four simple necessary relations $p_1 p_2$, $p_2 p_1$, $n_1 n_2$, $n_2 n_1$, that occur between the flowing of electric current in two soldered pieces of metal and the heating or cooling of the soldered joints. However, since such instances exemplify necessary relations of a *different type* than the majority of causal relations, and it is necessary relations that, by all probability, are the most prominent characteristic of causal relations, I find it appropriate to exclude connections consisting of four simple necessary relations from the scope of causal relations and to give them a different name. Together with so-called relations of *necessary coexistence* that represent the same kind of necessary connection, they may be said to fall under a common category of *complex* or *mutual dependence*. Such a relation obtains, e.g., between increasing the length of a lever's arm and decreasing the weight needed to balance the other arm, because the occurrence of one of these phenomena implies with necessity the occurrence of the other.

Thus, based on these considerations we may lay down another rule: *the occurrence of an effect does not necessarily bring about the occurrence of a cause, and the non-occurrence of a cause does not necessarily bring about the non-occurrence of an effect.*

Therefore, excluding two simple necessary relations, the causal relation also consists of two non-necessary relations: when P_2 has c_2, P_1 does not have to have c_1, and when P_1 does not have c_1, P_2 does not have to not have c_2. If we use symbols (p_2, p_1) and (n_1, n_2) for these non-necessary relations, we may represent the relation that connects a cause and an effect with the following formula:

$$Z = p_1 p_2 + n_2 n_1 + (p_2, p_1) + (n_1, n_2).$$

The above analysis leads to an important but not well-known consequence: *a causal relation combines necessary and non-necessary relations.* Of course, we also need to keep in mind that the view that a causal relation contains necessary relations is at present only an assumption, and the purpose of this consideration is simply to show what this assumption needs to be if it is to be non-contradictory and compatible with facts.

Simple necessary relations that are supposedly involved in a causal relation are much more significant than non-necessary relations; this is also why some of their features leave a characteristic mark on the overall relation. I would like to consider two of these features in more detail. Both simple necessary relations are, first, asymmetric. Because two objects, A and B, are in a *symmetric* relation if A is to B, as B is to A, e.g., brother-brother; but if A is in a different relation to B than B to A, as, e.g., father-son, the relation is *asymmetric*. Such an asymmetric relation occurs between two objects if they are connected by relations p_1p_2 or n_2n_1; for p_1p_2 signifies that having c_1 by P_1 brings about with necessity having c_2 by P_2, and having c_2 by P_2 is brought about by having c_1 by P_1, it does not, however, signify that having c_2 by P_2 brings about with necessity having c_1 by P_1. The same applies to relation n_2n_1. In general, no simple necessary relation is symmetric. An appropriate combination of asymmetric relations may indeed create complex symmetric relations, such as, e.g., relations of mutual dependence in which A necessarily brings about B, and B necessarily brings about A. *A causal relation, however, does not contain such a combination, thus this relation is asymmetric.* Members of asymmetric relations are not synonymous; that is why we normally use different names for them – in this case we use words "a cause" and "an effect" – whereas for members of symmetric relations we usually use the same word, as in, e.g., brother-brother, alike-alike.

Second, both these simple necessary relations included in a causal connection are transitive. When a relation has a peculiarity such that when it occurs between objects A and B and between objects B and C, it also has to occur between objects A and C, we call it transitive; otherwise, it is intransitive. For example, the relation of identity is transitive, so when $a = b$ and $b = c$, a has to be equal to c; whereas a relation of fatherhood is intransitive, as when X is the father of Y, and Y is the father of Z, X is not the father of Z, but is the grandfather of Z. Relation p_1p_2 is transitive because when p_1 entails with necessity p_2 and p_2 entails with necessity p_3, p_1 necessarily implies p_3 too. The same applies to relation n_2n_1. *Since a causal relation involves transitive necessary relations, we may call it transitive.*

This peculiarity of a causal relation is the basis of the concept of direct and indirect causes. Suppose that we are given three objects P_1, P_2, and P_3 that stand in relations with another such that when P_1 has c_1, P_2 has to have c_2, and when P_2 has c_2, P_3 must have c_3, but not conversely; from this it follows that when P_1 has c_1, P_3 must have c_3. Thus, we can say that both having c_1 by P_1 and having c_2 by P_2 are *causes* of having c_3 by P_3; however, we should call the first the *indirect* cause, and the second the *direct* cause. There are many examples of direct and indirect causes. Thus, if at point A, we irritate a motor axon that in B covers a muscle fibre,

A -----------------------------B

then after a very short moment a contraction of this muscle will occur. The nerve's irritation at point A is the cause of the muscle contraction, but only an indirect one, as we imagine that the irritation moves through the axon from one spot to another, bringing about some physiological changes, and that it is only the last change within the nerve ending in B that is the contraction's *direct* cause.

I believe that these considerations will be sufficient to illustrate to the reader the direction and the way in which investigations concerning a question as complicated as the problem of causality should be carried out. Only by a thorough logical analysis of every concept, and not – as Hume believes – *psychological* findings concerning the genesis and origin of concepts, may this as well as any other metaphysical question move forward and eventually be solved completely. I will be able to show in one of the following sections [viz., section 11] how great mistakes and misunderstandings appeared in philosophy due to underestimating the formal logical factor and overestimating the psychological element.

10   *Relations of Simple Dependence and the Concept of Necessity*

The same necessary relation that supposedly occurs between a cause and an effect may obtain not only between concrete objects, but also between abstract objects, such as, e.g., mathematical concepts. Thus, if some number is divisible by 6, it *must* be divisible by 3, and if it is not divisible by 3 it *cannot* be divisible by 6. So, between some number's divisibility by 6 and its divisibility by 3 there are necessary relations signified by p_1p_2 and n_2n_1; however, just as in the case of causal relations, relations p_2p_1 and n_1n_2 do not hold, because a number's divisibility by 3 does not necessarily bring about its divisibility by 6, and a number's indivisibility by 6 is not necessarily connected with its indivisibility by 3. This necessary connection consists therefore of two simple necessary relations and two non-necessary relations, and like a causal relation it is asymmetric and transitive.

A similar relation may also connect the truth or falsity of some judgments. If it is true, e.g., that "all men are mortal", it *must* also be true that "some men are mortal"; and if it is not true that "some men are mortal", it *cannot* be true that "all men are mortal". From the falsity of the general judgment, however, the falsity of the particular judgment does not necessarily follow, just as the truth of the particular judgment is not necessarily connected with truth of the general one. Thus, a logical connection between judgments that in traditional formal logic are signified as *SaP* and *SiP* consists of two simple necessary relations p_1p_2 and n_2n_1 and two non-necessary relations, and, like a causal relation, it is asymmetric and transitive. This relation may also obtain between numerous other kinds of judgments, the listing of which is a significant logical task; for this relation is a widely recognized and important relation of *reason and consequence*. The same two rules that I laid down in the previous section with respect to cause and effect are well known with respect to reasons and consequences, and they go as follows: (a) *the truth of a reason implies with necessity the truth of the consequence, and the falsity of a consequence implies with necessity the falsity of the reason;* (b) *the truth of a consequence does not necessarily imply the truth of the reason, and the falsity of a reason does not necessarily imply the falsity of the consequence.*

We see from these examples that the relation of reason and consequence, as well as certain necessary relations obtaining between mathematical concepts, have the same features that are characteristic of a putative necessary relation obtaining between a cause and an effect. Therefore, we may employ one common term for all necessary relations represented as follows:

$$Z = p_1p_2 + n_2n_1 + (p_2, p_1) + (n_1, n_2),$$

regardless of the objects they connect, calling them relations of simple dependence. I choose this name because there are related relations which consist of four simple necessary relations p_1p_2, p_2p_1, n_1n_2 and n_2n_1, and no non-necessary relation and which I previously described as *relations of complex or mutual dependence.* Like the relation of reason and consequence, the causal relation thus belongs to the kind of simple dependence relations.

Thanks to the close relationship between a causal relation and other relations of simple dependence, the concept of *necessity*, which is the putative basis of the causal relation, may be further defined. For it is not difficult to give the meanings of the expressions "something must be" or "something cannot be" when we are focused, e.g., on mathematical concepts. That a number must be divisible by 3 if it is divisible by 6, means nothing other than simply that it would contain a contradiction, if it were not divisible by 3 while being divisible by 6. For to be divisible by 6 means to be divisible by 2 and divisible by 3; so whoever claims that some number is divisible by 2 and is divisible by 3 but is not divisible by 6 makes two contradictory claims and creates a contradictory abstract object. The same applies to every other instance of a necessary relation which occurs between abstract objects: a part *has* to be smaller than a whole, that is, were it not, a contradiction would be involved; a circle *cannot* be a square, that is, were it a square, it would be a contradictory object; the truth of the judgment "all men are mortal" *must* be connected with the truth of the judgment "some men are mortal"; that is, if the latter judgment were true even though the former were not, a contradiction would be involved.

This is how necessity may be reduced to contradiction. Generally speaking, the concept of necessity or the concept of "what must be or cannot be" may be described in the following words: *object P must have feature c, that is, if it did not have it it would be a contradictory object;* or: *object P cannot have feature c, that is, if it had it it would be a contradictory object.* And by a *contradictory object* I understand an object that *has* a certain feature and at the same time *does not have* it, such as, e.g., "a square circle", "wooden iron", "a circle with a rational radius the area of which is the same as that of a square with a rational side" (an irrational number would then have to be rational) etc.

Within the domain of *ideal* abstract objects, thus, within, e.g., the scope of necessary logical or mathematical relations, in each case we may easily see that the foregoing definitions are correct. We create these objects regardless of experience, and we know with all certainty which features they have, because we gave them these features. So, we can say with complete certainty when these objects would involve a contradiction and show beyond doubt both the necessary relations that occur between them and the connection of these necessary relations to the concept of contradiction. Within the domain of *real* abstract objects and concrete objects we cannot always, beyond doubt, see contradiction; as we do not know *all the* features of concrete objects, nor we do know which features these abstract objects – the scope of which covers concrete objects – have to have. That is why very often in these cases we can only *guess* that there are necessary relations, and we assume them with more or less probability. But because in any case when we are inclined to accept such relations, as in, e.g., the causal relation, they show the same features that the undoubtedly necessary relations obtaining between ideal abstract objects have, we can, and we have the right to describe a *real*, that is, *physical, necessity* in the same way in which we describe a *logical* or *mathematical necessity*. The fact that a man *must* die would, therefore, mean that the totality of the features that make up the living human organism cannot be reconciled with the feature of immortality. Admittedly, we cannot grasp this contradiction, because we cannot fully explore human nature and define it as though it were some mathematical concept we create, but the mind of the Supreme Being that created the world can see it as clearly and distinctly as we can see in our conceptual creations.

I understand in the same way as well the necessity that supposedly occurs between a cause and an effect. That a platinum wire must heat when electric current is flowing through it means, therefore, that if it did not even though electric current were flowing through it, it would involve contradictory features; that a wheel mill must be turning when water is falling on it with an appropriate force means that if it were not turning, even though water were falling on it, it would involve contradiction; that a man whose heart was stabbed with a dagger must die means that if he remained alive with a hole in his heart, he would be a contradictory object. We are deeply convinced that there are no contradictory objects in nature, and that God who created this entire visible world removed all contradiction from His creation, in the same way we do from our scientific theories.

And this is perhaps the place at least to indicate a way to make plausible the assumption that a causal relation involves some necessary relations. To accept that between two objects P_1 and P_2 there is a relation such that when P_1 has c_1, P_2 must have c_2, but not conversely, it is sufficient to determine in experience the following three groups of facts:

(a)   *In each case where P_1 had c_1, P_2 had c_2* (e.g., whenever electric current was flowing, a platinum wire would heat);

(b)   *in each case where P_2 did not have c_2, P_1 did not have c_1* (whenever a platinum wire did not heat, electric current would not be flowing through it);

(c)   *there were cases where P_2 had c_2, however P_1 did not have c_1* (heated platinum wire, even though no electric current was flowing).

If we ever determine facts of this kind in experience, their simplest explanation is the assumption that between having c_1 by P_1 and having c_2 by P_2 there is a combination of necessary and non-necessary relations, which is the essence of the causal relation. And this is where the probability of this assumption lies. I do not know whether there is any other way of justifying this hypothesis; this is also how, after all, we argue for the probability of the judgment that gold is an element. It has turned out in every case so far that gold could not be chemically decomposed; the simplest explanation of these facts is that gold is not chemically composed at all. According to Jevons and Sigwart's *inverse* theory of induction, that seems to me to be the only proper presentation of the logical structure of inductive inferences, the only way that a law of nature may be justified is by showing that consequences that follow from deductive inference under this law are compatible with the facts of experience.[13] The more facts a given law explains, the more it allows for predicting certain facts, or even for discovering new ones; the more justified we are in taking this law to be an accurate expression of the facts.

It is easy to see that the foregoing three conditions, all consequences of the concept of the causal relation, provide as well three *rules* that allow for

---

13   In Polish philosophical literature there is a work describing inverse theory of deduction [Łukasiewicz 1903]. In this work, unfortunately unfinished, author presents Jevons and Sigwart's views on the essence of inductive inference in more detail, and he defends them from a criticism that was raised by Erdmann. However I believe that theory of inversion is, in principle, right, I also think that it shouldn't, as in this work, rely on the relation of reason and consequence, because except of this relation, there are also other necessary logical relations, such as, e.g., relations of contrariety and subcontrariety, which may be a basis for both deductive and inductive inference.

determining whether a causal relation occurs in each particular case. These rules are, however, somewhat different from Mill's four methods of inductive investigation; the former rely on a precise analysis of the causal relation, whereas Mill's methods were based on a vague and mistaken concept of cause bereft of analysis. I am aware that I am making a serious objection here against widely recognized rules of investigation, and I am raising a question that is very significant for science as a whole. But, in a monograph as short as this, I cannot consider it in more detail; I hope, however, that in one of my future works I will be able not only to show how insufficient and mistaken hitherto recognized methods of inductive investigation are, but also to create new methods of scientific inquiry that will expose Mill's theories as merely weak attempts in this field, and that are based on an extensive *theory of necessary relations* which, with the exception of causal relations, takes into account other kinds of necessary relations. A broader approach will perhaps also allow me to give yet different arguments for both my understanding of the concept of cause and my overall philosophical standpoint that I have already repeatedly tried to distinctly underline above.

11   *The Causal Relation Cannot Be Reduced to a Relation of Reason to Consequence; Efficient and Cognitive Causes*

I described in the previous sections the features of the causal relation and I indicated how the necessity that connects a cause and an effect should be understood; now I would like to address certain misunderstandings that could easily arise had not the view I hold been properly explained.

I have been trying to show that a causal relation, if it may be understood as a necessary relation at all, has the same features that, e.g., the relation of reason and consequence has. This thought, entertained already by Spinoza, may incite the suggestion that I simply reduce the causal relation to the relation of logical consequence, and physical to logical necessity. I would like to clearly separate myself from this possible interpretation of my view, and I will offer reasons for distinguishing between these two kindred relations. I want as well to consider this issue because there already exists, in Polish philosophical literature, a theory that attempts to reduce the causal relation to the relation between a reason and a consequence.

Bronisław Bandrowski, the author of this theory, gives it a very clear and precise formulation: according to him, a causal relation occurs between two objects *A* and *B* if an existential judgment "*A* exists" is the reason of an existential judgment "*B* exists". The necessity with which an effect follows a cause

lies in this logical necessity, and methods of determining a causal relation are
actually methods of determining a relation of reason and consequence.[14]

---

14   [Bandrowski 1904] and a separate offprint. It is a very clearly and precisely written dissertation which ensures its exceptional place within our scientific literature. The author
explains his views on the causal relation on p. 31. Having correctly noticed that the necessity involved in a causal relation cannot, according to Sigwart, rely on the concepts of
substance and force, Bandrowski continues as follows: "The necessity with which an
effect follows a cause has to have a different meaning. The definition of the causal relation will allow us to determine this meaning. Let us signify an effect with letter B and its
complete cause with letter A; a causal relation may then be expressed with the following
sentence: "If there is A, there is B". It is beyond doubt that all causal relations may be
expressed in this form, and there is no anxiety that this definition could not be applied
to some instance of a causal relation. The only objection that may be raised against it is
that as a definition it is too broad, and that other than the causal relation it also includes
other relations; because of this, it will have to be completed later such that it applies
only to the causal relation. Now, however, we will consider further consequences of the
fact that the causal relation may be expressed in the foregoing way. Such a conditional
sentence does not express anything other than that between the propositions that appear
in it as an antecedent and a consequent a certain logical relation occurs, a relation of
reason to consequence. The definition of this relation, that is highly significant in logic,
is as follows: "Proposition R is the reason of proposition N, if the truth of proposition R
is necessarily connected to the truth of proposition N; it follows from this that the falsity
of proposition N is necessarily connected to the falsity of proposition N. From this, the
following definition of the causal relation follows: "A is a cause and B an effect if the proposition "A exists" is a reason of the proposition "B exists", that is, the latter proposition is a
consequence of the former". It is exactly here that lies the necessity with which an effect
follows a cause. The analysis of speech brought us to understand that the relation of reason to consequence is involved in a causal relation. But this analysis is neither the only
nor the strongest argument. Rather, most importantly, it follows from the fact that the two
relations have a lot in common: for both are characterized by necessity and a necessity in
one direction: the truth of a reason is necessarily connected to the truth of a conclusion,
but not conversely; in the same way, with existence of the cause, the existence of the
effect is necessarily connected, but not conversely. Furthermore, it follows from the fact
that our entire knowledge consists of propositions and relies on logical relations between
propositions. In our thought operations, we do not have phenomena which are cause and
effect, but only propositions asserting that these phenomena exist. In a similar vein, we
do not deal with a relation obtaining between objects, but only with a relation between
propositions asserting that objects exist. Thus, I do not deny that there may be some real
relation (*reale Notwendigkeit*) between things, but for our thought processes this relation
is represented merely with a relation of reason to consequence between propositions
asserting the existence of these objects. We shall now turn to defining what the difference
is between a causal relation and other instances of a relation of reason to consequence. It
depends on the meanings that we give to symbols A and B in the above formula, that is, on
what kind of objects we take to be causes and effects. For there is no doubt that a causal
relation obtains only between what can have its beginning in time; what lasts eternally
can be neither an effect nor a cause. Therefore, we can only talk about a causal relation
when something comes to be, ceases to exist, or undergoes a change. Causes and effects

Reflection on what kind of objects a relation of reason and consequence connects shows why this view is mistaken. If someone claims that this relation obtains between *judgments*, and by judgments he understands some mental phenomena, then he reduces the necessity that supposedly obtains between real objects of *one* category (e.g. between physical phenomena) to the necessity connecting real objects of a *different* category (that is, mental phenomena). This is how Höfler seems to be understood the question, who clearly states that a relation of reason and consequence occurs between judgments if accepting the truth of the first judgment is necessarily connected to accepting the truth of the second.[15] Accepting that something is true is, however, a psychic act, it is spiritual phenomenon; thus, a relation of reason and consequence connects, on this view, certain spiritual acts. Setting aside the objection that a logical necessity would then be some kind of real necessity, concrete examples may show that this view is mistaken. For there are cases where, e.g., someone accepts truth of a judgment that a certain number is divisible by 6 but does not think about this number being divisible also by 3; and so, he does not entertain a judgment about this number's divisibility by 3. Accepting the truth of the first judgment, which in this case is a reason, is not connected to accepting the truth of the second judgment, that is, the consequence, because this second judgment as a spiritual phenomenon does not even exist. Furthermore, it may be that someone accepts, e.g., the truth of a judgment that in a quadrangle all sides are equal but does not want to accept the claim that in such a quadrangle the diagonals cross under a right angle, because he does not know the rules of geometry well enough, or he does not understand the relevant proof. Thus, here too, accepting the first judgment is not connected to accepting the second, even though it is easy to see that, as for their truth and falsity, between the two judgments: "a given quadrangle is equilateral" and "its diagonals cross under a right angle" the following relation obtains:

---

are thus real changes; that is also what we have in mind when we say that causal relations obtain between phenomena". I quoted these paragraphs *in extenso*, because, on the one hand, I find the fact that Bandrowski independently came to views similar to mine on the essence of a causal relation (he admits, e.g., that there is a correspondence between a causal relation and a relation of reason to consequence) to be a significant argument for my claim, and, on the other hand, I wanted to show an example of a psychologist way of thinking which beyond doubt is revealed in this very attempt to reduce a causal relation to a relation of reason to consequence.

15 [Höfler 1890: 136]. We find here the following definition of a relation of reason to consequence: "Ein Urteil *F* ist dann eine "Folge" eines "*Grundes*" *G*, wenn mit dem Fürwahrhalten von *G* das (vorgestellte) Fürfalschhalten von *F unverträglich*, und somit das Fürwahrhalten von F notwendig ist." Translation: "Proposition *N* is then "consequence" of "reason" *R*, if with accepting truth of *R* is *inconsistent* with (presented) accepting falsity of *N*, and thus, accepting truthfulness of *N* is necessary."

$$Z = p_1p_2 + n_2n_1 + (p_2, p_1) + (n_1, n_2),$$

that is, they are connected by a relation of reason and consequence.

Admittedly, a relation of reason and consequence does not occur between psychic phenomena. If it did, then perhaps it would be some kind of causal relation; instead, it obtains between the *truth* and *falsity* of judgments, that is, between certain *features of spiritual phenomena*. It is not as difficult as it seems to determine what these features signify; one just needs to realize what the function of judgments is.

We saw in the first chapter that an expression "to present something to one-self" is ambiguous; for on one hand it means to have a mental image before oneself and on the other hand to think about the object signified by this image. Hence, each expression or combination of expressions that signifies some presentation, e.g., "the skeleton of Casimir the Great, lying in the Wawel", has a double function: first, it expresses that the speaker presents to himself an image of the skeleton, and second, it indicates the actual skeleton lying in Wawel's cellar. Each *utterance*, that is, a verbal expression of a judgment, has two similar functions: e.g., the utterance: "the skeleton of Casimir the Great lies in the Wawel" expresses, first, a mental act, some conviction of the speaker; second, it indicates a real relation that occurs between king Casimir's skeleton and the Wawel. And in every other case an utterance expresses, on the one hand, a belief, that is, some internal assertion or negation, and, on the other hand, it signifies that something is or is not, that is this or that, that is, in general, that an object has a certain feature or does not have it. And just as a presented object, this internal image, is a kind of sign or symbol of a *signified* object, the mental act that we call a conviction is also a sign or a symbol of the relation of having a certain feature c by an object P.

What this relation of having or non-having a certain feature by a given object is, I cannot define; I can only *point out* such cases, when, e.g., I say that "Casimir the Great's skeleton lies in the Wawel", that "electric current flows through a platinum wire", that "financial securities have decreased in value", etc. Everyone knows what these expressions are about; and everyone will definitely admit that having the feature of "flowing" or "decreasing" is not a mental phenomenon, but something that we either accept or deny in our acts of judging.

Given these considerations, it is not difficult to define what the truth or falsity of judgments means. *A judgment is true if we accept the having of feature c by object P that this object has, or we deny the having of feature c by object P that this object does not have; a judgment is false if we accept the having of feature c by object P that this object does not have, or we deny the having of feature c by object P that this object has.* This is a time-honored, good definition of truth: *veritas est adaequatio rei et intellectus*; only distorted modern metaphysics or idealistic, albeit logically far from ideal, claims of the theory of knowledge perceive some difficulty in it.

The features "true" and "false" are therefore relative features that a conviction may have depending on what it concerns. Necessary logical relations that occur between these features may have two kinds of source. There are, first, convictions that due to their form stand within necessary relations, regardless of the content we put into this form. Forms of this kind of convictions are discovered by formal logic which creates rules of reasoning when it determines, e.g., that a relation of reason and consequence occurs between judgments of forms SaP and SiP, or that in the first figure with the truth of the premises:

$$MaP$$
$$SaM$$

the truth of the following conclusion is necessarily connected:

$$SaP.$$

However, necessary relations may occur as well between certain judgments because of their content. Since convictions are signs or symbols of relations of having or non-having a certain feature by a given object, when between having c_1 by P_1 and having c_2 by P_2 a necessary relation occurs, then also between the corresponding judgments – strictly speaking, between their features of truth or falsity – the same necessary relation occurs. The difference between necessary relations that connect two judgments because of their content and those that connect them because of their form may be explained with the following example.

The judgments [being parts of the sentence] "someone is a man, therefore he is mortal" are not connected by any necessary relation because of their *form*, because the truth or falsity of the judgment SaM is not necessarily connected to truth or falsity of a judgment SaP, nor conversely. However, because of their *content* they probably do stand in the relation of reason and consequence, since we suppose that with the totality of features that are the essence of a man the feature of being mortal is necessarily connected, but not conversely. For these judgments to be connected as well by a necessary relation involving their form, a further premise needs to be added: a judgment of the form MaP. That results in a syllogism according to the mode *Barbara*:

All men are mortal,
someone is a man,

––––––––––––

therefore, he is mortal.

In all instances of certain judgments being connected by a necessary relation because of their content, the necessity that connects them is *derivative*
and follows from the fact that the *objects* that these judgments concern are
connected by necessary relations. Now, this applies also to those existential
judgments that concern the occurrence of a cause and an effect. *We accept that
two objects A and B (a cause and an effect) are connected by a necessary relation,
not because we suppose that a judgment "A exists" is a reason of a judgment "B
exists", but, the other way round, we suppose that there is a necessary logical relation between these judgments because we suspect that there is a real necessity
connecting objects A and B.* This can be determined by any example. Hence, if
we suppose the truth of the judgment: "electric current flows through a platinum wire" and the truth of another judgment: "the wire is heating" are connected by the relation of logical consequence, we do not find this assumption
relative to these judgments' acts or their form, but in our conjecture that there
is a real necessity connecting these two phenomena. Thus, not *logical relations*,
not *thought processes*, but *real necessary relations* are in these cases, from the
logical perspective, something that is πρὂτερου πρὸς ἡμᾶς.

It follows, in my opinion, that real necessary relations cannot be derived
from logical necessary relations, and a causal relation cannot be derived from a
relation of logical consequence. Both these necessary relations have the same
features, both are relations of simple dependence; but they differ from one
another in that they occur between different kinds of objects. A causal relation connects certain *concrete* objects, whereas a relation of reason and consequence occurs between *abstract* features of truth and falsity that we ascribe to
judgments. And if Bandrowski claims that methods of determining the causal
relation are actually reduced to methods of determining the relation of reason
and consequence, then he is correct only insofar as both these kinds of necessary relations involve the same features and the methods for discovering them
are methods of determining the relation of simple dependence.

In relation to this consideration, purpose of which was to remove possible misunderstandings and clarify my view on the essence of the causal relation, I would like to present a certain very curious conceptual confusion that
turned out to be problematic precisely due to attempts to avoid it. Modern
philosophy prides itself on making a distinction between efficient and cognitive cause – *ratio fiendi et ratio cognoscendi*, unknown to the ancients.
Whoever has read Schopenhauer dissertation, *On the Fourfold Root of the
Principle of Sufficient Reason*, could see repeatedly how significant this distinction is for Schopenhauer, and how critical he is of the unclarity of thought
that seeks to undermine this distinction. Admittedly, if by a cognitive cause
we understand a reason and by an efficient cause a *cause simpliciter*, then

the distinction is correct, although perhaps not as significant as we normally assume. Nevertheless, numerous examples with which philosophers attempt to explain this distinction are chosen so unfortunately that they arouse the suspicion whether these philosophers fully understood the difference.

This can be shown in the following way. We suppose that when electric current flows through a platinum wire, the wire *must* be heating; it follows that when the wire is not heating, electric current *cannot* be flowing through it. Philosophers accept the necessity inherent in this second relation, but they normally transfer it from the domain of real objects to the domain of inference and claim that when the wire is not heating, we can only *conclude*, with great probability, that there is no electric current in it. That is how the conviction arises that, whereas the occurrence of phenomenon A is an *efficient* cause for occurrence of phenomenon B, the non-occurrence of phenomenon B is merely a *cognitive* cause for the non-occurrence of phenomenon A. A similar shift from real relations to logical relations is shown very distinctly in a classic example, quoted by almost all philosophers, of the warming of a room and the rise of the mercury in a thermometer. If the room is warming, the mercury level in a thermometer must rise; here a real causal relation occurs: the warming of a room is the efficient cause of mercury rising in the thermometer's bulb. If, on the contrary, the mercury level rises or does not rise, we conclude that the room did or did not grow warm. Here we do *not* admit there being a real necessary relation between the rising or not of the mercury level and the warming or not of a room; the former phenomenon is merely the *cognitive* cause of the latter, that is, in other words, a judgment concerning the existence or non-existence of the former phenomenon is the reason of a judgment concerning the existence or non-existence of the latter.

If, based on these examples, one wanted to define the concept of cognitive cause in such a way that he employed the term to name a phenomenon not in any real necessary connection with another phenomena – i.e. by the expression "cognitive cause" – and he only took a judgment concerning the occurrence or non-occurrence of this phenomenon to be the reason of another judgment stating the occurrence or non-occurrence of some other phenomenon, he would be exposed to a serious logical error. For to admit that the warming of a room necessarily brings about the rising of mercury in a thermometer is also to admit that, conversely, the mercury *not rising* necessarily brings about the *non-warming* of the room. This expression is somewhat extraordinary, but whoever does not accept it *is in contradiction*. For if relation p_1p_2 occurs between two concrete objects, relation n_2n_1 must also occurs between *the same* objects. And whoever claims that the latter relation connects *only* the truth or falsity of existential judgments concerning these objects cannot accept a real relation in the former case either, which, as explained in my previous considerations, I find mistaken. If we claim furthermore that the truth of the judgment "the mercury level in a thermometer rose" necessarily implies the truth of the second judgment "the room warmed", we can assume this necessary logical relation only because we assume a *real* necessary relation between these phenomena. For it does not follow from the *form* of these judgments that they are in a necessary relation. We can also see here that the phenomena: "the warming of a room" and "the mercury level rising in a thermometer" are in a relation of complex *dependence*, because in addition to relation p_1p_2, they are also connected by relation n_2n_1.

That the expression "the rising or not rising of the mercury level in a thermometer necessarily implies the warming or not warming of a room" sounds somewhat odd, or even paradoxical, perhaps results from the ingrained difficulty we have to understand a cause other than as an acting object. It seems to us that we understand perfectly well how heat works in increasing the volume of bodies; but that, conversely, we cannot understand or even suppose that bodies extending or not may somehow act on heat. However, all who are free from the anthropomorphic view of nature will not see any difficulty with these expressions.

Therefore, I believe that this "great" discovery of modern philosophy leads only to confusion and may expose us to logical errors. I do not see a better means for avoiding these errors than by removing, once and for all, the concepts of "efficient and cognitive cause" from philosophy. The expressions "cause and effect" and "reason and consequence" suffice perfectly to distinguish between real and logical relations of simple dependence; "anything beyond this comes from the evil one".

12   *The Temporal Relation in the Causal Relation*

Whereas scholars have very different opinions on what the essence of the causal relation is, in *one* respect everyone seems univocally to share a conviction, namely, that the causal relation involves a *temporal relation*. But as for the *kind* of this temporal relation there is again a diversity of opinion. In particular, two competing views struggle for the victor's palm: some, as Hume, maintain that a cause is always *prior* to an effect, hence they call it the *antecedent*; others, such as Sigwart, claim that cause and effect must occur *simultaneously*.[16]

---

16   Cf. Hume's definitions of cause in [Hume 1739–1749: footnotes 4 and 7]. [Sigwart 1879a: vol. II, p. 148, 149]: "(Es) lässt sich, genau genommen, nicht von einem Wirken eines *A* auf ein *B* reden, solange nur *A* sich verändert und *B* noch gar keine Veränderung zeigt; besteht das Wirken in dem Hervorbringen des Effektes, *so wirkt die Ursache eben darin, dass sie*

On this controversial question I wish to take an intermediate position, since I claim that both of these views are false.

To justify this claim with respect to the latter view, first, I will in particular show how insufficient a certain argument is that seems to support this view. Thus, one may think that since the occurrence of a cause *necessarily* brings about the occurrence of an effect, the cause and the effect must occur at the same time. This argument is mistaken. One may very well think, without contradiction, that there is a cause that occurs today that will yield an effect in one hundred years. Only then, and not any earlier, will it *have* to exist. A certain object must exist when its non-existence would prove that it contains a contradiction. However, form this it does not follow that contradiction would be involved were it not to exist *at this moment*. A temporal relation between a cause and an effect cannot be explained based on this kind of *a priori* arguments; instead, by relying on the principles of the inductive method we need to examine the causal relation as manifest in concrete instances.

And there are examples of causal relations where a cause and an effect do not occur simultaneously. Consider the example from physiology discussed earlier. Let line *AB* represents a motor axon the ending of which covers a muscle cell in *B*:

$$A\text{------------------------------------}B$$

If in moment t we irritate the axon's ending at point A, in moment $t + \tau$ there must be a muscle's contraction in B. The nerve's irritation is here the cause, the muscle's contraction the effect. Thus, the cause and the effect do not occur in this case simultaneously, but are separated by some finite, albeit small quantity of time. Someone might, however, argue that this is not plausible, because we know that the nerve's irritation at point A is merely an *indirect* cause of the muscle's contraction; *direct* causes must occur simultaneously with effects. But this argument is mistaken. For we accept that the nerve's irritation in A brings about a constant series of physiological changes in the axon that relate to one another in such a way that each prior change in the series is an indirect cause of the ensuing one, and the last change in the series is an indirect cause of the

---

den *Effekt hervorbringt;* das Wirken der Ursache *A* und das Hervorbringen des Effekts an *B*, die Veränderung von *B* muss *gleichzeitig* sein". Translation [Sigwart 1879b: 103]: "If we are to be accurate, we cannot speak of the efficient action of an *A* upon a *B* so long as *A* alone changes and *B* shows no sign of change. If the action consists in the production of the effect, *the cause acts just in that it produces the effect*, the action of the cause *A* and the production of the effect in *B* must be *simultaneous*."

muscle's contraction. Since the muscle's contraction ensues after a finite quantity of time τ after the nerve's irritation at point A, then particular intermediate causes and effects between the first cause and the last effect cannot exist simultaneously but must follow one another. If all these causes and effects existed simultaneously, the muscle's contraction would have to occur in the same moment in which the nerve's irritation in A occurs. So direct causes are not in this case simultaneous with their effects either, but they directly precede their effects in time. Similar reasoning may be applied to many other instances of causal relations, e.g., in the domain of mechanical or light, electric, chemical phenomena ... It can be shown in each instance that an effect follows a cause, and that does so *directly*. Thus, it turns out that the theory of the simultaneity of cause and effect, held by Sigwart, is wrong, and it seems that Hume's view, according to which a cause is a direct predecessor of an effect, is correct.

Nevertheless, nor is this view compatible with the facts, especially in Hume's formulation whereby a cause and an effect are *adjacent* in time and *directly* succeed one another. That there are *indirect* causes which, as the above example shows, do not have to precede their effects by an infinitely small quantity of time, is proof thereof. And it cannot be maintained that indirect causes are not causes at all; the adjective "indirect" simply makes the concept of cause more precise, that is, it *determines* it, just as the adjective "genuine" determines the concept of gold but does not change, that is, does not *modify*, its meaning in the way that adjective "Rzeszowian" *modifies* the meaning of gold.[17] From §9 we know that an indirect cause is in exactly the same relation with an effect that direct causes are with their effects. Thus, there are causes, indirect ones, that do not directly precede their effects in time.

It seems, however, that even instances of direct causes can be found that are not adjacent in time with their effects. We know of experiences of hypnosis in which a person under hypnosis is told to do some determined thing after waking. These experiences are very often successful. So, we might say that a direct cause of this person's movement, an hour after waking, is the preceding instruction of the hypnotist. Do we have to suppose that during all this time there are constant intermediate changes in the hypnotized person's nervous system between the instruction and the movement, in the same way that the axon's changes are intermediate between the nerve's irritation in A and the muscle's contraction? Whoever understands a cause as an acting object will probably disagree with this view. But just as *actio in distans* in a spatial sense

---

17   "Rzeszowian gold" is an alloy made by goldsmiths from Rzeszów, reminiscent of gold in appearance and weight, and sold by peddlers as "true" gold in Little Poland in the 18th-19th centuries. [JJ&ES].

involves no contradiction and is perfectly understandable, we may accept the concept of *actio in distans* in temporal sense, too. We simply have to rid ourselves of the conviction that in nature everything happens in a constant manner, that *natura nihil facit per saltum*. Series of changes in phylogenetic development show how mistaken this banality is. The domain of social phenomena, where there is almost no continuity of changes, probably provides numerous examples of causal connections in which a cause and an effect do not directly follow one another.

These considerations do not imply the fallacious view that a cause is the effect's precedessor; it is just that it should not be defined as an object directly preceding an effect. But it seems to me that there are also such instances of causal relations where a cause and an effect occur *simultaneously*. If a heavy body, e.g., a book, lies on some firm and solid basis, e.g., on a table, it must remain in a state of rest despite attracting earth force. Between the book's lying on the table and its not falling there is a supposed necessary relation of the form:

$$Z = p_1p_2 + n_2n_1 + (p_2, p_1) + (n_1, n_2),$$

which is a causal relation. Indeed, in our everyday life we say, too, that the lying of a body on a solid basis is the cause of its not falling. However, it is not plausible that the book's lying is some direct or indirect "antecedent" of its not falling. Both members of this causal relation, lying and not falling, occur simultaneously. Thus, it follows that a cause does not have to precede its effect.

These examples show that in some instances a cause precedes an effect, in others – it is simultaneous with the effect. It follows that both Hume's and Sigwart's theses are mistaken. It might seem, thus, that the correct view is Mill's, who does not devote much attention to this controversy and is satisfied with a claim that in any case an effect does not precede a cause.[18] So let us now consider this assumption.

I claim, first and foremost, that there are no *a priori* arguments that would prove that an effect cannot precede a cause. For by a causal relation I understand a necessary relation which can be presented using the formula:

$$Z = p_1p_2 + n_2n_1 + (p_2, p_1) + (n_1, n_2),$$

---

18   [Mill 1843: ch. IV, §7]: "I have no objection to define a cause, the assemblage of phenomena, which, occurring, some other phenomenon invariably commences, or has its origin. Whether the effect coincides in point of time with, or immediately follows, the hindmost of its conditions, is immaterial. At all events, it does not precede it" [...].

and which can be expressed, in short, by saying that when P_1 has c_1, P_2 must have c_2, but not the other way round. This necessary relation does not involve any temporal relation; a temporal relation is added to a causal relation only because both P_1 and P_2 may have features c_1 and c_2 at different moments of time. *But whether P_1 has c_1 before P_2 has c_2, or simultaneously, or perhaps later, does not, in any way, influence this necessary connection, nor conversely, does this necessary relation, in any way, influence the temporal one.* Therefore, whoever agrees with my definition of a causal relation must agree that *a priori* it is possible that there are such instances of causal relations where some *future* phenomenon or event necessarily brings about a *present* phenomenon. The only way in which this assumption could be falsified is by experience, that is, by determining that so far, we have never observed reversed causal relations in nature.

It seems to me, however, that the state of science today does not make room for such a proof. We cannot maintain that there are no future causes of present phenomena, because no one has ever sought such causes. And if we note that we do not perceive necessary connections in nature either, and that often it is only after arduous intellectual work that we can suppose what the cause is of a given phenomenon, then we should also admit that a merely general and superficial survey of the data of experience does not justify rejecting this logically possible view.

Moreover, actual necessary connections running from the future back to the past may even justify this view. Consider again the already familiar example from physiology. If we irritate a nerve leading to a muscle in moment t, the muscle's contraction must follow at moment $t + \tau$; from this it follows that if at moment $t + \tau$ the muscle's contraction does not occur, the nerve's irritation cannot exist at moment t. This is, therefore, an example of a simple necessary relation $n_2 n_1$, the first member of which, non-having c_2 by P_2 occurs later than the second member, non-having c_1 by P_1. Since the non-occurrence of an effect necessarily leads to the non-occurrence of the cause, we may at least say that there are such events whose non-occurrence in the future necessarily leads to the non-occurrence of other events in the present.

The non-occurrence of some events is, however, necessarily connected to the occurrence of events that are contradictory with the former. Hence, if at moment $t + \tau$ the muscle's contraction does not occur, then it is not contracted at this moment, but elongated. So, we may say that non-contraction of the muscle at moment $t + \tau$ necessarily leads to the non-irritation, that is, the absence of change to the nerve at moment t, but not the other way round. Between the non-contraction of the muscle and the non-irritation of the nerve there is, therefore, a necessary relation

$$Z = p_1 p_2 + n_2 n_1 + (p_2, p_1) + (n_1, n_2),$$

that is, a causal relation. Thus, we have an example of a causal relation where an effect precedes a cause.

I do not know whether this reasoning, although precise and logical, will suffice to convince everyone; for the thought that I am presenting here is so new and unusual that it is not easy to grow accustomed to it. We shall simply have to get used to it. Throughout the philosophical literature there seems to be only one book that addresses this question in an exceedingly precise and scientific manner. It is a little known, rarely read work in German, *Elements of Empiricist Teleology* by Paul Nicolaus Cossmann.[19] The author argues that each biological state is a function of two factors: a certain past state, from which an organism develops, and a certain future state, which an organism pursues as the goal of its development. Thus, e.g., the biological state of a chrysalis is an effect not only of a previous state in which it was a caterpillar, but also of its future state as a butterfly. It is obviously clear that such temporally reversed causal connections have a lot in common with final causes.

There are views in science, especially in philosophy, that have arisen over an indefinite period of time and that, being transmitted in the tradition from one generation to another, have acquired such great inertia that no one thinks or dares to address them. It seems to us that these views are obvious and cannot be doubted, and we would never think to question their logical basis. Among such views is the claim that everything that happens in the world must have a certain cause in the past. We imagine that every phenomenon or event that occurs in a given moment is a single link in a chain of phenomena tied by a causal node, i.e., it is an inevitable consequence of some other phenomenon that just occurred a moment ago, and it is an irrevocable perpetrator of a third which is about to occur in a moment. We take it that there are numerous such causal chains; they are tied to one another and entwine in various ways, and each "now" is some kind of huge depiction of this tangle that reveals nothing but causes in the past and nothing but effects in the future. All phenomena from causes to effects flow like a sort of river from the past to the future; we just do not know whether this river has a source, some first cause, or whether it flows eternally and incessantly, without a beginning or an end.

It is a pretty simple picture, but it seems to me that it is hanging in the air. Anyone who ever studied even *one* field of empirical science knows what a labyrinth of facts research can bring forth, and how numerous and complicated are the necessary relations connecting particular facts with one another.

---

19   [Cossmann 1899]. It is an extremely clear and detailed work based on a rich biological material. I draw attention to it, because both in Poland and abroad it is almost completely unknown.

Would the whole of nature be less complicated than each of its segments, and can it be represented in the naively *schematic* way the above view proposes? I admit that this thought seems as improbable to me as, e.g., the claim that the sun is situated in the middle of earth.

If my remarks in this section managed to raise at least a suspicion among philosophers against the view that the present is simply formed by the past, if they managed to somehow shake their dogmatic belief in this less than obvious principle and incline them to revise their previous arguments, I could then say with confidence that my efforts in this work have not been wasted.

4

13   *The Concept of Complete Cause; A Cause and An Effect Do Not Have to Be Changes*

At the beginning of chapter 2 I noted that investigations concerning the logical analysis and construction of the concept of cause need to be carried in two directions: first, it needs to be examined what kind of *relation* connects a cause and an effect, and, second, it needs to be defined which objects in this relation may be causes. I consider the first of these completed; now I proceed to the second one.

This task is already simplified, as we have an unquestionable criterion for objects that may be called causes. For two objects A and B are in a causal relation, if A necessarily implies B, but not the other way round, B does not necessarily imply A. Thus, an object that does not necessarily bring about some other object cannot be a cause. I already used this criterion when, while discussing the substantial theory of causality, I showed that it is not correct to call a man a cause of a weight's movement, because there may be a man and the weight does not have to move. Since this way of speaking very often leads to misunderstandings, philosophers have tried to avoid this difficulty by creating the concepts of *complete* cause and of *partial* cause.

I will explain these concepts using an example taken from Schopenhauer. If a body is to ignite, then this phenomenon must be preceded by the following states: (1) the capacity of this body to connect with oxygen, (2) the proximity of oxygen, (3) a certain temperature. When all these conditions are satisfied, the effect, that is this body's igniting, must follow.[20] Together *all* of these

---

20   [Schopenhauer 1813a: §20, p. 47] I quote the whole paragraph, as it includes the definition of cause that I discuss later: "Wenn ein neuer Zustand eines oder mehrerer realer Objekte eintritt, so muss ihm ein anderer vorhergegangen sein, auf welchen der

conditions are the *complete* cause of this phenomenon; separately each of them is merely a partial cause because when a flammable body, e.g., a tinder, is in the atmosphere of carbonic anhydride, it will not ignite despite the sufficiently high temperature. So too, in the example of the weight's movement because of a man's activity, the man may only be called a partial cause of this phenomenon of movement.

I am not in favor of retaining the terms of complete and partial causes. As the above examples show, the adjective "partial" does not determine but only modifies the concept of cause. A partial cause is not a cause at all, because its occurrence does not necessarily lead to the occurrence of an effect; every cause, in the strict sense of this word, must be complete. Instead of talking about complete and partial causes, we should rather, for terminological reasons, use the expressions "a cause" and "a condition", and by "conditions" we should understand all those states or phenomena that must occur for some whole to be a cause.

---

neue regelmässig, d.h. allemal, so oft der erstere da ist, folgt. Ein solches Folgen heisst ein Erfolgen und der erstere Zustand die *Ursach*, der zweite die *Wirkung*. Wenn sich z.B. ein Körper entzündet, so muss diesem Zustand des Brennens vorhergegangen sein ein Zustand (1) der Verwandtschaft zum Oxygen, (2) der Berührung mit dem Oxygen, (3) einer bestimmten Temperatur. Da, sobald dieser Zustand vorhanden war, die Entzündung unmittelbar erfolgen musste, diese aber erst jetzt erfolgt ist; so kann auch jener Zustand nicht immer dagewesen, sondern muss erst jetzt eingetreten sein. Dieser Eintritt heisst eine *Veränderung*. Daher steht das Gesetz der Kausalität in ausschliesslicher Beziehung auf *Veränderungen* und hat es stets nur mit diesen zu thun. Jede Wirkung ist, bei ihrem Eintritt, eine Veränderung und gibt, eben weil sie nicht schon früher eingetreten, unfehlbare Anweisung auf eine andere, ihr vorhergegangene Veränderung, welche, in Beziehung auf sie, *Ursache*, in Beziehung auf eine dritte, ihr selbst wieder notwendig vorhergegangene *Veränderung* aber *Wirkung* heisst. Dies ist die Kette der Kausalität: sie ist notwendig anfangslos." Translation [Schopenhauer 1813b: §20, p. 38]: "When one or several real objects pass into any new state, some other state must have preceded this one, upon which the new state regularly follows, i.e. as often as that preceding one occurs. This sort of following we call *resulting*; the first of the states being named a *cause*, the second an *effect*. When a substance takes fire, for instance, this state of ignition must have been preceded by a state, (1), of affinity to oxygen; (2), of contact with oxygen; (3), of a given temperature. Now, as ignition must necessarily follow immediately upon this state, and as it has only just taken place, that state cannot always have been there, but must, on the contrary, have only just supervened. This supervening is called a *change*. It is on this account that the law of causality stands in exclusive relation to *changes* and has to do with them alone. Every effect, at the time it takes place, is a *change* and, precisely by non-having occurred sooner, infallibly indicates some other *change* by which it has been preceded. That other *change* takes the name of *cause*, when referred to the following one – of *effect*, when referred to a third necessarily preceding *change*. This is the chain of causality. It is necessarily without a beginning." It seems to me that the value of this work and the significance of Schopenhauer in philosophy are by far overestimated.

To be completely strict and accurate, one needs to be careful not to omit some condition from the examination of causal relations without which a given object is not a cause at all. Thus, e.g., it is not simply the nerve's irritation that is the cause of the muscle's contraction, but the irritation of a nerve that is *not damaged, not ligated*, that is *in its regular state* is the cause of the contraction of the muscle that is *not weary, not sedated*, etc.; it is not like the water's falling on a mill wheel that is a cause of this wheel's turning, but the falling of a certain *amount* of water from a certain height on a properly constructed wheel, that is *not too heavy*, is *not tied to* a strong chain, etc. If in the previous sections I did not clearly list these conditions, I did so without affecting the relevant considerations, because in these cases such conditions go without saying, and they don't influence the results of the investigation. It was about giving the simplest, somewhat schematic examples, from which I was trying to remove any complication or awkwardness of expression.

Keeping in mind that only an object may be a cause that necessarily implies another object, we should now turn to the question of which objects may be causes.

First of all, it is apparent that only *concrete, real* objects can be causes. This results from the definition of the causal relation which may be defined as *a relation of simple dependence occurring between concrete objects*. It is this, as I already underlined above, that distinguishes a causal relation from other relations of simple dependence, especially the relation of reason and consequence, and the same necessary relations that occur, e.g., in the domain of the abstract objects of mathematics. Such definition is, however, not sufficient, as there are many kinds of concrete objects, such as things and features, phenomena and relations. Thus, we need to further specify the *kind* of concrete objects that may be causes.

Excepting scholars who accept the substantial theory of causality according to which a cause is always some thing or substance, most claim that a cause and an effect are some sort of *phenomena* or *changes*. This view is clearly represented by Schopenhauer who insists that the principle of causality concerns nothing but changes. This view may seem mistaken, because if a cause involves several more or less permanent conditions, then it cannot only be a change. Thus, e.g., the nerve's irritation leads to the muscle's contraction only given the conditions that the nerve is not damaged, not ligated ..., and the muscle is not fatigued, not sedated, etc. In this case, only the nerve's irritation and the muscle's contraction are changes, but the more or less permanent states of the nerve and the muscle obviously are not. This difficulty, however, may be avoided, if we take these states to be features of the objects whose changes are in a causal relation, and we say that the irritation of the nerve that *has such and such features* is a cause of the contraction of a muscle that *has some other features*. This could also be done in every other case of this kind, construing a necessary connection that would occur between the *real changes* of two objects that have some determinate features.

There are two questions that this view raises: first of all, what are these changes that the causal relation is supposed to connect, and, second, does this relation involve changes alone? To answer these questions we must, first and foremost, define the concept of change.

We say that a concrete object undergoes a change if it is different now than it was before. When a body is falling it is at every instant in a different place, now it is here, before it was there; it changes its position; when due to electrical current the platinum wire is heating, its temperature is different at every instant, now being higher, earlier lower; changing in every moment; when sugar is melting in water, its appearance begins to differ: it becomes smaller, fissures, its contours become blurry; just a moment ago we clearly saw a cube, now we hardly see a shapeless lump. In each of these cases we may distinguish above all two factors: a relation of *difference* that we signify by the word "different" and a *temporal* factor that we describe with the words "now" and "then". This temporal factor is usually a relation of *temporal succession*; in the examples above the objects are different in the *immediately succeeding* moment than they were in the preceding one. But this does not have to be. If an electric bell rings more loudly now than before, there is, indeed, a change in two immediately succeeding moments – there was silence a moment ago and now suddenly you can hear a ring – but there occurs as well another change of a different temporal relation, a change that we establish by saying that the ring is now *louder* than in *the past*, e.g., before replacing the battery. Thus, we should describe this temporal factor with a general expression of temporal difference.

There is a third factor that needs to be added to the above two, a certain relation of *identity*. We say that *one and the same* object undergoes a change, that *one and the same* object is different now than it was before. Removing the apparent difficulty that seems to follow from having one and the same object that is different at different times does not require bringing up metaphysical assumptions concerning permanent substances and variable accidents; all we need is to accept that an object undergoing a change consists of a group of features, of which some endure and others become different. Suppose that an object P (e.g., a falling stone) has at moment t_1 features abc_1 (shape, weight, spatial position), and at moment t_2 features abc_2 (the same shape, the same weight, a *different* position); we then have two groups of features, abc_1, abc_2, of which the first two endure and the third is different. We signify the whole of the *same* features by one name, and we speak of one and the same object (of the falling stone) undergoing a change, whereas the *different features* that attach to this object at two different moments of time (this or that spatial position) are its change. These connections may be represented by the following scheme:

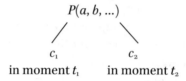

$$P(a, b, \dots)$$

$$c_1 \qquad\qquad c_2$$

in moment t_1 in moment t_2

Finally, we can distinguish a fourth factor in change: these *different* features c_1 and c_2 that are inherent to *one and the same* object at two *different moments* of time must be *species* of the same *kind* (*genus*). If, e.g., c_1 stands for a spatial position, c_2 cannot stand for a color, or temperature, but some different spatial position; if c_1 stands for a degree of heat, c_2 cannot stand for a volume or a shape, but some different degree of heat. The same holds for all the other cases. Hence, we normally use the same name for features c_1 and c_2, and we speak of a change of a position, a quantity, a temperature, a quality, an intensity, etc., of some object.

Given all the factors of change listed above, we may therefore say:

A real change is a relation of difference that occurs between two features of the same concrete object which are inherent to it at two different moments of time and which are species of the same kind. That this definition is correct may be seen in every example.

The bigger the difference of features that are inherent to a given object at two different moments of time, the bigger the change is. In many cases, this difference can be specified quantitatively.

Closely related to the concept of change is the concept of *phenomenon* which seems to be nothing else than *a series of changes of the same kind in the same real object.* Thus, e.g., the stone's falling is a series of changes of the stone's position, the platinum wire's heating is a series of changes of the wire's temperature, the sugar's melting in water is a series of changes of the solidity of the sugar's elements, the nerve's irritation is a series of physiological changes of the nerve that we don't know much about, etc.

Given these definitions, we can now solve the question whether a cause and an effect must *always* be changes or phenomena. Seemingly, yes. Plenty of cases can be adduced where changes and phenomena are members of a causal relation, e.g., the flowing of electric current and the platinum's heating, a nerve's irritation and the muscle's contraction, water's falling and the wheel's turning, etc. In each of these cases we assume that, e.g., the temperature of the wire must be different now than it was before because its electrical state is different; that the spatial features of the muscle must be different now than before because the physiological state of the nerve is different from it was before, etc. However, if we look at these examples more closely and consider why we suspect that causal relations hold between these relations of *difference* of features, we will see that we do so because of other causal relations that *do not occur* between changes. To say that, e.g., a change in the current's intensity generates a change in the wire's temperature we need to suppose that when a current of intensity i flows through the wire, the temperature of the wire has a certain value t, and when the current's intensity is i', the wire's temperature must be t'. So, when the current's intensity changes from i to i', the wire's temperature must change from t to t'. But if we supposed that temperature t is compatible with both i and i', we could not say that a change of i to i' necessarily brings about a change of t to t'. Thus, a change does not have necessarily to bring about another change, it only leads to it when the changing features of two objects are in some necessary relation, that is, when, e.g., a relation of cause and effect obtains between the electric current having intensity i and the platinum wire having temperature t. *However, it is not the changes, that is, certain relations of difference, that this relation connects here.* Therefore, based on these considerations we may claim that causal relations occurring between changes are only *derivative,* and they result from the fact that an object having a changed feature is normally necessarily connected to some other object having a changed feature. It seems obvious that Schopenhauer's view is mistaken.

That this view is false results also from many other instances of causal connections in which there is no change at all. We say that certain features of a human organism necessarily bring about its mortality, but, conversely, mortality certainly does not lead necessarily to these features of the organism. The cause of a man's *mortality* (not that he *dies* at given moment) are therefore certain hidden features of his organism. Thus, we have an example of a necessary connection occurring between objects that even on the surface do not seem to be changes.

That this view, according to which a causal relation occurs only between changes, is so common is due to certain features of the human mind. Each change surprises us and often even worries us; we want to know why an object is different now than it was before. We usually see that this change was preceded by another change. Hence, we ask what caused this last change, and it seems to us that it must have been some yet another change. This is how the convictions are formed that a causal relation connects nothing but changes, that every change has some cause that directly precedes it, that the chain of causes and effects is infinite, that the concept of first cause is in some way contradictory, etc. These are still naïve and non-scientific articulations of experiential data, much like the simple peasant's belief that the sun revolves round the earth every day. That such views can still be taken as axioms in philosophy (*vide* Schopenhauer) is a distinct proof of the progress of ... astronomy. Perhaps at the end I will be able to present, even if only in a few points, the view on necessity in nature that I consider the only correct one.

14   *What Is a Cause and What Is an Effect*

Anyone who has carefully followed my considerations so far has certainly noticed the direction towards which they are headed and realized what my position is regarding what a cause and an effect are. It is not things or their features that are the members of a causal relation, in rare cases changes or phenomena, but *relations of having a certain feature by a given concrete object.* In the whole *ArB*, which I used initially as a symbol representing a causal connection, *r* is a weave of necessary and non-necessary relations, and members of this weave, *A* and *B*, are relations of the form: "P_1 has c_1", "P_2 has c_2". Of these members the effect is the one that must occur when the other one does.

I will present two arguments to justify the validity of this view. I claim, first, that *members of each causal relation that can be found in nature may be expressed in the above form.* Examples, I believe, are not necessary. When a causal relation connects certain changes its members also may be expressed in the above form, because "to have a different feature now than before" is to have some feature of difference. Those who consider this argument to be false is obliged to give examples of causal relations that according to them cannot be presented in this form. It will then be up to me to show that they are mistaken.

Second, that members of a causal connection are relations of having a certain feature by a given concrete object follows from the concept of causal connection. A causal relation is a certain necessary relation. And no object may be necessary, or non-necessary, *by itself*: it is not the electric current that is necessary or non-necessary, but its *flowing*; it is not the platinum wire that is necessary or non-necessary, but its *heating*; it is not the muscle that is necessary or non-necessary, but its *contracting*; not God is necessary, but His *existence*, etc. In other words, necessary or non-necessary can be only that, e.g., the electric current *flows*, that the wire is *heating*, that the muscle *contracts*, that God *exists*, etc. Making this difference more accessible to psychologists, one might say that necessity and non-necessity are not inherent to objects of *presentations*, but to objects of *judgments*. Since a cause and an effect are both necessary or non-necessary, as an effect must be when there is a cause, and a cause does not have to be when there is an effect, both a cause and an effect must be something that judgments are about. And because every object of a judgment may be expressed by saying that *P* has or does not have *c*, also *members of a causal relation must be expressible in this way, with the proviso that their form is always positive*: P_1 has c_1, P_2 has c_2.

It seems to me that whoever thinks about this argument carefully will have to agree. There is only one objection that someone might raise: we often say that the *existence* of some object causes the existence of another. Members of this causal relation cannot be expressed by saying "P_1 has c_1", "P_2 has c_2", because existence is not a feature of objects. Already Kant showed that existence is not a concept of something that could be added to another concept and change its content. A hundred real dollars do not contain anything beyond a hundred possible, or imagined, thus, unreal dollars.[21] It might be concluded from this that existence is not a feature, because if a feature is ascribed to one of two objects, but not to the other, then it is impossible for one of these objects to comprise exactly what the other comprises.

How mistaken Kant's famous expression is, is very obvious. There is a huge difference between "a hundred possible or presented dollars" and "a hundred real dollars". A hundred possible dollars cannot be clutched, tucked away in a pocket, used for payment, etc. Is anyone so naïve as to claim that merely possible food may feed someone, that the thought of a locomotive may run over somebody, that a utopia presented in some philanthropist's head may save humanity from poverty and suffering? A functional, actually existing organization of society, even if it has numerous flaws, is obviously something different from and much more than the utopias of dreamers.

It is really very difficult to define the concept of existence. It may be that it cannot be defined at all, just as the concept of the color red cannot be defined, or an abstract object, or having a certain feature by a given object, etc. Be that as it may, one cannot maintain that an expression "A exists" cannot be expressed by saying that "A has a feature of existence", and thus, that there are causal connections that cannot be represented by the form "P has c".

However, the concept of existence brings us also to the second objection that may be raised against my view. Namely, one might claim that the simplest and the most general form of members of a causal relation is not "P has c",

---

21   Cf. [Kant 1781a: vol. III, p. 472 and 473]: "Sein ist offenbar kein reales Prädikat, d.i. ein Begriff von irgend etwas, was zu dem Begriffe eines Dinges hinzukommen könnte". And then: "Und so enthält das Wirkliche nicht mehr als das blosse Mögliche. Hundert wirkliche Thaler enthalten nicht das Mindeste mehr, als hundert mögliche". Translation [Kant 1781b: 567]: "Being is obviously not a real predicate, i.e., a concept of something that could add to the concept of thing." And then: "Thus the actual contains nothing more than the merely possible. A hundred actual dollars do not contain the least bit more than a hundred possible ones."

but "*A* exists", "*B* exists". It is thus always the existence or the occurrence of certain concrete objects that are members of a causal relation. I indeed agree that each member of causal relations may also be expressed by this existential form; I do not think, however, that this form is correct. Because, first, this form is a particular case of the form "*P* has *c*" in which *c* stands for existence; second, it leads to an unnecessary complication, because why would we say that the existence of the electric current's flow causes the wire to heat when it suffices simply to say that the flow of the electric current causes the platinum to heat; third, it blurs, to some extent, the variety of causal relations by seemingly creating everywhere the same causes and effects – the *existence* of something; and fourthly, it gives reason to the objection that it is not the existence of the electric current's flow that is the cause, but the existence of this existence, and so on, *in infinitum*.

That every member of a causal relation can be expressed in the existential form follows from a certain meaning of the concept "to exist". We often use this expression in the meaning "truly to be", that is, to be an object of a true positive judgment. Admittedly, if two relations of having a certain feature by a given object are connected by causal node, then the truths or falsities of judgments concerning these relations are connected by the relation of reason and consequence. I showed, however, in §11 that a causal relation cannot be reduced to the relation of reason and consequence, or, conversely, that the real necessary relation cannot be derived from logical necessary relations. These are two different kinds of relations of simple dependence.

To remove all possible misunderstandings I would like to underscore, finally, looking over the entire course of reasoning thus far, that by a cause and an effect I understand only *having* a certain feature by a given object, not non-having a certain feature. If two objects are connected to one another in such a way that non-having c_2 by P_2 necessarily brings about non-having c_1 by P_1, then having c_1 by P_1 is a cause of having c_2 by P_2. It is worth noting that by changing features c to their opposites c', each such relation may be transformed into another that obtains between having c'_2 by P_2 and having c'_1 by P_1. This causal relation differs, however, from the previous one, because it does not occur between the same members.

Here I end my investigations of the concept of cause. The results thereof are so numerous, and in part so new, that I will try once again to review them before the reader's eyes by providing an enclosed and rounded whole.

15   *Summary of Results*

The purpose of this work has been to give a logical analysis and construction of the concept of cause, thus, to discover the features of the abstract object called cause and to examine the relations obtaining between them. It has not been about constructing some ideal abstract object but creating a real concept whose scope includes concrete, real causes.

Using an *inductive* method, I determined, first of all, when it is that we signify some concrete objects by the expression "cause". It turned out that we use this word only for objects which are *correlative with respect to an effect,* and which stand to an effect in a *necessary relation* such that an object that is a cause necessarily *brings about* an object that is an effect. Having compared various instances of causal relations I then showed that *an effect does not have necessarily to bring about a cause,* and for terminological reasons I excluded from the concept of cause such instances of necessary relations in which both members necessarily imply one another. Having again compared concrete examples of causal relations, I came to the conclusion that they do not involve any special *temporal relation* that would require us to define a cause either as an object simultaneous with the effect or one preceding it. I also showed, on the basis of concrete examples, that a causal relation does not have to occur between nothing else but *changes.*

In examining these features using a *deductive* method, I proved in particular that a causal relation involves another necessary relation running in the opposite direction, which states that the *non-occurrence of an effect necessarily brings about the non-occurrence of a cause*; this is also how I showed that the non-occurrence of a cause is not necessarily connected to the non-occurrence of an effect. Using the deductive method, I discriminated further features of the causal relation: *irreversibility* and *transitivity.* The concepts of *direct* and *indirect* causes are connected with the latter. In examining members of causal relations, I showed that they are *relations of having a certain feature by a given object.*

Throughout this study, I had occasion to consider theories I find mistaken. Thus, I attempted to show the falsity of the *substantial* and *empiricist* theory of causality, the falsity of the view that a causal relation can be reduced to the relation of *reason and consequence,* and that a cause must be an *antecedent* or occur *simultaneously* with the effect. Finally, I tried to justify the claim that the terms "efficient" and "cognitive" causes, "complete" and "partial" causes, should no longer be used.

While discussing the necessary relation that connects a cause and an effect, I defined the concept of *necessity,* and I pointed out kindred relations of reason and consequence as well as other unnamed relations of the same kind among abstract objects, calling them all connections of *simple dependence* and distinguishing them from connections of *complex dependence.*

This short summary of the main results of this work should convince everyone that it was not without reason that I claimed at the beginning that so far investigations of the concept of cause have not conformed to the requirements of logic, and that they needed to be carried out again. And because the exact analysis and determination of the concept of cause is the basis for solving all the other problems concerning causality, it follows that the previous views on these problems require a scrupulous revision, even if only a small part of my claims turns out correct. I did not hesitate to state that I find commonly held convictions about necessity in nature to be merely premature and non-scientific formulations of experiential data, that is, initial and unsuccessful trials in this direction.

In conclusion, I would like to bring these numerous results of my work together and point out necessary relations among the particular features of the concept of cause. I would like to present the reader with the internal, logical construction of this concept by listing its constitutive and consecutive features.

The first *constitutive* feature of the concept of cause is a relative feature: an object *whose occurrence necessarily implies the occurrence of some other object, that is, an effect.* From this feature a *consecutive* feature directly follows: an object *whose non-occurrence is necessarily brought about by the non-occurrence of an effect.*

The second *constitutive* feature of the concept of cause, independent of the first, is a relative feature: an object *whose occurrence is not necessarily brought about by the occurrence of an effect.* From this feature a consecutive feature directly follows: an object *whose non-occurrence does not necessarily bring about the non-occurrence of an effect.*

From a combination of these two consecutive features, two further *consecutive* features of the concept of cause follow: an object *that is in an asymmetric and transitive relation with respect to an effect.* These two constitutive and four consecutive features of the concept of cause are therefore relative features w_1, w_2, w_3, ..., that characterize an object as a cause.

From these relative features a *consecutive* feature that is absolute necessarily follows: an object *that is a relation of having a certain feature by a given object.* For only this kind of relations can be connected by necessary relations.

The third *constitutive* feature of the concept of cause, independent of the two previous ones, is an absolute feature: an *actual, real* object.

These features suffice to give a clear and precise concept of cause. If by definition of a concept we do not understand a definition *per genus proximum et differentiam specificam*, but as a list of all its constitutive features, we may formulate the following definition of the concept of cause:

A cause is a real object that necessarily brings about some other real object, but is not necessarily brought about by this second object.

Because a causal relation is a certain relation of simple dependence, and a cause is the first member of this relation, we may describe it also as follows:

A cause is the first member of a relation of simple dependence that connects real objects.

We may give analogous descriptions of an effect: thus, *an effect is a real object that is necessarily brought about by some other real object, but that does not necessarily bring it about, or: an effect is the second member of a relation of simple dependence that connects real objects.*

I think that if these simple and clear definitions ever succeed in finding common acceptance in science, we could avoid many mistakes and controversies, and we would manage to broaden greatly the horizons of our knowledge.

16   Conclusion

Below the title of this dissertation I affixed the motto: *Arceo psychologiam*; I could add, *sed non odi*. I appreciate and value the results of psychology based on a thorough investigation of the phenomena of internal experience, but I react with all my energy against the central standing of psychology in the philosophical sciences. My views grew out of opposition to the great systems of modern philosophy, such as Hume's or Kant's; this is the background of the present dissertation.

When I think about the history of modern philosophy, ever since Descartes wanted to base all human knowledge on new foundations putting forward his famous "*cogito, ergo sum*" and formulating the concept of "*clarae et distinctae perceptionis*", whence Locke, following a failed metaphysical debate one evening, came up with the idea of examining the sources, certainty, and limits of human knowledge, and Hume and Kant, inspired by this idea, made noetic studies the heart of their philosophies, I cannot resist the conviction that this entire psychologistic direction of philosophical thought led into a wilderness. Marvelous systems have been created of the theory of knowledge, but they are fantastic and non-scientific. And when I look for the causes of this *fall* of philosophy, as I would call it, I see one and the same phenomenon: the lack of *historical education* of the great representatives of modern philosophy, the absence of the *scientific tradition* stemming from the ancient and the medieval masters of scholasticism.

Hume's and Kant's struggle with metaphysics is not a struggle with metaphysics. Neither Kant nor Hume *knew* what metaphysics is; their works show no indication that they ever looked into Aristotle.[22] They would be as efficient in

---

22   The index of names added by the editors to [Hume 1739–1740] doesn't anywhere include the name of Aristotle. The following quote from [Hume 1748: 41] [...] shows how poor

the struggle against Darwin's theory that arose only after them. Perhaps this was not their fault; the proper concept of metaphysics went missing somewhere in modern philosophy, and with the exception perhaps of the neo-scholastics, no one knows today how the mother of all sciences should be understood.

Aristotle gives two definitions of "first philosophy", which, for completely external and accidental reasons, was called *metaphysics*. In one of these definitions, he describes it as a study of the first principles and causes of being; in the second – as a science of what is insofar as it is, that is, of being in general, and he confronts this science, as general, with particular sciences.[23]

What Aristotle calls being, τὸ ὄν, and what the scholastics signify by the expression *ens*, is what I understand by an *object*. As professor Twardowski has already shown [Twardowski 1894: 37 and 38], an object is that which can be presented in some way, and, therefore, what is not nothing, but something, means the same as being, that is, the scholastic *ens*. According to the

---

Hume's understanding of Aristotle was: "Though it be too obvious to escape observation, that different ideas are connected together, I do not find, that any philosopher has attempted to enumerate or class all the principles of association". Obviously, Aristotle already formulated laws of association. The following quote from [Kant 1783a: §1, p. 41] shows how Kant understands metaphysics: "Die Prinzipien derselben (d.i. der Metaphysik) müssen also niemals aus der Erfahrung genommen sein, denn sie soll nicht physische, sondern metaphysische, d.i. jenseits der Erfahrung liegende Erkenntnis sein". Translation [Kant 1783b: 15]: "The principles of such cognition [...] [i.e., of metaphysics] must therefore never be taken from experience; for the cognition is supposed to be not physical but metaphysical, i.e., lying beyond experience".

23   In the first book of *Metaphysics* Aristotle considers who may be called wise. Namely, he is wise who knows about everything in general, although he does not know the details, who knows difficult things, knows them thoroughly, and may teach others about them; and of sciences the higher is that which is itself a purpose for itself and that requires and does not serve. Then he says (*Metaphysics*, A 2, 982, b. 8): "ἐξ ἁπάντων οὖν τῶν εἰρημένων ἐπὶ τὴν αὐτὴν ἐπιστήμην πίπτει τὸ ζητούμενον ὄνομα, δεῖ γὰρ ταύτην τῶν πρώτων ἀρχῶν καὶ αἰτιῶν εἶναι θεωρητικήν." Translation [Aristotle 1928: 981]: "Judged by all the tests we have mentioned, then, the name in question fall to the same science; this must be a science that investigates the first principle and causes". A definition that Aristotle gives at the beginning of book IV (*Metaphysics*, T 1, 1003, a.21) is definitely more important: "Ἔστιν ἐπιστήμη τις ἣ θεωρεῖ ἰὸ ὂν ἣ ὄνκαὶ τὰ τούτῳ ὑπάρχοντα καθ᾽ αὐτό. Αὕτη δ᾽ἐστὶν οὐδεμιᾷ τῶν ἐν μέρει λεγομένων ἡ αὐτὴ οὐδεμία γὰρ τῶν ἄλλων ἐπισκοπεῖ καθόλου περὶ τοῦ ὄντος ἣ ὄν, ἀλλὰ μέρος αὐτοῦ τι ἀποτεμομεναι περὶ τούτου θεωροῦσι τὸ συμβεβηκός, οἷον αἱ μαθηματικαὶ τῶν ἐπιστημῶν." Translation [Aristotle 1928: 1002]: "There is a science which investigates being as being and the attributes which belong to it in virtue of its own nature. Now this is not the same as any of the so-called particular sciences; for none of these treats universally of being as being. They cut off a part of being and investigate the attribute of this part; this is what the mathematical sciences for instance do." It is difficult to formulate the concept of science of objects in general more clearly.

scholastics, not only what exists (*ens habens actualem existentiam*) has being, but also what merely could exist (*ens possible*), and even what cannot exist, but can only be presented (*ens rationis*). Thus, the scholastic *ens* is *aliquid*, "something", and it is the highest concept, *summum genus*. The concept of object comprises all these features. Aristotle's first philosophy, as the science of being in general would not, therefore, be anything other than the science of objects in general.

Each *particular* science deals with a certain determinate kind of objects. Physics or chemistry study objects of external experience, psychology aims at finding laws for objects of internal experience, mathematics concerns objects that are not in experience at all. But perhaps there may also be a *general* science that would study objects of all kinds, dealing with the most general features of all objects. This is precisely what a general science *of objects*, that is, metaphysics, is.

It seems that just this is the proper meaning of Aristotle's first philosophy, and that his second definition was only the result of a certain solution to questions concerning objects. In his study of the most general features common to all objects, Aristotle thinks that these features are the four *causes*, namely, the formal cause, the material cause, the efficient cause, and the final cause. In his investigation of these causes, he arrives at certain *eschatological* views, thus, e.g., he claims that a chain of efficient causes cannot be infinite but has to have some *first* cause, etc. And since he ascribes great significance to investigations of causes in general, especially first causes, it is not surprising that he described the science of being in general, which brought him to exceedingly important results, as the science of first causes.

That metaphysics as a general science of objects leads to these kinds of ultimate questions is clear. But its first and most important tasks, on which all further results are based, lie elsewhere. Pointing to a few domains of metaphysics will perhaps suffice to indicate the proper domain of metaphysical investigations and to convince everyone how broad the scope of this science is, and how important its tasks are.

We know that along with *real*, that is, *concrete* objects (this or that man, painting, ...), we also distinguish abstract objects (a man as such, a painting as such, ...); and among abstract objects some have some *real* meaning (a man, a painting), some are purely ideal (a four-dimensional figure, a square circle ...). There are also other ways of *dividing* objects; systematically and thoroughly to divide all objects into particular categories is one of the most important aims of the investigation of objects, that is, metaphysics. Aristotle already attempted to accomplish this in his work on categories.

Furthermore, each object may stand in some relation to other objects; to examine and systematize this variety of relations, define and formulate their general features and laws is not the aim of any particular science but of a separate *theory of relations* that is a part of metaphysics.

Objects connected by relations form complexes, combinations, wholes of a higher level (a melody, a country, an organism). The examination of the features and laws of these wholes, that may be constituted by objects of any kind, doesn't belong to any particular science, but is the task of a separate *theory of wholes* which is a part of metaphysics.

Among various wholes, regular wholes whose simplest form is a series call for a special attention. So far, mostly mathematicians have worked on the theory of series. But not only do numbers form series; a series may be formed by objects of any kind. Thus, a general *theory of series* also belongs to the study of objects, that is, metaphysics.

Finally, a general *theory of necessary relations* belongs to the scope of this science. Even though not every object can be a member of a necessary relation because these connections obtain only between relations of a certain kind, each object can be a part of a member of a necessary relation. In this sense, necessary relations can occur between objects of any kind. Indeed, every particular science, be it empirical or *a priori*, not content merely to describe facts or objects, formulates laws and discriminates necessary relations between the objects it deals with; no such science, however, studies the features of the necessary relations that connect these objects. This is the task of the investigation of objects, that is, metaphysics.

No one has attempted so far to provide a systematic account of necessary relations. Modern philosophy was simply bereft of any understanding for this kind of questions. Of the various necessary relations it paid attention to causal relations only; but it investigated even these in its usual, psychological way. So, it only asked *whence* comes this concept and sought its psychological analysis and genesis; it considered, further, whence came the *conviction* about pervasiveness of the principle of causality, locating the source of this conviction either in certain facts of experience, as with Hume, or in some innate forms of the human mind, as with Kant. What this causal relation is, however, what features does it evince, or what the principle of causality *signifies*, these questions were dealt with only very superficially. But these are after all basic questions, whoever does not address them before pursuing further investigaions, acts against the scientific method and exposes himself to error.

If these philosophers, who together with Kant assume the "Copernican" standpoint in philosophy, instead of looking for mythical forms of cognition and creating strange metaphysical systems which they call "the theory of knowledge", could once look beyond their subjective horizons, they would see a new and very interesting world of objects and phenomena. They would learn that a causal relation, which they find so important, is just one of innumerable different necessary relations, that along with it there are also relations of complex dependence, contrariety, subcontrariety, contradiction, and many others yet unnamed; that these relations can occur between both abstract and concrete objects, and that they bring them together, tie them into various wholes; that almost everywhere as well certain non-necessary relations are, and must be, involved in them, etc. This could perhaps raise a doubt, viz., whether the principle of causality, which is supposed to be a "synthetic *a priori* judgment", really is as certain as it seems to be; and whether the concept of "synthetic *a priori* judgments" has any scientific value at all, and the question of how such judgments are possible any rational sense.

I suppose that everything in the world is tied together by some necessary knot; I don't think, however, that this knot is just a causal relation. If we consider the variety of necessary relations that obtain between creations of the mind as simple as integral numbers, the divisibility of some number by 6 necessarily brings about its divisibility by 3, but *not conversely*; the divisibility of some number by 3 necessarily brings about divisibility of the sum of this number's digits by 3, and *conversely*; the divisibility of some number by 2 and its divisibility by 3 together necessarily bring about its divisibility by 6, and so on; and if we consider how infinitely larger the variety of real objects and phenomena is, can we not suppose that necessary relations in the real world are much more complicated than within the domain of such simple abstract objects? Imagine that we have the power to put all our mathematical concepts in some concrete form such that they would have colors and shapes and positions in time and space, constituting the magical world of a fairy tale in which there were beings similar to us, with similar mental life. These beings would certainly toil at discovering regularities among phenomena, aspire to glean their essences and examine the necessary relations connecting them. If they were thinking rationally, they would soon learn how great the variety of these relations is, and how mysterious and complicated their configuration is. This is exactly the position in which we find ourselves. We live in a world which we did not create, but which is the work of Omnipotent God, the creation of His eternal thought just like our abstract concepts. We suppose that the same law of contradiction that governs the domain of our creations and is the basis of all necessary relations, also governs the real world around us. Thus, let us investigate these necessary relations where they occur in the clearest way: in the domain of abstract objects; perhaps then we could create a theory that with regard to reality would allow us better to grasp and understand this world's structure.

The present investigation into causality is but a fragment of this more general theory. The directions of study that I presented in it and the results at which I arrived are new and often even unexpected. I am aware that moving along on such a bumpy road, I could have easily tripped and fallen; hence, I tried to properly justify each of my theses in the appropriate way and to present them clearly and unambiguously, so that no one could doubt what my thinking is. Therefore, I hope that if there are any mistakes in this work, they will be easy to find.

Translated by Zuzanna Gnatek

Bibliography

Aristotle (1928). *Metaphysica*. Oxford 1966: Clarendon Press.

Bandrowski, Bronisław (1904). O metodach badania indukcyjnego [On Methods of Inductive Examination]. [In:] *Sprawozdanie Gimnazjum Franciszka Józefa za rok szkolny 1903/04* [Francis Joseph's Gymnasium Report for school year 1903/04]. Lwów, pp. 1–43.

Cossmann, Paul Nikolaus (1899). *Elemente der empirischen Teleologie*. Stuttgart: Zimmer.

Höfler, Alois (1890). *Logik*. Wien, Prag & Leipzig: F. Tempsky & G. Freytag Verlag.

Hume, David (1739–1740). *A Treatise of Human Nature*. London 1890: Longmans, Green and Co.

Hume, David (1748). *An Enquiry Concerning Human Understanding*. [In:] *Essays Moral, Political and Literary*. Vol. II. London 1898: Longmans, Green and Co.

Kant, Immanuel (1781a). *Kritik der reinen Vernunft*. [In:] *Kants Werke*. Vol. V. Berlin 1904. Akademie-Ausgabe.

Kant, Immanuel (1781b). *Critique of Pure Reason*. Cambridge 1998: Cambridge University Press.

Kant, Immanuel (1783a). *Prolegomena zu einer jeden künftigen Metaphysik die als Wissenschaft wird auftreten könen*. Leipzig 1888: Philipp Reclam jun.

Kant, Immanuel (1783b). *Prolegomena to Any Future Metaphysics That Will Be Able to Come Forward as Science*. Cambridge 2004: Cambridge University Press.

Łukasiewicz, Jan (1903). O indukcji jako inwersji dedukcji [On Induction as an Inversion of Deduction]. *Przegląd Filozoficzny* vol. VI, f. I, pp. 9–24; f. II, pp. 138–142.

Meinong, Alexius (1882). *Hume-Studien*. Vol. II. *Zur Relationstheorie*. Wien: Kaiserlichen Akademie der Wissenschaften. Sitzungsberichten der Philosophisch-Historische Klasse. Band CI.

Mill, John Stuart (1843). *A System of Logic Ratiocinative and Inductive*. London: John W. Parker.

Schopenhauer, Arthur (1813a). *Über die vierfache Wurzel des Satzes vom zureichenden Grunde*. Leipzig 1896: Philipp Reclam jun.

Schopenhauer, Arthur (1813b). On the Fourfold Root on the Principle of Sufficient Reason. [In:] *"On the Fourfold Root on the Principle of Sufficient Reason" and "On the Will in Nature"*. London: George Bell and Sons, pp. 1–189.

Sigwart, Christoph (1879a). *Logik*. Vol. II. Freiburg am B. 1893: J.C.B. Mohr.

Sigwart, Christoph (1879b). *Logic*. Vol. II. London & New York 1895: Swan Sonnenshein et Co. & Macmillan et Co.

Twardowski, Kazimierz (1894). *Zur Lehre vom Inhalt Und Gegenstand der Vorstellungen*. Wien: A. Hölder.

PART 2

Resonance of Łukasiewicz's "Analysis" in the First Half of the Twentieth Century in Poland

∵

CHAPTER 1

Criticism of the Concept of Causal Connection

Marian Borowski

Krytyka pojęcia związku przyczynowego
Przegląd Filozoficzny Vol. x (1907), I. IV, pp. 492–508

∴

In everyday life, as well as in science, we constantly use causal connections. They are meant for us to conveniently capture and express such connections between phenomena that we consider necessary – in contrast to accidental connections and combinations. I will not go into the question whether there is any justification for surmising necessary connections in nature.

In logic, the following general scheme of the causal connection has been established: phenomenon *A* is the cause of phenomenon *B*, since if *A* occurs, then *B* must occur. Therefore, since phenomenon *B* does not occur, its cause *A* also cannot occur. Two simple relations of necessity can be distinguished: (1) between the occurrence of the cause and the occurrence of the effect; (2) between the non-occurrence of the effect and the non-occurrence of the cause. Both these relations can be deduced from each other, such that they could even be considered two sides of one and the same relation.

On the other hand, there is neither a connection of necessary dependence between the occurrence of the effect and the occurrence of the cause, nor between lack of a cause and lack of an effect.

> The occurrence of an effect does not necessarily bring about the occurrence of a cause, and the non-occurrence of a cause does not necessarily bring about the non-occurrence of an effect.
>
> ŁUKASIEWICZ 1906: 27

> The effect is admittedly a constant consequent of a cause, but the cause is not a constant antecedent of an effect.
>
> BANDROWSKI 1904: 27

| DOI:10.1163/9789004522244_003

Ch. Sigwart [1872–1879: Vol. II, § 95, 13, p. 279], J.St. Mill [1843: Vol. III, Ch. x, § 3], A. Höfler [1890: 66] and many others speak similarly. If, for example, we put a burning match on dry gunpowder surrounded by oxygen, etc., then an explosion must occur; however, the absence of a burning match is not necessarily combined with lack of an explosion. It can occur due to an electric spark, impact, pressure, concentration of sunlight through a lens, etc. If there is no effect, there can be no cause, but if there is an effect, there need not necessarily be a certain cause. Since the explosion of gunpowder does not occur, the totality of the conditions together with the burning match could not occur, but if there is an explosion, it is not necessarily preceded by this cause. It is therefore assumed that, although the same causes must bring about the same effects and the various effects are due to different causes, the same effects do not have to correspond to the same causes, but there may be effects due to different causes.

The last theorem, which is a negative part of the current concept of causation, does not seem right to me because it corresponds neither to the postulates of our mentality nor to real relations in the world of physical phenomena.

According to the criticized view, an effect is not necessarily related to its cause – it may have other causes, and the concept of exclusivity is comprised in the concept of the necessary connection. "Any A *must* bring about B" means that nothing other than B can be brought about by A. Also "B must be brought about by A" means that B can be brought about by nothing other than A. Admittedly, the word "must" is also used in the following phrase: some A must bring about (be brought about by) either B, or D, or C, etc. But this blurs the proper meaning of the word "must" and can be replaced without any damage in this case by the word "can". Similar expressions are used due to inexact and inaccurate determination of the necessary connection. After all, if in a given case A brings about B, and not, for example, D, this happens due to the special conditions of α. Thus, A itself does not bring about B necessarily. Only A with the attribute α brings about B necessarily, but then also *exclusively*. A itself is not necessarily related either to B, or to C, or to D, since without special attributes such as α, β, or γ, A cannot bring them about. When we precisely identify the arguments for the necessary connection, it turns out that it contains the feature of exclusiveness. Therefore, the supporters of the criticized concept of necessity, who claim that the effect is not exclusively related to a given cause, must consider and actually do consider the relation of effect to cause as a relation that is *not necessary*.

Moreover, it should be noted that once it is accepted that a given effect can be caused by several different causes, which cannot be indicated by any common sign, basically nothing hinders the assumption that the possible causes of a given effect can be very numerous, and even that there is an infinite number of them. Then the relation of effect to cause presents itself as completely accidental, and the inference of the effect from the cause cannot be logically justified in any way. Since it is clear that, if a given effect can essentially be the result of the most various combinations, then its occurrence is not different from a completely accidental occurrence, because the case is also a consequence of any state of affairs. Thus, according to the concept of causation in use today, some phenomenon A, considered to be a cause, necessarily brings about phenomenon B, while B is not necessarily caused by A but relates to it in a probably quite *accidental* way.

The artificiality of the construction of such a connection is visible. It does not satisfy our mind's postulate to connect everything, if possible, with necessary and comprehensively defined connections, and does not correspond to our conviction that physical reality does not feature any randomness and ambiguity in ordering phenomena, and finally, it does not explain that in fact we conclude to the cause from the effect by the correct use of certain rules.

Also, this view is not in accordance with our innermost, deepest concept of necessity. Namely, if we want to be aware precisely of the necessity of bringing about phenomenon B by phenomenon A, we think that the nature of phenomenon A, its essence, is that it brings about phenomenon B. Phenomenon A would be internally contradictory if it did not bring about B. Therefore, if one accepts that it is also in the nature of other phenomena to bring about the same effect B, then one must suppose that their natures are the same, and therefore, that the causes bringing about the same effect are essentially the same.

It is interesting that the methods formulated by J.S. Mill to establish a causal connection also lead, if strictly applied, to establishing a connection of a different appearance. For example, according to the method of agreement, the detail occurring in various complexes of phenomena preceding a given effect should be considered as the cause when it is common to all these complexes. According to this method, it is necessary to eliminate details that differ from each other until all that remains is the same – it is the proper cause. At bottom, therefore, the conviction is that the same effects are brought about by the same causes.

In his logic, Sigwart [1872–1879: 474] criticizes this method of agreement, claiming that it leads to comical and impossible results. If, for example, we are looking by means of this method for what is common in various complexes of phenomena preceding the death of the biological organism, we will find only life itself as the only common moment – and, therefore, life should be considered the cause of death! I will soon be able to show that this example demonstrates not so much that the Mill's method is misleading, but rather that Sigwart's application thereof of is less than loyal.

Likewise, the method of difference, i.e., seeking the cause of a given phenomenon in how the complex of phenomena that precedes it differs from the complex after which this effect does not occur, is based on the principle that various causes have various effects. If many different causes could have the same effect, then it would be pointless to take into account many different complexes or to make changes to a given complex, as the method of variations does. However, this is not how things are; causes that differ from each other do not bring about the same effects. Finally, the correlation of given effects to known causes, as prescribed by Mill's fourth method, is also based on the assumption that the same effects are brought about, in each case, by the same causes and that, in particular, the quantitative relations between the phenomena, that are the cause and the effect, are permanent.

Summing up the objections mentioned hitherto, one can say: the current concept of causal connection does not correspond to our logical postulates, because: (1) it does not define both members of the connection either precisely or necessarily; (2) it conflicts with our understanding of necessity as something inherent in the nature of things; (3) the methods of inductive examinations currently in use are based on assumptions which are non-compliant with the form of the causal connection in question.

These arguments cannot be convincing for someone who does not consider the causal connection to be a necessary connection, and who does not consider Mill's methods to be accurate. For that reason, I will pay more attention to the analysis of specific examples, especially since everyday experience speaks very clearly against my position.

However, before I go into casuistry, I want to draw attention in advance to some errors, constantly repeated in constructing appropriate examples.

Namely, in our everyday talk and unfortunately all too often as well in scientific discourse, we neglect to define the terms of the causal connection, i.e., the cause and the effect, both strictly with regard to quantity and univocally with regard to quality. Usually, cause is understood too broadly and too sketchily, or effect is understood too narrowly and specifically. Also, often the scope of the cause includes that which is not the proper cause but instead an indifferent circumstance, or some part of the effect is wrongfully excluded from the whole effect. What is necessary and sufficient to bring about an effect should be called the cause, and, consequently, the effect is everything that unconditionally follows a given cause. This postulate does not prejudge any theory of causal connection. If we assume that there is any connection between real phenomena at all, whether it a necessary connection or some more closely undefined dependence, in any case whatever does not contribute to the effect and can be left out without any harm cannot be included in the cause; and, on the other hand, whatever does not suffice to bring about an effect cannot be considered the cause of something. It is also clear that the scope of the effect must include everything that owes its being to a given cause and nothing more.

This postulate does not entirely prejudge the question whether a given effect can always be brought about by the same causes. This is because I label as necessary the particular elements of the cause that cannot be removed without preventing the effect, and not in the sense that these elements could not be replaced by any other elements without affecting the effect.

The second frequently repeated error in seeking examples of a causal connection consists in paying insufficient attention to strictly direct causes. Only the last cause is the proper cause, i.e., the necessary and sufficient cause.

Having drawn attention in this way to these common errors in the determination of cause and effect, I can turn to the analysis of examples. According to popular belief, a person's death can occur due to some illness, due to poisoning, shooting, etc. A gunpowder explosion can be brought about on one occasion by a blow, on a second occasion by an electric current, a spark, or by applying a burning match. A stone will move along a certain path due to the action of one force or several attaching to one another at a certain angle. The phenomenon of heat can be brought about by a mechanical phenomenon, e.g., by impact, friction, an electrical or chemical phenomenon, etc. It is not difficult to see that in these cases the common view takes the scope of the effect too narrowly in comparison with the cause, or it takes the scope of the cause too broadly in comparison with the effect. The narrowness of the scope of the effect is revealed in that we do not consider that the total effects of poisoning, shooting a person, etc. always differ. The effects here are different complexes of phenomena and changes, and these complexes have only a certain part in common, namely the very death of an individual, whereas the remaining elements are different. This is because at death different bodily tissues are damaged in different ways for various reasons; sometimes they are accompanied by physical changes, sometimes by mostly chemical changes. In the event of a burst of gunpowder brought about by a hammer blow, in addition to the explosion itself there will occur: the crashing sound of the impact, the dissipation of the hammer's mechanical energy, the mechanical reaction of the powder to the impact etc. Were we to carry out the explosion in some other way, only some elements of the effect will remain the same. When dragging a material body with two forces interacting at a certain angle, it is necessary to include in the effect not only the movement of the body in the resultant direction, but also the lateral tension derived from the action of the components perpendicular to the resultant. Heat can be obtained from various other phenomena, that is, energy, but not from each in the same way and in the same devices. Taking these circumstances into account, it is clear that the entire effect will be different in each case. Moreover, the heat from various sources is probably not completely the same. For example, light derived from various sources, despite apparent identity, shows differences on closer examination. In order for an experiment with the interference of light rays to succeed, they must come from the same source and be spatially restricted to the fullest extent possible. We know that the same holds for so-called radiating heat. With a different type of heat, we cannot, however, identify any differences in quality despite its origin from various sources. This may be due to the familiar theory that heat is a disorderly motion of ether particles, or of matter, as opposed to light or electricity, which rely on ordered ether motion.

In the examples above, if we want to consider as a cause various complexes of phenomena, then the effect will always consist of complexes. A certain individual, total cause can bring about only a certain definite total effect, and *vice versa* a state of affairs that is the total effect can only be brought about by a certain total cause. We should always only take the same effect as generally as we take the cause.

Incidentally, based on the superficial experiences on which ordinary views rely, it is possible not only to conclude that various causes have the same effects, but, conversely, that the same causes have different effects. For example, one and the same heat brings about a chemical process in one case, and electric current or vapor pressure in a second case; the movement of a material body can bring about the movement of another body in one case, and heat in a second case, etc. Here, however, the human mind is more cautious and demands in each case that the total cause and all the conditions of the given effect be provided. Why, in analogous cases, that same mind does not care about indicating and describing the total effect probably depends on matters of a practical nature to which I will return.

This leads to the same conclusion, namely, that various causes have different effects, and the same effects always have the same causes, including the case where we want to consider as the effect only a certain moment in the complex of consequences, e.g., the mere death of a man without accompanying circumstances, the explosion itself of the gunpowder, the mere phenomenon of the movement of the material body along a certain path without the side effects, or just the phenomenon of heat. In such a case, it is also necessary to tighten the complex of phenomena on the side of the cause and to eliminate everything that is not necessary to bring about this special effect which we have in view. However, the ordinary view neglects this indication and usually takes the cause much to broadly and generally. If we try to analyze the total cause and its total effect into individual elements and parts, physical as well as metaphysical, then it will turn out that in each case the same special effects are also due to the same special causes. When, in the total effect of various causes, we encounter a certain common element, on the side of the causes we can find the corresponding common element; and it will turn out that just this element is sufficient and indispensable for bringing about this special effect. It is not difficult to see, namely, that all causes that cause a gunpowder explosion have a certain common moment which is that the temperature rises to a certain degree. The remaining elements that make up the complexes of phenomena called causes are different and not necessary to bring about an explosion as a particular element in a total complex of consequences. Two forces appropriately selected and inclining toward each other at a certain angle drag a given body in the same direction, e.g., to the east, as would a single force having the size and direction of the resultant. A common element, however, in both these various causes is the direction of the acting forces, the direction to the east, because from the forces inclining toward each other at a certain angle only their components, falling in the direction of the resultant, are operative.

The remaining components do not contribute at all to the effect in question, viz., dragging the body to the east, but they bring about separate special effects, such as lateral tensions. Medicine has reduced the proper causes of human death to two: heart failure or asphyxia, and there is hope that in the future it will succeed in analyzing one moment common to both, the ultimate cause of death. The phenomenon of heat can arise from various causes, from a chemical process, an electric current, mechanical work. And here, however, one can indicate the same element which is the proper cause of heat. According to the most widespread theory in physics, all physical phenomena rely on different movements of material particles or ether particles: a mechanical phenomenon is a uniform and ordered motion of particles, light and electric phenomena are periodic vibrations of ether, thermal phenomena are unstructured vibrations of ether, acoustic phenomena are vibrations of the air or some other material environment, and even static phenomena of voltage or mechanical pressure rely on latent molecular motion, etc. Thus, the common acting moment when heat is created from various sources may be considered to be the movement of the smallest physical elements, or rather some of their special components, the emergence of which, in a way, is the work of various devices to generate heat – different devices depending on the difference of the sources.

Nevertheless, the issue from the energy point of view is straightforward. All phenomena are only various forms and symptoms of energy, i.e., the ability to do work. Energy is one and the same in all phenomena; it takes

different forms depending on the conditions it encounters and the principle of increasing entropy. When, for example, a mechanical phenomenon
is transformed into thermal energy, then, according to the energy theory,
one and the same energy quantum has changed its form according to the
device into which it was imported, for example instruments for inducing
heat by friction (Joule's grinder), and according to the law of increasing
entropy directing changes of energy's forms. This law requires that energy in
the absence of interfering devices should shift from the state of aggregation
to the state of dispersion, or from a more conservative form to a form with
greater dispersibility, which is the form of heat versus the mechanical form.
The same, *mutatis mutandis,* can be said, for example, about the generation
of heat from electricity, etc.

Also, a physicist-phenomenalist, who does not want to see the "essence" of
all phenomena in mechanical motion or energy but takes them as they appear
to him, must agree that in seemingly different conditions of heat induction the
proper and sole cause is always one and the same thing. In order for a thermal
phenomenon to arise, (1) other phenomene must *disappear;* (2) the conditions
cannot create other types of phenomena. Heat is the natural end-product of
all physical processes. When an electrical phenomenon comes into being, it is
necessary that some other physical phenomenon as well as some special conditions, which are able to somehow disrupt the balance of the electrical factor,
disappear. These conditions in the face of disappearing mechanical phenomena will consist in mounting resistance to them, and in the face of chemical
or thermal phenomena in choosing certain sites among them and directing
them in a certain way. From a phenomenalist point of view, these matters will
not yet be "explained". An auditory phenomenon arises for seemingly different reasons such as, for example, vibrations of a string, blowing into a trum-
pet or pipe, some chemical process (the hiss given off when slaking lime), etc.
However, in each of these cases, the proper cause is the introduction of air into
the vibrations at certain periods.

Undoubtedly, from the point of view as well of the physics of electrons, the
same causes can be found for the same effects. In any case, it is in the nature
of every theory, as an "explanation", that it tries to find or construct equivalents
in antecedents for the given uniformities and similarities in the consequences.
Interference phenomena in the domains of light and electricity strongly suggest the the same causes. Since magnetic fields affect light rays just as they
affect cathode rays, it suggests that in the case of light electrons are involved.
The similarity of the behavior of electric charges toward atomic valences in
electrolysis to that of atoms in chemical reactions leads to the theory of the
homogeneity of these elements, etc.

It must be admitted that in many cases the state of our knowledge does not allow us to state strictly and demonstratively the proper causes and the proper effects. However, the more accurately we can analyze physical phenomena the more clearly it turns out that the same effect can only be caused by the same cause. The science of physics seeks to determine the connection between phenomena strictly and unambiguously. The causes of a given physical phenomenon are not sought in just any amount of energy, motion, or size of the preceding phenomenon – but only in the quantity and quantity corresponding exactly to the effect. The law of energy conservation, or the law of constant quantitative relations between the disappearing phenomena and the phenomena emerging in their place, and the law of entropy, defining the value of various energies or phenomena and the direction of physical processes, all these allow science to identify in the same measure both the antecedents of a given phenomenon and its consequences, and to identify the cause both explicitly by the effect and *vice versa:* the effect by the cause.

The psychological reason that in everyday life we have become accustomed to determining causes and effects strictly and precisely is, to a large extent, found in their temporal properties. We can determine the effect in more detail because there is a causal link in each case, one either present and given to us perceptually, or a future one, and then we usually have in view a very special, intended or expected effect without its attendant circumstances to which we are indifferent. On the other hand, the cause can be given either as something past or as something present. In the first case, it presents itself to us in a general way and allows us to include in it many things not belonging to it, especially since we usually have in mind more or less indirect causes; in the second case, i.e., when the cause is given to us in the present tense, practicability requires taking and applying the cause a little more broadly in order to guarantee that one has not left out any moment indispensable for bringing about a certain special expected effect. We look into the future microscopically, we see in it a few things, but clearly, either as the goals of our activity or prediction in the event of passive behavior, whereas we look into the past macroscopically, we remember important and minor items in a more or less equal way.

In addition to this psychological motivation, theoretical understanding of the causal connection on the model of the relation of reason to consequence often applies, for from the truth of the consequence one cannot infer the truth of the reason. Therefore, it should be noted: (1) it is impossible to maintain precisely an analogy between logical relations and causal relations among physical phenomena, because logical operations concern judgments, or more or less general terms, and in nature there are no facts corresponding to them – there are only particular, concrete natural facts; (2) it is probable that with the current formulation of the relation of reason and consequence, the reason is understood too broadly and the consequence too narrowly and too specifically. If we consider only what is necessary and sufficient to justify something as the reason of a given consequence, then it may turn out that the reason and consequence are strictly in line with each other, and that the reason can be inferred from its consequence. This result seems to be consistent with the application of the principle of quantification of the predicate in logic.

The position I have taken here in the matter of causality has several consequences that are inconsistent with the popular view of these matters. These consequences can be raised as objections against my position, and therefore I will deal with them more closely.

And so, since it is assumed that all differences and similarities on the side of the effects correspond to suitable differences and similarities on the side of causes and *vice versa*, it should also be assumed that the connection between cause and effect is reciprocal and equally strict in both directions. Meanwhile, the everyday view considers the cause not to be related to the effect as necessarily as the effect is to the cause, and, according to this view, something active is called a cause, and an effect is something passive and exclusively dependent.

It is not difficult to show that where the effect and cause are strictly simultaneous there is a bilateral connection between them. This is evident when dependencies are treated in a mathematical formula. For example, we signify with the formula $s = vt$ that the size of the path traversed by uniform motion depends on the speed of motion and its duration. However, nothing stands in the way of considering with the same meaning the length of time needed to traverse a certain path at a given speed, depending on the size of the path to be traversed at a given time. Neither the path, nor the time, nor the speed are essentially either independent or dependent quantities. The patterns $s = vt$, $T = 2\pi \sqrt{l / g}$ (duration of swing), $\alpha = 2\pi / T$ (angular speed) all sound quite natural. It cannot be said, however, that the product vt "brings about" the size of the path S, or that the quotient S / t "brings about" speed, because we want to deal here only with the dependence between co-temporal elements; whereas the terms "bring about" can only be used where there is a time difference between cause and effect.

Changing the volume of body depends on applying heat to it, but also *vice versa*: applying heat to the body depends on the change of volume; i.e., heating would not occur were there no change in volume at the same time. It is a conventional matter which of these cases we will call cause and which we will call effect; this depends on practical reasons. And so, since we heat the body, and at the same time the body expands, we call heating the cause, and the expansion the effect. If, on the other hand, we expand the body and at the same time it absorbs heat from the environment, then the first is called the cause and the second is the effect.

Gas pressure in a closed vessel depends on the pressure exerted on it frow without, but at the same time the amount of exertion depends on the amount of pressure, and were there no pressure no force could be exerted.[1]

The mutual dependence of cause and effect also occurs when the effect follows the cause in time. In a twisted spring there is a so-called potential energy that triggers the spring movement after removing the obstacle. I argue that the existence of this potential energy is dependent on the subsequent movement, as well as *vice versa*. After all, the essence of the potential energy (tension or pressure) lies in the fact that if the obstacles are removed, it causes movement. If this movement were not brought about, one could not talk about potential energy or the phenomenon of mechanical tension. It must be admitted, with the same degree of obviousness with which we claim that the potential energy in the spring would arise from the movement that encountered resistance, that this energy must bring about movement once resistance is removed. For electric current to occur, pre-existing conditions are needed, namely: the occurrence of some uncompensated difference in potentials; further co-temporal conditions are needed, for example, that there be no dielectric body nor too much resistance; and it is necessary that this current bring about at least partial equalization of this difference in potentials. For example, by removing from some closed system the possibility of equalizing the potential differences, it is impossible to create electrical currents. A magnet would not be a magnet if it did not exert ponderomotoric effects; chemical reactions could not take place if they did not emit or absorb heat; heat would not be heat if it did not radiate to the surroundings, etc., etc.

These claims seem paradoxical. However, I know of no rational reason why the future should be considered more dependent on the past than the reverse, and the present state should be determined only by the previous state without any regard to the next state. After all, the future is neither less real or unreal, nor real in a different way than the past! With the same certainty with which we claim that everything must have its cause in the past, we should say that everything must have its consequences. Just as a given phenomenon could not exist without causes, so could it not exist without bringing about effects.

Our physical principles apply in the same way to the past, the present, and the future. For the same reason that we believe that some phenomenon, matter

---

1 Cf. the different interpretaion of the same examples made by W.M. Kozłowski in [Kozłowski 1906: 201*ff*].

or energy, cannot arise from nothing we also believe that they cannot disappear without a trace in the future. To be sure, ordinary experience does not indicate that physical processes depend on their subsequent stages, but again this is only due to imprecise determination of causes and effects. A candle, for example, burns in the same way, regardless of whether it brings about photochemical or thermal effects; the rifle bullet travels in the same way, whether it strikes a rock or a human, etc. However, one could argue in the same way that these phenomena also do not depend on their antecedents. Lighting a candle is not affected by whether it was lit in this way or that; the gun's firing is not affected by whether it was caused by a blow or a spark. On the other hand, one cannot say that the energy of light or the bullet's travel occur from nothing, nor can it be said that they disappear without a trace. Equally, the circumstances of transforming the chemical energy of coal and oxygen into heat and light energy, and then again the light energy into the chemical energy on the photographic plate, and, similarly, the chemical energy of gunpowder into the kinetic energy of the bullet, and the latter again into potential, mechanical or thermal energy when encountering resistance – fall strictly under one and the same law of increasing entropy. Every phenomenon, therefore, is connected by the same laws to its past as well as its future. It could not exist without being brought about in a strictly determined way, just as it could not exist without causing its effects. One can easily identify it in each individual case if one determines precisely the right causes and the right effects. For example, the necessary and sufficient effect of the flight of the bullet (taken separately, without the accompanying circumstances) is not to kill a man, to crush a rock or to swing a heavy pendulum – but only a part of these complexes of phenomena, namely overcoming some resistance on a certain path. Without bringing about this effect under the emerging conditions, the kinetic energy of the bullet's flight could not, as such, exist at all.

The present would certainly be different, not only if its past but also its future were different. These kinds of relations are called dependencies.

The world in which neighboring phenomena are connected by a mutual and equivalent dependence can be symbolized as a net, such that each individual eye is supported by all neighboring ones. No phenomena can be fully understood if one does not know all its preceding and contemporaneous conditions as well as its consequences. The finalistic treatment of phenomena is nonetheless more legitimate than a causal one, and it is even indispensable in many cases where biological or social organisms are involved. However, I am not thinking about returning to the old teleology. The former teleology was naively anthropomorphic, operating with "intent", "aim", "striving", and "prior thought". On the other hand, the theorem concerning the equal dependence between preceding and the following phenomena involves no trace of the influence of spiritual elements and analogies to people carrying out previously laid plans. There is only consistent determinism – which happens to be very similar to determinism in the spirit of Laplace, so often evoked in philosophical writing.

The reason why it is so difficult to come to terms with the thought that the relation of the past to the present is not closer than the relation of the future to the present is, among other things, the fact that we know very little about the future in comparison to the knowledge that the memory of the past provides. Based on our limited knowledge of the future we hypostatize it as having little reality and small significance for the present. Likewise, lack of knowledge of the causes for some human behavior is often considered to be total absence of causes [and instead as] behavior by free will.

Determinism requires a single-valued correlation of phenomena in time, i.e., the irreversibility of physical processes. Meanwhile, both Ernst Mach [1905: 273] and his opponents derive the conclusion that physical processes are symmetric in time from the principle of the interdependence of causes and effects. Nothing could be more wrong. After all, the fact that the current phenomenon is equally dependent on the preceding one and on the successive one does not indicate that these phenomena could be inverted in time. Phenomenon A can cause phenomenon B, but phenomenon B cannot cause phenomenon A, although they are nevertheless strongly connected to each other. Phenomenon A would not exist if it did not bring about B as B would not have existed if A had not brought it about – but they cannot change roles between them. Similarly, I call something, for instance, "bigger" only in comparison to some other, "smaller" thing, and *vice versa* – but it does not follow that the smaller thing could be the bigger, and the larger the smaller. The particular parts of an organism, just like a machine, are closely related to each other in their functioning, but they can neither change places nor functions. The principle of the strict and comprehensive dependency of phenomena excludes any freedom and the possibility of inverting the order of phenomena in time or space.

The principle of the interdependence of cause and effect also sheds some light on the traditional dispute whether the cause precedes the effect or whether it is contemporaneous. If, in fact, the cause of a given phenomenon is everything that is necessary and sufficient for the existence of this phenomenon, then past and present as well as future phenomena and circumstances should be included in this cause. There is no avoiding one of these kinds of phenomena, and each type alone is not enough for the existence of a given phenomenon. One can, however, use the word "cause" in a narrower and improper scope, namely either with regard to the emergence of a given phenomenon one can take into account only the preceding phenomena; or with regard to its *duration*, one can take into account only contemporaneous phenomena; or finally with regard to its *ending*, one can take into account only the subsequent phenomena. But there is no real meaning here, because there are no phenomena given to us in experience that do not come forth, do not last for some time, and do not change.

My argument criticizing the current concept of casual connection can be summarized retrospectively as follows: the view that physical phenomena are connected equally strongly with one another by a causal connection, no matter which is the antecedent and which the consequence, results from the claim that equal effects are brought about by equal causes, whereas different effects are brought about by different causes, and that different causes always have different effects and that the same causes have the same effects. This claim results again from determining the cause as what is necessary and sufficient for the occurrence of the effect, and the effect as all that to which, as its cause, it owes its being. These definitions are completely synonymous. They originate from the concept of unambiguously defined dependencies between physical phenomena. Adopting such a concept is inevitable if a real connection between phenomena is at all supposed, i.e., it is supposed that phenomena do not happen at all by chance.

The above conclusions, however, do not imply accepting any connections of dependence or necessity in nature. They retain their formal value also for those who deny the human mind the right to see a real connection beyond the factual occurrence of phenomena and their constant consequences and argue that the category of "necessity-contingency" has no application in the real world. To hold this position, we also want to determine the necessary and sufficient antecedents, or the consequences of a given phenomenon, to signify precisely the elements that constantly succeed or accompany each other. The postulate of unambiguously defining quantitatively and qualitatively what we call cause and effect, and claiming that they are completely interdependent, originates with the supporters of this position. Should we, however, be satisfied with the form of mathematical functions when presenting physical processes? The answer to this question is not easy because the formal properties of the relation of constant succession or accompanying and the relation of necessary connection are the same. I find attempts – so frequent in philosophical literature – to show that we experience the constant succession of phenomena in a way different from the connection of necessity to be wrong. The answer to the above question can only come from considering what we mean by "necessity", that is, by examining the content of this concept, and then by considering the relation of the human mind to the outside world – in an epistemological and metaphysical direction.

This paper was delivered on 23.07.1907, in the afternoon [during a session of the Philosophy Section of the 10th Congress of Polish Physicians and Naturalists].

Translated by Jacek J. Jadacki and Edward M. Świderski

Bibliography

Bandrowski, Bronisław (1904). *O metodach badania indukcyjnego* [On Methods of Inductive Research]. Lwów: I Związkowa Drukarnia.

Höfler, Alois (1890). *Logik.* Wien, Prag & Leipzig: F. Tempsky & G. Freytag Verlag.

Kozłowski, Władysław Mieczysław (1906). Przyczynowość jako podstawowe pojęcie przyrodoznawstwa [Causality as the Basic Concept of Natural Science]. *Przegląd Filozoficzny* vol. IX, f. 2–3, pp. 180–222.

Łukasiewicz, Jan (1906). Analysis and Construction of the Concept of Cause. In this volume: pp. 3–66.

Mach, Ernst (1905). *Erkenntnis und Irrtum.* Leipzig: Joann Ambrosius Barth.

Mill, John Stuart (1843). *A System of Logic Ratiocinative and Inductive.* London: John W. Parker.

Sigwart, Christoph (1872–1879). *Logik.* Vol. I-II. Freiburg am B. 1889–1893: J.C.B. Mohr.

CHAPTER 2

Causality and Functional Relation. A Study in the Theory of Knowledge

Zygmunt Zawirski

Apud me non omnia mathematice fiunt.
   Przyczynowość a stosunek funkcjonalny
   Studium z zakresu teorii poznania
      Przegląd Filozoficzny vol. XV (1912), f. 1, pp. 1–66

∴

1

We are witnesses to an important matter in the history of science; voices are rising from all sides, demanding a revision of the most important scientific concepts, a revision of the "cognitive tools", with the help of which the mind tries to get to know and understand the reality surrounding it, or as others say, how the mind adapts to reality. These voices and the attempts to revise and reconstruct the most important concepts of science from many sides are the result of a certain discovery in the last century. A fact of extraordinary significance has been discovered: that science develops, and not only in terms of content, the amount of accumulated information – this fact did not need to be discovered – but that science develops in terms of its form, that as science develops the fundamental character of the cognitive relation of the human mind to the surrounding reality is subject to evolution. These changes concern not only the material from which the edifice of knowledge arises, but also relate to these cognitive means and tools, these forms of cognition with the help of which the human mind builds knowledge, these chief concepts without the help of which no science can be done, and which are the foundation and "scaffolding" for this construction called science. The demand to reform the basic concepts of science also flows from the understanding that without inspecting and improving tools, construction cannot proceed and develop, that if we are opposed to thinking about improving our tools, we will diminish the productivity of scientific work.

The study of the values of fundamental scientific concepts has always been an object of concern for philosophers and philosophy, especially that branch which has taken as its object of investigation the source, values and ranges of knowledge, and which has been called the theory of knowledge, transcendental logic, epistemology, noetics or the like. The development of this branch of philosophy dates back to the flourishing of philosophy in modern times, although its roots were already present in ancient philosophy and in medieval disputes over universals. However, not all modern philosophers who devoted their life to this area of philosophy agreed unanimously how this scientific assessment of concepts should be carried out, what the touchstone should be, what is to be the measure of their scientificity. Using the work of Locke, Berkeley, and Hume, and drawing his own conclusions from their attainments and errors, Kant attempted, in the *Critique of Pure Reason,* to indicate firmly and reliably what the criterion of the value of concepts should be, and how science should be protected once and for all from any skepticism or dogmatism. After all, science is a fact! Just look – he said in a way – at the edifices of the mathematical natural sciences which triumph in Newton's works. Just be aware of why they are possible, and you will discover the Archimedean support point. So, to know what you can talk about, being neither a physicist nor a biologist, first collect everything that can only be decided on the basis of reason itself, without looking at experience, experiments and observations, and you will have various "*a priori*" concepts and principles. But this is only the beginning. Among these concepts and purely rational principles, look further for those in which all judgments about experience are based, which are therefore a condition and the basis of scientific experience. Only those concepts and principles have right of citizenship in science that serve to grasp empirical data, only the "form of synthesis" of the details of experience, and therefore, the concepts that are an indispensable means and condition for collective scientific work. All other concepts and purely rational principles, even if they were also necessary and *a priori*, are not equal in scientific character. We have deliberately given the foregoing formulation to Kant's thinking to draw attention to an important detail, so far forgotten by many people, that "apriorism" in Kant's theory of knowledge takes a secondary place. After all, not only are "categories" *a priori*, but so are "ideas"; but only the first have scientific value because only they are "conditions for the possibility of experience". Not only should the Kantian "*a priori*" be understood in a purely logical sense, or even in an only methodological meaning, as Riehl wants, rather than in a psychological or metaphysical meaning, but it can, in my opinion, even be completely abandoned without affecting the nucleus of Kant's arguments, at least where his theory of experience concerned and understanding why he gives certain concepts priority in science over others.

Thus, a demarcation line was established, which was supposed to separate, once and forever – among general rational concepts and principles, among all products of the mind, among all thought constructions that have ever appeared, appear and can appear – scientific concepts from those which cannot have a scientific character in the strict sense of the word. Concepts that do not express any empirical data, that do not serve to capture certain details of experience, have no scientific value. For this reason, Kant included not only mathematical concepts in the set of concepts authorized in mathematics, but also such concepts of past metaphysics as substance and causation so criticized by Hume, while rejecting as not equivalent so-called "ideas" such as the concepts of freedom, the absolute, etc. This does not mean, of course, that ideas and what flows from them do not have any value for science. They have their value as well, but not the same as the former, because they do not enter into the *constitution* of scientific experience; scientific work in the field of physics and psychology confidently go forward without them. They may, however, have – at least some of them – a *regulative* value, i.e., scientific researchers should not lose sight of ideas altogether so as not to grant absolute value to empirical details and close their eyes voluntarily to many things, remembering that they have no means to deal with the whole of the universe, that on the basis of physics or astronomy nothing can be shown about the existence or non-existence of God, that they cannot see the proof of the existence of the Deity in the first impulse that the planets must have received or *vice versa*, just as they should not consider the non-existence of God to be demonstrated when they can provide a physical explanation of how the nebulae were formed.

In this effort to delineate and demarcate concepts in terms of their cognitive value, we see the superiority of Kant's theory of knowledge over all previous ones. Locke's theory of cognition did not adequately insure science against the misuse of its concepts; after all, Locke believed in the possibility of proving God's existence based on experience. Hume put the concepts of Newtonian physics on the same level as the concept of God. The reason for this was the fact that, before Kant, the theory of cognition, if it was not based on any metaphysical assumptions, was mainly guided by psychological analysis. Kant first tried to show the inadequacy of the psychological method used by Hume, distinguishing the question of fact from the question of justification [Kant 1781: 103], the psychological deduction of the concept from transcendental deduction.[1] The way a concept actually develops cannot determine its usefulness in science. Today, psychology tries to base every idea on some imaginative background, something concrete and evident, so both categories and ideas can have their psychological genesis; in this respect, psychology treats all concepts equally: scientific and non-scientific, those that have their objects in experience, as well as those that do not have their objects in experience. But that is not the end. Based on how the concept of, e.g., force develops, it does not follow that physicists should not be allowed to use these terms, since, as strictly defined, this way serves to express and capture certain empirical data. On the other hand, Hume, relying on analysis and psychological genesis, measured all these concepts by the same yardstick, and his resulting skepticism shook the whole of science. Admittedly, he did not want to draw practical consequences from his considerations; he took pity on science and spared its life, although he showed that science did not deserve it. Kant, on the other hand, proved that science does not need Hume's grace, because science has a different criterion, according to which it estimates the value of its own concepts.

However, Kant's demarcation should not be taken absolutely. The categories and concepts that follow only have significance as long as they express empirical data; they have value only for that data, and beyond that, they lose all value. This matter is closely connected with the distinction between cognition and thinking. We can think about everything, but we can cognize only what is given in experience. By means of categories, one can learn only when one gathers certain empirical data which are applied to what is transcendent; this ceases to be knowledge and becomes only thinking.

However, Kant's position did not satisfy everyone. The former psychological approach initiated by Locke and Hume took hold, and after merging with the new biological approach it became a very serious opponent. As a classic example of a position diametrically opposed to Kant's, let us take the philosophy of Richard Avenarius and the entire current of critical empiricism. They accuse Kant of having overlooked one great thing that has now been fully realized.

---

1 Strictly speaking, Kant distinguishes metaphysical deduction (i.e., the deduction of concepts and principles as *a priori*) and transcendental deduction (which explains how what is *a priori* can refer to objects and become the basis of universal judgments in the field of experience) from empirical (psychological) deduction. A first-class meaning should be assigned to the transcendental deduction; however, in Kant's case, they both closely connect with each other. For example, the deduction of categories from the table of judgments, as closely related to the function of judging things in general, is only an aspect of metaphysical deduction, and transcendental deduction, which seeks to demonstrate how certain concepts are the basis and the condition of scientific experience, is separate from it.

Science is no longer a ready fact (of course, not only as to the content that has grown and grows, but also some of its fundamental concepts). The edifice of Newtonian natural science, which Kant was fixated on and which he took part in building (in the natural works of the pre-critical period), is not an unshakeable accomplishment; science is becoming, it undergoes development, the relation of the human mind to reality has its own history, and this history has its own laws. Kant's position is historically conditioned, a criterion of the values of scientific concepts can be drawn from these laws of development regarding the relation of the human mind to reality, and the demarcation line that is supposed to separate authorized concepts in science from unauthorized concepts will look different than it did for Kant. The concepts of substance and causality that Kant situated within the field of demarcation are found outside this field today. Inside this field, they could have existed at a historically determined time. Kant takes the ready state of science as his starting point and asks how this state is possible, and in response to this question he ends up authorizing in science all the concepts that, as a form of the synthesis of empirical data, are a condition of scientific experience. Avenarius, as a starting point, takes the human individual together with an environment and utterances, dependent in some way on the environment, and he considers each successive state of science a modification of the pre-scientific state. Investigating the development of these utterances, i.e., experience, and thereby science, he discovers the law of progressive elimination, according to which the state of knowledge about the world, proceeding along a spectrum between a certain constant quantity, the "universal concept of the world" (*Universalbegrift*), and a certain variable quantity, "annexal concepts" (*Beibegriffe*), approaches in its development this constant quantity thanks to the fact that the annexal concepts, being biologically unsustainable, gradually disappear.[2] To discover this law, Avenarius not only takes into account the development of scientific concepts, thus creating a natural history of philosophical systems in the history of cultural humanity, but also takes into account the pre-scientific stages of animism, fetishism, etc., and predicts the future stage, because, in today's state of science, the process of elimination is far from finished. On the other hand, he tries to justify the law itself both biologically (physiologically and psychologically) as well as

---

2   The physiological version of this law in [Avenarius 1888–1890: vol. I, 198]; psychological [law] in [Avenarius 1888–1890: vol. II, 389]: "Wenn einer positiv entwickelungsfähigen Vielheit von Weltbegriffen genügend Raum und Zeit zur Variation zugestanden wird, so nähert sich der Inhalt der Weltbegriffe, von beliebigen Anfangswerten aus, dem reinen Universalbegriffe an." The summary of the arguments is in the "*Anhang*" to the work [Avenarius 1891].

logically. By applying the biological concept of purposefulness to mental life, and therefore to all mental work, he also demonstrates the method of elimination to be the result of work according to the smallest expenditure of force and therefore compatible with the principle of the economy of thinking, when:

> Vom Denken eines Gegebenen alles das auszuschliessen, was es nicht selbst enthält, heisst, nicht mehr Kraft auf sein Denken verwenden, als der Gegenstand selbst erfordert.
>
> AVENARIUS 1876: 39

From the above, it is evident that the concept in Avenarius is a relative thing, since it depends on the particular state of science; this relativism, however, can be eliminated, since we will look at the value of concepts from the position of this universal concept of the world, and then we will see that it does not follow *a priori* from the criterion of the value of scientific concepts as defined by Avenarius, and that this criterion must be simply incompatible with the Kantian criterion. This is because, according to Avenarius, what is to become the universal content of the concept which, as an absolute constant, all variations of concepts about the world are approaching, cannot be something fundamentally new, but rather, must be what is common to all concepts of the world. Therefore, it is not possible to predict in advance whether what Kant counted as an indispensable inventory of science will be preserved until a universal concept, common to all world views, is established. However, Avenarius is of a different opinion and quite unequivocally indicates in his "natural concept of the world" what should become the content of the universal concept, but, as Avenarius himself pointed out, his ideas of the "natural concept of the world", developed in *Der menschliche Weltbegriff*, can be questioned without violating the arguments of the *Critique of Pure Experience*.

Against such a general background of issues in the theory of knowledge concerning the position of certain concepts in science, which we presented in the form of the opposing philosophies of Kant and Avenarius, a whole series of disputable specific questions have arisen, including the one for which we undertook this study, namely: just how useful today is the concept of causality in science, and should it be replaced by the concept of function, be it that employed in mathematics or one similar to the latter? The question cannot be resolved other than by analyzing the concepts of causation and functional relation, and then comparing them, showing the scope of their applicability, and thus their usefulness in science, and the answer will follow if one of them can be eliminated and replaced by the other. Therefore, deciding on the value of these concepts, we will use criteria similar to those of Kant and Avenarius, and so, we will ask whether the concept in question is really useful, and even necessary and requisite, as a condtion of work in science which always consists in systematic ordering of our knowledge, connecting empirical data in a unified whole that is consistent, free from contradictions; we must also pay attention to whether these concepts correspond to the principle of the economy of thinking, because it turns out that many interpretations are possible, and, as some claim, even infinitely many interpretations, each of which can be a logical whole, free of contradictions and consistent with experience, of which one, the simplest, must be chosen. By the same token, it is self-evident that, in all of this, we will also take care that the concepts are clearly defined, do not contain contradictions, and are as consistent as possible with the experience they are meant to serve.

By concepts, we mean, in the first place, certain creations of our mind, certain mental contents, and we do not intend to enter here into the matter of whether the objects of these concepts exist independently of our consciousness, i.e., we carefully exclude the metaphysical side of our question, which is not our focus. If we treat concepts as products of the mind, we do not stand on psychological ground because we are not concerned with what this or that person thinks of causation; we do not mean individual psychic acts, but rather what is expressed in them, so undoubtedly a certain meaning, a certain objective content, or, let us even say, ideal objects, when it comes to it, but with the proviso that, by considering concepts with respect to their meaning, we cannot abstract from the cognizing subject. What we have said may seem strange for proponents of Husserl's school who consider that taking the cognizing subject into account in respect to logic in the widest meaning of the word is symptomatic of psychologism, and who do not consider even Kant free from the errors of psychologism. We appreciate Husserl's antipsychologism in the domain of formal logic, and in this domain we even attribute some merit to him for cleansing logic of various psychological errors. Nevertheless, if Husserl's logic is to replace the old theory of knowledge, then complete abstraction from the cognizing subject and from the subjective source of our concepts is, in our opinion, erroneous and dangerous. If, on the one hand, the boundaries of logic and psychology are clearly demarcated then, on the other hand, this approach erases the boundary between logic and metaphysics, and this throws up new dangers. We consider treating concepts only as objects, regardless of whether there is any cognizing mind that creates these concepts, and renewing the "Platonic" view of the essence of concepts [Łukasiewicz 1906: 4] only as a skillful trick, made in order to free oneself from certain answers about the relation of our knowledge to reality.

After these introductory remarks, in which we tried to characterize the background of the relation between the concepts of causality and functionality, and in which we briefly outlined our own position, or rather assumptions about certain issues of a more general nature, we proceed to the proper question. We will deal first with the concept of functional relation, then with the concept of causality, and then comparing them, in terms of content as well as applicability, we will try to evaluate the methodical value of both.

2

Many are the meanings connected with the word "function", in life as well as in science. Even a cursory review of the different ways it is used will make us aware of this ambiguity. And so, in certain expressions, "function" means almost the same as "action". Biology, especially physiology, talks about the functions of various organs, the function of the heart, lungs, functions of digestion, nutrition, reproduction, and in general about the vegetative and animal functions of an organism, etc. In this sense, it is said that one organ fulfills, hinders, or facilitates a function, or that it replaces the functions of another organ. Similar to this biological meaning is the everyday meaning of the expression "function", when we talk about activities, tasks, or duties that certain people or institutions have to meet, deal with, and perform. So, we hear about the functions of certain offices or committees; we meet expressions such as "in small towns a doctor performs the functions of a veterinarian",[3] "the secretary of the embassy fulfills the function of an ambassador", some people's fingers replace the functions of the fork. In some of the foregoing phrases, the word "function" is closely connected with related words, such as "functionary", "functioning", [...] and, in these sayings, the meaning of the word approaches the etymological meaning, i.e., the meaning originally possessed by the words "*functio*" and "*fungor*" in Latin, i.e., the meaning of "exercising", "performing", or "doing something".

In addition to these meanings, one should also add the use of "function" in relation to activities and matters of cognition, talking about psychic functions and the functions of the cognizing subject, e.g., about the *a priori* functions of transcendental apperception in Kant:

---

3   In the Polish original, Zawirski also gives here the example "komisja funkcjonuje lub "funguje" w pewnej porze"; in English, we will say in this case that the commission is working or "holding office" at a certain time [JJ&ES].

Alle Anschauungen als sinnlich, beruhen auf Affektionen, die Begriffe also auf Funktionen. Ich verstehe aber unter Funktion, *die Einheit der Handlung*, verschiedene Vorstellungen unter einer gemeinschaftlichen zu ordnen ... Alle Urtheile sind demnach Funktionen der Einheit ... Die Funktionen des Verstandes können also insgesammt gefunden werden, wenn man die Funktionen der Einheit in den Urtheilen vollständig darstellen kann.

KANT 1781: 114–115

From the above words, we see that Kant, using this expression, has in mind not so much the activity itself, but rather the characteristics of this activity, namely the unity that is revealed in it.

A similar shift in the meaning of the word "function" has taken place in a different direction. In some expressions of everyday speech, "function" means not only an activity, but rather a certain disposition to it, and thus a *duty*, a *task*, or a *role*. And the last meaning was transferred by some linguists to grammar, who call the science of the meanings of parts of speech and the individual components of words (suffixes, endings) the "science of functions". The function of a word is its meaning, the function of a suffix or a prefix is the role it plays in the meaning of a given word, e.g., the suffix "-ing" in "a writing" indicates an acting person etc. And here, this expression already takes on an intermediate meaning, between the biological meaning of "activities" and the mathematical meaning in which "function" simply means a quantity dependent on a different quantity. For while this part of grammar tracks the dependence of the meaning of a word on its structure, namely how the meaning changes the change of grammatical forms, here we are dealing with the concept that mathematics has connected to this expression.

The mathematical meaning of the function that we will now deal with is the least fluid, the most precise and the most special, but at the same time considerably distant from the everyday and biological meanings. The point here is only the purely logical dependence of one quantity on another or on several others. The function is called a quantity dependent on another, which is called "argument" ("azimuth") or generally an "independent quantity" (to be brief, we will speak only of one quantity), when they are related to each other in such a way that each special value had by one of them (i.e., the dependent quantity) depends on the value that is assigned to the other. However, it is not necessary that only one value of the independent variable must correspond to a certain value of a dependent variable; yes, there may be several of these values, but they are always related to the values of an independent variable according to a certain law, which precisely defines this connection. This law of dependence is usually given in the form of an equation; if, for example, the equation is due to the dependent variable of the second degree, then two values of the dependent variable will correspond to each value of the independent variable. The dependency connection does not have to apply to all variable values; it is enough if it exists within certain limits, at a certain interval, the extent of which also depends on the law defining the dependence. Thus, the exact definition of the concept of a function in the mathematical sense reads: "The variable quantity y is called "the function of another variable quantity x" in the interval from $x = a$ to $x = b$ if each value of x in this interval is assigned one or more values y, according to a certain law". The above definition only applies to the functional connection of two quantities; analogous definitions can, however, be stated for the dependence of one quantity on several independent quantities. When we have two independent values, each dependent value of a given dependent quantity corresponds to each pair of independent quantities, etc. An example of the functions of one variable is the dependence of the circumference of the circle on the length of the radius; any change in the radius' length entails a corresponding change in the circumference's length as a dependent quantity, whereby the radius can assume all values from zero to infinity; therefore, the dependency exists in the interval from o to ∞. An example of the function of two independent variables is the area of a rectangle, depending on the size of the base and height. A certain defined quantity of the area of the rectangle corresponds to each pair of values of the base and the height. In the above mathematical meaning, the word "function" has nothing to do with the concept of activity, but only signifies a certain quantity, remaining to another or to other quantities in a certain purely logical relation of dependence called "functional dependence".

The application of the concept of "function" to particular sciences, such as physics or astronomy, entails extending this concept at least in that we relate it not only to the detached quantities but also to the objects themselves subjected to measurement, and it is said also of the functional dependence of individual features of objects. And so, the period of the pendulum is a function of the length of the pendulum, vapor pressure is a function of temperature, the intensity of light is a function of the distance from the luminous point, the distance covered by a body in motion is a function of its speed and the time during which the movement lasts, the number of vibrations of a taut string is a function of its length, thickness and tensile loads. This concept of function, referring to real objects, could be named "real function", or, as others prefer, "concrete function", as opposed to a mathematical function, related only to the

quantities themselves, regardless of whether or not these quantities are the
result of measuring specific objects. However, we stipulate that by introducing
this distinction, we do not want to prejudge the question whether the concept
of a real function is identical to the concept of a mathematical function, or if
it shows other characteristics distinguishing it from that function. To demonstrate that this distinction is not only our artificial invention, it suffices to read
the paragraph contained in the Larousse dictionary under the word "fonction".
After describing the concept of a mathematical function, there is the following
remark:

> Il convient de donner à ce mot un sens plus étendu. En effet, d'abord, il
> n'est jamais nécessaire que les doneés d'une question soient fournies en
> nombres pour qu'on puisse en obtenir la solution: elles peuvent tout aussi
> bien l'être en nature. En second lieu, des opérations physiques à effectuer
> sur certaines grandeurs peuvent être aussi bien définies en elles-mêmes
> que par les opérations arithmétiques qui y correspondraient. Enfin, on
> ne saurait maintenant et on ne saura jamais, a quelque degré de per-
> fectionnement que la science parvienne, remplacer par des opérations
> arithmétiques bien définies la plupart des opérations physiques qu'on
> peut concevoir, et en raison desquelles cependant la chose produite a
> une relation parfaitement nette avec celles dont elle est provenue. Il con-
> vient donc d'admettre pour les grandeurs ainsi définies physiquement le
> nom de *fonctions concrètes*.
>
> MARIE 1885: 68–69

All the above cases of using the word "function" indicate to us two fundamentally different meanings, alongside several intermediate meanings, which are
less determined. In the first meaning, "function" means "action"; in this sense,
biology makes broad use of this word, and the everyday use approaches this as
well. In the second meaning, "function" signifies something that depends on
something else; the latter meaning undoubtedly came about under the influence of the first by introducing this word in the 18th century to mathematics.
By referring, however, to ideal objects, it lost its active aspect and was reduced
to signifying the pure relation of dependence without any admixture of act
or activity. And this became the reason for advocates of the method of elimination in philosophy to replace the concept of causality, which, after all, is
related to the ontological concepts of action and force, activity and passivity,
with the simpler concept of functional dependence containing fewer superfluous accretions.

3

If we are talking about a functional relation that would be able to replace the relation of causality or even be compared with it, then this may be either a purely mathematical functional dependence, or a functional dependence in the meaning of a concrete, real function, a concept which has only come about as a result of applying the concept of a mathematical function to real connections. In both these terms, as in causality, the relation of two members is involved, while the usual concept of function as an activity can hardly be reduced to the concept of relation; rather, it could be reduced to the concept of an object having some kind of permanent feature. And because we do not have an exact definition of a concrete function as distinct from a mathematical one, and because some philosophers, such as Mach, referring to the elimination of the concept of causality and replacing it with functional dependence, clearly mean the concept of a mathematical function, we must first submit the concept of a mathematical functional relation to a deeper analysis.

As we have already mentioned, the concept of this relation contains the concept of the dependence of certain quantities of this kind, such that each value of one or several quantities constituting one member, one side of the relation, corresponds to one or several strictly defined values of the quantity on the second side, the second member of the relation. Because the quantity which in the sequence of certain mathematical operations may assume different values is called a "variable quantity" as opposed to the constant quantities of calculus, we can say that a functional relation refers to the *connections of some variable quantities*. The members of this relation have their names; on the one side, we have an independent quantity or quantities, i.e., arguments, and on the other side, we have a dependent variable, i.e., a function. Thus, a function is a concept that is co-relative to the concept of argument, as well as cause and effect, reason and consequence, husband and wife, teacher and student, debtor and creditor. Something is considered a function because of the argument; something is considered an argument because of the function. One concept supposes the other; one without the other would not make sense. To signify the functional relation in mathematics, a separate symbol has been introduced; if there is only one quantity on both sides, then the independent variable is marked with the letter "x", the dependent variable with the letter "y", and the relation with the letter "f", written as: $y = f(x)$; or more generally, in the unresolved form due to "y": $f(x,y) = 0$. Individual values of variable quantities could be called "changes, which quantities run through". This course of changes can be presented in tabular form by means of series of constant numbers corresponding to each other, either graphically (geometrically) by means

of a curve and one continuous line, if the function is continuous in the entire
dependency area, or by intermittent forms, i.e., several curved sections, or even
loose points in the opposite case, when the function has places of a break in
continuity. The third way to express functional connection is analytic when we
present this connection with an equation.

Without going into further mathematical details, we will consider the logical
nature of functional dependence. In each case, the dependence is determined
by a certain law that finds its expression in the equation. Considering the nature
of this co-dependence of variables, we come to the conviction that it is based
on a necessary relation, that here there is a relation of necessary dependence
the negation of which would lead to contradiction. For by adopting a certain
value for an independent variable and substituting it for "x" in the equation,
which determines the connection of the two variables more closely, and making transformations on both sides of the equation based on logical reasoning,
we reach the appropriate value for the dependent variable. Thus, obtaining a
certain value for a dependent variable follows necessarily from accepting a certain value for the independent variable, while rejection of the latter must lead
to the rejection of the former. We cannot go into the question here of whether
this necessity is only logical or whether this necessity has another, deeper basis.
This matter is connected to a view of the source of the necessity of mathematical judgments in general. According to Kant, the necessity of these judgments
is not only logical, because then they would be only analytical judgments, but,
first of all, is due to the nature of pure mental images. That the radiant change of
a wheel entails changes in the circumference of the wheel is due to the nature
of space, and this is, according to Kant, the source of the necessity of judgments
of geometry. Without going into the matter of the necessity of the judgment of
mathematics regarding the functional connection of certain quantities, we will
analyze the content of this necessity to see whether it is the same as the dependence between reason and consequence, between cause and effect, or if it is
of a different nature. As we know, the necessary relation between reason and
consequence is such that the truth of the reason results perforce in the truth
of its consequence, and the falsity of the consequence results perforce in the
falsity of its reason; however, *vice versa*, we cannot say that the consequence is
false, if the reason is false, or that the reason is true, if the consequence is true.
Following the example of Łukasiewicz [1906], we can present this relation of
necessity with a symbolic formula which will facilitate capturing it. Thus, having signified the necessity of the implicated truth of the consequence from the
truth of the reason by '$p_1 p_2$', the necessary connection between the falsity of the
consequence and the falsity of the reason by '$n_2 n_1$', and unnecessary relations
between the truth of the consequence and the reason, and between the falsity

of the reason and the consequence by $('p_2 p_1')$ $('n_1 n_2')$, we can present the whole relation with the formula:

$$Z = p_1 p_2 + n_2 n_1 + (p_2, p_1) + (n_1, n_2).$$

The same relation of necessity occurs, according to Łukasiewicz, between cause and effect. On the other hand, as to the relation of functional dependence, it turns out, on closer examination, that it cannot be subsumed under the above formula. Admittedly, here also, from the acceptance of a certain value for 'x' a certain value for 'y' necessarily follows, while rejection of a certain value for 'y' entails the rejection of a certain value for 'x'; however, here the dependency also exists in the opposite direction. Increasing the circumference of the circle results perforce from increasing the radius' length, as well as conversely increasing the radius' length from increasing the circumference; it is also evident that rejecting a certain value of the circumference of a circle results in rejecting a certain value of the radius, as well as conversely, rejecting a certain value of the radius results in rejecting a certain value of the circumference. No side is more privileged than the other; we can assign any values to the functionally related quantities to examine what values will result for the other; we can take any as a starting point to track the other. The roles of the argument and function, the dependent variable and the independent variable are interchangeable; one can rearrange them, and the dependency will be what it was. If 'x' is a function of 'y', then 'y' is a function of 'x'; whereas, if A is the reason for judgment B, B is not the reason for A; reason and consequence cannot change their roles. In mathematics, this property of functional dependence is expressed by the confirmation that the functional dependence is symmetric. This property is closely related to the nature of the necessary connection which binds the function with the argument. Using Łukasiewicz's notation, we can express this type of necessity with the formula:

$$p_1 p_2 + n_2 n_1 + (p_2, p_1) + (n_1, n_2).$$

In contrast to the relation of necessity between reason and consequence, which is the relation of a simple connection, this type can be called the relation of *mutual or complex necessity*.[4] And this is the main and most important

---

4   The above difference should be documented by a difference in terminology. We leave it, however, for the special theory of relations. Our terminology has none other than a provisional meaning the purpose of which is to avoid misunderstandings as to what we mean in individual cases.

feature that distinguishes functional dependence from other necessary connections. Several derivative features result from it.

The first derivative feature is the already mentioned symmetry, in that
the members of the connection can exchange their roles. The ratio of line
dependence is, however, asymmetric ratio. Here, however, we want to emphasize a certain difference that occurs between the functional connection, as
symmetric, and other symmetric relations, such as equality, similarity, and
brotherhood. In the latter relations, the members are synonymous and have
the same names, such as brother-brother, similar-similar. Whereas, in the functional relation, the members have different names and different meanings; the
function is not the same as the argument; the argument is not the same as the
function. Here, reversibility means interchangeability of roles, i.e., each side
has the equal right as the other to play the role of function or argument.

Finally, the connection of functional dependence is a transitive relation.
We use this expression in the sense that Łukasiewicz did in "Analysis and
Construction of the Concept of Cause". The "transitive" is therefore a relation
with this property, such that when it occurs between the members A and B, and
B and C, it must also occur between the elements A and C. Such is the relation
of causality, reason and consequence, and similarly, the functional connection.

If 'x' is a function of 'y' and 'y' is a function of argument 'z', then 'x' is a function
of argument 'z'; if, for example, the surface of a straight cylinder with a constant
height is a function of the circumference of the base, and the perimeter of the
base is a function of the base radius, then the perimeter is a function of the base
radius. Of course, the functional dependence of 'x' on 'z' does not have the same
shape as the functional dependence of 'x' on 'y' or of 'y' on 'z'. Therefore, caution
is used in labelling and expressing the dependence of the other letters; so:

$$\text{if } x + f(y), \text{ and}$$
$$y = \varphi(z), \text{ then}$$
$$x = f[\varphi(z)], \text{ or } x = F(z).$$

The same holds for other transitive relations. For example, if A is the cause of B
and B is the cause of C, then the causal connection between A and C does not
look the same as between A and B or B and C. Hence, the distinction between
direct and indirect causes. Similarly, it is impossible to identify a logical relation
between reason and immediate consequence with a relation between reason
and further consequences. The role played by a judgment which determines the
truthfulnes of the judgment following the first one is not identical to the role
that this judgment plays relative to the judgments indirectly conditioned by it.

The result, therefore, of our analysis[5] is as follows. Contained in the concept of a functional connection is the relation of necessary dependence, however not the relation of the necessity of a simple, but rather the necessity of mutual interdependence, and consequently the functional connection is a symmetric relation; this is the difference between this connection and the connection of logical reason and consequence, and the connection of cause and effect, in its ordinary understanding. However, like the last two relations, the functional connection is a transitive relation.

The concept of a mathematical functional relation is the only one that is strictly defined, and therefore the logical analysis of this concept did not present great difficulties. It is conceivable that this concept is the only possible concept of this relation; we can settle this matter by considering all uses of this word outside mathematics in such cases where it was a matter of a certain dependence, and by investigating what the author meant in each of these cases. Only based on such research would it be possible to decide whether there existed or does exist a different concept of this connection that fundamentally differs from the mathematical one, and whether it can be defined in an unambiguous manner, free of contradictions.

Anticipating the outcome of this research in advance, we declare that we have not found a strict definition of a concept of functional relation that fundamentally differs from the mathematical one, but in many cases it can be used in a non-mathematical sense though remaining similar, more or less, to the mathematical one. Wherever the functional connection is referred to, there is always a kind of dependence of two phenomena to indicate the appropriateness of two series of changes without making assumptions; hence, a functional connection can be used wherever the concept of causality is an option but seems not very appropriate or accurate, or is saddled with material difficulties. Sometimes the use of this word flowed from a more obvious dislike of the metaphysical concept of causality in the old style that imagined some mysterious internal nexus binding the events in the world by a kind of ideal thread, as well as from unwillingness to utilize the concepts of action and force with which the concept of causality is still linked. Let's take a few examples.

Richard Avenarius makes very broad use of the concept of function in his system, taking his disregard for the concept of causality to such an extent that in his basic work, *Kritik der reinen Erfahrung*, he completely ignores the concept. In his small study, *Philosophie als Denken der Welt*, he came out against

---

5   In carrying out this analysis, we have modelled ourselves on the cited work [Łukasiewicz 1906].

causation because of the concepts of force and necessity connected with it. Not only should the concept of force be dismissed as obsolete anthropomorphism but necessity as well, because we do not experience necessity; it falls along with the concept of force, "because force is what compels, and necessity is compulsion". With the rejection of "force and necessity", all causality must fail because there is nothing left of it but a permanent succession. However, and this is characteristic, the author is in favor of maintaining necessity "to signify a certain degree of probability (certainty) with which we expect, and should expect, the appearance of an effect". Similarly, despite the criticism and elimination of the concept of force, the author retains it as a "temporary" and "shortened expression", such that in the end causality is legitimate as long as it expresses empirical relations, especially the idea of the continuity of becoming. In the *Critique of Pure Experience*, there is no mention of causality but only *conditioning* [Avenarius 1888–1890: vol. I, 25–30], systematic pre-conditions (*systematische Vorbedingungen*), complementary conditions (*Komplementärbedingungen*) from which the occurrence of change is able to materialize. The author considers all reality as well as every individual to be a system of dependent variables. Speaking of conditions, he always means conditions of change; a condition is the change of quantity v_1 with which the change in quantity v_2 appears. Nor is there even mention of the temporal succession of a conditioning and conditioned change; the condition is completely timeless, purely logical, just as the value of an independent variable is a logical condition of the dependent variable acquiring a certain value. Speaking of the dependence of changes, he continues to rely on the sign of the mathematical function, and so he describes the changes in the brain system (C) as dependent on the components of the environment R (*Reiz*) and S (*Stoff*), i.e., as $f(R)$ and $f(S)$, i.e., that the organism is a function, on the one hand, of such environmental components which by acting on system C, arousing excitement, force it to do some work, absorb its force, consume its energy, and, on the other hand, the components of the environment that nourish, strengthen and reinforce it, refreshing the energy reserves consumed by those factors, the action of which absorbs them, balances them [Avenarius 1888–1890: vol. I, 32, 86, 201], and thus sustains the continuous rhythm of life. In this definition, factors R and S are understood as independent variables and the changes of system C as the sum of the values functionally dependent on them. This sum in some cases equals zero; this is the most favorable case, the state of equilibrium, *maximum* behavior when the body's nutrition balances itself with its work $f(R) = f(S)$, that is $f(R) + f(S) = 0$; otherwise it manifests a certain positive or negative difference (*Vitaldiferenz*). The entire development of system C runs in a series of continuous fluctuations and oscillations of various orders, which correspond to certain mental states, that is, in the language of Avenarius, values of E (*Empfindung* in the broadest sense). Here again, values of E, i.e., mental states, are understood as dependent variables, are called functions of the independent vital series, i.e., changes of system C as independent variables.

In one still very important point of his system Avenarius does apply the concept of function. Namely, while following the development of system and systems C, he comes to the conviction that this development cannot last indefinitely. Certain components of the environment are repeated, which results in certain common properties of systems C in all human individuals, and as a result also some ultimate property of system C develops as conditioned by what is most often repeated in the environment and in the properties of systems C: an ultimate property, as capable of the most frequent repetitions – as the highest order of multiponibles [in Avenarius: invariants], it must also be as constant as possible. Historically, however, the developing multiponibles are never pure; they always have a certain individual color, whether they are idiosyndems [in Avenarius: individual human implementations of invariants], which include, besides the ultimate property, factors that are not conditioned by what is most often repeated in the surroundings and properties of systems C. Let us denote that constant component by 'a', the individual variable by 'A' and their connection in multiponible individual, or idiosyndemy, by 'y'; we will receive as an analytical expression for historical, individual multiponibles of the highest possible order:

$$y = f(a, \alpha).$$

However, it follows from the biological law of human development that the 'α' activity must constantly be limited and eliminated. As the conditions for the development of individuals, generations, peoples, and humanity extend beyond the accidental conditions of time and place, these individual components disappear. The farther in the future the individual is born and the more this individual's family circle is synonymous with humanity, and the smaller the world is, the more 'α' approaches zero and 'y' approaches the size of the constant. With regard to the above, Avenarius interprets this to mean that the approach of idiosciences to the absolute constant is a function of time and space, while the absolute constant is what is most often repeated in all components of the environment and in all systems C.

To translate all this into the language of psychology, we will say that idiosyncrasies are historical concepts about the world that have occurred in various individuals, nations, and in different philosophies; this ideal multiponible of the highest order, this absolute constant, is the universal concept of the world; this component of 'α', subject to elimination, is the same as the aforementioned annexal concepts (*Beibegriffe*); and the biological right of development is the law of progressive elimination, according to which the concept of the world approaches a certain absolute constant, etc.

We lingered over this point more closely not only because it is an interesting example of applying the concept of function, but also because this illuminates the source of this current of thought from which grew the call to eliminate certain scientific concepts and in part therefore the matter that has prompted the present study.

Let us now ask, in what sense Avenarius used the above-mentioned examples of the concept of function? He was the first to attribute to the concept of function such great significance that he was able to do without the concept of causality.

Such reference of the concept of function to concrete dependencies, to physiological and psychological changes, would correspond exactly to what we previously called the real function, but without prejudging whether such a function is fundamentally different from the mathematical one. Well, we believe that where Avenarius uses a mathematical symbol he undoubtedly has in mind a strictly mathematical functional relation. Nowhere, however, does he justify the use of this concept; he does not consider whether all the features of the functional relation can be transferred to real connections, and only in one place does he state laconically that the function is used "in the sense similar to the mathematical one" (*in einem dem matematischen angenäherten Sinne*) [Avenarius 1888–1890: vol. I, 182], saying that the approximation of the final property of system C to an absolute constant is a function of time and space. It is regrettable that he speaks so briefly in this matter and evidently avoids explaining himself as to *why he is moving away from the mathematical concept.* Before we give the ultimate answer regarding this concept of the applied function, we will include several other voices in this matter. As regards the application of the concept of function to the dependence of mental states on brain activities, this issue is raised in Professor Twardowski's study, "Psychology in Comparison with Philosophy and Physiology". In this study, the author accepts the application of this concept to the dependence of mental activities on brain changes if taken in the mathematical meaning, but opposes the use of the function in the above-mentioned case if it is taken in the colloquial meaning, as the equivalent of the act [Twardowski 1897: 95]. The above commentary was met with violent criticism in a review by A. Mahrburg who objected to Twardowski that the concept of mathematical function is of no use here, because the concept is symmetric, while this cannot be said about the dependence of mental states on the brain.

But let us now turn to the author who was the first to put the matter on the cutting edge of the sword, creating therein a scientific discussion, viz., Mach, who proclaims the utter unsuitability of the concept of causality in natural science, demands that this concept be removed from the scientific dictionary and replaced with the much more accurate and a more useful concept of function. At the same time, Mach quite clearly and unambiguously meant the concept of a mathematical function. In the last edition of his *Analyse der Empfindungen*, Mach testifies that he had already turned against the concept of causation in [Mach 1872], demanding that it be replaced "by the mathematical concept of function, i.e., concepts regarding the mutual dependence of phenomena, more accurately the dependence of phenomena on each other's properties" [Mach 1872: 74]. Phenomena in nature are rarely so simple that in a given case one can distinguish one cause and one effect, as if this primitive and "pharmaceutical" way of looking at the world can be used according to which there is always a some degree of cause for some degree of effect. According to the author, the objections raised against the notion of functional relationship by German critics (Külpe, Cossman) can be easily removed; the concept of a function can be freely extended or limited according to the actual state. Take as an example, says Mach, the behavior of gravitational masses. According to the old view of causality, when mass B approaches mass A, it is the result of the movement of mass A towards B. Meanwhile, when we consider the matter thoroughly, it will turn out that masses A, B, etc. give each other mutual acceleration which occurs simultaneously with the appearance of the masses. These mutual accelerations determine the velocities that the bodies achieve, such that the positions of masses A, B, and C are determined at each subsequent time. "The physical measure of time, again, is based on the measurement of space (the rotation of the earth)", so that even here, when determining the positions of the masses, it turns out that there is a need to refer to mutual dependencies. This simple example already indicates to Mach that the old formula is unable to comprehend the entire diversity of relations that occur in nature.

> So kommt auch in anderen Fällen alles auf *gegenseitige abhängigkeit* hinaus, über deren Form selbstverständlich von vornherein gar nichts ausgesagt werden kann, da hierüber nur die Spezialforschung zu entscheiden hat. [...] Alle genau und klar erkannten Abhängigkeiten lassen sich als *gegenseitige Simultanbeziehungen* ansehen.
>
> MACH 186: 75

We will not quote here everything that Mach says about causality. His views on causality are scattered throughout all his natural philosophy and have already been discussed even in Polish philosophical literature [Kozłowski 1906: 195]; the argument is more or less the same everywhere. The main argument in favor of the concept of function is that all dependencies in nature will be, contrary to the prevailing convictions concerning causal dependence, understood as *mutual* (bilateral) and *simultaneous*. Moreover, the superiority of the concept of function over the concept of cause lies in the fact that the first requires greater care in considering dependence, that there is no incompleteness, indeterminacy, and one-sidedness in the latter. The concept of causality is always just a crude, temporary remedy (*Notbehelf*). In general, we take two parts of the most intriguing phenomenon of cause and effect, and closer analysis always shows that the supposed cause is only the completion of circumstances that determined the effect.

The same thoughts are repeated and sustained by Mach in his last work [Mach 1905] [...]. The chapter "Die Voraussetzung der Forschung" is devoted to the replacement of the concept of causality with the concept of a functional relation. Mach's criticisms are directed to the very primitive and pre-scientific concepts of causality and mostly concern secondary issues. The same argument is repeated, however, that the cause and effect follow each other and are asymmetric in the ordinary sense, while closer examination of the dependencies occurring in nature demonstrates their reciprocity and simultaneity. In addition, he draws attention to the various benefits derived from equations of physics, which ordinary causal consideration of phenomena does not give. As science evolves – says Mach – the concept of causality is used less and less often. The moment we are able to determine facts with the help of measurable quantities, something done directly for time and space, and that can be carried out by artificial means with regard to other sensory elements, in that moment the concept of function allows us to show connections between elements much better. This is true not only when these elements in a larger quantity depend directly on one another, but also when the elements depend on each other indirectly by means of a chain of intermediary elements. This is visible in the equations of physics. If more elements are connected by one equation, each of them is a function of others; the concept of cause and effect can then change roles. If we consider two bodies that, being good conductors of heat, come in contact and are isolated from all others, then changing the temperature of one is the cause of the temperature change of the other and *vice versa*. However, if there are intermediaries in the exchange of temperature between these bodies, the change in the temperature of one is not enough to know the change of temperature of the other; it will be necessary to write as many differential equations as there are bodies, and each of these equations generally contains variables that refer to all bodies. If we succeed in obtaining one equation that contains only one variable, we can integrate it, etc. This example is meant to show philosophers that the common concepts of cause and effect are completely inadequate, and in the face of such a scientific means as the concept of function in physics, they are completely superfluous.

Mach's outcomes have sparked a lively discussion in the scientific world, and in the Polish philosophical literature we already have works that address this issue, either going in the direction indicated by Mach and arguing for the elimination of the causal method [Kodisowa 1907], or pointing to some inaccuracies in Mach's arguments, such as [Kozłowski 1906] with whom we would like to be associated. Kozłowski rightly claims that, undoubtedly, "the mathematical determination of regularity is the ideal of knowledge, and that where we have it phenomena are completely mastered by the mind". Ineluctably the question arises whether Mach's proposal does not amount to progress "as a shift from a qualitative to quantitative research stance". On the other hand, there is doubt that the concept of function exhausts the entire content of the laws of nature. This is an adequate representation of fact. Is there something hidden behind the concept of a function that constitutes its default complement, and without which it loses all meaning? Well, such an assumption is "an indispensable component of all mathematical formulas, expressing the laws of nature", according to Kozłowski, and:

> The relation of dependence exists here only from certain parameters to others, not as reciprocal, as if it were ordered by itself via a mathematical form of law.
>
> KOZŁOWSKI 1906: 201

Both causality and the functional connection express a certain dependence, however the causal connection is one-way or rather asymmetric, while the functional connection is symmetric. But that is why mathematical patterns of laws of nature are not enough to adequately present facts. So, to determine the connection between the path of uniform motion, speed, and time, we have the mathematical formulas:

$$s = vt \quad v = s/t \quad \text{and} \quad t = s/v$$

All three are equilibrated from a mathematical position and:

> From each of them the other two can be derived; only the first equation has a physical meaning, and its form requires a default complement that only 's' depends on 'v' and 't', but not *vice versa*, because neither time nor speed are dependent on distance, although they can be calculated from it.

The same applies in other cases. Thus:

> Every mathematical function, when used for the expression of a law of nature, contains the default reservation concerning the unilateral

dependence of parameters ...,[6] and unilateral dependence is the nature of causality. The previous statement means that every mathematical function, as long as it expresses physical relations, contains a causal statement by default. It therefore follows that not only can functional dependence not replace causality, but that it takes on meaning only in application to real phenomena.

KOZŁOWSKI 1906: 202

With this we finish this series of quotations from others. It is abundantly clear that those authors who wanted to replace the concept of causality with the concept of functional relation, or who did in fact replace causality with the concept of function, as Avenarius did, had in mind a mathematical function – though they did not want to get into the problem whether and to what extent we are allowed, when applying the concept of a mathematical function to real and specific dependencies, to transfer all the properties of a mathematical concept to these relations; they were cautious stating that the concept is merely similar to the mathematical one (Avenarius), or that the mathematical concept can be somewhat narrowed or broadened (Mach); in short, that by modifying the concept of a mathematical function one must specifically imagine ad hoc a new concept of function that would replace causation, releasing us once and for all from all anthropomorphisms and inaccuracies so far afflicting this concept. None of these reformers has indicated where this modification should occur. Just how this modification should be carried out and whether it is necessary at all are questions that can only be answered after a thorough analysis of the scientific concept of causality, and after coming to understand the use of mathematical functions when applied to real connections. Kozłowski's remarks concerning Mach indicate that one can be aware of the different concepts of functionality and causality, but still recognize the equality of the two concepts in science, not demanding the elimination of one in favor of the other. This is because the concept of function gives us some benefits that cannot be expected from the law of causality itself. However, there can be no question of the complete replacement of the law of causality, because a functional connection, if it is to be an adequate representation of facts, supposes a causal relation in advance. Real dependencies are not reciprocal as are functional dependencies in mathematical formulas; therefore, these mathematical formulas are not enough to understand the real connection of

---

6   In the equations, those quantities whose various values provide individual detailed equations belonging to one species are called parameters.

phenomena, and in order to be aware of real phenomena with their help we need to refer to causality. However, it is possible to consider this matter differently, as Mach does, who not only does not seem to admit the uni-directional or one-sided and irreversible character of causal dependence, but comes directly to the conclusion that real, causal, as well as functional dependencies bear the mark of interdependence, reciprocity, and simultaneity. Of course, simultaneity is here, in our opinion, a side feature, but the first moment is the most important, which Mach relies on heavily, i.e., that deeper consideration of real connections led him to believe that all dependencies are reciprocal (*"gegenseitige Abhängigkeit"*). Mach, therefore, contradicts the unilateral dependence of phenomena, that is, he demands a radical change of the concept of causality and calls for the adaptation of new concepts concerning real dependencies rather to the concept of mathematical function. He supports his claims with a number of examples. How these examples should be interpreted and whether his position is correct can be determined by analyzing causality, even if only briefly, and then comparing this concept with the mathematical concept of a function that is, at any rate, the only specific predecessor of a possible new concept of functional dependence.

4

To justify the various attacks on causality it must be admitted that no other scientific concepts have undergone such great changes as causality in their development, from the stages of animism and fetishism to the scientific definition of the present moment, and that today, after all, there is no unanimous agreement as to which feature of this concept is its necessary ingredient. There is no agreement concerning its temporal nature, the nature of the dependence of cause and effect, or even what the term "causation" is supposed to refer to. However, the situation is not quite so desperate, and only a small bit of due diligence in regard to the facts to be taken into account makes it possible to settle all these matters without any doubt. We caution, however, that ours is not some self-enclosed investigation of causality but rather a commentary on a few basic points with the assistance of the latest Polish works on causality by Łukasiewicz, Kozłowski, and Borowski.

We omit, therefore, various elementary matters, such as the fact that causality signifies a certain relation, in particular, the relation of connection; that the members of this relation have separate names, "cause" and "effect"; that the concepts of cause and effect are co-ordinate just like the function and the argument in a functional relation; we will proceed immediately to consider the points of contention. The first is the temporal nature of the causal connection, i.e., the problem whether the cause and effect succeed one another, whether they are simultaneous, or only whether the cause does not precede the effect, or finally, whether temporal order is completely indifferent; next, whether the causal connection should be considered a necessary connection and how this necessity should be understood; and therefore whether it is a relation of simple necessity, which we called unilateral, unidirectional necessity, or the relation of a necessary, mutual, reciprocal connection. A view on causality is connected to views on action, force, and condition. And finally, the question remains, what does causality concern: only changes or also states of coexistence without changes?

The philosophical criticism of the concept of causality in Hume, who for the first time obviously made everyone aware that we do not perceive the effect of the cause as a result of the force by which the cause produces the effect, and that neither external experience nor internal experience gives us the basis for this kind of belief, has led many to believe that nothing more should be seen in causality than the continuous succession of phenomena. However, succession is not enough, which has been confirmed many times. On the other hand, there is no doubt that a certain temporal order may indicate that in some cases we may discern a causal connection. To recognize a certain connection as causative, we must acquire the conviction that a given connection is necessary. This necessity is usually determined by examining whether what we have called the cause is necessary and at the same time sufficient for the effect to occur. Only a subtle analysis of facts can inform us about this indispensability and sufficiency, but we can never vouch for the accuracy of this analysis. We should remember that it is always possible that we have omitted some condition because of its relative constancy (e.g., the presence of the earth in relation to falling bodies in ancient writings), or that we include more factors than necessary because we are not familiar with other possible cases of the occurrence of a phenomenon [Borowski 1909: 450] (e.g., the necessity of oxygen for fire turned out to be illusory, because some bodies can burn in an atmosphere of gases other than oxygen). Thus, in every particular case, where causality is applied, the necessity we assume is always only probable, since the empirical basis of this necessity, i.e., the statement of constancy and uniformity in a limited form, never guarantees the absolute stability and universality required by a necessary connection. Some empiricists, such as, for example, Avenarius, when combating the concept of force and action in causality also reject necessity, considering that to retain this feature while rejecting action is inconsistent, since neither is visible in experience and cannot be determined empirically. Such a position, however, arises from the fact that Avenarius equates necessity, which for us is the logical feature of a causal connection, with the physical constraint exerted by force. Elsewhere, Avenarius accepts necessity if it is to express the degree to which an effect is expected. Here, however, two things are again confused: on the one hand, the necessity of the connection that we must accept if we wish to explain logically the regularity of events and, on the other, the degree of its probability in particular specific cases. For it is difficult to call necessity simply the probability of expecting an effect. It is another matter that force of habit in waiting for an effect may for many people be the psychological source of the concept of necessity, but this is only the psychological genesis of the concept, and this genesis cannot influence the logical value.

What is the nature of this necessity which we accept in every causal connection? Łukasiewicz [1906] has already analyzed this necessity; he considers it to be the sole and completely exhaustive property of causality. According to this analysis, it is a type of simple necessity which, following Kozłowski, we also call a one-sided connection, the same that we encounter in relation to consequences, as opposed to mutual and reciprocal necessity in functional dependence. This necessity, as we know, can be presented with the formula:

$$p_1 p_2 + n_2 n_1 + (p_2, p_1) + (n_1, n_2).$$

While the existence of an effect results from the existence of a cause, and the non-existence of a cause results from the non-existence of an effect, conversely, the existence of a cause does not necessarily result from the existence of an effect, and the non-existence of an effect does not necessarily result from the non-existence of a cause. It follows from this view that the connection is irreversible, and, moreover, transitive as well as functional.

However, this is not the only view of the nature of causal necessity. Łukasiewicz already has drawn attention to the fact that some real connections are of a different type, namely that of mutual dependence. Whereas, Mach asserts that all real connections are mutual and bilateral, and that as a result the cause and effect are symmetric! However, he does not try to define this mutual connection anywhere. In philosophical literature, on the other hand, we have an extremely valuable work by Borowski on this matter: "Criticism of the Concept of Causal Connection" [Borowski 1907]. Borowski concludes that the above formulation of causal dependency does corresponds neither to the "postulates of our mentality nor to real relations in the world of physical phenomena". Assuming that the existence of the effect does not result from the existence of a cause, but that the effect could have arisen from various causes, we thereby admit that the connection of effect to any given cause is accidental. In fact, we often conclude from the effect to the cause, and we suppose that it is in the nature of the cause that it brings about a certain effect.

Therefore, if one accepts that it is also in the nature of other phenomena to bring about the same effect [...], then one must suppose that their
natures are the same, and therefore, that the causes bringing about the
same effect are essentially the same.

BOROWSKI 1907: 69

Borowski claims that his view is consistent with Mill's methods and supports
this view with an analysis of concrete examples. He draws attention first and
foremost to the fact that we usually take causes too broadly and sketchily,
while the effect is taken in too narrow and detailed a manner, and often we do
not pay attention to strictly direct causes and hence we assume that the same
effect is attributed to various causes. Closer analysis shows that the effect then
is not strictly the same, for example when it is claimed that an explosion of
gunpowder can occur for various reasons, or that death has various causes; on
closer examination, it turns out that in death:

Different bodily tissues are damaged in different ways for various reasons; sometimes they are accompanied by physical changes, sometimes
they are accompanied by mostly chemical changes.

BOROWSKI 1907: 71

Similarly with the explosion of gunpowder.

In the event of a burst of gunpowder brought about by a hammer blow, in
addition to the explosion itself there will occur: the crashing sound of the
impact, dissipation of the hammer's mechanical energy, the mechanical
reaction of the powder to the impact etc. Were we to carry out the explosion in some other way, only some elements of the effect will remain the
same.

BOROWSKI 1907: 71

So, if we take the entire individual complex as the causes that brought about
the effect, we also need to take the whole complex as the effect, i.e., everything
that has occurred and not only one moment. If, on the contrary, we want "to
narrow the complex of phenomena on the side of the cause as well and to
eliminate everything that is not necessary to bring about this special effect",
the principle will also turn out to be true in this case. Where there is a certain
common element in the effect (e.g., death for various reasons, an explosion
of gunpowder among various circumstances), there must also be a common
element to be found in the cause. The author is deeply convinced that by

following this method, i.e., either taking the whole effect or by narrowing the dependence only to individual elements, one can always achieve the one-to-one correlation.

We attach great importance to Borowski's remarks because he drew attention to many details that had not been taken into account before. We think that in many cases such a bijective correlation can be achieved, but we doubt whether it always happens. Borowski sometimes seems to be in a difficult position. For example, investigating the common cause of the effect called "death", and only considering death without incidental circumstances, he states that:

> Medicine has reduced the proper causes of human death to two: heart failure or asphyxia, and there is hope that in the future it will succeed in analyzing one moment common to both, the ultimate cause of death.
> BOROWSKI 1907: 73

And in another place he says:

> It must be admitted that in many cases the state of our knowledge does not allow us to state strictly and demonstratively the proper causes and the proper effects.
> BOROWSKI 1907: 75

Therefore, we must consider the author's thought as a difficult hypothesis to prove. In many cases, the author would have to resort to quite hypothetical causes; in others, the cause would be to be something so general that actually ascertaining such causal connections would represent a very low cognitive value. This can be seen even in the examples that the author himself analyzes. And so, as heat can arise for various reasons – because it is known that all kinds of energy turn into heat – the author, when trying to define a common cause, comes to the following formulation of this cause:

> In order for a thermal phenomenon to arise, (1) "other phenomena must disappear; (2) the conditions cannot create other types of phenomena".
> BOROWSKI 1907: 74

Similarly, in other cases the author's response looks quite strange. When it comes to the fact that the same body movement can result either from several constituent forces or from one force acting in the direction resulting from those forces, the author answers that the common cause is the "direction of acting forces" (?). To grasp what Borowski understands by acting forces, we would have to formulate a special comment.

Borowski's thought is very prolific, but for now is also highly hypothetical and artificial. We need to reckon with the actual state of positive knowledge and therefore we will remain with the original formulation of causal dependence as a simple necessity, according to which the inverse connection, i.e., the necessity of the same cause with the same effect may occur, but this occurrence is not necessary.

Mach's statement that all causal dependence is mutual, bilateral, can also be understood in a different way. From the example he cites, it should be clear that he is not so much talking about the one-to-one correlation of cause and effect, that is, about Borowski's view, but rather about the dynamic nature of the connection, about something that remains in connection with metaphysical concepts of activity and passivity. Mach draws attention to the fact that, considering the gravitational relations of two masses A and B, we usually consider the approach of one of them the cause, and we only consider the change of body B's position as the effect, while in reality both bodies reciprocally condition their respective speeds: both are simultaneously cause and effect, both behave actively. Mach's abovementioned complaint, however, concerns only those very primitive concepts of causality according to which cause and effect are understood to be two things of which only the first behaves actively and the other passively. Today, even the defenders of the old metaphysics, who as take as their starting point in determining causality the concept of force and action, thus conceiving the matter in a manner different from that of Mach. This is evidenced by the metaphysics of Lotze [1883: 40–41], who explicitly points out that the cause can never be understood as only one thing, but always as at least two things that by their relations become the cause of some change, and this change as a result includes not only a change of one of these bodies 'a', but also the change of a second body 'b', and the change of their relation 'c'. Thus, in Mach's example above, one does not have to attach the concept of a cause to one of these bodies and the concept of effect to another, but the cause is identical with the mutual attraction of two bodies with certain masses, and the effect is identical with changes of their speed.

Only the above view is justified today, and only it can free us from various fruitless inquiries about the passive and active behavior of various bodies. In the expressions of everyday speech, this principle is not always respected, and one often treats individual objects as causes which, due to their own properties, have an advantage over others and experience only very minor changes. We will draw attention here to a few examples of such expressions, and their analysis will allow us to determine the temporal nature of causation – because the feature of necessity, in our opinion, does not exhaust the content of the concept of causality – or the object of this concept, i.e., the limitation of causation for changes. And so, in everyday speech, we hear that the sun is the cause of the earth's movement, while scientific analysis shows that the sun exerts influence on the movement of the earth as does the earth itself. The movement of these bodies, i.e., earth and sun, is influenced by the entire earth-sun system, in which each subsequent phase is the result of the previous one. The earth does not revolve around the sun, but both the earth and the sun move around a common center of gravity which is not at all in the center of the sun. Everyday expressions are only justified in that the movements of the sun compared to the movements of the earth are very small and reduce to tiny nods and swings while the earth makes huge circles, because according to their masses the movements of the earth are as many times smaller than the movements of the sun as the mass of the sun is greater than the mass of the earth. Kepler's laws regarding planetary motion are purely descriptive, except perhaps for the last law, which explains the periodically recurring changes in planetary motion speeds as a result of distance changes. On the other hand, a true causal explanation of all the motions of the earth-sun system can only be given by some exact cosmogonic theory, which would explain the current system of positions and speeds of the system's bodies as a result of previous changes and development phases.

Likewise, we should explain the example that was the object of Wundt's polemics with Sigwart, namely, whether the cause of a body's fall to the earth is the earth or its attraction, as Sigwart claims, or the fact that the body (a stone in this case) had previously been raised, as Wundt argues. We think that Wundt is much closer to the correct approach to things, that the stone's movement is influenced not only by the earth, but also by the stone itself, i.e., the whole earth-stone system to which constant changes must always be referred to explain previous changes. The mere presence of the earth is not enough, because it also exists when the stone is lying motionless on the ground. In the above way, one should also interpret many cases given by advocates of the simultaneity of cause and effect as proof of this simultaneity, for example, the attraction of two magnets, where we also perceive their deflection. The reason for the movements is, in addition to the magnets themselves, or their "magnetic forces", their contiguity.

As for the temporal character of the causal connection, not only is it not indifferent; it is an indispensable feature of the concept without which causality loses its proper sense and significance. After all, the task of causality has always been and still is to inform us of the temporal course of events and explain why phenomena occur in just this rather than in another temporal order. It is true that there have been many controversies over whether causality

concerns only successions or also or only simultaneity: in recent times, however, some have stated that the temporal nature of causal dependency is quite
indifferent; that the causes not only do not have to precede or be contemporary with the effects, but that they may even occur in the future. We encounter the defense of this position in one of the most serious works on causality
in the Polish literature – i.e., in "Analysis and Construction of the Concept of
Cause" by Łukasiewicz. The author of this study assigns too much importance
to his formula of the necessity contained in causality, such that he is willing
to remove from causality anything that does not fit his formula. Because this
formula, which we have already quoted, expresses only the relation of a simple
necessity, also present in the relation of reason to consequences, it therefore
does not follow *a priori* from this formula, as the author claims, that it is false
to claim that a future phenomenon may bring about with necessity a present
phenomenon. However, the very fact that temporality does not follow *a priori*
from this formula should make us pay attention to whether this formula is sufficient, and whether the analysis of phenomena alone entitles one to define
causality in this way. In fact, the author himself acknowledges that the matter
should be resolved only on the basis of experience, but he states that "today's
state of science does not allow for making such an argument". One cannot
claim that there are no future causes of present phenomena simply because
no one has ever found such causes! And:

> A merely general and superficial survey of the data of experience does
> not justify rejecting this logically possible view.
>
> ŁUKASIEWICZ 1906: 44

However, based on the current state of science we will allow ourselves to point
out that, among phenomena where future conditions seem to condition past
states, there are biological phenomena in which we ascertain the presence of so-
called purposefulness that Cossman had in view and to whose work Łukasiewicz
drew attention. Nevertheless, these phenomena were carefully separated from
causal phenomena, because apparently no one could fathom how an inexistent
future state can condition a present state in the same way that a preceding or
contemporaneous phenomenon can, and either they tried to explain these phenomena like others by referring to the action of only such factors in the body
whose presence could be determined and whose mode of action was familiar
from elsewhere, or novel causes were invented understood, for example, along
the lines of human actions where the future state already exists as a preconceived goal and, as such, influences an action. That is how different *causae finales*
arose, Aristotle's forms, Reinke's dominants, or something similar. Therefore, we

will continue to carefully separate these phenomena, and we admit that for us the influence of future phenomena on the past, placed on the same plane with the usually accepted understanding of causality, seems mystical. We can agree that both these forms, causal and purposeful, have common features which can be logically and jointly defined, but it should not be the case that, by subsuming them under a common rubric, their factual differences are disregarded that fundamentally change the nature of the causal tie, because in this way we fall back into the errors of the old scholasticism which, ignoring the facts, wanted to decide everything on the basis of the logical analysis of concepts.

But admitting that the empirical proof contrary to the considered view cannot be given on the basis of the present state of science, the author tries to justify his view experientially, pointing to factually occurring causal ties where the effect precedes the cause. He considers an example from physiology: a nerve's irritation at time t results in a muscle contraction at time $t + \tau$; this implies that non-contraction of the muscle at time $t + \tau$ brings with it necessarily the nerve's non-irritation at time t, but not *vice versa*. Therefore, between the muscle non-contraction and the nerve's non-irritation the following necessary connection holds:

$$Z = p_1 p_2 + n_2 n_1 + (p_2, p_1) + (n_1, n_2),$$

and, therefore, a causal relation in which the effect precedes the cause. The entire proof is carried out *ex definitione*. Because a certain connection of necessity corresponds to the formula considered sufficient to establish causality, a causal connection inheres in it. The example used by Łukasiewicz plays the role of a lure; the author could have equally well used another example, because wherever the existence of effect B results, in the ensuing moment, from the existence of cause A, it can be said that the non-existence of A results from the non-existence of B at the previous moment. And taking as a starting point these negative features, one can in this way create new connections of necessity between them, which for Łukasiewicz are *eo ipso* new connections of causality.

However, on page 52 of his work, the author voices a reservation that by cause and effect he understands "only having a certain feature by a given object, not non-having a certain feature. If two objects are connected to one another in such a way that non-having c_2 by P_2 necessarily brings about non-having c_1 by P_1, then having c_1 by P_1 is a cause of having c_2 by P_2." This confession, taken for itself, would be a lethal blow, dealt by the author himself, against his own example, but the author rightly and skillfully states:

> It is worth noting that by changing features c to their opposites c', each such relation may be transformed into another that obtains between

having c'_2 by P_2 and having c'_1 by P_1. This causal relation differs, however, from the previous one, because it does not occur between the same members.

ŁUKASIEWICZ 1906: 54

The whole passage is a strange dialectic, because if all non-possession of properties can be transformed into the possession of contradictory properties, and the author recognizes such necessary connections as new causal connections, what is the point of the initial reservation, that cause and effect cannot apply to non-having [some property]?

We will therefore continue with the view that temporal character is not indifferent to causal connection in such a way that the effect may lie in the past and the cause in the future. Minimally, this temporal character would therefore be reduced to the assertion, as Mill put it, that the cause cannot precede the effect, although this does not yet resolve the question whether the cause is simultaneous with the effect or whether it precedes it temporally. However, restricting the causal connection to succession is possible if we free ourselves from the imprecise, popular view of causality, reifying cause and effect, which claims that cause and effect are two things, one of which acts and the other experiences the action, and if we do not try to resolve the question of causality based on the logical analysis of concepts without regard for the facts, as did the rationalists. After all, the arguments in the matter marshalled throughout the whole course of modern history were such that a cause that has no effect is not a cause, and an effect that outlasts the cause is causeless, or that if the effect were separated by a temporary pause from the cause, it could not be brought about by the cause, etc. The temporary course of events is, moreover, more intense than everything else, and we attempt to account for it by means of the concept of causation the construction of which would be impossible were all dependencies simultaneous.

Besides, we can leave this matter aside because in comparing causality with functionality the matter of simultaneity or succession of cause and effect is indifferent, as functionality is, in general, not related to time; therefore the succession or simultaneity of cause and effect make the concept of causality neither similar to nor distant from the concept of functionality. We have to admit some temporal character in a causal dependence, and we can talk about a temporal order, even admitting a certain simultaneity of changes if it is accessible to our senses, because, as Kant rightly pointed out, it is not a matter of the passage of time (*Zeitablauf*) but of temporal order (*Zeitordnung*).

> Die Zeit zwischen der Kausalität der Ursache, und deren unmittelbaren
> Wirkung kann verschwindend (sie also zugleich) sein, aber das Verhältnis
> der einen zur anderen bleibt doch immer, der Zeit nach, bestimmbar.
>
> KANT 1781: 191

Hence, we will speak of temporal order, not excluding partial simultaneity
from causal dependency as long as it seems visible to us.

In what follows we want to revise a certain variety of opinions as to the
objects of the causal relation, the first of which is the matter of the concepts of
condition and force. The concept of condition developed under the influence
of the concept of force, and the latter remains in relation with the old reified or
"substantial" theory of causality according to which causes are certain things
that, despite the various changes they are subjected to and the relations they
can enter into, maintain a relative stability and stand out more than others.
It was necessary to provide such a reified cause as a thing with a certain force
which, as a permanent property of the body, had the ability to cause change
and was the cause when changes occurred. At the same time, however, with
the introduction of the concept of force it became necessary to introduce the
new concept of condition, as the occasion whereupon the force acts. For if the
body acts, i.e., brings about effects only thanks to the force it contains, then
to explain why this force, which is actually the source of action, does not create an effect constantly, but only in certain cases, the concept of conditions
had to be established, such that they allow or send a signal to the force to act.
Thus, by introducing the concept of condition, despite reifying the cause,
there was an attempt to reckon with the facts in which the causes turned out
to be events, and in which "the effect can only occur if there are changes in the
system of things that are carriers of forces" [Wundt 1883: 587; "Entwicklung
des Causalbegriffs"]. Therefore, the cause of certain events, called effects, was
always *force* + *condition*.

Apart from this concept of a condition as an occasion for the cause to operate, identified as a thing combined with forces, a new concept of condition
appeared in the history of philosophy in the 19th century. This concept became
broader, just as the concept of force had already been broadened, inasmuch as
the bodies that experience the effects of the actions of other bodies have also
been endowed with resistance to these actions. In this way, forces started to be
attributed not only to bodies behaving actively, for example causing movement,
but also to bodies when their passive behavior was attributed to forces such as
resistance, inertia, friction, stiffness, impermeability etc. The decomposition of
the concept of cause, initiated by the distinction of force and condition, went
further. Because an effect often consists of more things endowed with forces,

and because further conditions, that allow forces to act, can be varied and are often also things (e.g., a spark for the explosion of gunpowder), therefore the representatives of the empiricist line (Mill) define a cause as the totality or the sum of the conditions necessary for a given change to occur. In this way, using this vocabulary, the condition lost the meaning of an occasion, sign or signal for the forces to act, and this name now referred to all the components of the cause, either permanently existing or appearing at the last moment, and needed for the effect to occur. All the constituent parts were given equivalent significance, the concept of force as the proper source of causality lost its privileged position, serving only to signify the "hidden conditions", and obtained a status equal to the status of the other conditions. Mill's concept of cause, as the totality of conditions necessary for the effect to occur, gained wide acceptance, thanks to his four inductive methods of detecting causal connections, in various logic textbooks, for example the spirit of this view is presented masterfully in the description of the concept of causality in Höfler's manual of logic.

There is no doubt that such a concept of cause has its advantages, especially in inductive research, which is about detecting all the factors of phenomena, not overlooking anything, and learning the significance of each detail. It is a convenient way of defining every detail of the cause, without getting tied up in the nature of these details in their real grouping, and is justifiable on the one hand by the fact that every detail of the cause necessary for the effect to occur is of equal weight, and, on the other hand, by the fact that the old concept of condition was so unstable that it was understood as either just a group of things, allowing them to reveal their actions, or else some small things that, compared to larger things, were reduced to the status of mere "stimuli" for the action of the latter.

However, there are some doubts of a different nature concerning this understanding of cause. And so Wundt is against the fact that the above definition broadens the concept of cause an extent such it is rendered useless in science.

> Because the sum of conditions for each event is also an infinite causal connection of things, because it includes not only all the extraneous circumstances in which the cause was active, but also all the underlying causes from which it resulted.
>
> WUNDT 1883: 597

The total cause of my writing at present is the whole world. Therefore, says Wundt – the concept of cause should be limited to only that condition from which the effect resulted quantitatively and qualitatively in a direct and complete manner.

Because only this condition is unambiguously determinable, while how far we want to go in calculating the extraneous circumstances among which the phenomenon occurs always remains to a certain extent at our discretion.

WUNDT 1883: 597

However, advocates of Mill's view do not want to leave room for such arbitrariness. The number of details to be included in the cause is limited by the requirement to include only what is necessary and sufficient for the effect to exist, something to which Wundt does not pay proper attention. It must be confessed however, that this reservation does not eliminate arbitrariness entirely. Because conditions can be taken either with all their specific and individual features, or else only their general features and properties can be taken into account, depending on what we want to consider as the effect: either the entire individual complex or a certain striking moment in the succession to which we have turned attention. There is always still arbitrariness in what we take as an effect in a given case, and this arbitrariness can be put to an end only by holding the equivalence quantitatively on both sides, which Wundt strongly emphasizes. It is not only the causes but also the effects that can be taken more broadly or narrowly; and thanks to the extent to which we will include both *antecedentia* and *consequentia*, in some cases the basic law that determines the dependence of cause and effect may change, as Borowski pointed out in his dissertation quoted above. For example, if we consider the cause of the movement of the clock to be the winding of the mainspring or the drawing of the weights, then this cause will appear to us in one way when we consider the striking of the hours and in another when we consider, as belonging to the effect, the depletion of a certain amount of energy in the friction of the studs, in the generation of heat and other side effects.

Wundt continues to draw attention to the need for a strict delimitation between the conditions that bring about change and certain permanent conditions which are not indifferent to the phenomenon under investigation, but which remain unchanged by other phenomena, the constant referencing of which would be very inconvenient. According to Wundt, the *factor that brings about change* should be called the proper cause to the extent that the effect can be quantitatively determined by this factor, and Wundt wants to define "conditions" as these durable permanent conditions which are not indifferent to the phenomenon, but whose constant consideration would overly broaden the concept of the cause and render it inconvenient in science. Thus, here the concept of condition is more general than the cause and has a meaning quite opposite to the role originally played by the condition with respect to force. Consider the following example. Upon release, a body's fall to earth was explained by the force of gravity, and the elevation itself of the body above ground level was an occasion, a condition under which the force of attraction revealed its action. However, according to Wundt, the opposite is true: the cause of the body's fall is its elevation above a certain level, and from this elevation we can quantitatively determine the fall, because the energy given off by a falling stone is equal to that depleted to raise it; whereas the attraction of the earth, or rather the permanent presence of the earth, is only a condition, a permanent condition, which does not necessarily need to be mentioned in every case of falling. And according to Mill's dictionary this example would appear as follows: the sum of conditions is the cause of the fall and comprises the earth's attraction and the body's elevation; all these conditions are treated equally, perhaps with the reservation that one condition is permanent and hidden, the other is temporary and visible.

To better highlight the differences of views, we include the following table of various concepts of the cause:

$$
\text{Cause} = \begin{cases}
(1)\ \text{FORCE + CONDITION (Sigwart).} \\
(2)\ \text{THE SUM OF THE CONDITIONS: permanent, hidden conditions,} \\
\quad\ \text{+ momentary, visible conditions (Mill).} \\
(3)\ \text{PERMANENT CONDITIONS + FACTOR CONTAINING CHANGE, AS A} \\
\quad\ \text{CONDITION } - \text{ as THE PROPER CAUSE (Wundt).}
\end{cases}
$$

Wundt gives the following two arguments to defend his view and vocabulary. (1) Only his method of defining the cause provides exclusively what is needed to define the cause quantitatively. (2) Only with the above understanding of the cause can one limit causality exclusively to changes.

However, upon closer analysis, it turns out that Wundt's position regarding the understanding of the cause cannot be absolutely maintained, even taking into account the moments which can be cited in support of his view. Above all, it is not true that quantitative equivalence, which physics seeks to ascertain for all changes, does not take into account and does not concern those permanent conditions, which are hardly indifferent to the character of changes. After all, for example, when a stone is released to fall to the ground [Wundt 1880–1883: vol. I, 603], it is impossible to specify the amount of work expended for changing the location of the body, that is, for its elevation, as well as the work that the falling body expends. This is impossible without taking into account the acceleration of the earth "g", without which we could not get the formula "mgh" for the amount of work (m = mass, h = the height from which the stone falls, the height to which the body has been lifted); therefore, the presence of the earth is all too well documented here.

The quantitative equivalence of cause and effect, where it can be demonstrated, is undoubtedly a very serious means allowing subtle examination of causal connections; but let us remember that it can be stated only for physical dependencies; whereas we are also looking for causal connections – as Wundt does as well – in the occurrence of psychic phenomena, listing preconditions and dispositions as causes. Dispositions would correspond to Wundt's permanent conditions, while current states preceding the next state would correspond to the factors bringing about a change, that is, to what Wundt calls "the proper cause". If we do not want to consider permanent conditions in the cause, we should not include dispositions here. However, we believe that it is impossible to reject psychological dispositions from the explanation of psychic dependencies given today's state of knowledge about psychic phenomena. After all, if the same motives cause different actions in different individuals, we cannot explain this in any other way than by the difference in dispositions. To be sure, it can be said that the motives of action are not strictly the same; they occur in different individuals with different characteristics. But because these individual differences in motives are not able to be measured, such that we could determine the ability of each to exert influence, we have to resort to dispositions to indicate how much a certain motive can weigh in the balance in a given individual, in this way replacing the lack of knowledge of the individual tone of the motive.

With regard to the second point, that one can limit causality strictly to changes only by reducing the cause to the factor comprising the change, then in this case, it must be clear and unpleasant to all, how much we are artificially stretching facts in order to suit certain theories. And we are also of the opinion that causality serves primarily to recognize the dependency of changes, but we do not want to exclude permanent conditions since they are necessary for the effect along with the change. The analysis of the facts only leads us to suppose that in the cause there must always be one factor containing change, and only in this meaning can causality be said to be limited to change. It is, however, a blatant contradiction to exclude certain permanent conditions even though they are not considered indifferent to the effect. Whoever, like Wundt, does not eliminate the feature of necessity from causality, for whom the cause is what is necessary for the effect's occurrence, cannot without contradiction exclude factors not indifferent to the effect. A partial cause, from which the effect does not necessarily result, is not, as Łukasiewicz rightly points out, a cause at all.

From the above-mentioned concepts of condition, the significance that Wundt ascribes to this expression is the least satisfactory. With all this, Wundt is not even consistent in his own terminology, because he also uses the word "condition" in the second sense, i.e., the occasion or opportunity for changes, as another example he offers makes clear. Suppose a stone, raised from the ground, lay for some time on a base and its fall was caused by knocking it off the base. Does this sudden precipitation, as a change of position, explain the emergence of the kinetic energy of the falling stone? No! We must refer to a change occurring further back, i.e., in order for the body to be on the base and there to represent a certain "store of work accumulated in it", it must have been removed from the surface of the earth. Wundt, considering just this change as the proper cause of removing the support which prevented the fall, calls it a "condition" [Wundt 1880–1883: vol. I, 597], which returns it to the original meaning of the condition. Wundt too slavishly abides by quantitative equivalences and does not take duly into account the fact that these equivalences are not always a faithful reflection of real connections, and that these equivalences, as abstract schemes, follow the dependencies of changes only in certain directions, while in reality these different directions intertwine with one another in the most diverse ways.

Wundt's terminology, as long as it is consistent, has the advantage that, more strongly than any other, it emphasizes the difference between the details of the cause, containing the change, and those factors that continue without change. Only these first factors can be exploited to show a certain *continuity of changes*, which some naturalists raise to the dignity of a first-class principle, and only these series of changes can serve as a guide and signpost for tracking causation. On the other hand, permanent conditions, if they mean certain "forces", indicate only something that is still going on, which is repeated in all causal connections. And here lies the deeper difference between temporary and permanent latent conditions. Besides, in using the word "condition", we turn to Mill's terminology with the proviso that, in using the name "condition" for all the details of the cause, we do not want to prejudge their position in the real grouping of reality's components. We also do not consider it possible to expel force from a scientific vocabulary. Forces, dispositions, and abilities preserve their place in the cause as some hidden, stable conditions. The expulsion of these concepts would make our way of expressing connections among facts impossible; we also saw that, *de facto*, everyone uses these concepts; even the most fervent opponents recognize that these words, and therefore the concepts related to them, should be preserved as shortened ways of expressing ourselves. The problem of the elimination of these concepts depends on the value we attribute to them. Although Kant retained the concept of action and force as related to the concept of causality,[7] although he did not base the

---

7 "Die Kausalität führt auf den Begriff der Handlung, diese auf den Begriff der Kraft, und dadurch auf den Begriff der Substanz" [Kant 1781: 191].

CAUSALITY AND FUNCTIONAL RELATION   121

definition of causation on it, Kant does not demand that these concepts be hypostasized, but he bases their objectivity on the necessity of capturing and expressing certain empirical data. The criticism of these concepts carried out by Kant is well understood to be their elimination.

The definition of force as hidden conditions is also justified for the reason that in many cases physical forces can be understood as a series of slight collisions of masses and, as we know, the mechanistic view tries to reduce all forces to masses in movement. However, it has not been able to do so with gravity. The force of gravity is always something foreign in all mechanistic views of the physical world. However, attempts do exist to redefine this force down to something relatively simpler. Such an attempt supposes that, for example, the moon and the earth do not attract each other (*vis a fronte*), but that, by a hypothetical space ether, they are pressed, pushed towards each other (*vis a tergo*). In this way, the force of gravity would be reduced to mechanical collisions, just as the kinetic theory explains gas pressure by means of the constant impact of gas particles against the walls of the vessel. However, such a reduction of *actio in distans* to *actio per contactum* could not be made for gravity in a way consistent with the facts and free of contradictions, although something similar was done in the theory of Faraday and Maxwell for magnetic and electrical forces [Höfler 1904: 77]. However, the latest theory of electricity (the theory of electrons) makes it necessary to recognize the principles of Newtonian mechanics as a detailed case of the laws of electromagnetism, true only in approximation [Smoluchowski 1907]. Of course, this reduction of certain dependencies to relatively simpler matters does not yet determine the value of the concept of force in general.

Here we want to draw attention to the detail that the metaphysical concept of force is by no means identical to the concept of force in mechanics, where the quantity of force is measured by the product of mass and acceleration. After all, in the formula for the expression of force $p = mg$, force only signifies something that coexists with motion, is proportional to movement, and which becomes equal to zero when acceleration is equal to zero ($p = mg = 0$, when $g = 0$); meanwhile, in the metaphysical concept, force means the ability to cause changes. In physics, there are actually three concepts that can be associated with the concept of force: (1) the "mg" formula; (2) the "mv" formula (v = speed), which means the so-called "amount of motion" or "momentum"; and finally (3) the formula for "energy" as the ability to perform work, and it is this concept that corresponds to the metaphysical concept of power.[8]

---

8   In fact, the former dispute of the rationalists regarding the measurement of force (Descartes-Leibniz) concerned not the formula "mg", but the formulas "mv" on the amount of motion

Therefore, the *hypostatization* of this concept, especially of *potential energy*, as the ability to perform work related not to body movement but to its position as a "store of work accumulated in the body", leads to the densest metaphysics. Finally, the metaphysical element can be found in a number of statistical determinations of bodies: when we talk about statistical measurement of forces, of impermeability, inertia, frictions, and resistance, etc. Without entering into the metaphysical and ontological aspect of these concepts, they can be approved in science from the point of methodical purposefulness, and even this must be done while trying to avoid contradiction with one's way of expressing oneself and thinking. By keeping the concept of force, we can also keep the concept of "action", as long as, having cleared this concept of all anthropomorphism and anthropopathism, we use it only to define the dependency of changes.

At the end of the definition of the object of causal relations, we want to pay even closer attention to the issue of the relation of the concept of change to the concept of cause and effect, which has been mentioned several times. It seems to be clearer and more obvious that the effect is a certain change than that the change must also be included in the cause. In the same way, the history of philosophy teaches us that it took a long time before the view "reifying" the cause was supplanted by the concept of cause as an "event". Wundt rightly considers this to be one of the greatest achievements of science; however, he erroneously excludes certain permanent conditions from the cause. We will not ponder what should be understood by change because this concept already has its exact definition [Łukasiewicz 1906]. On the other hand, we will consider how convincing the arguments are of those who today still want to expand it so that it relates not only to the dependency of changes, but also to the connection of coexistence of the features of unchanging objects. And so, they pay some attention to the fact that the necessity of the connection among certain changes is somehow derivative when it results from the necessity of coexistence of certain features. This is undoubtedly an accurate remark, but it does not force us to include all these necessities under one heading. After all, we can establish a separate category for these necessities, i.e., for example, a sort of Kantian category of mutual interaction, according to which everything that coexists remains in a relation of mutual dependence. The above argument can be decisive for someone who considers the relation of necessity the only and exclusive feature of the concept of causality. One could, however, also refer to a certain expression of everyday speech, such as, for example, that the cause

---

and $mv^2 / 2$ on "living force", i.e., the kinetic energy of bodies. Looking at the matter of the values of concepts from the position of methodical expediency, the whole dispute must be considered a struggle over words.

of the stone lying on the table is the table, where, therefore, neither the cause nor the effect is a change. However, referring to certain expressions of everyday speech cannot be decisive here. All the expressions of everyday speech are ambiguous, especially the words "cause" and "result". After all, these concepts have gone through different stages of development and all these phases are reflected today in the use of words. Even today you can still encounter expressions from the most primordial stages of animism, such as "The candle does not want to burn". Therefore, to bear in mind every similar use of words and to try to account for each of them is impossible and even absurd. Each consistent implementation of the unambiguity of certain terms must be combined with the violation of certain expressions of everyday speech. This happens, for that matter, in every science. Let us compare only the meaning of expressions such as "acid" in chemistry or "energy" in physics with the meaning of these expressions in ordinary speech.

Thus examples like that of the stone and table prove nothing; they could be multiplied indefinitely. More important than these examples, where cause and effect are things in which nothing changes, would be those in which the cause would be a change and the effect would not, or *vice versa*, where the effect would be a change and there was no change in the cause, where, therefore, some changes would not be the result of other changes, but rather they would have come about, so to say, by themselves. Certain events would indicate the truthfulness of the first of these assumptions; namely that in some cases the effect of some changes is an unchanging state, if not an absolute quiescence, then at least a relative equilibrium. However, such cases do not contradict our understanding of the members of the causal relation. The result of the effect can last extremely long, in abstraction even to infinity, such as a monotonous straight-line movement, such as the result of a momentary impact; therefore, it is immaterial how long the product of an effect lasts as long as it can only be explained by another change, when we refer to it as a different previous state and understand it as a change. Thus, the above understanding of the members of the causal relation as changes does not exclude understanding certain states of relative equilibrium as effects, or, more precisely, as a residue of an effect, if we want the effect to refer only to the moments of change.

Undoubtedly, Lotze wanted to state the same thing, saying that a cause is always at least two things held in a certain relation. However, we do not want to adhere to Lotze's definition because only external physical changes could be, with difficulty, defined in this way, but we would not be able to refer this definition to the interdependence of psychic states with regard to which there cannot be talk of two things. By attaching causality to the dependency of changes, we want thereby to say that if nothing happened anywhere, if reality was a state of absolute deadness, silence, rest, immutability, in a word, if there were no changes, there would be no need to speak of causality; unless we would like to answer the question of why there is anything at all, why there is something rather than nothing, why reality is reality; but we doubt whether such a question would have any scientific sense at all and whether it could be placed on the same level as the problem of causality. According to physics, this could happen if all the differences between objects were eliminated, and if energy were evenly distributed throughout the universe. Can such a state ever be realized? [...] [According to me,] such a state is a scientific fiction, and [...] the principle of increasing entropy, raised to the dignity of an absolute principle indicating some absolute one-directional changes in the universe [Kozłowski 1906], has no scientific basis as such.

The above considerations lead us therefore to define causality as a necessary connection concerning the order of changes in time, the connection in the majority of cases of simple necessity, and in some cases of mutual necessity, and we rejected Borowski's claim only because it cannot be carried out absolutely for all dependencies. The result is modest and not very original, if we understand "originality" as establishing an utterly new thing; however, we are convinced that only the above definition corresponds to the nature of facts, and the work undertaken to reach the above definition was necessary to discuss the relation of causality and functionality.

5

Having established the content of the concepts of causality and mathematical functionality as the model for a new concept of functional connection that can be formulated and that would replace causation, we can easily compare the two and answer the question whether a new concept is needed here to eliminate the old one.

Both concepts have certain common features: they refer especially to the relations of *connections, necessary connections* especially, and there is some similarity as to the members to which these relations pertain; in causality, in fact, it is the dependence of real changes, whereas in functionality it is the dependence of certain values which can be taken by the variable values associated with the above relation, and thus of the dependence of certain *changes of quantities*. There is also some similarity with regard to derivative features; both relations are *transitive*, i.e., in a situation where the above relations between members A and B, and B and C obtain, they also exist between members A and C. But the similarity ends at this point.

The differences that occur between the two concepts concern both essential, constitutive features as well as derivative, consecutive ones. The first two include: (1) the *necessity* of functional *dependence* is *mutual*, or bilateral, whereas in causality we usually have *simple necessity*, because real dependence can be demonstrated mutually only in some cases; (2) the functional connection is *timeless*, or purely logical, whereas causality *concerns* any *order of the phenomena in time*. Among the derivative features there is also a deep difference: the first concept signifies a *symmetric* relation, and the second one signifies an *asymmetric* relation. Let us consider these features more closely.

If Borowski's theory that in the causal connection there is a one-to-one correlation of cause and effect were accurate, then the first difference as to the nature of necessity would have to be abandoned. Since, however, we have recognized that this mutuality cannot be demonstrated in all causal relations, we must retain this difference. Because causality involves only simple necessity, we must call this relation only a unilateral many-to-one correlation. However, it should not be presumed that the functional connection, because it expresses mutual necessity, must be, inversely, a mutual one-to-one correlation. Such a one-to-one correlation exists only in those functional connections where single different values of the one quantity correspond to single different values of the other quantity. Such connections include, for example, the connection between the circumference and the radius of the circle:

$$y = 2 \times \pi r.$$

However, there are also functional connections where several, and sometimes even infinitely many, values of the one quantity correspond to the single values of the other quantity. Such connections include trigonometric functions, e.g., $y = \sin x$.

Here, when "x" takes on all finite positive or negative values, "y" can only take values between "-1" to "+1" and therefore all values of "y" must be periodically repeated. And so, $y = 0$, when $x = 0, \pm 180°, \pm 360°, \pm 540°, + $ *in inf.* Therefore, the inverse function:

$$x = arc. \, sin. \, y$$

is infinitely polyvalent. Infinitely many values of the function correspond to one argument. Therefore, one cannot talk about a one-to-one correlation, which excludes the polyvalency of members of a certain argument of the relation. However, the lack of this one-to-one correlation does not at all disturb mutual necessity. This is because we proceed with necessity from a certain value of one side to a certain value of the other side, just as these other values of the other side lead with necessity to this one value of the first side, which we have chosen as the starting point. Therefore, the many-to-one correlation is not something that must be combined with mutual necessity, because although mutual necessity exists in all functional connections, the one-to-one correlation exists only in some functions. And in causality, the lack of the one-to-one correlation cannot result from the lack of mutual necessity. Mutual necessity would exist in causality, even if one cause had different effects, if only there were always a passage from these different effects to only one cause. Simple necessity is connected in causality with the unilateral many-to-one correlation because in considering of the dependence from cause to effect one cause corresponds to one effect, and in considering this dependence from the side of effect this is not the case.

Nor should one confuse the polyvalency of functionally dependent elements with the fact that there are several arguments in some functional dependencies. These functions are many-to-one relations, and some functions have one argument because the opposite members of the functions are not individual arguments, but always a certain system of values of these arguments put together. For example, if the surface of a rectangle is a function of the base and height, then one member of the relation is the value of the rectangle's surface, the second member is the pair of values for the base and height, and the relation is at the same time a one-to-one correlation, although there are two values on the other side.

Functional and causal necessity gives rise to further reflections when we compare them. Functional necessity concerns only a connection of quantity; causality, first of all, concerns a connection of quality; and because the quantitative cognition of phenomena makes it possible to define connections of quality more and more accurately if they are available, providing, so to say, a higher degree of cognition, for which reason the functional connection is also of great importance in those natural sciences which make extensive use of mathematics, and causality itself in natural science, combined with a knowledge of quantitative dependencies, can be more accurately implemented, enabling the quantitative equivalence of cause and effect to be stated. However, the concept of a function does not necessarily have to be limited to quantity; nothing prevents us from also recognizing quality in functional connections. We have seen that Avenarius also used this concept for such matters whose quantitative definition is almost impossible, saying, for example, that worldviews are a function of time and space. But the above extension of the concept entails a fundamental change in its logical character, because the connection between the two sides of dependence ceases to be necessary at this moment. We do not know any logic or mathematics of quality which would make connections between qualities so obvious to us. In any case, we would then have to look for some other source of necessity than given by mathematics alone, which only studies relations between quantities and magnitudes.

But let us go back to the basis of the necessity of all possible functional quantitative connections. We called causal dependence necessary; it is a theorem demanded by the existence of science and scientific experience. Some call it a postulate, but we prefer to reserve this term for claims of a different nature. This necessity, however, at least in every particular case of causal connections, must be considered probable. Something similar exists in connections of functional necessity. Functional necessity is also conditional to some extent. Because in order to derive logically the value of a dependent variable from an independent variable, one must assume a certain shape of a function that we ourselves assign in the task. As long as the shape of a function is not specified in the form of an equation, the dependence of the first quantities is not logically obvious. And so, while I only have the general symbol $y = f(x)$ I do not know how "y" depends on "x"; but if I define the shape of the function exactly with the equation, e.g., $y = ax + b$, then I can find an appropriate "y" for each value "x" and then I see that these values belong to each other with the necessity that their negation would lead to contradiction with the adopted shape, e.g., for $x = 0$, y must be $= b$ and *vice versa* for $y = b$, x must be $= 0$. The individual shapes of functions may have different sources; some may be a recognition of the relation between geometrical quantities, and others may be a system in the equation of practical problems. Additionally, we may try to define quantitatively the changes taking place in reality, arranging them in certain equations that allow us to derive new connections of the same kind from this equality without looking at the facts and, thanks to this, to anticipate new facts. The more subtle the observation and the more precise the equation, the greater the benefit of this equation, because the greater number of detailed cases can be derived from it. By introducing to science such a subtle research tool as the infinity calculus, we greatly increase the value of these connections. However, assuming that the observation was accurate, and that the deduced conclusions were true, we must assume that this connection, once expressed in the equation, is true always and everywhere, that it is stable and universal. Therefore, the general assumption of the certainty of the equations of physics and generally of applied mathematics is the belief in the uniformity of nature, in the necessity of all real connections. For, where the shape of a function is not dictated to us by reality but depends on us, there the necessity of connections exists as long as we want to be bound by the assumption once adopted. For equations of applied mathematics the assumption is reality, which is treated as one great mathematical problem. The change of the assumption does not depend on our arbitrariness. Therefore, the necessity of dependence in functional relations, so long as they concern empirical reality, where, therefore, the functions are of an empirical origin, is only borrowed. Thus, mathematics does not contribute and cannot contribute to reality any new certainty or any new necessity except those which we have already assumed for reality without mathematics in real connections. Mathematics can only reveal new details of these dependencies, which then become discoveries only when we verify them.

And yet the necessity in functional connections is not the same as in real connections! Why this is so and whether something follows for real connections, we will answer at the end of this section, but presently let us complete the review of the further differences between causality and functionality.

Causality concerns a certain connection of phenomena in time, it concerns their temporal order, while in functionality the time factor does not enter the game at all, and this is an important difference that cannot be forgotten and whose strict observance will release us, as we shall see, from a great deal of nonsense. Mach wanted to bring the two concepts closer together, referring to the fact that all causal relations are not only mutual, but also simultaneous. The proof of the first feature cannot be established, and the second point has no evidential power. Simultaneity, as a time attribute, divorces causality from functionality as much as succession. Functional connections, if they relate to real connections, can refer to both simultaneous and temporally distant members. On the other hand, not taking into account the temporal character of causality in general causes other fatal confusions of the concepts.

This is true especially in understanding the reversibility or irreversibility of both concepts. As we have seen, only the functional connection has the feature of reversibility, and causality is asymmetric. This irreversibility results both from the fact that the relation of cause and effect is not a relation of interdependence, or mutual necessity, and also because the order of cause and effect is not symmetric. Mach, on the other hand, considers causality a symmetric relation in time! It seems to him that since the dependence of cause and effect is mutual, one can inverse the cause and effect much like function and argument. There is an apparent confusion of the concepts of mutuality and reversibility. Even if the causal connection were a relation of mutual necessity, as Borowski's theory supposes, it is not yet possible on the basis of this feature alone to deduce that the members of the causal relation are convertible if another feature of this connection does not allow it. Mach's attention was already drawn to this inaccuracy by Borowski [1907].

After all, the fact that the current phenomenon is equally dependent on
the preceding one and on the succesive one does not indicate that these
phenomena could be inverted in time. Phenomenon *A* can cause phenomenon *B*, but phenomenon *B* cannot cause phenomenon *A*, although
they are nevertheless strongly connected to each other. [...] The principle
of the strict and comprehensive dependency of phenomena excludes any
freedom and the possibility of inverting the order of phenomena in time
or space.

BOROWSKI 1907: 79

Mach undoubtedly was also seduced by the circumstance that the dependencies of phenomena, occurring at a certain place and time, are repeated
in another place and time in such a way that members of the same kind of
quality occur in reverse order. So, in one case, the volume of a body changes
as a result of a change in temperature, and in the other, conversely, the body
temperature changes as a result of a change in volume (e.g., when gas con-
densation causes the gas to warm). This is undoubtedly a kind of reversibility,
but it means something other than reversibility in a functional relation that
consists in the interchangeability of positions of argument and function. In
causality, the reversing that occurs means only that members of the same kind
of concepts may appear in different order in different places and at different
times, not that in the same place and at the same time cause and effect may
change their roles. Admittedly, it could be remarked that after all, in a functional relation as well, it is not the case that the argument is a function and,
simultaneously, the function is an argument: that by taking a certain quantity
as an argument, they cannot simultaneously assign the same role to the second
quantity. This is a just remark, but in any case, this choice is arbitrary, whereas
in the meantime, in the temporal course of phenomena, all arbitrariness is
excluded. In a functional relation, no quantity has a greater right than another
to be made the point of departure to consider changes of the second, while in
causality the temporal course indicates only one position for each phenomenon, and the supposition itself that all phenomena could change their roles
would amount to introducing total chaos into reality.

From our position, we must also condemn certain paradoxical expressions
regarding the connection between cause and effect. Words like "depends",
"results", "evokes", if we are referring to causal relations, mean only that, but
also all that which constitutes an integral part of the concept of causal relation.
And that is why when these words are used to discuss causal connections they
should not be taken in a different sense. We must therefore condemn all such
expressions as "the present depends on the future" or "the cause results from

the effect" or the like. Even if we accept, as Borowski wants, that there is not a one-sided, but rather a bijective, correlation between cause and effect, then such expressions are also not justified, as long as we retain a certain temporal character for causal dependencies. Somebody will say that opposition to such expressions results rather from the unscientific understanding of causality as an action that can come from the cause and not from the effect. Undoubtedly, an anthropomorphic element, which turns against the similar use of words, remains present in language; however, even after rejecting this anthropomorphic element, expressions are unjustified when a certain order of time has preserved causes and effects that cannot be reversed. When it comes to the bijective correlation of the future to the present, the effect to the cause, this can be expressed without uttering paradoxical expressions. Certain of Borowski's expressions are even erroneous, for example [the statement that]:

> The existence of the potential energy is dependent on the subsequent movement, as well as *vice versa*. [...] If this movement were not brought about, one could not talk about potential energy.
>
> BOROWSKI 1907: 77

This is not true! One can also talk about potential energy where change has occurred at the expense of work, and where the body, as a result of the occurrence of certain conditions, can never even replenish this store of work. After all, some assume that the universe may come to an absolute state of equilibrium, in which the energy of the world, however quantitatively intact, will lose the ability to do work.

For the same reason, we also condemn the "logical necessity" of certain "paradoxical expressions" in Łukasiewicz [1906: 38–39], i.e., the necessity which flows only from ignoring the temporal character of causal connections.

Now we will answer the question of how to understand the application of the concept of mathematical function to real connections, when the properties of this concept do not correspond to the properties of causal connection, and whether, on the basis of certain properties of a mathematical concept, one can determine something about the nature of these real connections. Well, causally related quantities can only occur in nature in such a way that only one of them is really independent (of course only relatively independent, that is, in relation to its effect), and the other really dependent (also only relatively dependent, i.e., in relation to its cause, and able to be comprehended as independent in relation to other changes, its effects). Given this dependence in the formula of the mathematical equation, disregarding the real order of this dependence and treating the data as having abstract quantity, I can take any quantity as a starting point for the calculations; I can take the really dependent quantity as functionally dependent or as functionally independent as well. For the concept of a function to be applied to the real course of phenomena, it suffices to state that changes in one quantity are combined with changes in the second quantity. Which of them, however, is really dependent and which is truly independent, that is completely neutral for the application of the concept of function. From the fact that the concept of function is symmetric, it does not follow that we must consider as symmetric the real relations for which we use this concept, because by using these relations we abstract in our calculations from the real order. More or less the same thought, although in a slightly different form, was already expressed by Kozłowski [1906: 201]. Taking into account the formula for a path of uniform motion:

$$s = v \cdot t$$
(the distance equals the product of speed and time)

I can reverse the dependencies in abstract treatment of these quantities by writing:

$$v = s \,/\, t \text{ or } t = s \,/\, v$$

Both of these equations are correct, since it is about the quantitative side of the phenomenon, i.e., about calculating the number of meters expressing the speed, or seconds during which the movement continued. But when *all* three equations are the same equations from the *mathematical standpoint*, and the other two equations can be derived from each of them, *physical meaning is possessed only by the first*, and its form requires a default complement that only "*s*" depends on "*v*" and "*t*", but not conversely, because neither time nor speed are dependent on the distance (although they can be calculated from it).

KOZŁOWSKI 1906: 202

In principle, we agree completely with the above position, but we must note that the example itself is unfortunate. This is because not all mathematical equations express causal relations; especially when time appears as the measured quantity in mathematical formulas we cannot consider the passage of time a causally dependent or independent quantity; although the amount of time that passes is not indifferent to causal relations because changes can increase proportionally or decrease with increasing time. And speed is also not something that would really bring about distance and conversely distance does not causally bring about speed, although speed can be assessed only from the quantity of paths. Speed is just a kind of characteristic of motion defining the relation of elements of distance to elements of time. Thus, kinematic patterns have nothing to do with causality, as long as there is no mention of the causes of movements or the causes of their changes.

But let us take a different, more general example. Mental phenomena all seem to depend on certain physiological changes, whereas many deny the reverse dependence of physiological on mental changes. If this statement were true, a number of psychological phenomena would really be dependent on physiological phenomena, but not conversely. Does this mean that it is impossible to apply here the well-known concept of mathematical function, which is symmetric? Not at all! To use the mathematical concept of function, it is enough to know exactly the connection (of course quantitative connection if we are to draw some advantage from using the symbols of mathematics), so that we can determine the value of one quantity from the other. The real dependence can run in one direction only, and we, nevertheless, can calculate both changes of the truly independent quantity from the truly dependent quantity or conversely. All these functional dependencies will be mathematically justified because they will be about the ability to calculate one from the other, but only one formula of functional dependence will have real significance.

But here a new question arises. If a certain temporal, asymmetric, character is assigned to the real dependence,, then – someone will say – it is clear that the causal dependence is asymmetric, and that functional dependence, since it abstracts entirely from time, can prejudge nothing about the temporal order. However, does the possibility of calculating one quantity from another, and conversely, not only truly dependent ones from truly independent ones, but also truly independent ones from truly dependent ones, not speak in favor of this theory, which presumes that all real necessity is mutual and that the cause and the effect can stand in a mutually single-valued correlation? Borowski actually draws this conclusion from the mathematical formulas in favor of the theory [Borowski 1907: 76]. In response to this question, we point out that, above all, we cannot rely on formulas from phoronomy (kinematics), which establish a connection of certain quantities with time, because, as we have already pointed out, time alone is neither a cause nor an effect. As for other quantitative connections that concern the transformation of quality, or, as physics says, the transformation of various forms of energy, where the matter is really only about causation in our understanding, they also prove nothing. This is because the formulas for the quantitative equivalence of various forms of energy can by no means be considered an accurate representation of real transformations as they do not specify under what conditions, when, and why just these rather than other energy changes occur. Does the claim that, with all transformations of heat into work, one calorie = 424 kilogram-metres of work, exhausts the whole connection between heat and work? Does it say anything about why such transformations occur in certain cases? A complete mutual dependence requires that, in both directions, changes should be as easy and occur under the same conditions. Meanwhile, we cannot say anything similar. We know, for example, that the transformation of heat into work is not possible to the same extent and in the same conditions as the transformation of work into heat.

Finally, we should take up the issue here, already noted, that qualities belonging to the same kind may occur in various places and times in a different causal order; in one case, a change in gas volume (by compression) may cause a change in pressure; in other, conversely, pressure causes a change in volume, and this interchangeability of various properties of bodies into others, and conversely, gives great value to general mathematical formulas which, having detected relations between quantities in one case ascribe them equally to other cases where the relation of quality is in the opposite order. Not all defenders of the law of causality have paid attention to this detail. However, that these cases do not prove anything in favor of functionalism and the interdependence of cause and effect is already due to what we have said, namely that changes of quantity in one direction do not take place with the same ease and in the same conditions in the opposite direction, and that the general formulas of mathematics do not give all the details of incidental dependencies, which, however, are not indifferent in the specific temporal course of facts.

With this we can end the comparison of causality and functionality and the matter of how to understand the application and authorization of this application of the concept of mathematical function to real dependencies. A few words should be added here about the meaning with which one can also speak about a condition in functional relations. In causality, we called all details of the cause, including forces, conditions because it seemed wrong to demarcate the conditions from the proper cause. In a functional relation, conditions can be called single argument values; but where the argument is one, the word "condition" would actually signify the whole reason why the function would take on a certain value. One could, however, extend the meaning of the condition in a functional relation, considering it to be the whole detailed shape of the relation given in the equation, which together with the value of the argument assigns the value of the function. Then it is no bother to also transfer this word to what gives rise to a certain detailed shape of the function. In this sense, we said that in functions of empirical origin (e.g., in the Gay-Lussac equation for gases: $pv = RT$) the conditions of dependence of the argument and function are always real relations, which provide the base to the construction of the equation, and therefore we called the necessity contained therein conditional and borrowed.

Now we can answer the question whether it is necessary to create a new concept of function in addition to the mathematical one and what its content could be. This concept can be created by extending the functional relation to the connection of qualities. But the ensuing value is small, because the basis for the necessity of such a connection of qualities would always be borrowed, as in empirical functions; but, moreover, we could not draw any conclusions about specific dependencies, because we do not have any mathematics of quality that would allow operations with qualities, analogous to mathematical operations on quantities. This means that all the benefit which we derive from a mathematical functional relation would drop out, and only a general, comfortable means of expression would remain. Of course, the principal nature of the relation, and therefore some reciprocity of this dependence and its reversibility, would have to remain, otherwise the functional relation would no longer have the right to be called functional. However, since the divergence of the concept of causality and the mathematical functional relation shows the impossibility of eliminating the first concept by means of the second, therefore this new concept of functional relation, modelled on the mathematical concept, cannot replace causation.

For the final assessment of the value of both concepts in science, i.e., causality and functionality (mathematical or generalized), let us consider the scope of their applicability. We do not limit causality to the physical world alone, but we also accept it in the psychical world. The temporal nature of the mutual dependence of states can be reduced to a quite distinct succession of psychical phenomena, and the principle of absolute determination of phenomena requires that here, too, we adopt for each of the consecutive states a relation of necessity, and the relation of simple necessity in particular, since we suppose here that the same effects result from the same causes, and conversely, the same effects may result from different causes; for example, the same decision may result at different times from the intersection of different motives, although it cannot be determined here either whether certain cases of the relation of mutual necessity will be found. Here, however, it must be stipulated that there can be no question that the absolute determination of psychical phenomena be only psychical, because these series of phenomena are often interrupted, and we do not see any relation between the successive states, e.g., when, in the course of intellectual labor, I receive a blow to the head and feel pain, I cannot conclude to some relation between mental labor and the subsequent pain. Therefore, the application of causality to psychical dependencies exists only within very narrow limits (laws of association, volitional laws of motivation);

besides, we have to refer to physical (physiological) changes whose relation to psychical ones is difficult to decide on the basis of experience.

The concept of function can be applied wherever we apply causality, but not conversely, because in a functional relation we can also include some constant dependencies, e.g., dependencies of spatial forms on each other, i.e., functions that are the result of geometric research; hereinafter all phoronomic [*scil.* kinematic] equations, which define only the very forms of movements, indicate a broader use of the concept of functional relation than causality. Wherever we come across causality, the concept of function can also be implemented; this results from what has been said above, namely that the use of this concept does not prejudge anything about real dependence, and, on the contrary, in empirical functions we must rely solely on these causal necessities. Examples of applying the concept of functional relation for real dependencies in the physical world are provided by the entire science of physics. However, we can do the same in the psychical world, saying, for example, that memories are a function of perceptions, or acts of will are a function of motives. If we could express these relations quantitatively, then we could invert mathematical formulas here and determine the number of memories from the number of perceptions, or conversely, the number of perceptions from the number of memories. However, as long as we cannot express this relation quantitatively, introducing it gives us nothing more than a new way of expressing ourselves. The philosophy of Avenarius provides many examples of the use of the concept of function. We can also apply the concept of function to social, economic, and political phenomena, wherever one can see series of changes corresponding to each other, regardless of when and whether the changes depend directly or indirectly on each other, if the mediation of other quantities has no impact on the series of examined changes. The concept of function is more general because it takes into account the temporal nature of dependence, and therefore we can grasp, in the form of a functional relation, relations of dependencies and those that are revealed to us in phenomena bearing the mark of finality, and thus in biological phenomena. Here, we can say that the development of an organism is a function of the typical form toward which the organism tends, and such an expression has none of the nonsense of the claim that the present state of the organism is the result of a future state. It is enough only to detect a certain permanent and necessary relationship, it is enough to discover a certain permanent and necessary connection, being of the simple necessity kind and asymmetric, because *reversibility in a functional relation has a purely arithmetical value,* and the unilateral dependence of the simple necessity is not disrupted by the fact that cases of such dependence cannot be considered from the standpoint of mutual dependence. Where, as in a causal relation, *B* results from A, but B does not necessarily result from A, that means that B may still result from something else, e.g., from A'. However, where I know that A' is absent, or I cannot ascertain the effects of its absence, I am allowed to consider the relation between A and B from the position of interdependence, assigning certain *quanta* of one quantity to appropriate *quanta* of the second quantity. Therefore, no dependence connection can be *a priori* excluded from the domain of applicability of a functional relation, and this has superiority over the concept of causality in so far as it is more general in its use. However, causality cannot be replaced by a functional relation because the latter is not identical with the concept of causality, it is based on causality in empirical functions, and the transfer of all properties of the functional relation to real dependencies would be equal to introducing chaos into reality.

6

Let us collect the results of our discussions and end with a few general remarks. The question we dealt with arose from the call to eliminate as useless certain concepts from science, either because of their vagueness or instability, or because they contain too many anthropomorphic elements and thus, instead of making it easier for people to orientate themselves in their environment, are concepts that make the matter of cognition more difficult. And we are also of the opinion that the principal concepts of science should be free from all ambiguities and as to their content as indisputable as possible, that the study of reality should be carried out with as few prejudices as possible, and especially where we transfer by analogy human affairs to reality, whose values we cannot assess in objective terms, great care should be taken. Many problems arise only because of misrepresentation. Thus, *the principle of the methodological purposefulness* of concepts must be strictly observed. In accordance with this principle, we have shown that both concepts, causality and functionality, must be preserved, because one cannot be replaced by the other, they have different content, and their applicability, although partly overlapping, is based on different foundations, the first having the task of capturing the temporal order of phenomena according to certain dependency relations, and the second, of examining the interdependence of certain magnitudes and qualities (if at all possible) by a purely logical approach, without taking into account their position in the real order. Mach's struggle against causality grew out of resentment toward very primitive forms of causality, out of incomprehension as to the foundation of the applicability of the concept of function to reality, and out of a certain inaccuracy in expressing himself.

The evaluation of concepts by virtue of their methodical purposefulness entered into force in the theory of knowledge undoubtedly under the influence of the development of its biological direction, which understands the matter of knowledge as a process of adapting the mind to its environment. If we agree to the validity of this criterion, this does not mean that we consider this biological position sufficient. The insufficiency of this position results from the biological considerations themselves, as can be seen in some general conclusions reached by Avenarius. As we mentioned, he tried to show that each view of the world is a function of a certain constant and certain variables that are gradually eliminated, bringing the development of concepts concerning the world closer to that absolute constant. Therefore, it follows that something that is not subject to development itself, something that is common to all world views, as Avenarius himself points out, takes part in the understanding of reality. And since there are some factors in the understanding of reality, some basic components of cognition, *invariable* components, applying them to the concept of development does not reveal anything about them. These *invariables, invariants* of cognition, when we agree that they exist, can also be detected and determined by purely logical and rational considerations, without resorting to the help of biology, when we realize what must be a necessary element of all scientific experience and science in general, without which science or rather knowledge of reality would be impossible.

We did not touch the metaphysical side of our problem here. But however the objectivity of our concepts might be defined, we must also accept these epistemological criteria of their value.

Translated by Jacek J. Jadacki and Edward M. Świderski

Bibliography

Avenarius, Richard (1876). *Philosophie als Denken der Welt gemäß dem Prinzip des kleinsten Kraftmaßes.* Leipzig 1903: Fues's Verlag.

Avenarius, Richard (1888–1890). *Kritik der reinen Erfahrung.* Vol. I-II. Leipzig: Fues's Verlag.

Avenarius, Richard (1891). *Der menschliche Weltbegriff.* Leipzig: O.R. Reisland.

Borowski, Marian (1907). Criticism of the Concept of Causal Connection. In this volume: pp. 67–81.

Borowski, Marian (1909). O pojęciu konieczności [On the Concept of Necessity]. *Przegląd Filozoficzny* vol. XII, f. 3, pp. 338–372, f. 4 pp. 449–475.

Höfler, Alois (1904). *Physik mit Zusätzen aus der angewandten Mathematik, Logik und Psychologie.* Braunschweig: Friedrich Vieweg & Sohn.

Kant, Immanuel (1781). *Kritik der reinen Vernunft.* Berlin 1889: Mayer & Müller.

Kodisowa, Józefa (1907). W sprawie eliminacji metody przyczynowej [On the Elimination of the Causal Method]. *Przegląd Filozoficzny* vol. X, f. 2, pp. 149–174.

Kozłowski, Władysław Mieczysław (1906). Przyczynowość jako podstawowe pojęcie przyrodoznawstwa [Causality as the Basic Concept of Natural Science]. *Przegląd Filozoficzny* vol. IX, f. 2–3, pp. 180–222.

Lotze, Rudolf Hermann (1883). *Grundzüge der Metaphisik.* Diktate aus den Vorlesungen. Leipzig 1901: S. Hirzel. (Dritte Auflage).

Łukasiewicz, Jan (1906). Analysis and Construction of the Concept of Cause. In this volume: pp. 3–66.

Mach, Ernst (1872). *Die Geschichte und die Wurzel des Satzes der Erhaltung der Arbeit.* Leipzig 1906: Johann Abrosius Barth.

Mach, Ernst (1886). *Die Analyse der Empfindungen und das Verhältnis des Physischen zum Psychischen.* Jena 1919: Gustav Fischer.

Mach, Ernst (1905). *Erkentnis und Irrtum. Skizzen zur Psychologie der Forschung.* Leipzig: Johann Ambrosisus Barth.

Marie, Maximillien (1885). *Histoire des sciences mathématiques et physiques.* Vol. VII. Paris: Their-Villars.

Smoluchowski, Marian (1907). Zarys najnowszych postępów fizyki [Outline of the Latest Advances in Physics]. *Muzeum* vol. XXIII, f. 1, pp. 43–60, 144–165.

Twardowski, Kazimierz (1897). Psychology vs. Physiology and Philosophy. [[In:]] [Twardowski 1999], pp. 41–64.

Twardowski, Kazimierz (1999). *On Actions, Products and Other Topics in Philosophy.* Amsterdam & Atlanta: *Rodopi.*

Wundt, Wilhelm (1883). *Logik. Eine Untersuchung der Principien der Erkenntnis und der Methoden Wissenschaftlicher Forschung.* Vol. II. Stuttgart 1893: Verlag von Ferdinand Enke.

CHAPTER 3

How Did the Problem of Causality Arise? An Outline of Its Development in Ancient Philosophy

Tadeusz Czeżowski

Jak powstało zagadnienie przyczynowości.
Zarys jego rozwoju w filozofii starożytnej.
WILNO 1933: Wileńskie Towarzystwo Filozoficzne

∴

The following outline arose from lectures given at the University of Vilna in the course of the autumn trimester of the year 1930/1931. Its purpose is not to identify the sources of different views in the area of the problem of causality, but to take a glance at the entirety of the problem's development in the connections of the successive systems and currents. Hence, the outline ends with a presentation of the views of the Stoics, Epicureans, and Skeptics, and does not encompass later philosophical-religious systems considered part of ancient philosophy. New elements which those systems introduced to the problem of causality are connected to the later, medieval way of thinking rather than to the former development of the problem; thus, the development of the problem of causality until the emergence of those philosophical-religious systems constitutes a self-contained whole to which the following presentation is confined.

Among the general introductions to the history of philosophy, the work by Windelband [Windelband 1892] is especially informative when it comes to the development of the problem of causality in ancient philosophy. In addition, the following works have been helpful to me: [Lang 1904], [Göring 1874], [Hartenstein 1888] and [Peter 1909]. The bibliography of the subject is provided by the more comprehensive handbooks of the history of philosophy.

Introduction

1

According to Aristotle's oft-quoted saying, the human mind is not satisfied with the knowledge that something is such and such and asks *why* is it so, it seeks the *causes* of what exists and aspires to an *explication* or *explanation* of reality. The question "why", however, is ambiguous, which means that its explication can also be understood in different ways. One should distinguish between at least three possible kinds of answers to questions beginning with "why". When we ask, "why did the fire start", we want to figure out what phenomena antecedent to the fact constituted the sufficient *condition* of the fire starting. When we ask, "why does the sum of the angles in a triangle equal two right angles", we are concerned with finding the sufficient *reason* of the geometrical theorem in question. Finally, when we ask, "why are you leaving the house" and get the answer "in order to arrange a matter at the office", the answer picks out the *purpose* of the action.

Thus, among the circumstances which we usually take into consideration while explaining some fact or phenomenon, we should distinguish, at the least, among: *sufficient conditions* of the phenomenon in question, i.e., its *natural causes, the reasons* of the statement by means of which we assert the phenomenon, and the *purpose* of the action whose symptom, expression or result is the phenomenon. It sometimes happens that one and the same phenomenon can be explained in each of these three ways. When trying to explain any historical phenomenon, e.g., the French Revolution, a historian seeks among other historical phenomena a complex of conditions which brought it about. A sociologist, in turn, will try to find the reasons for the claims of the historian who discloses the origin and course of the revolution. The reasons in question will be certain sociological laws – certain general statements asserting the conditions in which social upheavals take place. This sociological reasoning could then serve as the basis of an act of reasoning leading to the conclusion that, given such and such a state of society, the revolution had to erupt. Finally, a historiosopher who seeks to understand historical phenomena as an expression of certain aspirations of humanity, will try to discover the purpose of the phenomenon under investigation, consistent with those aspirations.

We ask the question *"why"* when we want to figure out the *cause* of things; thus, all three modes of explanation we have distinguished remain closely connected to the concept of cause, and distinguishing among them is already the result of a relatively advanced analysis of that concept. In the course of historical development, each was a hue or variant of causal explanation.

2

When trying to reach answers which would serve as an explication of things and their properties, we also ask *"from what"*, and *"how"*, or *"in what way"* something arose. The first of those questions corresponds to another hue of the concept of cause – one of special importance in the earliest period of Greek philosophy. Cause in this sense is ἀρχή, the beginning of a thing. One can distinguish between two other ways of understanding that concept corresponding to the two meanings of the statement that a table is made of wood. In the first meaning, we have in mind the matter of the table; it is in this sense that we can say, pointing at the table: "This is wood". In the second meaning, when we say that the table is made of wood, we have in mind the tree trunk out of which the parts of the table have been made; we cannot point at the table and say: "This is the tree trunk". It is in the first meaning that we say that an outfit is made of velvet, while in the second one we say that bread is made of flour – but is no longer flour. We are going to call that from which a given thing arose *matter* when we have in mind the first meaning, and *element* when the second meaning is intended.

The question *"how"* or *"in what way"* is answered by pointing out the factors *through* or *as a result of* which the thing to be explained arises. The same factors also constitute causes – at least in some sense, in accordance with the original meaning of the word. The factors in question are usually inferred; we conclude that they existed even though we only have before us their final result. Sometimes they are also treated as the hidden "essence" of the phenomena given in experience. Thus, they are *hypothetical causes* – as opposed to empirically given natural causes, which we have discussed above; they were understood as forces or processes acting on our body and calling forth sensory impressions, or as the movements of atoms perceptible as the physical properties of bodies, or, finally, as the movements of the soul, manifesting themselves in the form of psychic phenomena.

3

The necessity of distinguishing in yet another way among the different hues of the concept of cause is shown by further example: A boulder falling from a mountain broke a tree growing in a valley. Was the cause the boulder – the object whose action resulted in an effect – or the phenomenon of the rock's falling? The first understanding corresponds to what is at play in the case of our own actions. I consider myself the cause of my deeds. "That man rendered his neighbor's unhappy" can be said about someone who harmed someone else. A man, and not his choice of this or that course of action, is considered the cause of a misdeed. The relations among human actions seem to be the prototype of all causal relations; we are inclined to understand causal relations just like we understand our own actions: someone or something, rather than a fact, process or phenomenon, is the cause. Such an account is called the *substantialist* understanding of causality. Seeing things from a different viewpoint, one can say that it is not the subject but some change which took place in it – and thus a fact, process, or phenomenon – that is the working cause, since before the change there was no action and thus no causal relation. The substantialist account of cause contrasts with the *phenomenalist* account, according to which it is not a substance, someone or something, but the phenomena that are causes.

4

The views on the *relation* between cause and effect are as different as the ways in which cause (and effect) are understood. There are two main positions on the issue. According to the first, usually connected to the substantialist understanding of cause, there is a real, objective, concrete connection between cause and effect consisting of the operation of forces; we experience those forces directly when they are exerted on our body or when we bring about an effect with some amount of effort. Something similar also takes place in the mental world – there too we encounter effort and work, and thus also causal connections of a psychical nature. The second view, contrary to the first, is usually connected to the phenomenalist understanding of cause. According to the position in question, the causal connection is not an objective, real connection, but an expression of the way in which our mind conceives of the course of phenomena. Thus, a causal connection is a connection which takes place not between things or phenomena but between our representations of them. We express the opposition between these two ways of understanding the causal relation by calling the first *realist* and the second *idealist*. This opposition goes in hand with transferring the problem of causality from metaphysics to the theory of knowledge. That is because when we understand a causal relation as objective, belonging to reality, the problem of causality becomes metaphysical. However, if we embrace the position that a causal relation does not connect real phenomena but representations which embody our cognition of things, then by the same token the analysis of causality, just like the analysis of any constituents of cognition, is an element of the theory of knowledge.

The history of the development of the problem of causality in the theory of knowledge is part of modern philosophy. In antiquity, the problem of causality was a metaphysical issue, but already with the demise of ancient philosophy – in the arguments of the skeptics – we can find thoughts leading directly to the transfer.

The history of ancient philosophy teaches us how the concept of causality gradually formed. We find therein the different hues of that concept, which we have distinguished above, as well as the beginnings of almost all the issues connected with the concept, which have constituted the content of philosophical considerations within that area to the present day.

Chapter 1: From Thales to Democritus

1   *The Older Ionian Physicists: Thales, Anaximander, Anaximenes (6th Century)*

The first philosophical question to appear when Greek thought began to search for a non-mythological explanation of the surrounding reality, was: From what did the world arise? This question not only signals the urge to *explain* phenomena, but also, asked in accordance with the tendency to generalization characteristic of the main philosophical problems, the pursuit of *unity* in the diversity of objects and facts, achieved by bringing them down to a common beginning, matter, or element – concepts which at that point had not yet been distinguished. *Thales* considers that common beginning to be *water* (or perhaps liquid in general). According to ancient testimonies, his belief was inspired by the observation that all living beings are moist. We can perhaps discern in his view a connection to the beliefs of primitive peoples, who took the blood of men and animals to be the element of their lives. Extending that observation to the whole of nature, animate as well as inanimate, was probably aided by mythological animism, i.e., the belief that all things live just as we do, which would not have been distant from the thought of that day; if the whole world is animate, its nature must be uniform and moist. The same animist viewpoint serves as an explanatory background for the hylozoism of Thales and his followers, i.e., for the view that the beginning of everything is itself animate; thus, the whole world developed out of it just as each vital entity does. Apparently, the need for an explication of such development, which at that time seemed natural and universal, must not yet have arisen; the questions, "how" and "why" did the world develop from its beginning, did not exist. For the while, the explanation was limited to the one version concerned with the beginning of the world as a whole.

The direction indicated by Thales was followed by his successors – two other thinkers categorized as older Ionian physicists or philosophers. They were satisfied by the form of the explanation of reality provided by the generalization that reduces the diversity of reality to a common beginning, but differed from Thales, and from each other, in their views on the question of what that beginning is. While Thales understood it in a very concrete way, seeking it in experience, *Anaximander*, who was younger than Thales, chose a new direction of reasoning. Namely, he believed that the *arché* (Anaximander was the first to use the term) should be infinite and indestructible and could not itself have arisen from anything, which means that it is uncreated and primordial, containing the seeds of everything; it is, so to speak, the primitive stage of the unity of all things which lay undifferentiated within it; hence it is still completely indeterminate. It is the primitive *chaos* (χάος), the infinite (τὸ ἄπειρον), and the indeterminate (τὸ ἀόριστον). In Anaximander – contrary to Thales – *arché* clearly occurs as element, not matter, but, as with Thales, the animate element alone forms the whole of reality.

The group's third member, *Anaximenes*, combined the views of Thales and Anaximander. Like Thales, and with the tendency to concreteness characteristic of the Greek mind, he sought the beginning within the data of experience, it being an element and the matter of things, but also ascribed to that beginning some features assumed by Anaximander, namely, infinity and eternity. He believed *air* to be the element joining those properties. What led him to his view was probably the fact that air is much more movable than water, and what is more movable has more life in it – and that air, as breath (πνεῦμα), no less than water, was considered to be the element of life. Fire, wind, clouds, water, and stones constitute different levels of air's density. At the same time, Anaximenes was the first to try to explain *how* different states of matter arise and, basing himself on observation, states the hypothesis that all this happens by heating and cooling. By raising this problem Anaximenes overtook both his predecessors while coming close to the younger physicists of later times.

2   *Heraclitus and Parmenides (Beginning of the 5th Century)*

The foregoing philosophical considerations were based on two assumptions. According to the first, a changeable and diverse real world exists, while according to the second the changeability and diversity of the world's phenomena emerges out of some primitive unity, a common beginning. Further development of philosophy is connected to the rejection of both these assumptions. Rejecting the first is the starting point of Parmenides of Elea, while Heraclitus of Ephesus starts from rejecting the second.

According to *Heraclitus*, there is no one element or one common matter shared by all things. Nothing is constant or unchangeable, *everything changes ceaselessly*. Heraclitus presents this universal changeability in a concrete way – as fire, which destroys everything, while it keeps assuming new shapes (fire is thus not the element of the world, like water or air according to the previous thinkers, but the concretization of the continuing changeability). Thus, the with Heraclitus generalizing observational data went in a different direction than in Thales' thinking, namely, in a direction more consistent with experience since he does not require that there be one beginning of everything that exists. Instead, Heraclitus finds the uniting factor that orders the ceaseless changeability in something else. Namely, changeability is subject to *regularity*, it is ordered and occurs in accordance with some measure. Heraclitus called the regularity of changes within nature destiny (εἱμαρμένη), reason (λόγος), justice or order (δίκη). Thus was uttered the principle on which all general laws governing generation are based, since were it not true, it would not be possible to formulate any such laws. Already Anaximenes, explaining the way in which different levels of air's density are generated, stated certain general laws, thus implicitly relying on the principle in question. When we state general laws, we also state the existence of causal relations, hence the principle of Heraclitus constitutes the assumption of all scientific research in which the causes of facts are sought.

Parmenides made use of a very different method. While Heraclitus, following his predecessors, reached his philosophical worldview by generalizing the data of experience, Parmenides applied rational analysis to the concepts of change and generation, discovering these concepts to be internally contradictory and concluding that nothing can arise or be subject to change – that whatever really exists must be unchangeable. Nothing can come into being, since to come into being is to come to existence from nothingness, and nothingness cannot generate anything. Moreover, nothing can change, since to change is to be and not be at the same time. In Parmenides, for the first time in philosophy, we encounter the distinction and contrast between two kinds of being. *Real being* is unchangeable; for Parmenides, who follows the teachings of his mentor, Xenophanes of Colophon, the deity – the all-encompassing, unchangeable, eternal unity – is such a being. The empirical world, the world of the senses, is the *world of illusion,* since changes, causes and effects occur in it only as illusions.

The views of Heraclitus and Parmenides were not only opposed to those of their predecessors but also mutually opposed. Thus, further development of thought in that earliest period of Greek philosophy, in the group of the so-called younger physicists, sought to reconcile the oppositions until critical analysis, destroying both positions, brought about a profound philosophical breakdown.

3   *The Younger Physicists: The Atomists (5th Century)*
The younger physicists took from Parmenides the principle that nothing can come into being and nothing perishes. However, while Parmenides concluded

on this basis that no change is possible, the thinkers in question, who, along with Heraclitus, acknowledged universal changeability, asserted that change-ability concerns the mechanical pattern of eternal, indestructible elements. Thus, the synthesis of the positions of Parmenides and Heraclitus led to an essential conceptual modification. In the first place, the original concept of the beginning of the world quite clearly became the concept of the world's *matter;* the elements of Empedocles, the homoiomeriae of Anaxagoras and the atoms of Democritus constitute the matter of the world. The original unity of the elements or matter in the works of the older physicists disaggregated into the plurality of material *elements* composing particular objects. Finally, apart from the question "out of what", there came the question "how" things come into being out of the plurality of material elements. Since the qualitative changeability of matter has been ruled out, the "how" in question could be understood only in a mechanical way, as the merging and separating of the molecules of matter – as physical *movement* in all its forms.

Empedocles of Acragas, the group's first representative, assumed the exis-tence of four elements or kinds of matter, namely, fire, air, water, and earth. The cause that connects them is love or attraction, and what pulls them apart is hatred or repulsion. The merging and separating of elements lead to cyclical changes in the universe. A more comprehensive elaboration of an analogous guiding thought can be found in *Anaxagoras* of Clazomenae. According to the latter, there are not four but an infinite number of matter's kinds corre-sponding to the infinite variety of things in the universe, which differ from each other in quality. The kinds in question are distributed in tiny molecules (homoiomeriae, ὁμοιομερῆ), and there are molecules of every kind in every-thing, while the quality of a thing corresponds to the nature of those mole-cules which occur in it in the greatest number. The cause of the merging and separating of molecules is their movement. Nonetheless, they do not move by themselves. Anaxagoras, following Heraclitus, believes that the world of mol-ecules and their movements is governed by regularity. To explain it, accord-ing to Anaxagoras, one has to assume that it is the *rational soul* of the world (νοῦς) that imparts movement to the molecules. The soul is the element of life and movement, and only reason can create the order governing the universe. Thus, Anaxagoras was the first to wonder about the problem of the beginning of the world in the sense of the ultimate cause of everything which takes place within it. Along with the concept of reason as the cause that orders phenom-ena Anaxagoras introduced to the problem of causality a new aspect, namely, the *purpose* of generation, since rational activity is purposeful.

The most perfect cosmological system of that period was the system of Leucippus and Democritus. Apparently, it was Leucippus who designed its principles, while Democritus put them to use. The principal thought – the solution of the contrast between the concept of being and the concept of change – is here the same as in the two previously discussed philosophers; the matter out of which the world is built is indestructible and unchangeable, and the changes concern the pattern of its molecules. The progress in relation to Leucippus' predecessors consists in a more perfect elaboration of both the concept of matter and that of change. To explain the differences in quality between things, Empedocles and Anaxagoras adopted a greater number of different kinds of matter. Democritus, in turn, probably under the stronger influence of Parmenides, came up with the thought which subsequently became dominant in modern physics, namely, that the diversity of sensory qualities, colors, sounds, and smells is only apparent, while there is veridical knowledge of geometrical and mechanical properties of bodies, their shapes, positions and movement, in which we see again the reflection of Pythagorean ideas (which will be discussed later). Hence, the conclusion that the matter of the world does not have sensory properties such as colors, sounds, and smells, and its molecules possess only geometrical properties, differing from each other in shape, position and movement. Everything consists of an immeasurably large number of the molecules of matter. The latter are what we would obtain if we were able to divide up the objects down to the ultimate limits. Democritus called those ultimate, indivisible molecules of matter atoms (ἄτομα). Atoms are indestructible and unchangeable, and all changes, like generation and destruction, take place only by connecting atoms and splitting them up. The task of science consists of explaining all differences among things given in experience by the properties of atoms, especially their movement. Thus, Democritus was a *mechanist,* since according to him the course of all phenomena can be explained by the movement of atoms, and a *materialist,* since he considered movement to be the property of matter and all phenomena to be material (Democritus' concept of matter already included the features of extension and movement, characteristic of matter in all materialist thought of later times); finally, he was a *determinist,* since he accepted the universal regularity of generation, making the position and movement of atoms at a particular time causally dependent solely on their position and movement at the preceding moment, ruling out the existence of chance. Democritus did not separate psychic from physical phenomena, also explaining the former by the movement of material atoms, though those that are smaller and faster moving. Democritus' materialist and mechanist determinism encompassed both animate and inanimate matter as well as the psychical world. Anaxagoras also embraced mechanist determinism and applied it as broadly as Democritus did, but the determinism of Anaxagoras was not materialist, since according to him movement is not an original property of homoiomeriae but was imparted to them by a purposeful act of Reason, governing the world.

The atomist theory of Democritus, reducing phenomena to atomic movements, introduces hypotheses whose purpose is to explain how phenomena work. Nonetheless, for Democritus atoms and their movements were not just hypotheses – he believed that the knowledge concerning them is knowledge of the same kind as that of the sensory properties of bodies, though surpassing the latter in precision; its content is what is real (ἐτεῇ), while the content of the knowledge of sensory properties is what is only apparent (θέσει). Democritus believed that the task of science is to find the causes, understood as just such real (ἐτεῇ) courses of phenomena. Thus, we encounter in Democritus, so to speak, two sides of causal explanation: according to the first, following the views of other physicists, causal explanation tell us "how" and "out of what" things arise. However, things and their sensory properties are illusions, behind which is hidden atomic reality. Thus, the other aspect of causal explanation consists of the discovery of the real nature of the illusion. The atomism of Democritus, considered as a causal theory, belongs to its age because of its application of the characteristic concept of material cause, providing an answer to the question "how" and "out of what", but also already shows some similarity to the views of Plato, in that Democritus, like Plato, sees the cause of "illusions" in what is "real", seeking the causes of the sense-world in some other realm, more real than the sense-realm.

4   End of the Period: Zeno of Elea and Gorgias (End of the 5th Century)

As we have seen, two basic concepts, that of unchangeable being and that of movement or change, have been present in philosophical systems from the time of Parmenides and Heraclitus; in the 5th century the cosmology based on these two essential concepts was subject to collapse due to being consistently subjected to the method of reasoning created by Parmenides. The method in question consisted of the analysis of the concept's content. By means of such an analysis, Parmenides reached the conclusion that the concept of change contains an internal contradiction, and it was believed that contradictory concepts do not represent anything real; therefore Parmenides did not doubt that pointing out a contradiction within the content of a concept amounts to the proof that its object does not exist. As a result, Parmenides considered the ever-changing world of the senses to be the world of illusion. Further philosophical investigations, however, included attempts to move past that consequence of Parmenides' reasoning by reducing the changeability of the sense-world to the movements of unchangeable molecules of matter. Zeno of Elea came up with a sharp criticism of such reasoning, showing, very much in the spirit of

Parmenides, that the concept of movement contains internal contradictions, hence concluding that movement does not exist. On the other hand, Gorgias of Leontinoi, usually considered a Sophist but close to the Eleatics in his way of thinking, carried out proofs – also by applying Parmenides' method – showing internal contradictions in the concept of being, entirely analogous to those encountered in the so-called logical paradoxes known from the ancient times and analyzed by contemporary logic, which, at least in part, has to admit that Gorgias' criticism was correct. Thus, the two essential concepts in the form they had been applied so far turned out to be useless, as a consequence of which pride of place was taken by other directions of thought standing in opposition to the speculation characteristic of the previous period of Greek thought.

Chapter 2: Plato and Aristotle

A   *Plato*

1   The Sources of Plato's Philosophy: The Sophists and Socrates

The period of cosmological speculation, which, as we have seen, ended with the negation of its basic assumptions by Zeno and Gorgias, was followed by a period of reaction coinciding with the appearance of the Sophists, professional teachers of wisdom, and characterized by a skeptical attitude towards cosmological topics. At the same time, the Sophists – given their tendency to apply the outcomes of knowledge practically, in social and political life – were interested in the human being, human thought and behavior, i.e., problems of psychology, epistemology, and ethics. This interest gave birth to the theory of epistemological subjectivism, developed mostly by *Protagoras* of Abdera (480–411). Protagoras believed that objective knowledge, the aim of the cosmologists' quest, does not exist, and that all human opinions are equal. What is true for a given person is what he is convinced about, and the truth of those who can persuade others to accept their beliefs is more powerful. Hence, the significance of the art of debate and argumentation, especially as cultivated by the Sophists. Thus, the philosophy of the Sophists was characterized by skepticism concerning cosmological issues, as well as anthropological interests, epistemic subjectivism, and emphasis on the art of argumentation, which constituted the beginnings of logic.

The same epoch was the time of *Socrates* (469–399); the latter, however, pointed out new directions for the development of philosophy. Like the Sophists, he gathered and publicly taught the youth, but, in contrast to them, he did not take any payment for his teaching. Following the Sophists, Socrates limited himself to problems concerning the human being and human activity,

and ascribed considerable importance to the art of argumentation and the correct method of investigation. Unlike the Sophists, however, he was not a sub-
jectivist: he was seeking one objective truth, valid for all. His chosen starting
point was quite simple: passing from subjective to objective truth consists of
rejecting everything about which human opinions differ, whereas what these
opinions share in common is free from subjectivity and constitutes the truth
which is objective. Socrates believed that different opinions do have such a
common content that the art of argumentation draws out; this, however, is not
easy to do, since people usually do not realize what beliefs they actually hold,
and these beliefs have to be, so to speak, brought to the surface in the course of
debate, so that it often turns out, to the surprise of many, that the real beliefs
of numerous individuals are unknown even to those who hold them. In this
way, by analyzing human opinions and singling out what was common to them
all, Socrates came to discover the real meaning of courage, virtue, bravery, and
piety (his reasoning focused on the area of human activities). To realize that
goal he created general concepts; statements conveying their content were
supposed to disclose objective truth.

Before Socrates, the Ionian philosophers and the Eleatics created and oper-
ated with general concepts. Both those groups, however, approached this goal
by applying ways of reasoning differing from that of Socrates. What Thales,
Heraclitus, and others did was to extend the content observed in an accessible
area of experience beyond that area, transferring, so to speak, the properties
of what they knew to the entirety of things. Such a procedure corresponds to
the primitive form of generalization called simple induction (*per enumeratio-
nem simplicem*) where enumeration, i.e., presenting a number of cases possessing some common feature, serves as the basis for ascribing that feature to
all unknown cases of a given kind. Parmenides, Zeno, and Gorgias applied the
method of creating concepts which today we would call axiomatic; namely,
they adopted some conceptual content as the starting point of their reasoning and on that basis drew conclusions, creating secondary and contradictory
concepts. Socrates, on the other hand, created concepts by the method of
abstraction consisting of the comparison of cases belonging to the scope of the
concept in question and the elimination of those elements of that content
which were found in only some cases under scrutiny. This is the method of
induction by elimination, whose chief varieties are called the method of agreement and the method of difference.

Socrates did not make any direct contribution to the problem of causality.
Nonetheless, he laid the foundation for the completely novel account of that
problem which can be found in the philosophy of *Plato* (427–347). Plato took
from Socrates, above all else, the conviction that objective knowledge exists,

and that it is different from the subjective opinions of particular people and attainable by creating general concepts encompassing the common content of particular opinions. Thus, Plato broadened the area of philosophical investigation dealt with by Socrates. The latter sought solely knowledge of the issues concerning man and his activity; in that he adhered to the mainstream of his time. Plato's investigations again encompassed the entirety of reality, like those of the cosmologists. In that he was probably inspired by the influence of yet another one of his teachers: Cratylus the Sophist, a follower of Heraclitus.

2   The Sources of Plato's Philosophy: Cratylus
Cratylus, like Heraclitus, taught that everything changes constantly, taking this to imply that it is not possible to make a true judgment about anything, since at the moment of making the judgment about a thing the latter is already something other than what we intended to judge about. While Socrates contrasted the changing subjective opinions of human beings with what is common to them all – objective truth – Plato found in the changeability of things ideal, constant, unchanging being, singling out what was not subject to change within the changeable. For instance, a man is different at every moment of his life, changing from young to old but always remaining a human; thus, his humanity is what remains unchanged throughout the course of change. The same essence of humanity is something constant in the immeasurable diversity of all people who are born and die. The generalizing procedure similar to the one deployed by Socrates, and later Plato, in order to objectively discern true knowledge among subjective and diverse opinions enables Plato to separate the unchanging world of beings corresponding to those general concepts from the perpetually changing sense-world. The concepts in question encompass common features, which exist unchanged in the changing world of phenomena. According to Plato as opposed to Cratylus, true knowledge of such unchanging beings is possible. What we find here seems on the face of it to be the same contrast between the changeability of phenomena and the unchangeability of being as set forth by Parmenides. But the roads to that contrast were different in both cases, which explains the differences between the two views. Parmenides chose as the starting point of his reasoning the most general concept of being, by means of purely rational speculation reaching the rejection of any connection between the being in question and the sense-world, claiming that the two are completely independent and dissimilar from each other. The sense-world became for Parmenides the negation of being, an illusion or irreality, while the concept of being was devoid of any content drawn from the sense-world. As logic teaches us, such concepts are created incorrectly and lead to

contradiction, which fact facilitated Gorgias' criticism of them. Plato wanted to reach knowledge of being as opposed to the sense-world, and even though he too considered the two to be completely different from each other, he preserved the connection between them by making the sense-world dependent on the conceptual world and reflecting its properties; accordingly, Plato had the means with which to equip the world of unchanging beings with varied content, diversifying it in accordance with the hierarchy of general concepts standing in manifold relations to each other.

Plato reached his general concepts in two ways. When he seeks true knowledge, he finds it, following Socrates, in what is common to all the various human opinions about things, while when he seeks for real being, he finds it, again, in what is common in the diversity and changeability of phenomena. Plato makes a clear distinction between those two ways of generalizing, calling the first induction, *epagoge* (ἐπαγωγή), and the second anamnesis (ἀνάμνησις), in which the soul recalls, at every occasion of perceiving sensory objects, the ideas it had once known in a direct way; the latter is, as we would say today, intuitive knowing (νόησις) of the essence of things among the diversity of phenomena.

3   The Sources of Plato's Philosophy: The Pythagoreans

Along with Socrates and Cratylus, the third source of Plato's philosophy was Pythagoreanism. The school of Pythagoras (around the middle of the 6th century) developed separately from the other schools: Philolaos (who lived at around the same time as Socrates) was its first literary representative. Pythagorean philosophy arose from specialized issues; the Pythagoreans busied themselves with mathematics, astronomy, and music, finding in these areas the regularities which could be expressed by means of numerical relations. Hence, generalization and conclusion, very different from those of Thales and other philosophers who sought for the principle of everything in existence and claimed to have found it in number. Further development of philosophical considerations gave that Pythagorean principle a more specific form. On the one hand, the distinction between two worlds, dating back to Parmenides, suggested an analogous distinction between numbers and the sense-world as well as the attribution to numbers of unchangeable being, as opposed to the changeability of phenomena. On the other hand, however, the teaching of Heraclitus concerning the constant changeability of the world of phenomena governed by the law of destiny also found direct application to the principle of Pythagorean philosophy; the law in question, governing the changeability of the world of phenomena, was numerical law, reflected in the course of phenomena.

Pythagoreanism gave yet another account of the relation of the world of numbers to the sense-world. The mystical teaching of the Pythagoreans set up contrasting pairs in all areas of being. The pair possessing the most fundamental significance was the contrast between the infinite and limitation; the infinite is formless, passive, and imperfect, while limitation provides the infinite with form, being something perfect and active. The world of sensory things harmoniously combines the infinite and limitation in such a way that bodies come into being when the infinite is delimited by virtue of shape in accordance with numerical laws.

Pythagoreanism was akin to Plato's thought especially in that, as with Plato, it distinguished between the world of changing phenomena and the overarching world of unchanging numbers; the road was short from there to joining the world of numbers with the world of ideas and introducing Pythagorean elements into the way the relation was understood between the world of ideas and the sense-world.

4   The Relation between Ideas and the Sense-World
Plato's claim that the world of phenomena is a reflection (εἴδωλον) of the world of ideas, which are their prototypes (παραδείγματα), also had Pythagorean coloring. According to another similar expression by Plato, phenomena "participate" (μέθεξις) in corresponding ideas in such a way that when they come into being, they, so to speak, draw closer to the ideas, only to stop participating in them the moment they perish. Later Plato describes the relation between the sense-world and the world of ideas as causal, stating that ideas are the causes (αἰτία) of the emergence of phenomena, but not in the sense that the activity of ideas brings about phenomena; ideas could not be conceived of as efficient causes since action is a change, while ideas are unchanging. Thus, ideas can be the causes of phenomena only by presenting the ends to be realized in phenomena, the ends in accordance with which phenomena come into being. The highest end is the good, conceived in the most general way possible, such that the idea of the good is the highest idea to which all other, less general ideas are subject, in the sense that the idea of the good governs the world and all phenomena are directed to it as their ultimate end.

However, apart from the relation of purpose, there is also a logical relation between phenomena and ideas and among different ideas. This is because ideas are general concepts to which phenomena are subordinated, and since there is a logical hierarchy among the ideas we can order them on the basis of their degree of generality. Plato identifies the relation of final cause and the logical relation of subordination between a sensory phenomenon and its corresponding idea. Hence, the novel conception of science in Plato's thought. According to Socrates, real knowledge is general and conceptual; for Plato the concept of a phenomenon is also its cause; hence, according to Plato, real knowledge is the knowledge of the causes of things. This concept of science was taken over from Plato by Aristotle, and thanks to him it gained currency to the present day, even though the concept of cause underwent a complete change.

Plato's position can be explained by the following example: Socrates, being a man, logically falls under the idea of man, but the idea in question is also the final cause of the existence of Socrates, whose life testifies to the pursuit of the idea of man. The idea of man is logically subordinated to the idea of living being; at the same time, the idea of living being is a higher end than the idea of man, since the life of Socrates, by virtue of being a realization of the idea of man, is also a realization of the idea of living being. The highest idea is the idea of the good, since every end is also some good. The life of Socrates, being a realization of the idea of man and of the idea of living being, is the realization of ends or goods which those ideas contain; that is why the ideas in question are particular cases of the idea of the good, subordinated to the latter as the most general. The most general idea is that of being. The term "being", understood collectively, means everything that can be thought, while in the distributive understanding it means anything, any object of thought. To grasp Plato's thought, one has to assume that the idea of the good does not differ from the idea of being – every good is some being, but also the reverse: every being is some good, insofar as we conceive of it as the end of any pursuit.

Joining the causal relation to the relation of logical subordination is in Plato a consequence consciously derived from the initial assumptions. For the Pythagoreans too, numerical relations are general connections under which particular phenomena fall – like under the concepts – on the one hand and the causes of those phenomena on the other. For instance, when they discovered that two chords of the same thickness and of lengths 1:2 result in the harmonious sound of an octave, they came to consider the numerical relation 1:2 to be not only a generalization under which all corresponding cases fall but also the cause of that chord. However, the difference between Plato and Pythagoreanism lies in the understanding of cause. Plato takes cause to be an end, while Pythagoreanism, it seems, takes it to be a certain relation of agency. Hence, identifying the logical and metaphysical relation, which in Plato is understandable as an element deliberately introduced into his theory, may indicate, in Pythagoreanism, the lack of an adequate distinction.

5   Matter as the Co-cause of Phenomena

The Pythagorean contrast between the infinite and the limited can also be found in Plato. For the question was raised, why are ideas only imperfectly reflected in phenomena? The explanation of the imperfection of phenomena had to be sought in something other than ideas. The existence of ideas is perfect and complete, while the existence of phenomena is a less perfect existence, since phenomena perish, which means that they somehow contain within them both existence and non-existence. Thus, non-existence (τό μή ὄν) is a co-cause (ξυναίτιον) of phenomena. Plato understands non-existence as the formless unlimited of the Pythagoreans or (in accordance with their thought) an empty space, which is shaped by assuming the form of ideas.

Contrasting existence given in ideas with non-existence as, respectively, the cause and co-cause of phenomena is one of the concepts crucial for the entire further history of the problem of causality. Plato identified the element of non-existence and passivity, devoid of any form with empty, unlimited space; in later modifications of Plato's teachings it became a synonym of matter to which inertia and spatiality were ascribed as essential features. Ideas, on the contrary, as non-sensory entities, are devoid of any materiality. There is reason to suppose that Plato, in his last writings, had already conceived of the world of ideas as the world of the psyche. Thus, contrasting both elements of the world of phenomena – the passive factor of the unlimited or non-existence and the ideas which shaped it – gave birth to the contrast between matter and spirit within the scope of this world. At the same time, introducing the division between the sense-world of phenomena and the non-sense-world of ideas as well as connecting them by the relation of the unilateral dependence of the former on the latter became the model of all later views which looked for the cause of the existence of the world of sensory experience within the extra-sensory-world.

6   The Principle of Determinism

Plato, following Democritus, asserted that nothing comes into being without a cause, and considered discovery of causes to be the goal of scientific investigation. Given the entirety of Plato's views, the cause of a thing should be understood as the idea which that thing reflects, i.e., the general concept to which it is subordinated as well as its final cause. Thus, the principle of universal causality is, on the one hand, an expression of the logical law according to which for each thing there is a general concept under which it falls, and on the other hand an expression of universal finality. To this principle, Plato adds another encompassing the whole empirical world – the principle according to which every cause (idea) is counteracted by a co-cause which limits its activity. Thus, when we subordinate something under a general concept, it is not entirely subordinated; no content of a general concept exhausts empirical reality. Individual features remain outside the content of the concept and are determined by it, so they need to be related to something which is not part of the world of ideas. Similarly, when we consider something as a realization of the ideal end, we find in it several moments which are either indifferent in relation to that end – they could turn out in more than one way – or even make it so that the end is realized in an imperfect way. Therefore, the moments in question need to be related to something which is not the ideal end. The duality of cause and its co-cause expressed by the connection of the above two principles in later philosophical systems takes the form of the contrast between the rational and final action of the spirit and the blind inertia of matter, where inertia expresses itself as the law of the necessary causal relation between physical causes and effects, while the spirit's pursuit of intended ends belongs to the area of the freedom of will.

Plato, explicitly describing the "co-cause" as the negation of existence, runs up against two difficulties. First, the co-cause limits the principle of determinism; though according to Plato not everything has its cause in an idea, the cause in question does not determine it entirely. Second, it is hard to understand how something non-existent could prevent an idea from becoming reflected in a sensory thing. To remove these difficulties, one would have to modify the assumptions of the doctrine of ideas as Aristotle did.

B   *Aristotle*
1   Plato and Aristotle
Confronting the problem of overcoming epistemological subjectivism and the skepticism of the Sophists, Plato came up with a solution by discovering the domain where certain and objective knowledge can be found, namely, the domain of concepts whose content is definite and unchanging. However, the knowledge in question was one-sided, unconnected to the empirical world of changing objects which come into being and perish. For that reason, there needs to be a return from this position back to the empirical world that requires thorough investigation in a way which takes into account the already acquired methods as well as the concepts of change and becoming, the causes of such insurmountable difficulties in the previous stage of the development of philosophical thought. Plato did not do that, since for him the empirical world was still the opposite of the object of knowledge. It was *Aristotle* (384–322) who overcame the negative stance concerning knowledge of the empirical world; the problem of becoming became the central issue of his philosophy along with the problem of causality.

2   Four Kinds of Causes

Aristotle distinguished between four kinds of cause: the material cause (ὕλη, *causa materialis*), the formal cause (εἶδος, *causa formalis*), the efficient cause (ἀρχή τῆς κινήσεως, *causa efficiens*), and the final cause (τὸ οὐ ἕνεκα, τἀγαθόν, *causa finalis*). Everything arises from some other thing (such as the house out of wood or stone) by taking on the features essential to it which matter does not possess (the form of a house is the spatial pattern of matter), and there is an agent, a person or thing, which makes matter assume a form (in the example above, a builder); moreover, every creation aims at some ultimate state which constitutes its end. When something comes into being, these four causes coexist. Coming into being consists of matter assuming some form. Matter is the potency (δύναμις, *potentia*) of a thing, the potency is actualized, i.e., passes into the state of reality (ἐνέργεια, *actualitas*), when matter conjoins with form. Thus, matter and form are the causes which, as it were, enter the thing itself, while the two remaining kinds of causes, agency and end, remain, so to speak, to the side. Sometimes the concepts of agency and end merge with the concept of form: when the sculptor sets about to make a statue, that sculptor already has in mind its form as the motive and end of the work; in the same way, a doctor has in mind the idea of health when approaching the bed of a suffering person, this idea calls forth his actions, is efficacious, and is also the end; moreover health is the form imparted to the suffering person, and the shape of the statue is the form assumed by the statue's matter.

3   Substance

From the conjunction of matter and form an individual object, or substance (οὐσία), arises. A substance is everything which actually exists as a conjunction of matter and form. The form of a substance consists of its characteristic properties; the substance endures as long as it does not lose these properties. For that reason, we can assert true judgments about a substance, predicating properties of it which constitute its form, that is, its essential features. Hence, the grammatical-logical definition of substance: a substance is what can be a subject in a sentence; the substance cannot occur in a sentence as a predicate since the latter is a property and thus not the substance but the complete form or a part of it. A substance is independent in the sense that it does not need anything else to exist, while the properties need the substance, since they are the properties of the substance and cannot exist in any other way than by being the properties of something. Substances are particular people, particular animals, etc. The form of humanity is constituted by all the properties which make a being human, in other words, the features common to all humans, which make up the content of the general concept of man. The form in Aristotle is the same thing as the idea in Plato. However, an essential difference in the views of the two philosophers is that Aristotle's form is part of the thing which it constitutes along with matter, while Plato's ideas are unconnected to things; Plato imagined them as beings outside the world, whose imperfect reflection is provided by concrete objects. Aristotle came out against that conception of Plato, considering it to be unjustified and redundant.

The form of a substance in Aristotle, like the idea in Plato, is the final cause of the substance, so the substance's coming into being is understood as the pursuit of the end constituted by the reception of the substantial form by matter. In this sense, Aristotle calls the form of a substance its *entelechia* (ἐντελέχεια) or immanent end. At the same time, he treats form as an efficient cause since, by becoming incorporated in matter, it makes the substance, made up of form and matter, come into being. Finally, form is the general concept under which the substance falls as an individual. Thus, we have in Aristotle the same dual relation between the substance and its form which we encountered in Plato as the relation between the sensory object and idea; the relation in question is ontological, causal, on the one hand, and logical, on the other.

In order to avoid terminological confusion, we need to note that Aristotle also makes use of the term "substance" (οὐσία) in a broader sense, distinguishing between primary and secondary substances; the term "primary substance" signifies what we meant above when talking about substance, while "secondary substance" is the object of a general concept, e.g., man in general.

4   Primary Matter and Pure Form

We already know that matter is a constituent of substance; in relation to the substance matter is a potency which is actualized, i.e., becomes a substance by conjoining with form. For instance, a block of marble is the matter out of which a statue can be hewed. But the block of marble itself is also a substance, it, too, consists of matter and form; although it does not have the form of a statue, thus being less determinate than a statue, it possesses the form proper to it, namely, the features which make it a block of marble. If, by means of a certain action, we subtract from it the features of marble, we will acquire the constituents out of which marble can arise, i.e., the matter of marble, which, in turn, will itself be some substance, more primitive than marble but possessing particular features. Let us assume, following Aristotle, that we continue this line of thinking, subtracting more and more features: the process we are conducting is going to end only when we think about completely indeterminate matter, devoid of any features. It will not be anything real, it will not be substance, but pure potency; in this way we will reach primary matter (πρώτη ὕλη, *materia prima*), the opposite of any form. That matter is not non-existence, as in Plato, but only pure potency. Aristotle believes that by conceiving of it in this way he manages to avoid the difficulty plaguing Plato: how something can arise out of nothing. The substance arises not out of nothing but out of potency. Coming into being is passing from potency to act.

Several substances which we passed through on our way to primary matter are also extended analogously in the opposite direction. Every substance we encounter contains the potency to change into something else, so every substance can be considered matter for some other substance. Aristotle believes that in that second process of determining matter further we necessarily reach the concept of pure form or pure act as the limit beyond which there is no further change of potency and thus no matter. Pure act is the opposite of first matter. It is the ultimate end as well as the ultimate agent of all changes, since the highest degree of the gradual actualization of matter is the achievement of the state in which every potency has changed into act. Pure act as the highest end is the same thing as Plato's idea of the good. It is unchanging, since within it there is no potency to change. Finally, it transcends the senses since everything in the sense-world is capable of further development.

In this way, Plato's division between the two worlds is recovered. For Aristotle, unchangeability and transcendence, ascribed by Plato to ideas, inhere in pure form. The entire sense-world comprises the constituent of potency, which makes it less than completely real. Thus, the concept of lesser reality, associated by Plato with the sense-world, took on new content in Aristotle. Here lesser reality consists of comprising potency for something else, the potency to change. A being of pure form is perfect, since its every potency has already been realized. The highest, unchanging reality, which is the ultimate cause of everything, in that all the changes of a substance tend toward it but it itself is not subject to any action, is pure act since every form is the active constituent of the substance, shaping matter. Its activity, however, cannot pass on to anything else; it is incapable of any action since action contains the moment of changeability ruled out by the pure form. According to Aristotle, the only activity which is not an action is thinking – and not the kind whose object consists of particular substances and changeable phenomena, but the kind whose only object is its own unchangeable content, νόησις νοήσεως, as Aristotle calls it, the thinking of thinking, the awareness of itself. The essence of immateriality is here clearly conceived as the spiritual being.

The concept of pure act created by Aristotle is of momentous significance for the history of philosophical thought, being nothing else than the concept of God dominant throughout the entirety of medieval philosophy until the advent of modern times. It is a monotheistic concept as opposed to the polytheism or pantheism dominant in antiquity. The highest being is defined in a personal way: as the absolute spirit. Transcendent in relation to the world, it is also the ultimate cause of everything.

5   The Principle of Determinism. The Contraposition of Causes
When Aristotle posits that the goal of science is to seek causes, he has in mind not all four kinds of cause but, following Plato, only formal causes, or ideas. The knowledge of formal causes enables us to know the properties and states of individual things (for Aristotle, every fact or phenomenon is the property or state of some primary substance), while the method of tying the knowledge of things to the knowledge of causes is provided by the classical theory of syllogism developed by Aristotle. When we seek the cause of Socrates' being mortal, we find it when we note that every man is mortal and Socrates is a man. Seeking causes is seeking general reasons, since in reasons we assert the properties of ideas on which the properties of substances depend.

But not all the properties of a substance are tied in this way to the properties of its form. As we already know, according to Aristotle one needs to distinguish between essential and contingent properties of the substance; only the former depend on the form since only they can be derived by means of a syllogism. Here we are reaching the end of deterministic explanation since – at least outwardly – the same limitation of the principle of determinism arises that we encountered in Plato's philosophy. Aristotle overcame the limitation in question by making the concepts of matter and contingency relative.

The accidental features of the substance are as real as its essential features; the accidental features of Socrates – his being ill or old and bald during some part of his life – are parts of his matter, being features of his body, which (let us say for the sake of simplicity, though not entirely in accordance with Aristotle's line of thought), like Socrates' matter, is "potency" relative to Socrates, but otherwise is itself real, i.e., is also a substance which has its own matter and form as well as essential and accidental features. Thus, Socrates' accidental features are also explicable via reasons and also possess a formal cause, but the latter differs from the formal cause of the features which in Socrates inhere as essential. Everything real is determined by formal causes and is subject to causal explanation, and the only difference between essential and accidental features is that their formal causes differ. Contingency is the expression of the *plurality* of formal causes in every substance, not the lack of cause. Aristotle, who prescinds from accidental features in his explanation of reality, takes into account the requirements of every scientific investigation which always departs from a definite viewpoint and makes an appropriate choice in the matter under scrutiny; every explanation is likewise an ordering of the matter in question, in the course of which we collect certain empirical data, separating them from the rest, thanks to which we can sort them under general principles.

The only undetermined part of matter is that which is not yet real, or, in other words, which involves *potency* to be realized in the future. For instance, the matter of a given man is such that at a certain moment he will act so-and-so; since his action is not yet real, it is also undetermined. Determination occurs when potency becomes reality, or when at a particular moment the man chooses his course of action and is in a particular state, which already falls under such and such a form. Here a new problem arises: why does potency at a particular moment change into reality which determines the undetermined – for instance, a block of marble becomes a statue, or a man chooses such and such an action? Aristotle answers this question stating that in every such case there is an efficient cause; in the first example, it is the work of the sculptor, while in the second it is the decision (προαίρεσις) of the person who makes the choice. One can also talk about contingency with reference to efficient causes: what is accidental in relation to some efficient cause is the effect of another efficient cause. At the same time, there is no contingency in the absolute sense, i.e., there is no contingency consisting of the negation of efficient causality: every motion, or passing from potency to act, has an efficient cause (ἅπαν τὸ κινούμενον ἀνάγκη ὑπό τινος κινεῖσθαι).

Thus, in Aristotle, the principle of determinism assumes a dual character. Everything real has a formal cause, and everything that comes into being has an efficient cause. Formal causes, which shape reality, and efficient causes, which provide the impulse for that shaping, act conjointly in the coming into being of everything. A form is also an end, and efficient causes are conjoined with material ones by actualizing the potencies of matter. In this way, the Platonic opposition between causes is recovered and is connected as well to the opposition between essential and accidental features of substances, acquiring a new incarnation. Essential features are also telic, while accidental features belong to the material constituent of the substance. The former are explicated by efficient causes, being the expression of non-telic, "blind" but necessary, actions of a material nature.

This opposition occurs in manifold forms throughout the history of human thought: as the opposition between finality and determination, spirit and matter, freedom and necessity. Noticing it in Aristotle's system, we have to ask whether it does not falsify both forms of the principle of determinism. Is it possible that the chain of efficient causes and their effects will ever be broken by the intervention of the final cause? And conversely: do final causes have any significance in the face of the unavoidable chain of efficient causes? In Aristotle's philosophy there is a gap consisting in the lack of a theory which would properly connect the action of formal and efficient causes, or the finality and necessity of the course of phenomena in the world. It is no wonder that in the next period of ancient philosophy considerations on the problem of causality will mostly focus on that question. The latter will give birth to the conflict constituting the essential content of one of the great metaphysical issues, namely, the problem of free will.

Chapter 3: Stoicism, Epicureanism, Skepticism

1   *New Philosophical Systems and Their Relation to Their Predecessors*
Shortly after Aristotle, two new philosophical systems arose which included the problem of causality among the issues under their consideration, namely, the system of *Stoic* philosophy created by *Zeno* of Kition (340–265) and *Chrysippus* (280–209) and the system of *Epicurus* (341–270). The two developed in parallel while being opposites. In accordance with the characteristic feature of the age, both focused on ethical issues and existential wisdom. They took ethics to be the most important of the three parts into which philosophy was then divided, and the other two were to provide the former with a foundation: logic or so-called (by Epicurus) canonics – the science of cognition – encompassed logical, methodological, and epistemological statements functioning as an introduction to philosophy, while physics, the science of the world, provided ethics with metaphysical justification. Such an approach brought both systems closer to the age of the Sophists and Socrates than to that of Plato and Aristotle; hence their content referred to the earlier philosophical currents whose tradition had incessantly been maintained along with that of the Platonic and Aristotelian schools. When it comes to ethical views, Stoicism and Epicureanism constitute the last link (through the schools of the Cynics and the Hedonists) in the chain initiated by the ethical teachings of Socrates. Socrates taught that the virtuous person is the one whose actions are directed by reason, and that such person is also happy. Hence, for the Stoics living one's life in a way conforming to reason was an ethical duty and the only source of true happiness, while Epicurus saw an ethical duty in the happy life, which he considered to be the only rational one.

Establishing the sources of Stoic and Epicurean physics is a more complex task. Each one of the previous stages in the development of philosophy gave birth to a different worldview. Democritus gave expression to the most developed form of the first of them, while Aristotle did the same thing for the second. When it comes to those aspects of their thought which interest us here, we can describe them as follows: according to Democritus everything that exists consists of uniform elements (atoms), and there is one, all-encompassing causality, while according to Aristotle one can distinguish in everything two constituents – matter and form – and there are two types of causality, namely, that which shapes the world in a manner analogous to the purposeful activity of a rational and free human being, and efficient causality, which corresponds to the unavoidable course of events in nature. Stoicism and Epicureanism produced two mutually contradictory syntheses of those two positions. The Stoics took from Aristotle the dualism of matter and form connecting it to the claim of the only universal regularity governing the universe; at the same time, they referred to that law as rational, which corresponded to the main postulate of their rationalist ethics. Epicurus' ethics required bestowing on man the freedom of the unhampered pursuit of happiness as its metaphysical presupposition. This presupposition was found by Epicurus in Democritean atomism along with the negation of the universal regularity of events in the name of the freedom in question.

2   *Stoicism*

As has already been mentioned, Zeno, following Aristotle, accepted the presence of the material and formal constituents in each thing. However, the two were supposed to be inseparably connected, such that there is no matter without form and no form without matter. In Zeno, the pure form of the universe plays the role which in Aristotle is played by pure form. It is not outside the world, as in Aristotle, but rather within it, penetrating it like the material human body is penetrated by the human soul. This is the reason which governs the world. Here Zeno connects the view of Aristotle with the earlier views of Heraclitus and Anaxagoras, since, according to Zeno, this world-governing reason is equipped with the features ascribed to it by all three of those philosophers. It is the highest law and norm under which everything in the world falls (Heraclitus), establishes the final order of coming into being (Anaxagoras), and, finally, like the Aristotelian *entelechia*, is an internal force shaping the organic unity of the universe.

Stoicism, inseparably connecting reason with matter, tries to overcome the opposition between the purposeful activity of ideas and the passive resistance of matter, the contrast so visible in Plato and, to a certain extent, also in Aristotle. According to Aristotle, form includes the features characteristic of the species, while the remaining "accidental" features belong to matter. Stoicism also ascribed those material features to form. According to the Stoics, every quality belongs to form. Matter is only what is subject to shaping, while everything already shaped constitutes form. At the same time, the distinction between the two is purely conceptual since there is no unshaped matter. Thus, the limitation imposed on form by matter completely disappears. Everything that exists has been anticipated in the purposeful activity of reason as divine providence (πρόνοια), while being a necessary outcome of the laws established by reason as destiny (εἱμαρμένη). Thanks to the laws in question, nothing happens without a preceding cause (αἰτία προηγουμένη), and that universal causal conditioning of every detail results in the world's constituting a unity whose parts are connected to each other in a purposeful and rational way. For that reason, Chrysippus staunchly opposed the possibility of chance, teaching that apparent chance-events, where something seems to arise without cause, prove only that we do not know their proper cause. The postulate of consistent determinism, extended to all individual phenomena, connects Stoicism to Democritus, and throughout the whole of antiquity only the Stoics attempted to introduce this postulate uniformly to all areas of knowledge. At the same time, the Stoics differed from Democritus in that their determinism was not mechanistic. The Stoics identified the causal necessity of destiny with divine providence taking divine will to be its source; thus opposing the reduction of all the processes taking place in the universe to the mechanistic activity of material particles, i.e., to impact and pressure. The physics of the Stoics allows the existence not only of mechanical, quantitative differences between things but also of qualitative ones, maintaining the distinctiveness of the qualitative, as opposed to mechanical, changes in things.

Just as the universe consists of matter and form – the latter being the reason which governs it – every separate particle of the universe has its own matter and form which is a particle of the world-governing reason and animates the particle to which it belongs, i.e., makes it an organic individual developing in accordance with its nature. A person also consists of body and soul, the latter being a particle of the highest reason. The rational human soul, as a particle of the highest reason, indicates to that person the same laws of behavior which constitute the laws governing the universe. Hence, the ethical imperative of submitting to the laws in question, which constitutes living in accordance with the rational nature of the person.

3   Epicureanism

According to Epicurus, the highest goal of humanity is happiness, which consists of making use of life and its gifts in a calm and cheerful manner. Science should serve the same goal by providing people with the knowledge of the natural connections between things to free them from superstition and resulting anxieties. Epicurus understood superstitions as belief in deities and in the supranatural order of things as well as the belief in the immortality of the soul and its torment in the afterlife. For Epicurus, the knowledge which provided sufficient explanation of the phenomena of life and nature and thus offered freedom from empty fears was atomism.

Epicurus followed Democritus in believing that the only thing one needs to assume to explain the world is the plurality of atoms, differing in shape and size and moving within empty space. All phenomena, the rising and perishing of all things and their properties, can be reduced to motion, atoms colliding and connecting or separating, with all qualitative differences being only apparent and reducible to quantitative mechanical differences. Thus, Epicurus took from Democritus his atomism and mechanism as well as the explanation of phenomena by means of the motion of particles, while rejecting the universality and necessity of the causal regularity governing the course of events.

Heraclitus' claim concerning the universal regularity of the universe in Democritus came to be connected, as we already know, with atomism, since according to Democritus each atom moves forward by means of its own original movement, and, as a result, can collide with other atoms. Atoms gather into groups whose motion is the resultant of the motion of the atoms thanks to the universal regularity thanks to which the motion of particular atoms yields particular kinds of resultant motion. Thanks to the regularity in question, every phenomenon is a necessary offshoot of the preceding phenomena with reference to which it can be rationally explained and anticipated.

Epicurus dissented from Democritus' determinism regarding two points. The first concerned the problem of the world's beginning or ultimate cause, while the second was connected to the constitution of motion. Democritus did not touch upon the first point, explicitly assuming that the motions of atoms are, like their size, shape and position, one of their primary qualities. Those qualities, primary according to the assumptions of the system, were enough to explain all the events which followed from them. The issue under scrutiny remained open, however, and has often been resolved by assuming that a supreme, divine, rational being exists, which gave the world its beginning; that was the view of Anaxagoras, Aristotle, and the Stoics. Epicurus was forced to reject that solution if he wanted to be consistent with the assumptions of his philosophy. Nonetheless, he considered it necessary to assert the existence of the moment that was the beginning of the world. According to him, it was the moment when an atom deflected from its original, "natural" course by which all atoms fell downwards; as a result of this deflection, the atom collided with other atoms, creating a vortex of atoms out of which the world emerged. The deflection itself, however – the ultimate cause of the world's coming into being – occurred without any cause, thus being a result of chance. Here we encounter a concept of chance different from the Aristotelian one. In Aristotle, the "accidental" belonged to the matter rather than the form of a substance, and, from the perspective of the form, lay outside the form and did not contribute to the latter's realization in the substance, thus not being purposeful. But for every property that is accidental in relation to some cause there is, according to Aristotle, some other proper cause; the concept of chance being thus relative. In Epicurus, on the other hand, being accidental is tantamount to the complete absence of cause, and in this sense whatever is accidental is so absolutely. While in Aristotle the existence of chance was the result of metaphysical dualism – the distinction between matter and form – in Epicurus it is tantamount to the rejection of the principle of determinism.

The second point on which Epicurus dissented from Democritean determinism is the rejection of the universal regularity of becoming. The laws which make some motions of atoms lead to other atomic motions, according to Epicurus, are not universally valid. They are binding in the external world where they allow events to be explained and predicted, but they are not binding when it comes to human behavior. The latter, like everything else, can be reduced to atomic motions, but here it is not the case that some motions of atoms necessarily result in other particular motions constituting human behavior; the result may be this or that behavior, i.e., some atomic motions may lead to such and such motions of atoms – no universal regularity governs it. That is because an individual is free, not subject to any causal necessity in behavior. Here everything is governed by chance – the opposite of determinism. Nonetheless, there is a difference with reference to both points to which Epicurus introduces the concept of chance. To be able to assert that something is the effect of some cause one needs to make two assumptions: first, that there is a regularity which makes particular effects correspond to particular causes; second, that something exists which, based on that regularity, is the cause of the effect in question. But when Epicurus rejects the claim that human activity is causally determined he, by the same token, rejects the first assumption, and when he rejects the claim that the deflection of an atom from the course of its straightforward fall has a cause, he rejects the second.

Epicurus' indeterminism as well as atomism and mechanism remain directly tied to his ethics. The latter is individualistic, with an individual's happiness as its main goal – hence the tendency to detach oneself from any ties that could restrict happiness. The ties in question result from an individual's threefold dependency: on the gods, on the species, and on causal necessity. Atomistic mechanism and the assumption of the world's accidental becoming serve to found the rejection of dependency on gods. Atomism allowed Epicurus to treat the individual as a group of atoms, independent of other groups and in no way tied to other individuals understood analogously, thereby sundering social connections based on the conspecificity of all humans. Finally, the assumption of indeterminism with reference to human behavior granted freedom from causal necessity.

We need to note that the three assumptions of Epicurus' physics – atomism, mechanism, and indeterminism – are not on a par methodologically. The task of atomism and mechanism is to explain reality; indeterminism is the assumption which limits the scope of that explanation but is not an assumption that by itself provides another explanation. Thus, the points with which Epicurus' determinism is concerned do not themselves have an explanation. We are forced to conceive them as the principal hypotheses of the system, which, not unlike atomism and mechanism, acquire their justification only in their applications within the philosophical system.

4   The Problem of the Freedom of Will

The opposition between Stoic determinism and Epicurean indeterminism is strictly connected with the problem of the freedom of human will which appeared as a new problem within metaphysics in connection with the concept of cause, but had already been the subject of earlier ethical considerations. The term "freedom of will" had become ambiguous quite early, and to understand the development of the problem correctly, we need to go back in time to its beginning.

The problem of the freedom of will arises against the background of considerations about the conditions of human behavior, initiated by *Socrates,* who asked, which behavior is good and what are the *conditions of good behavior.* In accordance with his characteristic method, Socrates looked for the definition of what is good in commonly held opinions on the matter. Everyone takes the object of their pursuit to be good; hence Socrates' general claim that the will always pursues the good and desires what reason presents it as being good. However, human reason is often mistaken in its understanding of the good; Socrates believed that every bad deed stems from a false opinion, which results in the absence of the real knowledge of what is good. Socrates' answer to our question is that the necessary and sufficient condition of acting well is having knowledge of what is good. Whoever acts wrongly acts out of a lack of awareness and for that reason does not act voluntarily. In other words, only a sage is free, and the man who does not have knowledge is not free. Thus, according to Socrates, the difference between acting freely and non-freely is an ethical difference, since acting freely is good and acting non-freely is bad; moreover, the difference in question concerns solely motives and their assessment: some motives are right and proper, others are improper and wrong. The person whose activity is directed by proper motives is free, whoever is directed by improper motives, is not. Freedom in this sense is sometimes called *moral freedom.*

On the Socratic understanding of freedom, the person who acts wrongly and the one who acts well are equally dependent both on their beliefs and their motives of action. They both act in the way stipulated by their beliefs, which are the causes of their actions; in both cases activity is conditioned psychologically in the same way. The question arises whether Socrates's belief is correct that the will always desires what reason shows it to be good, or, in other words, whether motives alone are enough to determine activity, or if there are internal factors other than motives which determine our activity, and, if so, how does our freedom depend on them. This question is connected to the problem of a man's responsibility for his behavior, an issue Socrates did not touch. Plato, who, in general, accepted Socrates' views on that matter, stated that a man becomes responsible for the errors of his actions when, contrary to reason's command, he allows anger or passion to rule over him. But the clear formulation of the problem can be found only in Aristotle. A person becomes responsible for his behavior only when we can talk about his merit or blame in connection with it. *Aristotle* asked about the *conditions of the responsibility for an action.* To say that someone is responsible for a certain action is to take him to be the agent of this act, for which reason Aristotle believes that the only deeds about which this can be said are those with respect to which a man, by his act of will, accepts or rejects certain motives and, as a result, behaves in such and such a manner. Only such an individual possesses freedom of the will, while one who acts under coercion or out of the lack of awareness of the matter at hand does not. Thus, Aristotle does not agree with Socrates that knowledge is the sufficient condition of acting well and that motives play a decisive role in behavior. According to Aristotle, a necessary condition of ethical behavior, apart from motives, is the subjective factor, the act of will, which consists in accepting certain motives and constitutes the proper foundation of action. Acts of will express qualities of character, which can be shaped by means of exercise and habit.

Aristotle accepted two kinds of conditions of ethical behavior: intellectual or emotional conditions, i.e., motives, and conditions of a dispositional nature, belonging to character. Only when the latter can manifest themselves in an act of will, unhampered by coercion or the lack of awareness, are we free in our actions. This is freedom different from that which Socrates talked about. We attest to it in internal experience when we engage the will and thereby experience our agency; hence it is called *psychological freedom of will.* It is the necessary and sufficient condition of the soundness of mind at the moment of performing an action.

The *Stoics* accepted Aristotle's position, but went even further in their considerations. The burning feeling of responsibility characteristic of their ethics required the assumption of freedom, necessary for soundness of mind to be ascribed to the subject. Therefore, they asserted staunchly that an individual possesses such freedom. At the same time, however, the Stoics' metaphysical views seemed to defy the possibility of accepting free will. As we know, the Stoics taught that reason, which governs the world, creates the law to which everything in the world is subject. The law in question makes up destiny, which brings about every event in the unstoppable chain of causes and effects: nothing in the world happens without a proper cause. If these principles are applied to human behavior, one can no longer assert that an individual does something or abstains from doing it freely, since every human deed results necessarily from some previously existing causes. If divine providence and divine destiny encompass human deeds as they do other events, the deeds in question are also determined in advance and unavoidable. The Stoics did not shy away from this consequence of determinism. Chrysippus believed that only if we assume that human deeds are causally determined in advance can we state that judgments about the future are true or false, since their veracity requires that the future existence of their subject has already been decided. Divine providence and the knowledge of future things, says Chrysippus, can concern only what is necessary in the future and not what is indefinite.

The opponents of the Stoics saw in these statements, consistently entailed by their metaphysics, the denial of the freedom of human actions, and this became the basis of their strongest objections to the Stoics. The Stoics, in turn, tried to show that, despite their acceptance of universal determinism – or rather in line with it – a man is the cause of his actions in the sense that he can be considered responsible for them. Chrysippus distinguishes between primary and secondary causes. Every deed necessarily follows from the causal cooperation of the essence of an individual and the pattern of external circumstances. The circumstances are only secondary causes, while the primary cause is the individual, whose reason gives consent to an action. When we ascribe responsibility to someone for some behavior, our ascription is based on that consent. Even though the rational soul of an individual is only a part of the reason which governs the world, in each person it constitutes an independent individuality, which alone is the source and cause (ἀρχή) of decisions and deeds. The following example can serve as an illustration of the distinction in question: when someone finds himself in a state of great poverty, that circumstance is for him something necessary, creating external coercion which the impacted person cannot change by himself, thus being the secondary cause of the theft which he is going to commit. But if he commits theft, it is the result of the drive residing in him as the main cause, a drive in which his whole moral being is expressed. The effect of that main cause is necessary, since everyone reacts to the impulses given in external circumstances in a way which is predictable given the properties of one's character. The properties in question belong to a person's individuality, they form the basis for the assessment of the individual, be it praise, rebuke, reward or punishment. That the individuality of a man is the result of the operation of the causes independent of him, according to the Stoics, does not influence the issue of the soundness of mind since one needs to distinguish between the question whether it is possible to assess a person's character ethically and ascribe to him responsibility for his behavior and the question whether human characters and behavior could be, in the course of the events, other than they are. They gave a positive answer to the first of these questions but a negative answer to the second.

Thus, in the minds of Stoics, an individual's actions are the final result of a number of causal connections. That is to say, it follows from the fact that the individual as the "main cause" decides on, i.e., consents to, the behavior; in this way the Stoics, like Aristotle, asserted the psychological freedom of will, considering the individual as the agent of his behavior. What is more, according to the Stoic teachings, the decision of the individual (or: the individual himself, at the moment of the decision) is causally determined by the properties of character which constitute the essence of that individual. Here Aristotle was their guide only to a certain degree, stating that such causal determination of the acts of will exists only where the character is strong, shaped by long exercise – the behavior of such an individual can be predicted in advance with a significant degree of certainty – while in the case of an individual whose character is weak the act of will is undetermined. The Stoics, accepting the determination of the act of will by the character of the man, were thus able to transfer ethical assessment from the deed to its subject and to assess the subject ethically on the grounds of his actions. Finally, according to the Stoics, the character of the individual is also causally determined by the factors which have shaped it. They believed that the latter dependency cannot have any influence on ethical judgments for which sufficient grounds are provided by the existence of both the previously mentioned connections along with the fact that the person is a rational individual.

The opponents of the Stoics, led by *Epicurus*, vehemently attacked Stoic determinism, stating that making the act of will dependent on the chain of causal connections liquidates its essence, and that a person cannot be considered the agent of a deed if his act of will is causally determined by the course of events in the universe. The ethical ideal of the sage requires, according to Epicurus, complete independence from the environment. For that reason, the causal chain assumed by the Stoics had to be broken at some point. That is what Epicurus did, denying the causal determination of the act of will as the effect of the properties of the acting person's character. According to Epicurus, an act of will devoid of cause arises in just this way: accidentally; only an action based on such an act of will is free.

In this way Epicurus put forward a new problem: the problem of the *conditions of the independence of actions*. The necessary and sufficient condition of the independence of actions is the freedom of will in a third meaning, viz., the *metaphysical freedom of will*. If one denies the causal determination of the act of will as the effect of the properties of the acting person's character, one supposes that in given circumstances, which constitute the motives of the act of will, the latter can have different versions. Thus, if one denies the dependence of the act of will on the properties of character, by the same token one denies any proper connection to the motives out of which it has arisen. Hence, the problem of Epicurus assumes yet another form, which is as follows: Can an act of will arise without a motive (or in spite of the motives) proper to itself, as *"liberum arbitrium indifferentiae"*? Stated in this way ther question had already been given a negative answer by Aristotle, who showed that causal conditioning of the act of will is not tantamount to coercion, which does away with its freedom in the psychological sense. Aristotle's claim was disseminated in the form of a fable, the paradox of Buridan, according to which an ass sitting between two piles of hay died from hunger, being unable to choose between them since both attracted him equally.

5   *The Stoic and Epicurean Concept of Cause*

In the context of their entire system, the concepts of cause and causal relation acquired new meaning in the philosophy of the Stoics. This was especially true with regard to the following points:

(1) Causes are things, i.e., individual objects or (in Aristotle's terminology) substances. That statement is a direct consequence of the Stoic assumption that there is no matter without form and no form without matter but only things within which one can distinguish matter and form. Thus, if causes can be called material, if they are seen in the way the thinkers of the cosmological period understood them, and formal, if conceived in accordance with the Platonic-Aristotelian understanding, causes as seen by the Stoics are *substantial*. At the same time, they are bodies in the materialist sense, which is implied by the Stoics' epistemological assumptions. We know that, according to Zeno, form is inseparable from matter, so everything is material in that sense, but the meaning in question does not correspond to the materialist understanding of the term since Stoic matter does not have physical features. The materialism of

the Stoics, i.e., their claim that there are only corporeal things, had a direct connection to their sensualism: since, as they believed, the only source of knowledge is the senses, which provide the perceptions of corporeal bodies, one can only talk about the latter.

Bodies, while acting on other bodies, bring about qualitative or quantitative changes in them; the effect is always some change or, generally speaking, some property or other of the body, i.e., what can be predicated about it (τὸ λεκτόν), which is why the Stoics claim that causes are corporeal while effects are incorporeal, since the latter are constituted by the properties of bodies, predicated of bodies, not being bodies themselves.

(2) The causal relation is understood by the Stoics as a relation of agency, that is, as a relation between bodies which consists of producing an effect. This is the *realist* understanding of causal relation. The Stoics see activity as mechanical – in the form of the exertion of pressure – but also divide it into mechanical and qualitative; however, the Stoics also tend to explain qualitative changes, following Anaxagoras, by connecting and separating qualitatively different elements, seen as similar to homoiomeriae.

(3) Finally, for the Stoics, there is clearly the moment of temporal succession between cause and effect: nothing happens without the *preceding* cause (αἰτία προηγουμένη). The moment in question was not easily visible in the concept of material cause, even less, in the concept of atemporal ideal cause, so it should be invoked along with the other concepts for the purpose of specifying the distinctiveness of the Stoic concept of cause.

All three of the moments we distinguished, specifying the Stoic understanding of causality, can also be found in Epicurean thought. The Epicureans likewise reduced all causal relations to the activity of one set of bodies – the complexes of atoms – on another set, seeing the activity itself mechanistically. The substantialist understanding of causes and the realist understanding of causal relation may not be as clearly expressed in the Epicurean as in the Stoic systems, but it is certainly implied there. The same is true with the problem of temporal succession in the causal relation. In spite of the deep differences between Stoicism and Epicureanism, which we have discussed before, both systems are close to each other as far as the understanding of causality is concerned, which implies that the connecting moments – namely, the *substantialist* understanding of causes and the *realist* understanding of the causal relation – can be taken as characteristic not only of Stoicism but also of the entire age of Hellenistic philosophy (until the religious-philosophical systems came on the stage), which constituted, so to speak, the third stage of the development of the problem of causality in ancient philosophy. At the same time, it can be considered the ultimate result of the development of that issue in antiquity. This understanding of cause and the causal relation lasted for centuries, until David Hume directed his criticisms against it.

6   *The Skeptical Analysis of Causality*

The realist and substantialist position on the problem of causality, common to both schools, came under attack by the skeptics even as ancient philosophy was waning. The skeptical arguments were collected and systematized by *Sextus Empiricus* (circa 150 AD); they all aimed at proving that a contradiction lurks in the statements concerning causal relations and it is impossible to take them to be true. This kind of proof is analogous to the one employed by the skeptics to show the impossibility of accepting any statements pertaining to reality other than those based on sensations. Thus, Sextus collected statements within different philosophical systems for and against the existence of causes with the aim of deriving the skeptical conclusion. From among the arguments of Sextus we choose those which are directed against the substantialist and realist understanding of causality.

If one states that causes include bodies and only bodies, what one means is that bodies act on other bodies, bringing about certain effects. Sextus argues that the activity of a body is not possible, and for that reason that bodies cannot be causes. His proof assumes that every activity takes place in space and that no body can act at a place where it is not found, or, in other words, there is no such thing as acting from a distance. Since the acting body and the body on which it acts are not in the same place but next to each other in space, the acting body would have to, so to speak, go out of itself to be able to act on another body, and that, in accordance with the assumption, is impossible. The supposition that the activity of bodies could be directed at something which is not a body but rather a thought (τὸ λεκτόν of the Stoics) is also unacceptable. Thought does not fill space, and we cannot as much as imagine an activity of a body which would not be spatial (i.e., would not happen by impact or pressure). Thus, we cannot imagine bodies acting on thoughts.

An analogous difficulty arises when we consider the temporal relation between cause and effect. Every activity lasts in time, hence the conclusion that the cause precedes its effect (since, if the cause were simultaneous with the effect, there would be no duration and every activity would take place in one moment; the third option, namely, that the effect precedes its cause, is ruled out in advance). If the cause precedes its effect, at some point in time there is the cause but no effect. If that is the case, however, the cause is not the cause and another cause for the effect which did not occur has to be found despite the existence of what we called its cause. The same reasoning can be applied to the new cause, hence nothing can be a cause.

This reasoning applies to the problem of activity the difficulties associated with the concept of the continuity of space and time, which have long been known as the foundation for the arguments of Zeno of Elea against the possibility of motion. The conclusion was the rejection of the substantialist understanding of cause. Along with substantialism realism also falls, since the denial of the possibility of action is the denial of the reality of the causal relation. The skeptics replaced realism with phenomenalism. According to Sextus, all relations between things are not real but only products of thought. One and the same object, without undergoing any change, occurs as an element of different and mutually contradictory relations. And, since it is impossible, says Sextus, that one and the same thing is both, e.g., larger and smaller in reality but is only presented to us in this or some other way, depending on what we compare it to, relational predicates should not be ascribed to things in reality but testify only to our thinking them. The same is true of the concepts of cause and effect: they, too, are only the descriptions of relations; therefore, in reality there are no causes and effects, we only add them to the presentations of things in our thoughts.

7   *Conclusion*

Two basic claims of the skeptics, namely, that the knowledge of the objective causal relation is impossible, and that the causal connection is something which we only add to the presentations of things in our thoughts, were articulated again a dozen or so centuries later by the thinker to whom modern philosophy owes the ground-breaking analysis of the concept of causality: David Hume. However, despite the compatibility between their statements, Sextus and Hume differ in their argumentation and starting points. The ancient skeptic proceeds by accepting the general assumptions pertaining to the content of the principal concepts of cause, effect, and activity, gradually reducing these assumptions to absurdity and concluding that no statements concerning causal relations can be accepted. Thus, if we have the concept of causal relation, it could not have been drawn from objective reality but is a product of an operation of our mind. The entire reasoning is conducted by means of *a priori* and deductive method and operates within the scope of metaphysics and logic, while Hume's considerations have an epistemological and psychological character. Hume examines the sources and content of knowledge concerning causal relations; on that basis he claims that this knowledge is based neither directly in our perceptions nor can it be deduced from knowledge of things, which means that cognition of causal relations between things is simply impossible. Our belief that causal relations exist is subjective and, according to Hume, can be explained by the fact that perceiving phenomena succeeding each other in a regular way produces in us a "habit", which makes us expect the same succession of phenomena in the future: we believe that it will occur. The result of Hume's analysis is thus not only the acknowledgment of the subjectivity of causal relation, negative at its core, but also the claim that the subjective causal relation corresponds to the constant succession of phenomena as the basis for associating the representations of cause and effect on the objective level.

Over the course of these considerations, we have seen that the ancient world gave the problem of causality, by turns, the form of questions directed to the matter of things ("out of what" and "how"), to form or reason, and, finally, to the acting things. The method of investigation introduced by Hume involves a new form of our problem, unknown in antiquity, where, when we ask for the reason why something happened, we have in mind some other preceding event, which is the *sufficient condition* for the event under explanation. That modern concept of cause contains one moment especially which distinguishes it from the concept of cause dominant in antiquity and which should be noted, namely, the moment of the *uniformity* of cause and effect. What should be understood thereby is that both cause and effect are – as phenomena – beings of the same kind, while Democritus' atom and sensory object, Aristotle's idea and substance along with its properties, the Stoic account of the acting thing and its incorporeal effect were not uniform in relation to each other. Thanks to that uniformity, which also enclosed the causes of empirical phenomena within the bounds of the empirical world, the issue of causal explanation lost its speculative character and became an inductive problem, passing from the realm of metaphysics into the area of particular sciences.

Translated by Sylwia Wilczewska

Bibliography

Göring, Carl (1874). *Über den Begriff der Ursache in der griechischen Philosophie.* Leipzig: Metzger & Wittig.

Hartenstein, Carl Wilhelm (1888). Über die Lehren der antiken Skepsis, besonders des Sextus Empiricus, in betreff der Causalität. *Zeitschrift für Philosophie und philosophische Kritik* vol. xciii, f. 2, pp. 217–279.

Lang, Albert (1904). *Das Kausalproblem.* Vol. I: *Geschichte des Kausalproblems.* Köln: J.P. Bachem.

Peter, Curt Leo von (1909). *Das Problem des Zufalls in der griechischen Philosophie.* Berlin: Leonhard Simion.

Windelband, Wilhelm (1892). *Lehrbuch der Geschichte der Philosophie.* Tübingen 1919: J.C.B. Mohr.

CHAPTER 4

The Problem of Causality in the Neo-scholastics

Józef M. Bocheński

Zagadnienie przyczynowości u neoscholastyków.
Przegląd Filozoficzny vol. XXXVIII (1935), f. 1–2, pp. 125–134

∴

When setting out to give a preliminary account of the debate on causality among philosophers who, in the majority of cases, are also Catholic priests, I would prefer to speak of "Catholic philosophers"; the latter expression characterizes the group in question better than the term "Neo-scholastics", since some of the authors I am going to discuss do not really have any connection to Neo-scholasticism apart from the formulation of the problem [of causality]. Nonetheless, because of my negative position concerning the existence of "Catholic philosophy",[1] I prefer to avoid that term and talk about "Neo-scholastics" instead, with the qualification that by the latter I understand the class of writers characterized above, no matter what meaning is usually ascribed to the term.

In recent years, the problem of causality has been one of the most hotly debated issues connected to Neo-scholasticism. Even just enumerating the most significant relevant writings would take too much space.[2] All the important Neo-scholastic journals discussed it at length; last year the Academy of

---

1   The problem of the existence of "Catholic philosophy" is currently subject to lively debate in the same circles. It was the topic of, among others, the last "study day" of the Thomistic Society in Juvisy [*La philosophie chretienne* 1934].

2   In what follows I will avoid providing literal quotes, since I do not consider this method to be expedient. Here I am listing the titles of some works from the range which is being discussed: [Descoqs 1925], [Droege 1930], [Engert 1932], [Franzelin 1933], [Fuetscher 1930], [Garrigou-Lagrange 1914], [Geyser 1929], [Geyser 1933], [Hessen 1928], [Isenkrahe 1915], [Isenkrahe 1922], [Mausbach 1930], [Munnynck 1929], [Nink 1928], [Sawicki 1925], [Skibniewski 1930] and [Straubinger 1930].

St. Thomas Aquinas in Rome announced a competition on the topic; even a historical monograph on the debate has been written.[3]

The debate in question, far from being a novelty in these circles, constitutes the third stage of the great argument concerning the same problem. Its first stage took place at the turn of the previous and current centuries at [...] academic congresses gathering Catholics in Fribourg, Switzerland, and in Brussels; the second stage was the exchange between de Munnynck and Lammine immediately before the Great War [viz., World War I]. The current stage encompasses the last 9 years (beginning with 1926) and differs from the previous ones, conducted in French, by taking place almost entirely throughout German linguistic territory, and, especially, by its complexity, due to the emergence of as many as three different directions of debate; also the number of writings devoted to the problem, along with the interest of Neo-scholastic circles, has greatly increased.

1

The contentious issue is the *value of the causality principle*. To explain the meaning ascribed to the problem as defined above (what is the value of the principle of causality?), I will discuss first Neo-scholastics' formulation of the principle of causality and then the concept of "value" in question. To simplify a little, I am going to use the following symbols: C for cause, E for effect, CP for the principle of causality, Wx for "x exists and is a relative object". The sign ~ will signify negation; thus, $\sim A$ will mean "not-A" with reference to concepts and "it is not true that A" with reference to judgments.

(1) Neo-scholastics understand by CP the claim that for every x, if x exists and is a relative object, there is some y different from x and in active causal relation to it: yCx, y is the cause of x.[4] When it comes to the definition of that relation, the group is in agreement: yCx means, first, that "if y occurs, x occurs", and, second, that "y exerts real influence on the existence of x". Thus, E is not only a logical but also a real *result* of C, which "provides" C with its existence. This means that here we are dealing with the *dynamic* definition of causality, close to the definition of Sigwart and akin to Meyerson's "theological" definition of C, which is ultimately a concept of so-called common sense.

---

3   [Heuser 1930].
4   $(x): . Wx . \supset : (\exists y) . yCx . x \neq y.$

It has to be noted that the crux of the whole debate is not whether in a given case we can ascertain what concrete object is the C of a given phenomenon, and how that can be done. This is a separate problem which, generally speaking, is not touched upon in the course of the debate. The attention is focused on the question of the value of CP in general, i.e., whether we can say with certainty that there is *some* C of a given E, and when that can be done. That is another point about which the Neo-scholastics agree.

(2) At the same time, there are some, at least apparent, differences of opinion concerning the definition of the class of objects which can be E-s. Some define the abovementioned "relative" object as what begins to exist, i.e., as what is such that it is possible to point out the time t at which E does not exist and the time $t + \Delta t$ at which E exists. Some others narrow the concept even further, defining it as change (motion) itself in the Aristotelian meaning (*fieri*); those who do formulate CP as "every change has a cause". In the majority of cases, however, it is about "relative being" (*ens contingens*), i.e., not the absolute, or about the being which participates (μετέχει) in its own content. On the latter account, a white wall, for example, can be a correlative of the causal relation because it does not possess whiteness to the absolute degree.

The difference in formulation in this respect plays some role in the debate, since by defining E one already indirectly points out the feature which is to ground the causal relation. Nonetheless, when it comes to the range of the objects falling under the concepts described above, it is practically the same, seeing that every object empirically known to us has all the features mentioned above. The exception is constituted only by the definition limiting the range of the concept we are discussing solely to "*fieri*" – but such a definition is encountered relatively rarely. Thus, the majority of the participants of the debate understand the formula CP as follows: "For every x, if x begins to exist, some y exists, and y is the cause of x".

It is worth noting that it is real existence (*exsistentia*) which is being addressed.

(3) With reference to the "value" ascribed to CP one can distinguish four different concepts, which I will signify with the letters V_1, V_2, V_3, V_4.

A. *The impossibility of the concept* (des Begreifen) of the relative object (in the sense explained above) existing without C. According to the consensus among the Neo-scholastics, such an object cannot be conceived – at least in the current stage of humanity's development – and there is a natural inclination to seek C for it.

B. *The impossibility of the thought* (des Denkens) of such an object. Some Neo-scholastic thinkers distinguish between the possibility of a concept and the possibility of a thought (unbegreifbar – undenkbar). The distinction is

Kantian – but the authors from the abovementioned group generally define the "unthinkable" object as *contradictory*. In this interpretation, the only concepts which cannot be thought are those which contain logically inconsistent features. The concepts $V_1 \sim V_2$ which cannot be "grasped" but can be "thought" are possible, at least in principle.

The values V_1 and V_2 belong to the order of thought, and while V_1 can be called the psychological value of CP, V_2 can be called its logical value.

C. *The impossibility of the existence of E* without *C in the empirical world*. It has to be noted that for many Neo-scholastics, not as in Kant, the phenomenal (empirical) world is transcendent, but it is not identical with the world in general, since it is possible for real non-empirical objects to exist. The thinkers who ascribe to CP the value V_3 restrict to the phenomenal world not only the range of *Er*-s but also range of *C*-s, or, better, the field of the causal *relation* itself; according to them, we cannot know if the causal relation can also probe beyond the world of phenomena.

D. *The impossibility of the existence* of *E* without *C within the ontic range* in general, without any limits. If one ascribes this value to CP, one has to state that *E* and *C* as well as the causal relation itself can, or in given circumstances must, also exist outside the world, not only the immanent world but also the phenomenal one. This value gives CP the broadest meaning: there is no relative object without *C*.

It is the latter value that is of most concern in the debate we are discussing; the value of V_3, and especially V_2 are marginally discussed, the latter because of the proof of the value of V_4.

2

Because of the unclear and erroneous views on the method of Neo-scholasticism, which can be found even in philosophical circles, it will be suitable to summarize the most important specific directives accepted by its representatives.

(1) All Neo-scholastics are in agreement about the *autonomy of philosophy*, both with reference to faith and to non-philosophical sciences.

(a) When it comes to the attitude towards faith, the Thomistic thesis of philosophy's independence from it is currently universally accepted, even by the proponents of the Augustinian current. According to St. Thomas, the role of philosophy with reference to faith is neither that of a set of axioms nor of a positive directive but only of a negative norm, i.e., for a Catholic, to reject some statement it is enough that the latter turns out to contradict the statements of faith.

The directive in question never openly appears in the debate under scrutiny. One even has the impression that it is not seriously taken into account by any of the contending groups; other contenders (the Thomists) do not need to apply it, since the internal logic of their system leads to the acceptance of theses compatible with faith. Within the third group, in turn, which will be discussed shortly (Geyser, Descoqs), an interesting phenomenon of subordinating philosophy to faith can be observed. The whole system of those philosophers appears to be determined by the directive in question. In what follows, we will explain why that is.

(b) Neo-scholastics also postulate the independence of their field from the non-philosophical disciplines. The independence in question can go so far that with some Neo-scholastics we have the impression of the complete lack of knowledge of the whole contemporary debate on causality in physics. In psychological terms, this can be explained by the significant mistrust of empirical sciences brought about by positivist and monistic interpretations of their outcomes on the one hand and by the modern critique of sciences on the other, while in objective terms, this can be explained by a completely different formulation of the problems within the empirical sciences and in Neo-scholasticism. Nonetheless, it is hard not to be surprised that neither one of the contending camps has attempted to support their claims with experimental-psychological proof. While the problem of causality has not been sufficiently worked out by psychologists, the Neo-scholastics, who have a number of laboratories and skilled workers at their disposal, could have conducted the needed research by themselves. Only Geyser, as far as I know, cites the writings of psychologists to support his claim.

(2) Another feature of the Neo-scholastics who debate the problem under scrutiny is their *intellectualism*. Bergsonian methods and defining truth in the pragmatist vein are unknown among them. Correct reasoning, the analysis of concepts, and a dry and concrete style are encountered everywhere in their work. This does not prevent a certain irrationalism in the conclusions of one of the groups, which, having come to believe in the impossibility of justifying CP intellectually, grounds it in religious feeling, etc. The scholastic training received by all the participants of the debate makes their method strictly logical even when they make irrational statements.

(3) In the end, there is another thesis common to the Neo-scholastics, objective rather than methodological, which is worth mentioning: namely, their realism. Among the philosophers in question, there are no epistemological idealists; at the same time, it is true that different shades of realism can be

found in their views, beginning from the Thomistic position approximated by the "radical realism" of Professor Kotarbiński and ending with Hessen's realistic phenomenalism, which only accepts "some equivalent" of the contents of knowledge within the transcendental world. As we are going to see soon, this difference in views on the epistemological problem and the neighboring problem of universals plays an important role in the contention under scrutiny.

3

When it comes to the method applied to our problem, excepting one author (J. Engert), *no one* currently appeals to induction to support their claims. This is understandable, since it is the *general* value of CP – which cannot possibly stem from induction – that is at stake. Three non-inductive methods do occur in the debate: deduction, the analysis of concepts, and the phenomenological method.

(1) The most commonly applied method is deduction, within which the methods of classical logic are applied since in Neo-scholastic circles logistics is little-known or consciously rejected, mainly under the influence of Maritain and Meyerson. In the vast majority of cases deduction takes the form of reduction to absurdity in accordance with the formula $\sim CP \supset . \sim p . p: \supset CP$.

(2) The broadly conceived analysis of the concepts of C, E, causality etc. is also applied. The analysis in question usually takes up the most space in the monographs discussing our problem; it is generally conducted in a very clear and careful way, with the use of many examples. In this respect, important results, or, in any case, a higher level of rigor than the one present in Neo-scholastic literature so far, have been achieved.

(3) Lastly, a certain group of authors, namely Professor Geyser and his students, make use of the phenomenological method.[5] I have to admit that, in spite of my efforts, I am unable to understand – which must be my fault – how the method in question can give the intended result. Geyser denies the possibility of reducing CP to some other, more certain claim; he also denies its obviousness. Nonetheless, by means of introspection he asserts the existence of causal dependencies in his psychical processes, while discovering in the "relative" object the feature of *always* grounding the causal relation. I do

---

5   As is known independently, Geyser opposes phenomenology. In spite of that, I believe that
     his method is at least very similar to the phenomenological one.

not know what logical law allows for passing from individual experience to a general statement.

It is worth noting, however, that the phenomenological method is only employed by a small group of Neo-scholastics; it is generally deduction and the analysis of concepts that are dominant.

4

After a long but necessary introduction I will now set about presenting the positions in the debate. In this respect the Neo-scholastics can be divided into three groups; of course, this division, like all such divisions throughout the history of philosophy or the humanities in general, cannot lay claim to absolute rigor and is somehow schematic. Nonetheless, it is based on the deep systematic assumptions of the systems in question, which makes it suitable for an introductory outline.

(1) The first group is constituted by the philosophers who ascribe the value V_1 to CP while negating the other values. This position can be symbolically expressed as $V_{1'} \sim V_{2'} \sim V_{3'} \sim V_{4'}$. This is how the late C. Isenkrahe, a mathematician from Trieste, and Fr. F. Sawicki, a professor of the seminary in Pelplin (who, unfortunately, wrote in German), formulated their position. The views of the most notable participant of the debate, J. Hessen, a professor of philosophy in Cologne, are very close to those of the group in question: his claim can be expressed as $V_{1'} \sim V_{2'}. V_{3'} \sim V_{4'}$. The difference is minor, since it concerns only the phenomenal (transcendental) world. It is also worth noting that, according to Sawicki, V_2 does not imply V_4, so that, while principally taking the position $V_{1'} \sim V_{2'} \sim V_{3'} \sim V_{4'}$, one does not consider the position $V_{1'}. V_{2'} \sim V_{3'} \sim V_{4'}.$ to be impossible.

The philosophers from this group deny that CP should be ascribed the value V_2, i.e., they believe that a relative object without C can be *thought* but cannot be *conceived*. Consequently, they assert the *synthetic* character of CP. The next step is to negate the value V_4, which could be rationally ascertained only on the condition that CP was an analytic judgment, and that the categories of mind have corresponding categories of being, which, in the opinion of these authors, cannot be rationally justified, at least with reference to the (synthetic) principle of contradiction and, of course, to CP itself.

In Isenkrahe, Hessen, and Sawicki the theses described above are based on lengthy and very careful analysis of the attempts to justify CP throughout history. The outcome is negative: no attempt has been satisfying, which means that there is no rational justification of CP. Hessen and Sawicki, in turn, look

for another foundation for the value V_4: while the former finds it in the postulates of religious feeling, the latter sees it in the "irrational faith in the rational
structure of being", where the structure in question, according to the author,
can be rational only if it allows for not only "thinking" but also "conceiving"
every being. Of course, "grounding" cp in this way, while it can have significant
meaning in terms of worldview, does not work for philosophy; because of that,
I include these authors in the group negating the value V_4. Besides, Isenkrahe
talks about this denial openly.

With reference to the value V_3, Hessen conducts a special proof based on
the obvious (in his opinion) fact of the existence of order in the phenomenal
world. The lack of the sufficient analysis of concepts and formal errors in his
reasoning make this part of Hessen's construct much less valuable than the
remaining parts.

(2) The second group is constituted by the philosophers whose views I am
going to express as $V_1. \sim V_2. V_3. V_4$. Here are included, in the first place, the
abovementioned J. Geyser, a professor of philosophy in Munich, a French Jesuit
P. Descoqs, and his German confrère, L. Fuetscher, as well as several other, less
important thinkers.

The first statement of these authors is the same as that of the group we
have just discussed: the value V_2 should not be ascribed to cp. J. Geyser has
undergone an interesting evolution in this respect: first he accepted the value
in question, then he began to hesitate and now staunchly denies it. Descoqs
and Fuetscher embrace the same position. The proof consists of the analysis of
all the reasoning used so far in order to prove the value of V_2, which turns out to
be insufficient: thus, cp is a *synthetic* judgment. So far, the views of the second
group do not differ from those of the first. The difference becomes apparent
only in the course of further debate, since Geyser and others, after asserting the
synthetic character of cp, try to prove its value V_4 and, by implication, also V_3.
Geyser does this by means of the abovementioned phenomenological method,
while others consider cp to be immediately (when it comes to the value V_4)
obvious (Straubinger) or deduce it from the synthetic but immediately obvious
"principle of reason" (Descoqs, Fuetscher). The latter states that "every being
has a reason for its existence" and is more general than cp since it claims that
"for every x, if x exists, there is some y in the relation R to x (y is the reason for
x)", which removes two elements: restricting x to the range of relative objects
and restricting y to the range of the objects different from x.[6]

---

6   $(x): ex\, x \supset . [\exists y] . yRx.$

It is worth adding for the sake of orientation that Suaresians are usually members of this group; Geyser himself identifies as a Thomist, although in my view he uses the word "Thomist" in a meaning different from the universally accepted one since his theses contradict Thomism in many points.

The writings of this group are characterized by being carefully mapped out. The works of Geyser are especially a paradigm of monographic workmanship, which, unfortunately, is so rarely to be witnessed nowadays in spite of the partial return to systematics.

(3) The third group is characterized by embracing the position V_1, V_2, V_3, V_4. Here are included: B. Franzelin SJ from Innsbruck, a Fribourg (CH) philosopher de Munnynck, R. Garrigou-Lagrange (both Dominicans), Skibniewski, Th. Droege, and a number of others, most of them Thomists. The latter two published complete monographs on the problem; the older treatise of Garrigou-Lagrange, whose theses are taken up by the others without any major changes, is worth special attention.

The thinkers enumerated above claim, first, that cp should be considered one of the so-called "first principles" of logic: its denial is not only inconceivable but also unthinkable. From that they deduce that cp is an analytic judgment. Their reasoning is based on a premise which is an element of the philosophy of logic, that, while rarely made explicit, is obvious to everyone who possesses some knowledge of Thomism, namely, the Thomistic theory of judgment. According to the Thomists, a judgment is basically always an analysis, and the only judgments which can be general, and thus necessary in the meaning B, are those whose predicates express the feature of the *general* concept expressed by the subject. In the judgment described as "synthetic", on the contrary, the predicate expresses the feature of some *particular,* individual subject. Thus, the necessity and generality of the judgment imply its analyticity.

At the same time, Thomists distinguish between two kinds of analytic judgment: within the first kind, the predicate is the feature *constituting* the subject, while within the second kind it is the *property* (ἴδιον, *proprium*) of the subject. It is difficult to explain the meaning of these somehow complex concepts; the practical difference consists in the fact that with reference to judgments of the first kind the connection between the subject and the predicate can be found through the analysis of the subject itself, while with reference to judgments of the second kind the predicate needs to be known and compared to the subject. According to Thomists (and Aquinas himself), cp is a judgment of the second kind.

The reasoning outlined above has an indirect character, since it starts with the feature possessed by all the judgments of the type to which cp belongs. In addition, Thomists conduct a direct proof through the analysis of cp itself. In this respect there are some differences between them but they mostly make use of the reasoning already formulated by Aquinas, supplementing it with a proof of the assumption which has in later times been rejected.

Aquinas' reasoning went more or less as follows:

Every being has the reason of its existence within or outside itself.

A relative object does not have the reason for its existence within itself.

A relative object has the reason for its existence outside itself – and C is just such reason.[7]

This reasoning, while formally valid, contains in its minor premise the claim whose proof has been provided by Aquinas himself; even now everyone considers the proof in question to be sufficient. When it comes to the major premise, or rather the principle of reason which it contains, the proponents of cp (or of ascribing to it the value V_4) follow Hume in rejecting it. Because of that, contemporary Thomists try to prove the principle of reason by means of reduction to absurdity, proving its analytical character and thus the analytical character of cp itself. To do so, Fr. Garrigou-Lagrange worked out the following method; he distinguished in the relative object (E) two elements: essence (what the object is) and existence; both these elements remain connected by some relation like coexistence, or, more precisely, "information" (for Thomists existence is the "act" (ἐντελέχεια) of essence). The information in question implies the existence of something connecting the two elements, without it the connection would be contradictory (the connection of unconnected elements); and the connective is reason.

Finally, Thomists deduce AP's value V_4 from cp's analytic character. The deduction is based on the one hand on their theory of judgment discussed above, and on the other hand on *metaphysical realism* (when it comes to the problem of universals), universally accepted by the school. Indeed, to embrace this position, one has to take all existing objects to be constituted by the same forms which are the content of concepts; hence, if some general concept contains some feature analytically, all objects falling under its range have to possess this feature in reality. In that light, for Thomists cp is an analytic judgment. Since, of course, the value V_4 implies the value V_3, Thomists also assert the latter for cp.

---

7   (1) $(x)::(\exists y)::.yRx::(y):x=y. \lor .x\neq y.$

     (2) $(x,y):.Wx. \supset: \sim: yRx.x=y.$

     (3) $(x)::(\exists y):.Wx. \supset: yRx.x\neq y. (1,2).$

     (4) $(x,y):yRx.x\neq y. \supset .yCx.$

     (5) $(x):(\exists y):Wx. \supset .yCx. (3,4).$

5

Here we have touched upon the phenomenon which seems to play the crucial role in the debate under scrutiny: namely, that the positions of those who debate *CP* precisely correspond to their views on the problem of universals. The phenomenon in question has rarely been discussed, but since it is of enormous significance and has many counterparts in other contemporary debates within different philosophical schools, I will attempt to provide a concise justification of what I have just said.

(1) The position of the first group is necessarily implied by the claims of the empiricist-nominalist current. The philosophers from this group negate, in the first place, the value V_2, with reference not only to *CP* but also to the principle of contradiction, which marks their distinct tendency to rule out any universals, a tendency characteristic of the current under scrutiny. Besides, Hessen quite clearly admits to it. If one embraces the position mentioned above, one cannot accept the value V_2 or, less still, the value V_4 of *CP*. The reason why V_2 cannot be accepted is that the only logically necessary elements of the position in question are tautological judgments; the reason for the impossibility of the acceptance of V_4 is that for a nominalist the value of a non-tautological judgment cannot transcend the scope of experience for a nominalist. *CP* cannot in any way be considered a tautological judgment and, at the current stage of the debate, no one considers it to be one.

(2) The position of the second group entails conceptualism, that is, namely, the philosophers who belong to it state that logically necessary judgments exist which nonetheless are not analytic, even in the second Thomistic meaning, which is tantamount to embracing the existence of *synthetic a priori* judgments. At the same time, synthetic *a priori* judgments are possible only insofar as we accept the existence of the universals *created* by the mind as far as their content is concerned, i.e., if we embrace the conceptualist position. It is true that neither Geyser and his school nor, less still, does Descoqs draw this conclusion. Still, it seems to have been definitely established since Kant, and it is difficult for the reader of the authors from this group not to get the impression that some extra-philosophical factors do not allow them to draw Kantian conclusions from their assumptions.

(3) The position of the third group entails realism. The matter is obvious and has already been explained, since the realist claim is the crucial constituent of Thomistic reasoning: forms exist which constitute objects and *the same* forms are the contents of concepts, acquiring generality in the mind. Here we observe an interesting phenomenon; Thomists, *a priori*, as it were, on the strength of their epistemological assumptions (metaphysical

realism), have to consider, insofar as they want to maintain their claim about the value V_2, CP as an analytic judgment; all the "proofs" of its analytic character – in my opinion, not always fortunate – are a marginal topic brought about by the necessity of defending it from fierce attacks of the opponents. The analyticity of CP, and thus also its value V_4, follow necessarily from the principles of Thomism.

Thus, it turns out that the essence of the contention consists in a disagreement concerning the problem of universals. This phenomenon is very common in the history of philosophy, including contemporary philosophy, in which the two strongest currents, namely, more or less positivist empiricism on the one hand and the "transcendental" philosophy principally dependent on Kant on the other, are based on nominalist and conceptualist assumptions correspondingly.

6

An impartial observer of the debate has to conclude that the latter is one of the most appealing displays of contemporary philosophical activity and entirely deserves to also be known outside Neo-scholastic circles. Above all else, the debate has already produced a few positive and interesting results. Several concepts (relativity, the causes of the analytic judgment, etc.), which engage both the metaphysician and the epistemologist, have been defined. Several older formulations of CP and other "principles" have been removed. The problem has been unambiguously grounded in epistemological foundations, and the hidden system of axioms, so often difficult to discern, has been uncovered. Finally, the debate brought into light a great deal of interesting historical material in connection with the positions of medieval and modern philosophers.

However, the most important thing explained by the debate in question is the impossibility of presenting a united position of what is known as "Catholic philosophy" on the problem under scrutiny. "Catholic philosophy" includes both quite radical rationalism and empiricism embraced in an entirely open way, diverse epistemological positions, radical irrationalism as well as typical intellectualism, and, finally different kinds of metaphysics and different theories of worldview. In a word, *de facto* there is no *Catholic philosophy* concerning the problem in question, i.e., there is no thesis uniting all Catholic philosophers, a number of whom are incomparably closer in their views to this or that "non-Catholic" school than to another "Catholic" current.

Another matter is whether *de iure* Catholic philosophy exists, i.e., which one of the groups we have mentioned, if any, has the right to call itself characteristically Catholic. That problem transcends the boundaries of our account. The Church has not said anything about the matter, leaving everyone free to debate it.

Translated by Sylwia Wilczewska

Bibliography

Descoqs, Pedro (1925). *Institutiones metaphysicae generalis.* Vol. I. Paris: Beauchesne.

Droege, Theodor (1930). *Der analytische Charakter des Kausalprinzips.* Bonn: Verlag S. Hofbauer.

Engert, Joseph (1932). Das Prinzip des zureichenden Grundes. *Philosophisches Jahrbuch* vol. XLV, f. 6, pp. 1–17; f. 7, pp. 159–176.

Franzelin, Bernhard (1933). Zur Klärung des Kausalproblems. *Divus Thomas* vol. XI, pp. 3–51.

Fuetscher, Lorenz (1930). *Die ersten Seins- und Denkprinzipien.* Innsbruck: F. Rauch.

Garrigou-Lagrange, Réginald (1914). *Dieu, son existence et sa nature.* Paris 1923: G. Brauchesne.

Geyser, Joseph (1929). *Das Prinzip vom zureichenden Grunde.* Regensburg: J. Habbel.

Geyser, Joseph (1933). *Das Gesetz der Ursache.* Münich: E. Reinhardt.

Hessen, Johannes (1928). *Das Kausalprinzip.* Augsburg: Benno Filster.

Heuser, Adolf (1930). *Neuscholastische Begründungsversuche für das Kausalprinzip.* Bochum: Pöppinghaus.

Isenkrahe, Caspar (1915). *Über die Grundlegung eines bündigen kosmologischen Gottesbeweises.* München: Kempten.

Isenkrahe, Caspar (1922). *Zur Elementaranalyse des kosmologischen Gottesbeweises.* Bonn: Marcus & Weber.

La philosophie chrétienne (1934). *Compte-rendu de la deuxième journée d'études: Juvisy, le III Septembre 1933. Société Thomiste.* Paris: Édition du Cerf.

Mausbach, Joseph (1930). *Dasein und Wesen Gottes.* Band I. *Die Möglichkeit der Gottesbeweise.* Münster: Aschendorf Verlag.

Munnynck, Marcus de (1929). Essai sur le principe de causalité. *The New Scholasticism* vol. III, f. 3, pp. 253–295.

Nink, Caspar (1928). De principiis contradictionis, rationis sufficientis, causalitatis eorumque inter se connexione. *Estudios Ecclesiásticos* vol. VII, No. 25, pp. 24–41.

Sawicki, Franz (1925). Der Satz vom zureichenden Grunde. *Philosophisches Jahrbuch der Görres-Gesellschaft* vol. XXXVIII, pp. 1–11.

Sawicki, Franz (1931). Das Irrationale in den Grundlagen der Erkenntnis und die Gottesbeweise. *Philosophisches Jahrbuch der Görres-Gesellschaft* vol. XLIV, pp. 410–418.

Skibniewski, Stephan Leo von (1930). *Kausalität*, Paderborn: Ferdinand Schöningh.

Straubinger, Heinrich (1930). Evidenz und Kausalitätsgesetz. *Philosophisches Jahrbuch der Görres-Gesellschaft* vol. XLIII, f. 1, pp. 1–17.

CHAPTER 5

The Negative Concept of Causality

Mieczysław Kreutz

Negatywne pojęcie przyczynowości.
Przegląd Filozoficzny vol. XLI (1938), f. 1, pp. 37–44

∴

The simplest way to express causal laws is with the following formula: After the occurrence of a particular cause a particular effect *must* occur.[1]

An essential tendency of such laws is to assert some necessity. Causal laws are not only about concluding that in a number of observed cases a cause was followed by the expected effect; in addition, they are supposed to state that that has always been so, both in cases we have observed and in those no one has observed, and that it will be the case in the future – in other words, that it cannot be otherwise. The necessity in question, which, as I said, plays an essential role in causal laws, is connected to complex issues and difficulties of a theoretical nature but also to the invaluable benefits and the great significance these laws have for human life and activity.

---

1 The conception of causality presented in the present paper is a topic I have investigated for a couple of years, doing my best to think it through thoroughly and comprehensively; I suppose that I would be able to dispel in a convincing way many of the doubts which may arise in the mind of the reader as well as to give a better justification for many claims of the paper, but that would require writing an ample volume. In planning the present paper, I was restricted by its purpose – a presentation at the Philosophical Congress – and had to fit the entire theory onto a few pages. [The author is referring to The World Congress of Philosophy in Paris, 1937. sw] Such a short account, however, has its advantages, namely, with such complex matters it can easily happen that a seemingly tiny detail, unnoticed by the author at the beginning, strips the entire theory of value. That is why it is better to declare and submit to criticism the principal points of the theory first and then set out to develop it in detail. I would be glad if some Polish philosopher were so kind as to investigate at length the value of my view, so that I could, as it were, try out its resilience, and, if the trial turns out positive, calmly set out to develop it more comprehensively. The Polish version of the present paper is a translation of the presentation in German and contains some minor additions.

The problems and doubts of a theoretical nature essentially come down to the following question: on what grounds can we make any judgments concerning events no one has observed or which have not yet even occurred and are only thought to occur in the future – in other words, how can we justify such judgments and how can we know anything about them?

If we follow Hume in holding that causal laws only assert the constant succession of some facts, we should formulate those laws differently, since, strictly speaking, we are not allowed to talk about constancy and should limit ourselves to concluding that in a number of cases observed by us or by some credible persons the succession of the same particular facts has occurred repeatedly. But that is not our goal, and such a judgment of a historical nature does not possess any major theoretical or practical value. If, in addition, we accept a general premise saying that what was the case in a number of observed cases is always the case, we end up with the form usually assumed by causal laws but also overstep our investigative rights. Such reasoning causes serious and well-justified protests, since, first, the number of observed cases is very small in comparison to the overall, perhaps infinite, number of all cases of the same kind which have really occurred, occur presently, and will occur in the future. Second, the aforementioned general premise does not qualify the needed number of observed cases and often does not agree with experiential data. Within such a theory of causality it is not possible in principle to differentiate causal laws from mere superstitions, since the latter are also based on the observation of a number of cases which have actually occurred. For instance, it is difficult to say whether the claim that aspirin or some similar medical substance has beneficial influence on the body is a superstition or a scientific law. Such theoretical deficiencies could well incline us to reject the concept of causality entirely, which some philosophers have indeed set out to do.

On the other hand, however, it is hard to accept the rejection of a concept which serves us so well, allowing us to predict some future phenomena in an accurate way. After all, causal laws are the foundation of empirical sciences as well as the practical activity of engineers, architects, farmers, doctors etc., and, in spite of theoretical reservations and doubts, complex devices do function, magnificent buildings arise, and difficult therapies enjoy wide popularity. We cannot reject causality lightheartedly; instead, we should first look for another solution of the problem of necessity, which presents the greatest difficulty of the entire cluster of issues in question.

The following reasoning, in my opinion, presents the right solution to the problem of what necessity consists of and how it can be identified. Necessity is based on the principle of contradiction, and the latter needs to be accepted without proof, if we do not want to give up all scientific activity or rational thought and activity in general, all of which would be rendered impossible were it not accepted. The principle, however, can be accepted as true without any reservations since it has not failed us even once throughout a few thousand years of human experience. As everybody knows, the principle of contradiction is negative in the sense that it does not lead to any positive declarations concerning what is or will be but only asserts that something is impossible.

In view of the above, necessity can also only be negative, which should be understood as the claim that, when talking about necessity, we do not prejudge that something must occur but only state that nothing can come to be unconditionally. Reducing necessity to the principle of contradiction in this way is the only known solution of the problem of necessity; as far as I know, no other solution has ever been proposed, so, if the term "necessity" is not to be an empty sound, it must be accepted.

I will try to explain this conception with the help of an example brought to my mind by reading Leibniz. If we forcefully push a billiard ball in the direction of a thick strong wall, we know with absolute certainty that when the ball hits the wall some change has to occur since the ball cannot move in the same direction and in the same way it did before reaching its destination. The reason we know this is that, if no change occurred, a state of affairs containing a contradiction would have to occur, namely, the ball and the wall would be at the same place at the same time, which cannot be reconciled in any way with the material properties of these two objects. We do not know what will happen at the moment when the ball hits the wall, or rather, we are unable to provide sufficient justification of our predictions on the matter. We can think of different changes which could occur, but the only thing we know with absolute certainty is what is definitely impossible. Nonetheless, since the ball hits the wall within a tightly filled space where there are many obstacles preventing the free movement of the ball or, more precisely, the free movement of the molecules of which the ball consists, we may be able to rule out a whole number of other eventualities – always on the basis of the principle of contradiction – so that in the end only one remains, which in the given state of affairs has to be realized. Thus, positive and justified predictions concerning future events are possible only by eliminating all eventualities containing a contradiction, which means that we need to have sufficient knowledge of such eventualities. That is why necessity is something purely negative, and, when we make use of this concept we should only assert the impossibility of the occurrence of some particular eventualities.

Such a view was already proclaimed in 1906 by Professor Łukasiewicz. In his paper, he has shown that both empirical necessity, with which I am currently concerned, and logical necessity of the kind which occurs in the statement that a number divisible by 6 must be divisible by 3, come down to the principle of contradiction [Łukasiewicz 1906: 29]. Łukasiewicz, however, did not discuss, and perhaps did not notice, some especially important consequences of such conception of causality, which I am now going to summarize.

1. Accepting this view on necessity forces one to recast the concept of causality completely. Contradiction is a relation and as such requires the existence of at least two elements, the so-called *termini relationis*; if a contradiction is involved, at least two objects must come into play. Thus, if one talks about causality in the material world, one needs to point out two elements between which a contradiction could occur. Cause and effect are definitely not such elements; what we need are two separate bodies which collide in a particular place and at a particular time. It is only at the moment of their collision that the danger of a contradiction becomes actualized, as I have shown using the example of a billiard ball. Since there no state of affairs containing a contradiction can come about, some change in one or both of the colliding bodies must take place. The question arises: what are we going to call, respectively, the cause and the effect? Cause can be understood in two ways: one narrower, the other broader. In the narrower meaning, the cause of change is the collision of the two bodies, while in the broader meaning the cause includes, apart from the collision itself, the bodies in collision. Analogously, what we understand by effect are either only those changes which occurred in one or both of the bodies at the moment of the collision or both bodies in their changed form. Thus, cause and effect should not be seen the way they are usually seen nowadays – namely, as opposed to each other – because both cause and effect are constituted by the same two bodies in which certain changes have occurred at the moment of the collision. The elements of the relation of impending contradiction are two separate bodies, let us call them A and B; some of their properties may contradict each other. At the same time, one should not talk about the contradiction between the cause AB and the effect $A'B'$.

The currently dominant theory reducing causality to a constant succession of phenomena allows holding the view, without an essential error, that if, for instance, I pour some water into an empty vessel, pigeons will fly out of it, a possibility ruled out in reality except for a magician's stage. That is because the theory of causality currently in vogue contains no postulates concerning the qualities of the phenomena which constantly succeed one another: any phenomenon can be the cause of any other phenomenon. The theory of causality presented here excludes examples like that of the pigeons since it maintains that only some minimal changes in the cause – in our example, water and the vessel – can constitute the effect. I will give one more concrete example to show that the theory of causality I am describing is more consistent than the older one with common experience. One cannot claim that, for instance, only bacteria are the cause of infectious diseases; the real cause of someone getting infected, e.g., with tuberculosis, is, in the narrower meaning of the term, the impact on or penetration of the organism by bacteria, and, in the broader meaning, both the bacteria and the individual organism which they have entered. The effect of the impact, in turn, is constituted both by the changes in the human body, which are called disease, and the changes in the life of the bacteria which have entered the body and begun to prosper inside it. It is a fact that, depending on immunity levels, not everyone contracts a disease after contact with pathogenic bacteria, so we cannot consider bacteria to be the only cause of the disease.

2. The theory of causality presented here entirely removes the anthropomorphic view that a cause is constituted by some working force (Sigwart), since, as I said, when we talk about cause, we only rule out some contradictory eventualities, saying nothing about any positive action. In view of that, to remain in agreement with the views of physics (the law of conservation of energy), we have to assume that the forces at work in the material world exist eternally, and their origin is an unsolved metaphysical problem. Within empirical sciences we can only observe the changes in the movement and shapes of bodies, i.e., the changes consisting of the transfers of those eternal forces, and only in this area can we talk about causes. At this point, the question of the origin of those forces oversteps the boundaries of science and belongs to metaphysics.

3. Reducing causality to the principle of contradiction implies the following methodological consequences:

(a) It lessens, or rather changes the difference, from qualitative to quantitative, between empirical and *a priori* sciences, since, once the theory has been accepted, all sciences are based on the same principle of contradiction. Therefore, all well-justified outcomes of any science are equally certain and true, and their value depends solely on whether the principle of contradiction is true and whether it governs the real world without restrictions or exceptions. If that were the case, the view, currently dominant but so difficult to assimilate, that, e.g., the Pythagorean theorem is absolutely certain while the claim that every human being will die or that every stone thrown into the air will fall is only very probable, would lose its grip. Nonetheless, to avoid misunderstandings, it needs to be noted that, in the realm of empirical sciences, causal laws which could be exhaustively justified in accordance with the requirements of the theory under scrutiny have so far been few and far between, which is why I drew attention to the quantitative difference between the two groups of sciences.

(b) The theory of causality presented here sets the boundaries which can and should be approached when inquiring about causes. Noting the frequent succession of two phenomena is almost never satisfying. For instance, when a doctor states that after the application of a medicine the state of the patient suffering from a particular disease improves, and puts his observation to practical use, this method, sometimes employed in the absence of any better one, is still considered a less valuable "empirical method". This is because in this case we feel the need for further explanation of why the medicine works as it does, an explanation unlike that by Molière. According to the theory presented here, one should move forward with the explanation until one encounters contradictions, which are then ruled out, and, by way of elimination, the only possible eventuality is discovered. Only then is the connection under investigation completely explained and the boundary of inquiry into causality reached, since any further questions concerning the genesis of the forces at work in the given case belong to the domain of metaphysics.

(c) The theory under discussion also seems to make it possible to predict some effects *a priori*, if only we know with sufficient precision the properties of the bodies whose contact constitutes the cause. Such predictions are possible even now within some disciplines, e.g., in chemistry (when it comes to the production of certain synthetic bodies). What is more, based on the theory in question it is possible, to some degree, to discern the cause on the basis of the effect, which, though done in practice (e.g., in medicine), has so far been considered unacceptable in theory.

4. If we try to apply the theory of causality presented here to metaphysics, then, if we accept some additional assumptions – e.g., the principle that only minimal changes, i.e., the smallest changes which allow the avoidance of contradiction, can occur as the effect of the collision of two bodies – then we will envision new directions which have not so far been explored by metaphysicians.

(a) On the grounds of this theory, indeterminism will become intelligible and acceptable without any dangerous consequences for the order of the universe. Let us assume that 10 different eventualities could occur as a result of the collision of two bodies. Then let us suppose that, on the basis of a thorough analysis, we have ruled 8 of them out as leading to contradiction. This will leave two, about which, after the most thorough investigation, we will be able to state that neither one issues into a contradiction, i.e., that both are possible, in which case, by definition, it is in no way necessary that one of them occurs and the other one cannot occur. That would be an undetermined case, not subject to any causal law, the case which, according to some physicists, occasionally happens in atoms and which constitutes an essential point of contention in relation to the problem of free will.

(b) If we reflect on the beginning of the universe, the theory of causality presented here leads to dualism and to a sort of pantheism. According to the theory in question, one cannot take any one object or substance to be the first cause; rather, one should assume that the first cause was constituted by two separate substances to whose contact the universe owes its beginning. Moreover, since the effect is only a minimal change in one or both of the objects colliding, the universe in which we live is at least one proto-substance, now somehow changed. I am not going to develop this idea further, but I chose to mention it since the thesis of the first cause plays a major role in metaphysical considerations.

(c) When it comes to the problem of the origin of mental life, the theory under scrutiny also leads to dualism. Mental phenomena of an individual are certainly a reaction to stimuli from the external world. This should be understood as stating that some physical processes which take place outside the human body exert an influence on it, i.e., impact it and bring about mental phenomena. After applying the theory presented here to this area, we have to assume that within the human body some immaterial part exists, i.e., some part of a mental nature, since otherwise the only effect of the organism's contact with the external world would consist of some physical changes, e.g., some neural processes, and not mental phenomena such as thoughts, feelings etc. That is why in this area too, dualism – i.e., the soul and the body whose spatio-temporal contact implies certain changes within the elements in contact – should be accepted. What constitutes the changes in some properties of the soul are mental phenomena.

Even though I do not attach much weight to the metaphysical consequences mentioned above, I hope that the theory of causality I have presented can be of some service when it comes to the scientific problems currently under debate, contributing to the explanation of an extremely dark and vague situation. While I realize that my theory has numerous shortcomings, I console myself with the thought that "*in magnis et voluisse sat est*".

Translated by Sylwia Wilczewska

Bibliography

Łukasiewicz, Jan (1906). Analysis and Construction of the Concept of Cause. In this volume: 3–66.

PART 3

The Concept of Causality in Poland Many Years Hence

∵

CHAPTER 6

Łukasiewicz on the Analysis of Concepts

Anna Brożek

1   Introductory Remarks

The first part of the paper "Analysis and Construction of the Concept of Cause"
[Łukasiewicz 1906] includes valuable methodological comments concerning
the procedure of the analysis of concepts Łukasiewicz applied to examine the
concept of cause. At the end of this first part of the paper, Łukasiewicz wrote:

> I have reached the end of these introductory considerations which I by
> no means consider to be an insignificant part of the study. For not only
> do they provide me with a weapon and an instrument for proceeding
> in the investigations that follow; they can also instruct the reader about
> what to pay attention to in *methodically* conducted works of this kind. A
> work lacking in scientific method is not a scientific work at all but merely
> fantasizing about science. I would like this to be remembered not only by
> dilettantes who feel entitled to address philosophical questions, but also
> true philosophers who too often proclaim with emphasis far-reaching
> metaphysical views, such as, e.g., that everything in the world has some
> cause, or that the principle of causality is some innate form of cognition,
> but because they have no clue what a cause is they do not satisfy the sim-
> plest rules of scientific method.
>
>   ŁUKASIEWICZ 1906: 11–12

This passage shows Łukasiewicz's strong interest in the methodological aspect
of philosophical research and his need for reflection about the methods used in
philosophy. Such a tendency was natural for a philosophical child of Kazimierz
Twardowski and a grandchild of Franz Brentano. However, Łukasiewicz's
emphasis on methods went much further than that of his predecessors and
finally became a kind of his *idée fixe*. Testimony to that was Łukasiewicz's later
(unfortunately unrealized) initiative to found the Methodological Institute.

It is a known fact that Łukasiewicz found the ideal of methodicality in
mathematical logic, and he was convinced that the tools of mathematical logic
could be applied in philosophy. In the 1920s, he also formulated the program
of "logicisation" in philosophy in which he proposed presenting philosophical

systems in the form of axiomatic systems (cf. [Łukasiewicz 1928]). From the "logistical" point of view, philosophical investigations that do not make use of the logical apparatus seemed poor and uninteresting to him. Łukasiewicz expressed it thus:

> When we approach the great philosophical systems of Plato or Aristotle, Descartes or Spinoza, Kant, or Hegel, with the criteria of precision set up by mathematical logic, these systems fall to pieces as if they were houses of cards. Their basic concepts are not clear, their most important theses are incomprehensible, their reasoning and proofs are inexact, and the logical theories which often underlie them are practically all erroneous.
>
> ŁUKASIEWICZ 1922: 111–112

However, Łukasiewicz was already a "logicoidal" philosopher in 1906. He calls his analysis of the concept of cause "logical" and contrasts it to psychological analysis. From the very beginning of his career, Łukasiewicz was set against the psychologistic inclinations of his teacher, Twardowski, and, let us add, his own colleague Władysław Witwicki. In the paper [Łukasiewicz 1906], Łukasiewicz reveals these antipathies and, on the other hand, his sympathies towards "good old" Aristotelian metaphysics and the Platonic interpretation of concepts.

In fact, Łukasiewicz's conception of analysis is "logical" in two senses: its object consists of logical concepts (and not psychological concepts) and its tools are taken from logic (for instance, he uses the concepts of consistency and reasoning).

Nevertheless, we must remember that Łukasiewicz's paper was written before his final "logistic conversion", and it is a fact that in the "logistic period", Łukasiewicz did not positively evaluate his early works, including the study on the concept of cause. He wrote this openly in *Diaries*:

> During my stay [...] [in Leuven] I prepared a dissertation on causality for the competition announced by the journal *Przegląd Filozoficzny*. I sent the dissertation to Warsaw under the emblem *"Arceo psychologiam"*, which was to mean "I stay away from psychology". The dissertation received the first prize, but in my opinion unjustly. It was to be an analysis and construction of the concept of cause, but I understood logic too little to do so properly. At present, I do not recognize this dissertation, even though Twardowski accepted it as my habilitation thesis.
>
> ŁUKASIEWICZ 2013, p. 66

Let us state clearly: Łukasiewicz's self-estimation was not, I think, objective in this respect. In fact, Łukasiewicz's comments on the method of analysis of concepts are significant, not only because they provide him with "a weapon and a tool" for his own investigations, and not only because they may be helpful to anyone who undertakes a similar task. Łukasiewicz's methodological comments are important also from a historical point of view. Firstly, Łukasiewicz's article is one of the earliest methodological papers in 20th century analytic philosophy. Secondly, Łukasiewicz's article was an essential element in the development of metaphilosophical investigations in the Lvov-Warsaw School, the Polish branch of the analytic movement.

In the present paper, I reconstruct Łukasiewicz's conception of analysis of concepts as presented by him in [Łukasiewicz 1906]. The reconstruction is placed in a certain conceptual scheme and supplemented with some comments on analytic methods as such.

2   Some Semiotic and Ontological Distinctions

At the beginning, some semiotic and ontological distinctions have to be introduced.

Take a certain real object as an example; let it be Maria Skłodowska-Curie. As a real object, she has many different properties. For instance, she is (was) a mammal, a Pole, a scientist, she is (was) intelligent, talented, and hardworking. She entered into relations with other objects, for instance she was younger and cleverer than her husband Pierre Curie. She shares some properties with other objects. For instance, she is spatio-temporal (as was a portion of polonium, discovered by her), and she is a human being (just like Pierre Curie). She also shares some properties with other women. Being-spatio-temporal, being-mammal, and being-rational are examples of such properties.

Now let us assume that there are two properties which are common to all and only women, that is, all tokens of the type: woman. One may say that these properties determine the set of women. Let these properties be: being-human and being-female. Such features can be called "specific (essential) features of women". Of course, apart from specific features, every woman also has certain individualizing properties, that is, properties characteristic of only one woman. Maria Skłodowska-Curie also belongs to other sets (she is also, for instance, a scientist and a Nobel-Prize winner, etc.); and she possesses some properties which are essential with respect to these sets.

From a biological point of view, women do not form a separate species. However, let us suppose that, from the point of view of a certain science, it is worth distinguishing such a species. Species may be understood simply as sets of individuals. However, it happens that genera are hypostatized. The fact is that sometimes scientists speak of genera and species as they would speak of individuals. For some philosophers, this is only a manner of speech. However, there are some "Platonizing" philosophers who postulate objects like "woman-as-such". Woman-as-such is understood as a substrate of only the specific properties of women or simply as a composition of these properties. Considering certain properties of a given object as separated from these real objects is sometimes called "abstraction", and these properties or the postulated substrates of these properties are called "abstract objects".

Now notice that people use terms to indicate objects or to assign some properties to objects. For instance, Maria Skłodowska-Curie is a designatum of the term "woman" (just as any other woman would be in fact). The set of all and only women is the denotation of this word. When we call someone "a woman" we ascribe to this object certain properties, namely, properties that are connotations of this term. These properties are considered essential properties of women.

Once the connotation of a given term is established, it may be expressed in a (connotational) definition of this term. Imagine that we look up the term "woman" in the dictionary, and we find a definition of this word. It is as follows: "[A woman is] a female human being". We may say that this definition indicates the meaning of the word "woman" in English, that is, the concept of a woman or the connotation of the word "woman". In an ideal (from the logical point of view) situation, the connotation of the word "woman" indicates the denotation of the word "woman": the elements of this denotation are all and only such entities that possess properties contained in the connotation of the word "woman".

All competent speakers of the English language can use the word "woman". In particular, they know what objects can be indicated with this expression. Consequently, some believe that we have the right to claim that there is something in the psyche of a competent language speaker using the name "woman" thanks to which this speaker applies this expression correctly. We will say that this person has a (psychologically understood) concept of a woman. What is the relation of the concept indicated in this definition to the concepts in the psychological sense had by users of the language? It probably varies, as our "personal" concepts of a woman may vary significantly.

In what follows, it is important to distinguish the following things:
(1)   particular, individual objects (for instance, Maria Skłodowska-Curie);
(2)   the set of particular objects (1) (for instance, the set of women);

(3)   properties that indicate elements of set (2) (for instance, being-human and being-female) which are essential with respect to this set and determine it;

(4)   the substrate of properties (3);

(5)   a given word (term) (for instance "woman");

(6)   designata of (5) (for instance, Maria Skłodowska-Curie);

(7)   the denotation of (5) (for instance, the set of all women);

(8)   connotation of (5) (for instance, being-human and being-female);

(9)   someone's mental representations of (1), (3), or (8) (psychological concept(s) of woman).

3   What Are Concepts According to Łukasiewicz?

Łukasiewicz's paper concerns concepts in the logical sense. What are they?

One may assume that the following objects are identical: the (logical) concept of a woman, the connotation of the name "woman", and the sequence of the essential properties of women. Such an identification makes similar the following procedures: the analysis of real objects (with respect to essential features), the analysis of meaning of words, and the analysis of (logically understood) concepts.

Of course, we do not have to make such an assumption, and there are some who would never agree to such an identification. Some philosophers also rightly notice that the ontological status of some of the objects involved is suspicious (for instance, common features, essential features, the substrate of essential features). However, from a methodological point of view these ontological difficulties are not a serious problem. Even an ontologically parsimonious philosopher makes use of terms that refer to more than one object and from time to time establish the meanings (connotations) of these terms. And if so, they should also know how to do it.

Nevertheless, the above distinctions are also needed to reconstruct Łukasiewicz's idea of analysis of concepts.

In his paper [Łukasiewicz 1906], Łukasiewicz makes some comments on the concept of concepts. He starts with the following statement:

> What these abstract objects are I *cannot specify* [my emphasis]; I can only point at them, in the same way that I can only point at objects of red color, but I cannot specify red color itself.
>
> ŁUKASIEWICZ 1906: 3

Then, however, Łukasiewicz shows that he *is able* to specify, at least to some degree, what concepts are and what they are not. At first, he makes some negative statements:

> For, as I would like to emphasize, by concepts, that is, by abstract objects, I do not understand psychic acts that are formed when we think about some concept, nor any spiritual "images" that can be given to us in an internal experience. What convinces me of this view are the following considerations. Whoever claims, for instance, that a geometrical circle is a closed curve does not make a claim about some psychic act or about some intangible, imitative image of a drawn circle which maybe appears now in his consciousness, but about some unreal object, for which this real mental image is a symbol, just like the expression "circle" is. Whoever makes claims about some mental act or about some imitative image and studies their properties is doing psychology; whoever makes claims about a circle and studies properties of a circle is doing geometry.
>
> ŁUKASIEWICZ 1906: 3–4

In this passage, Łukasiewicz reveals his anti-psychologistic view. He simply refuses to understand concepts as something mental (presentations or their contents). What does Łukasiewicz state positively about concepts?

Firstly, he calls them "abstract" objects.

> Thus, by concepts I understand meanings of such expressions that do not indicate concrete objects, in other words, *by concepts I understand abstract objects.*
>
> ŁUKASIEWICZ 1906: 3–4

Secondly, he identifies them with meanings of terms such as "a man in general" or "a circle in general".

> A man in general, a circle in general, indicate unreal abstract objects.
>
> ŁUKASIEWICZ 1906: 3

Thirdly, he declares that he is sympathetic with the Platonic interpretation of concepts.

> A circle as an abstract object is always one and the same, and it does not exist in time, nor in space, nor in any man's mind.

I do not doubt that nowadays only few will agree with the last sentence. Thus, I would like to show, in at least a few words, the logical error that caused this old, the only correct, "Platonic" view on the nature of concepts to disappear almost completely in modern philosophy. [...]

Man in general, circle in general, cause in general are neither objects of internal experience nor words; universalia neque sunt conceptus, neque nomina. I rehearsed the arguments above using the example of a circle; be that as it may, whoever has grasped the difference between presented and signified objects will immediately see that these considerations are correct.

ŁUKASIEWICZ 1906: 4, 5

Finally, Łukasiewicz states:

As I aim to give a logical analysis of the concept of cause, I will not therefore investigate what I present to myself, that is, what happens or appears in my consciousness when I think about a cause, or what someone else presents to himself while doing so – for that would be a psychological analysis that I am not concerned with; instead, I will try to specify what the word "cause" signifies. I will try, in other words, to study the *abstract object* that is the meaning of the word cause.

ŁUKASIEWICZ 1906: 6

Let us note that Łukasiewicz did not introduce a distinction between two functions of terms (such as the distinction between denotation and connotation); he only makes use of the concept of content (this is Twardowski's heritage). Without the distinction between two kinds of semiotic functions of terms, he thought of concepts as correlates of terms "*x*-in-general". Of course, the use of such terms is the source of many misunderstandings.

In Łukasiewicz's paper, there is also the following surprising statement:

Abstract objects, that is, those wholes consisting of various features connected by relations, *are constructed by the human mind* [my emphasis] when we seek either to grasp scientifically given experiences or to create systems of truths regardless of experience and reality.

ŁUKASIEWICZ 1906: 8

It seems that Łukasiewicz's concept of concept was not completely devoid of psychological elements, as he believes in their psychological genesis.

4   Why Is Analysis of Concepts Important for Philosophers?

Philosophers have been analyzing concepts from the very beginning. Socrates walking through streets of Athens and asking people what justice is; Aristotle meticulously elaborating definitions of terms; Thomas Aquinas making subtle distinctions; Gettier modifying the standard approach to knowledge – these are all examples of philosophical analyses carried out by philosophers.

However, analytical procedures are encountered in every scientific discipline. There are, for instance, mathematical, physical, chemical, biological, psychological, and sociological analyses. Various types of analyses differ with respect to the objects analyzed, the tools applied, the initial hypotheses, etc. Nevertheless, the analysis of concepts in philosophy plays a special role; it is sometimes even said that whenever one undertakes an analysis of concepts, he plays the role of a philosopher. Conceptual analyses are needed especially when changes occur to scientific paradigms.

Concepts submitted to philosophical analysis may derive from various sources: from particular sciences (including some segments of philosophy) or from everyday language. It is sometimes assumed that the distinguishing feature of philosophically significant concepts and claims is that they are multidisciplinary. It is said that a philosopher primarily researches concepts which occur in more than one specialist language, that is, such concepts as "property", "essence", "cause", etc.

Łukasiewicz was aware of the role of conceptual analysis in a philosopher's work. He stressed that analysis of concepts precedes any further investigations; in particular, it has to precede establishing the logical value of theses:

> Whoever wants to address any question concerning the "problem of causality", needs to know what a cause means; otherwise, he acts against the rules of a scientific method and exposes himself to errors. [...] To know what a cause is, one needs to analyze this concept thoroughly.
>
> ŁUKASIEWICZ 1906: 3

Let us add that conceptual analysis is a necessary step within other methods of philosophy, such as paraphrase of theses or axiomatization of theories. Establishing the sense of words is also the necessary starting point of any philosophical discussion.

5   What Are the Components of Concepts and How Can They Be
       Represented in Ontologically "Neutral" Methodology?

Independently of the ontological status of connotations, species, and logical
concepts – which is basically irrelevant in the analytical procedure – they all
are successfully represented in this procedure as sequences of properties. In
particular, it is assumed that concepts can be (at least) represented with con-
junctions or disjunctions of properties. This is exactly what we do, providing
terms with definitions (indicating their connotation). For instance, the concept of a woman consists of the conjunction of properties: being human and
being female. A disjunctive concept is, e.g., the concept of color: something has
a color if it is red or blue or green, etc.

The terms "sequence", "conjunction", and "disjunction" in their basic sense
refer to sentences (or states of affairs as semantic equivalents of sentences). In
the absence of generally accepted "better" terms,[1] I use them to refer to properties in such a way that: object x has the sequence of properties W_1 and W_2
when one of the two situations occurs: (a) object x has properties W_1 and W_2;
(b) object x has the property W_1 or object x has the property W_2.

It was said earlier that the concept of woman (the connotation of "woman")
may be identified with the sequence of properties that determines all and
only elements of the class of women.[2] Suppose that the following sentences
are true:

(1) All and only women have property W_1.
(2) All and only women have property W_2.[3]

The conjunction of W_1 and W_2 determines the class of women. However, any
singular property of this conjunction does this equally well. In such a situation,
is it only a question of choice which property, W_1 or W_2, will be taken as our
concept?

Sometimes, researchers assume that even if (1) and (2) hold together, one of
properties in question is somehow more important than the other or that even
one property is somehow entailed by the other – and therefore we have:

$$\bigwedge x\,(W_1 x \rightarrow W_2 x).$$

A problem arises here: is there any entailment or simply co-occurrence?

---

1   Łukasiewicz's equivalent of my term "sequence", i.e., the words "collection" and "whole",
    seems to me worse if we accept the disjunction of properties as a possible concept.
2   I use the term "the class of x-es" as a synonym of the term "the set of all and only x-es".
3   Both the properties, W_1 and W_2, can be single properties, as well as sequences of properties.

Łukasiewicz was convinced that concepts (as with any abstraction from concrete objects) possess some properties. He wrote:

> Any object, concrete or abstract, has some properties or features. The properties of a man include "alive", "rational" ...; the properties of a circle – "curved", "closed" ... Features of different objects never form some chaotic collection, but an ordered whole, thanks to being connected to one another by various relations. Among relations that can connect the features of an object, the most important for us are necessary relations. Thus, we take it, for instance, that between the features of a man, "alive" and "rational", there is some necessary relation, as we suppose that where there is no living organism nor can there exist the life of mind.
>
> ŁUKASIEWICZ 1906: 6

It should be emphasized that formulations such as the above quotation from Łukasiewicz are not the most fortunate. Here are the reasons for this "misfortune".

Let's assume that individual I_1 has property W_1. This property W_1 is an individual property of individual I_1. So, when we say that some individual I_2 other than individual I_1 also has property W_1, we express it inaccurately: individual I_2 can have at most individual property W_2 more or less similar to individual property W_1. Properties such as W_1 and W_2, i.e., individual properties similar to one another are sometimes combined into a class: let it be in this case class W. Some philosophers – call them Platonists – identify such a class, i.e., class W, with an appropriate general property, and they say about appropriate individual properties W_1 and W_2 that they fall under general property W, or that they exemplify this general property W. Let us retain the terms "individual property" and "general property" without deciding what their ontic status is but only acknowledging that the relation between an individual property and a general property that is exemplified by the first (individual) property can be represented by the relation of being-an-element (in the sense of set theory). Let us also assume that we know what the relation of possessing is, namely, the relation which holds between a given individual and its individual property. Let us call this relation "R".

Well, to avoid misunderstandings, and sometimes even paradoxes, which have their sources in careless phrases such as those in the above quotation from Łukasiewicz, we should remember the following things.[4]

---

4 It is worth noting that Tadeusz Kotarbiński's nihilistic position as to general objects (according to which general objects do not exist because they are contradictory) resulted from his

Firstly, the properties belonging to concepts are not individual properties, but general ones.

Secondly, the relation between a given concept and a certain general property belonging to this concept (let us signify this relation with letter S) is not identical to relation R; we cannot say that this concept *has* (possesses) the aforementioned property.

Thirdly, among properties being in relation S to a certain concept in relation S, and thus "forming" this concept, there hold various "necessary" relations described, for example, in such a way that one of these properties necessarily entails the other. I would like to make it clear that holding these relations can be accepted without getting involved in any hopeless ontological controversies. Namely, we can represent these relations –particularly that general property W necessarily entails general property U – as follows. Let me signify by means of letters W_k and U_k some individual properties that are exemplifications of general properties W and U, respectively. Then we have:

$$\bigwedge x \, [(x \text{ has property } W_k) \to [(x \text{ has property } U_k)].$$

The conceptual distinctions introduced above allow a proper understanding of Łukasiewicz's division of the constitutive and consecutive properties belonging to concepts:

> With respect to the necessary relations within which features of an object can stand, we normally distinguish two categories: we call *consecutive* those features of an object that result with necessity from its other features, and we call *constitutive* those features from which the former consecutively *result*. A consecutive feature of a circle, for instance, is "equality of all its diameters", because this feature results with necessity from a constitutive feature of a circle: "equal distance of all points of the circumference from the middle".
>
> ŁUKASIEWICZ 1906: 7

---

not distinguishing between properties *belonging* to concepts and properties *possessed* by these concepts (e.g., reality belongs to the concept of woman, and unreality is possessed by this concept; generality does not belong to the concept of woman, and non-generality is possessed by the concept [Kotarbiński 1949: 36–37]). In Poland, Roman Ingarden was one of the philosophers who were conscious of these nuances; Ingarden said that the properties belonging to concepts create the *content* of these concepts.

6   Analysis of Concepts

Let us agree that "to analyze" a given object means to indicate the parts of this object. Analysis is an intentional action. Accidentally breaking a glass is not an analysis, even though certain parts of this glass are extracted as a result of its breaking. Analysis is guided by a leading question ("What elements does this object have?", "How many parts does this object have?", etc.). Anything which has any parts of any kind (or which we suppose has these parts), or anything which is a part of something of any type, can be the object of analysis. Therefore, in fact, any entity can be the object of analysis.

Thus, to give an analysis of a concept means to indicate its parts. If we agree that the general properties of concepts are their parts, then to analyze a concept means indicating the properties of which this concept is composed. The final result of analyzing the concept of x is the definition of the term "x" (or, in other words, is the essential description of x).

This is what Łukasiewicz states:

> To give a logical analysis of some concept, that is, of some abstract object, means finding all its features and examining the relations among them, with a particular attention to the necessary relations, that is, singling out the constitutive and consecutive features. To give a logical analysis of the concept of cause means therefore finding all features of the abstract object called a cause and examining the relations among them while at the same time indicating the constitutive and consecutive features of this concept.
>
> ŁUKASIEWICZ 1906: 7

Łukasiewicz points to some difficulties of this conception of analysis. Firstly, he is aware that it is impossible to indicate all properties of objects (even abstract ones). Secondly, a more serious objection is explained as follows:

> When a chemist wants to examine the chemical composition of calcium carbonate, he needs to have a sample of this substance in front of him; and when a psychologist wants to study the immanent state that appears when someone presents a concept to himself, he needs to have this psychic state in front of him [my emphasis]. Calcium carbonate can be found in nature and a psychic state can be brought about in oneself. Abstract objects, however, do not exist in the real sense, like pieces of calcium; it is only the human mind that creates them. Some have a given meaning, like, e.g., the concept of circle in geometry; thus, whoever wishes to analyze a circle

knows what they are to analyze. *But other abstract objects are not specified like this, the concept of cause being one of them* [my emphasis].
ŁUKASIEWICZ 1906: 7–8

Łukasiewicz's comment here reveals two problems. Firstly, it signals the problem of what the basis (corpus) of analysis is; secondly, it raises the problem of the constructive element of analyzing. These two problems will be discussed in the following sections.

7   Foundation of Analysis

How to establish the properties that constitute a given concept? It seems that analysis of a given concept can be founded on varied material.

The foundation of the analysis of a concept can be (purely) objective, (purely) linguistic, or mixed. Let me signify the first foundation with the term "objective basis", and the second with the term "linguistic basis" of analyzing.

When performing an analysis with an objective basis, we must have direct access to the object under investigation; e.g., an objective analysis of the concept of woman takes place when we examine a real woman; an objective analysis of polonium takes place when we observe and research a real piece of polonium. The linguistic basis for analysis can be a set of language utterances concerning the analyzed entity. In the case of analysis of the meaning of a given expression, the following entities can constitute such a basis: (a) the existing definitions of an analyzed expression; (b) complex expressions (viz., language contexts) in which an analyzed expression occurs (possibly with situational contexts in which it is uttered); (c) lingual intuitions of the person uttering an analyzed expression. Let us note that in the case of our own lingual intuitions, we are also ultimately dealing with our actual or imagined uses of a given expression. In such a case, a linguistic basis can be called "introspective" as opposed to "extraspective", in the case of the utterances of others.[5]

In any case, the material for the analysis which is the point of departure for definitions is sometimes selected more or less randomly.

Take objective bases. We rarely have access to all designata of an expression the connotations of which we seek (i.e., to all entities falling under the analyzed

---

5 Some (e.g., phenomenologists) are inclined to believe that the meaning of expressions can be attained in nonverbal ways. I am not going to prejudge whether this is actually true, but if it is, this foundation can be called an "extraverbal basis". Obviously, we would only have access to our own extraverbal basis.

concept). Therefore, we rely on a certain selection of these objects: either random or selected because of certain criteria (e.g., typicality or, conversely, non-typicality).

The case is similar with linguistic bases. Let us take option (a), that is, relying on our analysis of existing definitions. We can establish in advance that the point of departure of our definition of a given expression consists in all existing definitions occurring in encyclopedias and dictionaries published in English between 1950 and 2020. However, sometimes we rely on a few definitions, randomly selected. As for option (b), we can make use of a linguistic basis in the form of a collection of works (either academic or literary) by a given author or coming from specific circles of speakers/writers. Finally, we can obtain our linguistic basis by way of experiment, that is, arranging suitable linguistic situations. It seems that this latter way of obtaining material occurs among philosophers affiliated with so-called experimental philosophy. Our own intuitions can also be more or less random, more or less critical, more or less "tainted with theory", etc.

Taking this or that foundation as the point of departure of our analysis is a question of methodological choice. It is however important to be fully aware of what, in a given case, the foundation is of our analytical research .

The following quotation shows that Łukasiewicz was aware of various possible foundations of analysis. He wrote about foundations of analyzing the concept of cause:

> In our everyday life, we use the expression "cause" very often, and we normally know what to call a cause and what not; however, we usually are not aware *why*, that is, due to what features we call some things, and not other things, causes. Hence, we always speak of some cause or other, but a cause *in general*, as an abstract object, is in our life only an empty sound. In science, this term is used to signify some *concept*; however, in this case, there is another difficulty, for different scientists determine this concept differently. Each of them creates therefore a different abstract object which he signifies with the same word. Thus, whoever wishes to analyze the concept of cause encounters a serious problem. What is it that he is to analyze? Certain concrete objects that we call causes in our everyday language, or abstract objects created by this or that scientist?
>
> ŁUKASIEWICZ 1906: 8

Łukasiewicz's analytical foundations in the paper on cause include some simple examples of causes and definitions given by other scientists and philosophers.

8   Constructive Elements of Analysis

For many reasons, it may happen that analysis of concepts has to be combined with reconstruction or even construction of this concept. Both reconstruction and construction usually have a "remedial" aspect; they are undertaken when the results of an analysis *sensu stricto* are unsatisfactory.

Suppose that the point of departure of our analysis of the meaning of "*T*" (the concept of *T*) are some objects habitually referred to as *T*s (instances of *T*), namely some objects called "*T*". Indicating the connotation of a given term (namely: the content of a given concept) with a given, habitual denotation of this term (given instances of this concept) can be troublesome.

Firstly, it is sometimes the case that for objects referred to with a given term it is impossible to determine a sequence of such properties which would be inherent to all and only those objects (therefore, denotation is not a predicative set). Then we face two options: either we accept that the term under investigation is ambiguous or we accept that it should not be used with reference to some discussed objects. Depending on the option, we can either ascertain the ambiguity of the term and provide a separate (non-eclectic) reporting definition for each meaning or indicate a connotation of the given term only for this subset of objects referred to with the term for which the proper (consistent) sequence of properties exists. The second option, that is, formulating a stipulative (regulative) definition, can have the result that some habitual uses of the defined term turn out to be incorrect in the newly defined meaning.

Secondly, it is sometimes the case that the denotation itself is not precisely determined, that is, it is impossible to determine whether certain objects belong to the denotation or not. We say that the term we want to define (or the corresponding concept) is vague. In that case, we may sharpen the denotation of the term so that determining whether a given object belongs to the denotation or not is always in principle (that is, with adequate objective knowledge of this object) feasible. In that way, a regulative connotative definition (which indicates the properties inherent to all and only elements of the sharpened denotation) is produced.

Let us consider a different situation, namely, that at the point of departure we have at our disposal an existing, explicitly stated connotative definition of a given term, apart from the implicitly provided denotation. It would then be natural to juxtapose the definition with its customary denotation and check whether the properties enumerated in the connotative definition actually are inherent to all and only designata, and therefore, if they well determine the denotation. If this is not the case, correcting the existing definition would be the next step. Then a regulative connotative definition (with respect to the existing one) is created.

It is also sometimes the case that, although the connotation indicated in the definition corresponds to a given denotation, a different sequence of connotative properties is sought for a specific purpose. This is the case, for example, when we wish to define a given term with concepts belonging to the language of a specific scientific discipline, or when we wish to adapt a term defined in one scientific discipline for the purposes of another. A definition which indicates a connotation of a term with a given denotation and for the purposes of a given scientific discipline can be called "an explicative definition". Using a finished conceptual network (of a given scientific discipline) to construct a definition is often connected with deregulation of the existing denotation.

It is good to be aware that, for instance, when we proceed to analyze a philosophical concept, the weight of the possible empirical material of our analysis is often huge. It includes both everyday utterances and philosophers' utterances, as well as often numerous proposals of more or less successful definitions. No wonder that this empirical material must sometimes be drastically limited if such a definitional undertaking is to be successful. Philosophical analysis of a given concept focuses then only on, e.g., the utterances of one philosopher or on several common definitions, or on linguistic intuitions of a philosopher-analyst.

Wherever analysis does not lead to reporting definitions, it is an analysis associated with the (re)construction of concepts. This situation was described by Łukasiewicz in the following way:

> There is, it seems to me, only one way around this difficulty. We need to accept that there is no pregiven abstract object called cause that we could analyze, and that such an object has to be yet *created*. And to create, that is, to construct, some abstract object, is to find certain features, consider which can be combined and which removed, and by this means arrive at a whole set of features connected by relations constituting the very object in question.
>
> ŁUKASIEWICZ 1906: 8

When it is impossible or improper from some point of view to indicate the analysis which satisfies all intuitions and is in accordance with every earlier usage of a term, it is necessary to propose a (re)constructed concept. According to Łukasiewicz, this is a standard situation in any discipline and one should not be surprised by it or by its consequences.

Perhaps this concept will appear as slightly different from usual definitions of a cause found in logic textbooks or works of metaphysics; perhaps it will not even be always consistent with what our everyday speech names as a cause in a more or less shaky and imprecise way. In case of such inconsistency, I will not be able to provide any remedy. It would simply require *breaking the habit* of calling a cause something that does not fall under the concept of cause, just as one needs to break the habit of calling carbonic acid the compound symbolized by CO_2, which is not an acid, but an acid anhydride.

ŁUKASIEWICZ 1906: 11

9 Ideal and Real Concepts and Requirements for Satisfactory Analysis

If scientists and philosophers are allowed to (re)construct new concepts, are there any restrictions of their fantasy in this domain? Łukasiewicz gives some suggestions in this matter.

Firstly, he distinguishes between ideal and real concepts. Let me quote his words *in extenso*:

When, for instance, a mathematician talks about a number *e*, or about a four-dimensional figure, when a logician forms the concept of reason and consequence, or of contradictory objects, he does not care whether in the actually existing world there are any concrete objects which correspond to these abstract objects. No one doubts that there is no four-dimensional figure or a contradictory object, such as, e.g., "wooden iron"; however, a mathematician calculates the dimensions of that abstract figure, and a logician examines the features even of contradictory objects. Such abstract objects that the human mind creates regardless of whether something corresponds to them in reality or not, and, thus, which are not intended to cover concrete objects, may be called *ideal* abstract objects.

A physicist, chemist, biologist, psychologist, sociologist … deal not only with concrete, particular objects, such as an instance of a ball rolling on a sloping gutter, a certain piece of calcium carbonate, a specimen of a nerve cell under a microscope, successive changes of afterimages in a given man's consciousness, the workers' strike in Łódź in 1892 – but also with abstract objects, that is, concepts [such as] acceleration of heavy bodies, a neuron in general, an afterimage in general, a strike in general.

Each of these scientists, while creating concepts of acceleration of gravity, calcium carbonate, a neuron, an afterimage or strike, seeks, however,
to construct abstract objects such that some concrete objects fall under
them. A chemist, for instance, certainly does not want even to hear about
a "calcium carbonate" that besides having one atom of calcium, one
atom of carbonate, and three atoms of oxygen, includes also two atoms
of hydrogen; for in all likelihood in reality there are no combinations of
chemical composition of H_2CaCO_3. Such abstract objects that the mind
creates *with regard to* reality, that is, which are supposed to cover some
concrete objects, we may call abstract objects with *real* meaning or simply real abstract objects.

ŁUKASIEWICZ 1906: 9

So, real concepts are concepts that correspond to some real (empirical) objects;
ideal concepts do not have to correspond to anything real. The first group is
characteristic for empirical sciences, the second group for the non-empirical
ones.[6]

According to Łukasiewicz, the only restriction placed on the analysis of
ideal concepts is consistency, or, let me say more precisely: consistency within
the properties *belonging* to these concepts. And real concepts must additionally correspond to their real instances:

An essential condition that all scientific concepts, both real and ideal,
must meet is that *they cannot have contrary or contradictory features*,
that is, features that necessarily exclude one another. It follows from this
condition that all scientific concepts must be unambiguous, that is, they
have to have some strictly defined features. For if at some time we assign
some features to an object and then different features at a later time, we
create an object that contains a contradiction. Unambiguity is therefore a consecutive feature of scientific concepts because it follows with
necessity from another feature which we can simply call the feature of
non-contradiction. "A geometrical circle" or "calcium carbonate" are, for
instance, scientific concepts; but "integer π" is not, because the features
"integer" and "irrational" exclude one another. Words denoting scientific
concepts are called *terms*.

---

6   Of course, some ideal concepts (such as the concept of circle or the concept of number) have
    some empirical source but finally they are considered independently of reality.

The feature of non-contradiction is sufficient when it comes to scientific ideal objects. However, real abstract objects, if they are to be scientific concepts, must also be *consistent with reality*, thus, they have to have such features that we either discover or at least surmise about the corresponding concrete objects. This is why we cannot, for instance, add two atoms of hydrogen to the chemical composition of calcium carbonate, because so construed the concept would not be consistent with the calcium carbonate that we find in nature.

ŁUKASIEWICZ 1906: 10

It would seem, therefore, that when constructing real concepts, any general property or any (internally consistent) sequence of general properties exemplified in the real world can be used in creating such a concept. In scientific practice, however, at least two additional conditions are imposed on such concepts. The first condition is that the newly introduced concept can be "embedded" in the already existing conceptual apparatus of a science, and thus that the objects which exemplify these concepts are related with some necessary connections to the objects that exemplify the concepts already belonging to this apparatus. The second condition is that the entire conceptual apparatus – enriched by means of a newly constructed concept – should be able to describe a particular field of reality in terms of an aspect "significant" for a given researcher or group of researchers.

10   Analysis and Local versus Global Methods

Let us repeat that analysis of concepts and establishing the senses of terms is a starting point of many further philosophical tasks, for instance establishing the logical value of theses or axiomatizing procedures. Thus, to analyze a certain concept may be a self-sufficient aim, but it may also be a step in a more complex procedure. This may be described by introducing the concept of local and global methods.

Assume that to achieve goal G, one must achieve intermediate goals G_1, G_2, and G_3. Assume also that we have a certain method of making G_1 occur. We shall then say that the method to make G_1 occur is local with respect to the global method of making G occur. Yet, the method of making G_1 occur could be a global method relative to the objective of making G_1 occur. (The same can be repeated with goals G_2 and G_3).

It should be stressed that the globality and locality of methods should be relativized to a given goal. For instance, the truth-table method is a global method

of checking whether a given formula is a tautology of classic propositional calculus. However, it is not a global method to check whether a given sentence
results from another (as, apart from checking for tautology, one would also
have to build a scheme of the sentence in question, etc.). An analysis of the
term "cause" is a global method of determining what this word means, but it is
only a local method in the process of responding to the question whether the
law of causality is true.

On the other hand, the method of analysis is also a composite procedure,
and to carry out such an analysis (and construction, if necessary) one has to
take several steps making use of some local (with respect to the analytic aims)
methods. For instance, there are methods of choosing the analytic corpus,
establishing the properties of objects, extracting the sense of words from the
context in which they appear, etc. Among these local methods a special role is
played by various kinds of reasoning.

Łukasiewicz stresses that in the analysis of real concepts, both inductive
and deductive reasoning have to be used.

> I noted in §4 that "in constructing the concept of cause I intend to create
> an abstract object such that it covers all concrete and real causes, the
> existence of which we admit both in the external world and in the world
> of spiritual phenomena; and I do not mean some ideal object to which, as
> with a four-dimensional figure, perhaps nothing corresponds in reality".
> [...] Thus, since I conceive a cause as some *real* abstract object, then I can
> follow only one path to create it – the inductive method. [...] However,
> neither in this nor in any other inductive research can we stop here. The
> features gleaned by means of the inductive method are but material that
> requires scientific elaboration. This involves defining the exact meaning
> of the features that have been uncovered, examining their consecutive
> features, indicating the relations among them and checking whether
> some contrary or inconsistent features have not slipped into the content
> of the concept. In such investigations, we will no longer be able to use the
> inductive method but will need the *deductive method*. All this labour is
> simplified insofar as others, by these or similar means, have already tried
> to discover certain features of the concept of cause; but it needs to be
> checked whether they have not made mistakes in their research.
>
> ŁUKASIEWICZ 1906: 24

The claim that in the investigation of empirical domains, when establishing
empirical concepts and empirical laws, both inductive and deductive elements

are necessary, was accepted long before the 20th century discussion between the inductionists and deductionists.

11 Closing Remarks

To end, I will (a) draw together the most important elements of Łukasiewicz's conception of analysis of concepts, (b) sketch the place of Łukasiewicz's conception within the metaphilosophy of the Lvov-Warsaw School, and (c) make some remarks on Łukasiewicz's conception through the prism of the history of analytic philosophy as such.

Let us summarize Łukasiewicz's standpoint concerning concepts and their analysis:

(1) Concepts are meanings of terms and (from the ontological point of view) they are abstract objects which are sequences of (general) properties. Concepts in the logical sense are not the contents of anyone's thought. However, concepts are *created* by a human mind.

(2) In the content of concepts, there are constitutive and consecutive properties.

(3) Analysis of a given concept consists in indicating properties – especially constitutive properties – belonging to this concept.

(4) If an examined concept is not "ready" (i.e., a given term does not have an established connotation), the concept should be constructed.

(5) The only restriction on the construction of ideal concepts is logical consistency.

(6) Real concepts are connotations of terms designating real objects. They must refer to reality.

(7) The construction of real concepts is based on establishing the properties of some real objects.

(8) The results of concept construction may be non-consistent with the semantic intuitions of persons using words to which a constructed concept is attached.

What was the significance of Łukasiewicz's conception within the Lvov-Warsaw School?

Łukasiewicz's conception was preceded and by all means influenced – both positively and negatively – by the conceptions of his teacher, Kazimierz Twardowski. A commonly cited example of a negative influence is Łukasiewicz's distinction between concepts in a logical sense and concepts in a psychological sense. His paper [Łukasiewicz 1906] may be immediately understood as a declaration against his teacher's psychologism. However, it is not the case that Twardowski ignored concepts in the logical sense, and that considering concepts as meanings of terms was Łukasiewicz's novelty with respect to his teacher. In his early works, such as [Twardowski 1898] and [Twardowski 1903], as well as in his textbook [Twardowski 1901], Twardowski already distinguishes between concepts in the psychological sense and concepts in the logical sense. All these works were certainly known to Łukasiewicz. There is no room here to discuss Twardowski's standpoint in detail; however, let me quote at least a short passage:

> Concepts that have been established by definition are called "scientific", "exact", or "logical". And since the concept of objects is also the meaning of the word indicating these objects, therefore people possessing scientific concepts constantly connect the same words with the same meanings. As a result, mutual communication is greatly facilitated, and at the same time one of the most important causes of erroneous reasoning is eliminated. The fixed terms are called scientific, because giving definitions of concepts, and therefore fixing them, is one of the most important tasks of scientific research.
>
> TWARDOWSKI 1901, p. 81

Twardowski states that logical concepts are the meanings of scientific terms. He adds that precise meanings are necessary tools in science and that fixing these meanings is an important task of scientists. What Łukasiewicz provides in his paper [Łukasiewicz 1906] is a proposal of how to fix the meaning of the term "cause". Moreover, he also reconstructs the procedure of establishing logical concepts before they are fixed and given in definitions. In this way, Łukasiewicz contributes seriously to Twardowski's philosophical program.

Later, younger members of the Lvov-Warsaw School provided further contributions to the theory of analysis of concepts. It is important to remember that following the "semantic turn", most of these contributions were provided within the conceptual scheme of the theory of definitions (cf. [Brożek et al. 2020], chapter 7). The most developed conception of conceptual analysis in the Lvov-Warsaw School was provided by Tadeusz Czeżowski under the label of "analytic description" (cf. [Brożek 2017]). Analytic description is a description of a real object that aims to indicate the essential properties of this object and, further, to formulate a real definition of the corresponding term. As in Łukasiewicz's case, the procedure contains constructive elements. Czeżowski states that analytic description plays a crucial role in philosophical investigations, and that it was broadly applied by Brentano and Twardowski. Surprisingly, Czeżowski never refers to Łukasiewicz's paper on the concept of cause. Generally speaking, Łukasiewicz's conception of analysis was never openly commented on by his colleagues from Twardowski's School.

Central-European analytic philosophy, as initiated by Brentano and continued by his followers (including Twardowski and his students), developed in parallel with other analytic movements. An analogy suggests itself between Łukasiewicz's antipsychologism and Fregean antipsychologism. Łukasiewicz would fully agree with Frege's claim that one should distinguish psychological questions from logical ones; there are also some common traits in how they deal with abstract objects. However, Łukasiewicz's did not know Frege's writings directly when he wrote [Łukasiewicz 1906]. In his *Diaries*, Łukasiewicz confessed:

> The first volume of [Edmund Husserl's] *Logical Investigations* made an impression in Lvov and particularly on me. I had long not liked Twardowski's psychologism, but now I refuted it completely. However, the second volume of *Logical Investigations* disappointed me. It again contained cloudy philosophical palaver which pushed me away from all German philosophers. I was surprised that there was such a great difference between two volumes of the same work. Later, it became clear to me that in the first volume it was not Husserl that was talking to me but someone much greater: Gottlob Frege, whose results Husserl used in his book.
>
> ŁUKASIEWICZ 2013: p. 65–66

Thus, at that time, Łukasiewicz knew Frege's idea only indirectly.[7] Łukasiewicz's conception also had other sources. First, there was his fascination with Aristotle and the scholastic tradition (marked in many places in his work). Second, despite the fact that Łukasiewicz himself considered his teacher Twardowski a psychologist, some elements of Twardowski's thought also reveal anti-psychologistic tendencies. One was the conception of object, which Łukasiewicz mentions and adopts in his paper.[8]

---

7 Łukasiewicz's paper on the concept of cause was prepared during his stay in Louvain, in the first half of 1905. Later that year, after returning to Lvov, Łukasiewicz first learned about Russell's work. At first, Marian Borowski, Łukasiewicz's colleague, asked him for help with Russell's article "On the notion of order". Then, Łukasiewicz bought the book *Principles of mathematics*, studied it carefully, and later considered it the best of Russell's books. This was also probably his second way to Frege (as *Principles* contains a big chapter on Frege's conception). Cf. [Łukasiewicz 2013: 67].

8 In this context, it is worth mentioning that another of Twardowski's students and Łukasiewicz's friend, Bronisław Bandrowski, in [Bandrowski 1905], formulates anti-psychologistic comments quite similar to Łukasiewicz's.

There are obvious analogies between Łukasiewicz's conception of analysis and construction and Rudolf Carnap's later conception of explication. Carnap was interested in logical analysis of concepts and in improving conceptual schemes of sciences from the very beginning of his career but his conception of explication was clarified in the 1940s. In [Carnap 1947], Carnap wrote:

> The task of making more exact a vague or not quite exact concept used in everyday life or in an earlier stage of scientific or logical development, or rather of replacing it by a newly constructed, more exact concept, belongs among the most important tasks of logical analysis and logical construction. We call this the task of explicating, or of giving an *explication* for, the earlier concept.
>
> CARNAP 1947: 8–9

The analogies between Łukasiewicz's and Carnap's ideas are clear. The aim of both procedures is to establish and fix the sense of terms. In both procedures the results often lead to changing the language habits of the users of the reconstructed language. In both conceptions, there is no place for the paradox of analysis. Finally, both Łukasiewicz's and Carnap's conceptions belong to the reconstructionist branch of analytic philosophy (as opposed to the descriptionist branch). It is certainly good that the translation of Łukasiewicz's paper has finally been published, for now there are no longer any reasons to neglect it in research on the history of metaphilosophy.

Acknowledgement

The text was prepared as part of the project 2015/18/E/HS1/00478 "Philosophy from the Methodological Point of View", financed by the National Science Centre (Poland).

Bibliography

Bandrowski, Bronisław (1905). *O analizie mowy i jej znaczeniu dla filozofii* [On the Analysis of Speech and its Significance for Philosophy]. Rzeszów: J.A. Pelar.

Bocheński, Józef M. (1954). *The Methods of Contemporary Thought.* Dordrecht 1965: D. Reidel Publishing Company.

Brożek, Anna (2017). Opis analityczny jako metoda filozoficzna [Analytical Description and a Philosophical Method]. *Filozofia Nauki* vol. XXV, No. 2, pp. 57–87.

Brożek, Anna et al. (2020). *Antiirrationalism. Philosophical Methods in the Lvov-Warsaw School*. Warszawa: Semper.

Carnap, Rudolf (1947). *Meaning and Necessity*, Chicago 1956: University of Chicago Press.

Kotarbiński, Tadeusz (1929). *Gnosiology. The Scientific Approach to the Theory of Knowledge*. Oxford & Wrocław 1966: Pergamon Press & Ossolineum.

Łukasiewicz, Jan (1906). Analysis and Construction of the Concept of Cause. In this volume: pp. 3–66.

Łukasiewicz, Jan (1922). On Determinism. [In:] [Łukasiewicz 1970], pp. 110–128.

Łukasiewicz, Jan (1928). O metodę w filozofii [Appeal for the Method in Philosophy]. [In:] [Łukasiewicz 1998], pp. 41–42.

Łukasiewicz, Jan (1970). *Selected Works*. Amsterdam & Warszawa: North-Holland Publishing Company & PWN.

Łukasiewicz, Jan (1998). *Logika i metafizyka* [Logic and Methaphysics]. *Miscellanea*. Warszawa: Wydział Filozofii i Socjologii UW.

Łukasiewicz, Jan (2013). *Pamiętnik* [Diary]. Warszawa: Semper.

Twardowski, Kazimierz (1898). Imageries and Concepts. *Axiomathes* vol. VI, No. 1, pp. 79–104.

Twardowski, Kazimierz (1901). *Zasadnicze pojęcia logiki i dydaktyki* [Main Concepts of Logic and Didactics]. Lwów: Towarzystwo Pedagogiczne.

Twardowski, Kazimierz (1903). The Essence of Concepts. [In:] [Twardowski 1999], pp. 73–97.

Twardowski, Kazimierz (1999). *On Actions, Products and Other Topics in Philosophy*. Amsterdam: Rodopi.

Witwicki, Władysław (1900). Analiza psychologiczna ambicji [Psychological Analysis of Ambition]. *Przegląd Filozoficzny* vol. III, No. 4, pp. 26–49.

CHAPTER 7

On the Causal Role of Limit Properties in Physics

Tomasz Bigaj

1   Background

Physics is replete with fundamental laws that take the form of differential equations – from Newton's second law of dynamics, through Maxwell's laws of electromagnetism, to Einstein's field equations of GTR. And yet philosophers cannot come to an agreement on the ontological status and role of derivative-based physical properties, such as instantaneous velocities or accelerations.[1] The typical problems discussed in this context are questions of whether instantaneous velocities and the like are truly instantaneous in the sense of characterizing physical systems at dimensionless temporal points, whether they can be used as parts of the momentary states of systems, whether (and in what sense) they are reducible to more fundamental properties, and so on. In this article, I will address yet another related question whether derivative properties can play a causal role – i.e. whether they can be causes and effects. I will discuss the main arguments against the supposition that derivative properties can participate in causal relations, and I will show that they are not conclusive. Derivative properties are not only capable of being causes and effects – they turn out to be indispensable in this role if we want to give proper causal accounts of physical phenomena.

A derivative quantity is a quantity characterized in terms of the mathematical operation of differentiation. We can explain the details of this operation using the standard example of instantaneous velocities. Let $x(t)$ be a continuous and differentiable function of position. The instantaneous velocity at a moment t_0 is typically defined as the first derivative of $x(t)$, i.e. as the limit of an infinite sequence of ratios $\dfrac{x(t_0 + \Delta t) - x(t_0)}{\Delta t}$ when Δt approaches zero. This limit, in turn, is explicated with the help of the famous Cauchy-Weierstrass

---

1   As an example of a difference of opinion in this area, see the extended debate between Frank Artzenius and Sheldon Smith on the nature of instantaneous velocities that began with [Artzenius 2000], followed up by a critique in [Smith 2003a], followed up by a quick tit for tat ([Artzenius 2003], [Smith 2003b]).

© TOMASZ BIGAJ, 2022 | DOI:10.1163/9789004522244_009

formula, which leads to the following condition that the instantaneous velocity $v(t_0)$ has to satisfy:

$$\forall \varepsilon > 0 \exists \delta > 0 \forall t \left(\left| t - t_0 \right| < \delta \to \left| \frac{x(t) - x(t_0)}{t - t_0} - v(t_0) \right| < \varepsilon \right) \tag{1}$$

In words: no matter how small a number ε we select, we can always make the

difference between the ratio $\dfrac{x(t) - x(t_0)}{t - t_0}$ and the number $v(t_0)$ even smaller

than ε by selecting arguments t close enough to t_0 (closer than some δ). For
obvious reasons, derivative properties are also referred to as limit properties
(or neighborhood properties). We will give a precise definition of limit properties in Sec. 4, from which it will follow that all derivative properties are limit
properties but not *vice versa*.

Formula (1) can admit two interpretations. The most natural interpretation
is that it is a contextual definition of instantaneous velocity $v(t_0)$, and hence
expresses a necessary truth on the basis of the meaning associated with the
symbol $v(t_0)$. Another possibility is that (1) is a law of nature, whose truth is
contingent only. Under the second interpretation the concept of instantaneous velocity is assumed to acquire its meaning independently of characteristic (1). Typically, the followers of this approach claim that the concept of
instantaneous velocity is primitive; thus, it does not admit any reductive definition. Unsurprisingly, this position is known in the literature as primitivism.
The first interpretation, on the other hand, bears the name of "reductionism",
as its proponents insist that instantaneous velocities are ultimately reducible
to trajectories and some of their mathematical properties.[2]

In the current analysis I will pay little attention to primitivism, focusing
instead on reductionism, which in my opinion better fits standard physical
practice. However, reductionism faces a serious challenge in the form of the
question about the exact relation between derivative properties and their

---

2   The main proponent of reductionism was Bertrand Russell, who revived the medieval 'at-
    at' conception of motion [Russell 1903: 473]. A similar view was defended by Kazimierz
    Ajdukiewicz [1948]. Among primitivists one can count Michael Tooley [1988], John Bigelow
    and Robert Pargetter [1990] and John Carroll [2002]. Primitivists believe that it is logically (or
    metaphysically) possible, even though not nomically possible, that an object could have an
    instantaneous velocity distinct from the actual value of the derivative of its trajectory.

ontological bases. If instantaneous velocities are reducible to positions (trajectories in space), then it seems that the instantaneous velocity $v(t_0)$ of a body should be reducible to the position of this body at t_0. But clearly fixing the position of the body at a given moment does not fix its velocity. A given position $x(t_0)$ is compatible with any value of $v(t_0)$, including zero velocity (when the object is at rest). Mathematically, the first derivative of a given function $x(t)$ at t_0 represents the slope of the function, i.e. the measure of how 'steep' the function is at this point. But the value of the slope at t_0 depends on how the function behaves in the vicinity of t_0 (in the neighborhood of t_0). It does not make sense mathematically to ask about the slope of a single point $x(t_0)$, because the concept of the tangent to a point is not well-defined, and the slope is just equivalent to the angle that the tangent makes with the horizontal line on the function's graph.

Considerations like these led some philosophers to the conclusion that derivative properties are not truly instantaneous, but instead characterize their bearers in some non-zero intervals. We will return to this issue later. For now let us move to the problem of causal explanations involving derivative properties in physics.

2   Causal Explanations in Classical Mechanics

A typical problem considered in classical mechanics is how to calculate the trajectory of an object given all the forces acting upon this object. The relevant law applicable to this case is of course the second law of dynamics, connecting the value of the net force $F(t)$ on an object at a moment t with the object's instantaneous acceleration $a(t)$ at the very same moment:[3]

$$F\left(t\right) = ma\left(t\right) \tag{2}$$

The second law admits an obvious causal interpretation, according to which the fact that the acceleration of an object takes on a given value at moment t is caused by the force exerted upon this object at t. However, in order to determine the trajectory of the object, we have to move from acceleration to the sequence of positions that the object occupies during its motion. Instantaneous acceleration is defined as the first derivative of velocity with

---

3   For simplicity's sake I will ignore the fact that force and acceleration are vectors, not scalars.

respect to time: $a(t) = \dfrac{dv(t)}{dt}$. Knowing the value of the acceleration of a body at time t is not sufficient to calculate the value of its instantaneous velocity; the acceleration merely tells us how fast the velocity changes at t, not what its absolute value is. In order to calculate the value of $v(t)$ we have to know what the *initial* velocity at a given preceding moment t_0 was, and we have to know the values of the acceleration in all the intervening moments between t_0 and t. The appropriate integral formula for velocity is as follows:

$$v(t) = v(t_0) + \int_{t_0}^{t} a(\tau) d\tau \tag{3}$$

If we wanted to give a causal interpretation of the above formula, it would most probably be something like this. The velocity of an object at time t is caused by the initial velocity at an earlier time t_0 and the values of the acceleration at *all* moments between t_0 and t.[4] Neither acceleration nor the initial velocity are *complete* causes (in the sense of being sufficient for the effect); they are only *partial* causes. (However, in accordance with common practice I will continue to refer to partial causes as being causes *simpliciter* of an appropriate effect.) The combination of the initial velocity and the acceleration function, on the other hand, *is* a complete cause of velocity $v(t)$.[5] It is worth noting here that while the causal relation between the force and acceleration is temporally instantaneous, in the sense that the cause and effect are simultaneous with one another, all the partial causes of velocity $v(t)$ lie in the past of t.[6]

---

4   The values of the acceleration at the endpoints of the interval (t_0, t) are irrelevant to the value of the entire integral and therefore can be dropped.

5   The distinction between partial and complete causes used above nicely fits into the framework of John Mackie's INUS conception of causation [Mackie 1965]. Mackie's definition of an INUS condition for a given event E is well known: it is an Insufficient but Necessary part of an Unnecessary but Sufficient condition of E. In our example both the initial velocity and the intervening values of acceleration are INUS conditions for the value $v(t)$: taken separately they are not sufficient for the velocity at t to assume a particular value, but they are necessary parts of the sufficient condition of $v(t)$ (for instance, given the actual circumstances, if the initial velocity was different, the value $v(t)$ would also be different).

6   Of course this past is *infinitesimally* close to t, as the values of acceleration at *all* moments preceding t are relevant to the value $v(t)$. Thus, there is no *temporal gap* between the complete cause and its effect. We will return to this issue in Sec. 5.

The same mathematical procedure leads from the values of instantaneous velocity at times earlier than t to the position of the body at t (and, consequently, to its trajectory). Again, the instantaneous velocity $v(t)$ does not determine the position $x(t)$ of the body, but only the rate of change of the position at t. The formula expressing position $x(t)$ has to contain the initial position at an earlier moment t_0:

$$x(t) = x(t_0) + \int_{t_0}^{t} v(\tau) d\tau \qquad (4)$$

The causal explanation for the fact that a body occupies position $x(t)$ at moment t can be thus given as follows. At an initial time t_0 the body occupied position $x(t_0)$ and had velocity $v(t_0)$. At every moment t' between t_0 and t, the value of the net force $F(t')$ causally determines the value of the acceleration $a(t')$, according to Eq. 2. For every moment $t' \in (t_0, t)$, the totality of all values of the acceleration in the open interval (t_0, t') plus the initial velocity $v(t_0)$, causally determine the instantaneous velocity $v(t')$, as prescribed by Eq. 3. And the totality of all values of the velocity at times between t_0 and t, together with the initial position $x(t_0)$ causally determine the position of the object at t (Eq. 4). In this picture the values of the force and the initial velocity and position act as causes, the position of the body at time t is the effect, and the intervening values of acceleration and velocity at times between t_0 and t are both causes and effects.

Figure 7.1 below illustrates the web of causal connections in the considered case. The value $x(t)$ on the right side of the diagram is causally determined by the (integrated) totality of the values of velocity in the open interval (t_0, t) plus the initial value $x(t_0)$. Each value $v(t')$ in turn is causally determined by the totality of values of acceleration in the open interval (t_0, t') plus the initial value $v(t_0)$ (the diagram contains only one such totality causally determining a particular value $v(t')$, but it is understood that analogous totalities should be attached via arrows to every other value of velocity). The blue typeface indicates that the appropriate values do not contribute to the value of the integral and merely set the limits of the integral (see ft. 4). This ensures that the causes of $v(t')$ and $x(t)$ are totalities of facts that temporally precede and yet come infinitesimally close to their effects. At the very beginning of the causal chain, each value of acceleration $a(t)$ is causally determined by the corresponding simultaneous value of force $F(t)$.

However, it is possible to substantially simplify the above causal story by eliminating from it the intermediate elements. Mathematically, all the

$$F(t_0) \rightarrow a(t_0) \left.\begin{matrix} \\ \vdots \\ \\ \end{matrix}\right\} \begin{matrix} v(t_0) \\ \vdots \\ \end{matrix}$$

$$F(t') \rightarrow a(t') \left.\begin{matrix} \\ \end{matrix}\right\} \rightarrow v(t') \left.\begin{matrix} \\ \vdots \\ \\ \end{matrix}\right\} \rightarrow x(t)$$

$$v(t_0) \qquad v(t) \\ x(t_0)$$

FIGURE 7.1   The 'three-stage' causal model of motion in classical mechanics

equations (1) – (3) can be replaced by one 'cumulative' equation connecting position $x(t)$ with the acting forces and the initial positions and velocities as follows:

$$x(t) = x(t_0) + v(t_0)(t - t_0) + \frac{1}{m} \int_{t_0}^{t} \int_{t_0}^{t'} F(\tau) \, d\tau \, dt' \tag{5}$$

According to Eq. 5, the only causally relevant factors contributing to the position occupied by the body at t are: the initial position and velocity at t_0 and the acting forces in the interval between t_0 and t. The accelerations and velocities present in this interval may be treated as epiphenomena with no causal powers. In this simplifying picture there is no relevant 'instantaneous' causation, where the cause and effect are simultaneous. All the causal factors responsible for the body's occupying position $x(t)$ occur earlier than t (even though some of them happen infinitesimally close to t). The appropriate causal diagram illustrating this causal model will be as follows (as before, parameters typeset in blue do not contribute to the effect).

$$F(t_0) \left.\begin{matrix} \\ \vdots \\ F(t) \\ x(t_0) \\ v(t_0) \end{matrix}\right\} \rightarrow x(t)$$

FIGURE 7.2
The 'one-stage' causal model of motion

2.1   *The Bathtub Example*

In this subsection I will briefly mention an interesting case of causal connections involving derivative properties, provided by an example of a bathtub with an open drain being filled up with water. This example has been used in philosophical literature to illustrate general methods of causal modelling in science, as well as to give support to some specific claims regarding causality and its connection with other philosophical concepts (e.g., decomposability and time-scale dependence).[7] In the current discussion I will use the bathtub example to draw the reader's attention to a curious case of an apparent causal circularity which can be resolved by appealing to some special features of derivative properties.

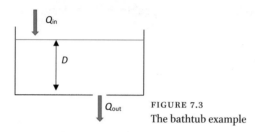

FIGURE 7.3
The bathtub example

The physical set-up is depicted on the diagram above. Q_{in} indicates the rate at which the bathtub is filled with water, while Q_{out} represents the rate at which the water flows out. Letter D stands for the depth of the water in the tub. The physics behind this process can be described in the following two equations connecting all the relevant parameters:[8]

$$Q_{out}(t) = c_1 D(t) \qquad (6)$$

$$\frac{dD}{dt} = c_2 \left(Q_{in}(t) - Q_{out}(t) \right) \qquad (7)$$

The first equation follows from the fact that the rate of the outflow is proportional to the pressure at the bottom of the tub, which in turn is proportional to the depth of the water according to a simple law of hydrostatics. The second equation indicates that the rate of change of the water level in the tub is

---

7   Cf. [Iwasaki & Simon 1993], [Weinberger 2019].
8   I am making some simplifying assumptions here, such as ignoring the size of the drain as another causal factor contributing to the value of Qout. For a more complete description of this case, see [Iwasaki & Simon 1993: 158–160] and [Weinberger 2019].

proportional to the difference between the inflow and outflow rates. In particular, if $Q_{in} = Q_{out}$, the depth of the water does not change and the system is in a state of equilibrium. However, we will consider what happens when the system is far from equilibrium, for instance when we unplug the bathtub at a certain moment t_0 when the water has a particular depth $D(t_0)$ and the inflow rate equals $Q_{in}(t_0)$.

In that case the initial outflow rate $Q_{out}(t_0)$ will be determined according to Eq. 6. This value, in turn, together with $Q_{in}(t_0)$, should determine the value of the time derivative $D'(t_0)$ in accordance with Eq. 7. And the derivative $D'(t_0)$ together with the initial value $D(t_0)$ gives rise to a new value for the depth of the water, which in turn influences parameter Q_{out}. Does that mean that Q_{out} causes itself in violation of the principle of no self-causation? In answering this question we have to properly keep track of time. The values $D'(t_0)$ and $D(t_0)$ do not determine a new value of D at moment t_0 (this would be contradictory, since we already know what the value of D at this moment is), but *right after* t_0 (infinitesimally close to t_0). Consequently, the new value of Q_{out} is taken at a moment after t_0, and this later value can be used to calculate a new value of the derivative D' at a still later time. In order to visualize this chain of causal dependencies we will make the simplifying assumption that time consists of a series of discrete moments t_0, t_1, ... Figure 7.4 below depicts the connections between the values of the relevant parameters taken at subsequent moments.

$$
\left.\begin{array}{l} D(t_0) \to Q_{out}(t_0) \\ Q_{in}(t_0) \end{array}\right\} \to \left.\begin{array}{l} D'(t_0) \\ D(t_0) \end{array}\right\} \to D(t_1) \to \left.\begin{array}{l} Q_{out}(t_1) \\ Q_{in}(t_1) \end{array}\right\} \to \left.\begin{array}{l} D'(t_1) \\ D(t_1) \end{array}\right\} \to D(t_2) \to \cdots
$$

FIGURE 7.4   The chain of causal dependencies in the bathtub case

It is worth noting that the existence of such a linear causal chain, as opposed to a circular one, is made possible by the fact that the property $D'(t_0)$, being a derivative, somehow involves the values of function D in the (infinitesimally) close future of t_0 (the exact nature of this involvement will be the subject of extensive scrutiny later in the article). This would be difficult if not outright impossible to achieve if we dealt with 'regular' non-derivative parameters confined to temporal points only.

3   Self-Causation, Common Causes and the Two-Property View

Let us go back to the general problem of causal explanations of the trajectories of physical bodies under external forces. Regardless of what specific causal model we decide to follow, one thing is certain: in classical mechanics the initial velocity of an object at moment t_0 plays an indispensable causal role in bringing about later positions of the body. However, this fact is precisely the source of the difficulty that is the central topic of this paper. Instantaneous velocities are limit properties whose ontological status, including their purported causal role, is controversial to say the least. We have already seen that there are two main interpretations of instantaneous velocities: reductionism and primitivism (with Marc Lange's dispositionalism being a third option). Under reductionism, velocities are not considered fundamental properties of objects, but instead can be reduced to ontologically more fundamental positions. But, as we have explained, this reduction is not at all straightforward. The value of instantaneous velocity at a given temporal point cannot be reduced to the position at this point but instead depends on the positions in its neighborhood. Thus, it is often said that a body's velocity reduces to relations among this body's positions. As Lange writes, according to Russelian reductionism "the body's [velocity] $v(t_0)$ is just a relation's holding among points in the body's trajectory at t_0 and neighboring points" [Lange 2005: 439]. Chunghyoung Lee echoes this view, claiming that the limit of average velocities "... is not a property belonging at an instant to a body but a relation among different positions at various different instants" [Lee 2013: 138–139].

If we take the above statements about the relational character of instantaneous velocities literally, an immediate difficulty regarding their causal role ensues. As Lange observes, it is natural to assume that if a relational fact is a cause of some event, every relatum of this relation is a cause of this event too [Lange 2005: 439]. And since by assumption, instantaneous velocity $v(t_0)$ is a relation among positions at instants other than t_0, presumably including instants that come after t_0, and $v(t_0)$ is a cause of *every* later position of the body, then it follows that some positions of the body at times later than t_0 are their own causes. This is the problem of self-causation in a nutshell. Another way to present it is in terms of causal explanation. The instantaneous velocity $v(t_0)$ is supposed to causally explain all the positions the body occupies after t_0, but since $v(t_0)$ itself involves some positions of the body after t_0, $v(t_0)$ cannot fulfil its role as an explanans (the explanation becomes circular).

The above sketch of an argument, as it stands, leaves a lot to be desired. To begin with, it is unclear how to characterize precisely the relations that instantaneous velocities are supposed to be reducible to. What exactly are the relata connected by these relations? Presumably they include some of the positions of the body at instances other than t_0. But which ones, precisely? As it turns out, no particular position occupied at a time distinct from t_0 can be said to definitely belong to the range of the purported relation. Take any time t, however close to t_0. Is the position of the body at t relevant to the value of instantaneous velocity $v(t_0)$? The answer is "no", because we can always take a neighborhood of t_0 that does not include t, and the trajectory of the body in this small neighborhood is sufficient to fix its instantaneous velocity at t_0. Thus, the velocity at t_0 can be taken as a cause of the position at t without implying that the position at t is somehow its own cause. It looks like the argument from self-causation is not only poorly stated – it is flat-out wrong.

Lange admits that the argument from self-causation can be refuted by adopting the following strategy: for every point t later than t_0 we select a neighborhood of t_0 not including t, and we interpret the instantaneous velocity at t_0 as being reducible to the relations among the positions taken within this neighborhood. However, he points out that this strategy has the undesirable consequence that the instantaneous velocity at t_0 is no longer treated as a *common cause* of all subsequent positions of the body. If we identify a particular neighborhood of t_0 as containing all factors causally relevant for the position the body assumes at t, then the trajectory in this neighborhood cannot causally explain the positions *included* in it, so for each moment within the initially selected neighborhood we have to choose an even smaller neighborhood to do the explanatory job. But this means, according to Lange, that we can't find a unique common cause for all the positions the body assumes after t_0.

The common cause argument is peculiar in that it seems to presuppose that by selecting a particular neighborhood around a temporal moment t_0 we are reducing the instantaneous velocity at t_0 to the sequence of positions taken within this neighborhood. If this were true, then in fact we would not have a single instantaneous velocity, but an infinite number of them, each associated with a particular choice of a neighborhood. But this is most certainly incorrect. Instantaneous velocities cannot be reduced to the trajectory within any specific neighborhood, since in any neighborhood of moment t_0 there are elements that are entirely irrelevant to the value of the velocity at t_0. The common cause argument seems to be based on a false premise which ignores the true nature of limit properties, which is that they can never be uniquely reduced to (or grounded in) any specific set of fundamental properties. In the next section I will approach this issue in a rigorous fashion using the distinction between grounds of properties *simpliciter* and mere *sufficient* grounds, and I will argue that instantaneous velocities are groundless properties, even though they possess an infinite number of sufficient grounds that form ordered sequences. As it turns out, both the argument from self-causation and the common cause argument are based on the incorrect presupposition of the existence of grounds for limit properties. In order to properly analyze these arguments, they have to be restated in terms that are appropriate for the peculiar case of limit properties, which do not possess grounds.

Before we begin a rigorous analysis of the relation between limit properties and their purported grounds, let me briefly address yet another strategy of how to deal with the self-causation problem that is discussed in the literature. Again, the idea goes back to Lange, who suggested that the problem of self-causation could be easily dispensed with if we defined instantaneous velocities as the time-derivatives of the position function 'from below' ('from the left'). The derivative from below at t_0 is calculated by taking a sequence

of ratios $\dfrac{x(t_0) - x(t)}{t_0 - t}$, where $t < t_0$. This variant of the definition of a deriva-

tive ensures that the values of the differentiated function $x(t)$ that it takes for the arguments above t_0 are irrelevant to the value of the derivative at t_0. If we defined instantaneous velocities in that fashion, they could be safely assumed to be causes of later trajectories without infringing upon the principle of no self-causation. However, an immediate objection to this solution is that it works in one direction only – it enables properties defined as derivatives from below to be causes, but not to be effects. Lange points out that if we assumed that a derivative-from-below property at t_0 is caused by some factor at t_0 (for instance instantaneous acceleration, interpreted according to the derivative-from-below proposal, is caused by a force), this seems to imply that the past positions taken at moments just before t_0 that ground this property are also caused by an event at t_0. Since retro-causation is no less problematic than self-causation, we should reject the supposition that on the derivative-from-below proposal, limit properties can be effects.

One possible response to the aforementioned difficulty could be to divide limit properties into two exclusive categories: those interpreted as derivatives from below, which can be causes but not effects, and those interpreted as derivatives from above, which can be effects but not causes. Lange calls this proposal the two-property view, and notes that its major problem is that it does not admit causal chains involving limit properties. For instance, according to the causal interpretation of motions under forces depicted in Figure 7.1 (Sec. 2), acceleration is both an effect of the total force acting upon an object and a cause (together with the initial velocity) of the object's subsequent velocity. Acceleration acts as an intermediary between the force on the one hand, and the velocities and ultimately positions on the other hand. However, on the two-property view this causal model is no longer available to us, since acceleration is a limit property, and therefore can be either a cause or an effect, but not both.

Kenny Easwaran does not consider this an insurmountable obstacle for the two-property view [Easwaran 2014]. He insists that we can causally connect past forces with future trajectories without assuming that acceleration acts both as an effect and a cause. Although his remarks are somewhat cryptic in places, I believe that his main idea is to follow the alternative causal model that I have outlined in Sec. 2 (Figure 7.2), according to which the causal nexus connects forces and initial positions and velocities directly with the trajectory of the body, without any active role played by acceleration. On this view acceleration is a sort of epiphenomenon that is caused by forces but doesn't literally cause anything.[9] However, under this proposal it remains problematic that we cannot give a proper causal explanation of velocities, as they belong to the category of past neighborhood properties that can only be causes and not effects. Of the three causal factors responsible for the occurrence of the future trajectory – the forces, the initial position and initial velocity – the latter is conspicuously distinct from the former two in that it does not admit direct causes that bring it about. This is rather surprising and calls for some further explanations.[10]

All these mental gymnastics prove to be totally unnecessary when we realize that the central problem we are trying to solve (the self-causation problem) is a mere artifact – a result of a sloppy treatment of the special category of limit properties. In the coming section we will try to rectify this situation by developing a rigorous way to express causal relations that derivative-based properties such as instantaneous velocities can enter into.

---

9   Here are some quotes from [Easwaran 2014: 853] that seem to support my interpretation of his conception: "… on the view I defend here forces cause accelerations, while accelerations are grounded in future velocities and positions. [...] Acceleration is an effect, and only a cause in the indirect sense that the future velocities that constitute it can themselves cause things even farther in the future. [...] Lange's chain would be problematic if accelerations at a time had to causally determine velocities at the same time. But the fundamental causal determination is just forces and velocities at a time determining positions and accelerations on a future neighborhood of that time." It should perhaps be added as an aside to the last sentence that forces with velocities are not sufficient to fix future positions – we also need initial positions for that purpose, as explained in Sec. 2.

10   To be fair, we should note that Easwaran admits that "[v]elocity [...] is only an effect in the indirect sense that it can be partly causally determined by events even farther in the past, and that velocities over time constitute accelerations, which are effects" [Easwaran 2014: 853]. This fragment suggests that some form of causal determination is available for velocities, but it is a mystery to me how precisely this is supposed to work given the assumption that velocity is a past neighborhood property.

4   Limit Properties and Grounding

In the analysis given below I will make extensive use of the concept of *grounding*, following Easwaran's approach in his 2014 paper. The broad idea behind this concept is as follows: if we believe that a certain property P is reducible to more fundamental properties Q, we can express this fact by saying that each instance of an object's possessing property P is *grounded* in some fundamental properties Q possessed by the object. Equivalently, we can say that an appropriate set of properties Q form a *ground* for property P. I propose the following definition that in my view correctly captures the essence of what it is to be a ground for a given property:

(8)   A set of properties Π of an object a grounds property P of x iff
       (a) by necessity, if a possesses all properties from Π, a possesses P, and
       (b) Π is the smallest of all sets satisfying condition (a) (i.e. no proper subset Σ of Π is such that by necessity, if a possesses all properties from Σ, a possesses P).

To that we will add a definition of the weaker concept of a merely *sufficient* ground, which is simply a set of properties satisfying the above condition (a):

(9)   A set of properties Π of an object x is a sufficient ground for a property P of x iff by necessity, if x possesses all properties from Π, x possesses P.

Def. 9 is based on Easwaran's proposal of how to characterize sufficient grounds (Easwaran 2014, p. 847), while def. 8 adds to that the requirement that *proper* grounds should not possess any redundant elements. As an illustrating example consider a property P_t defined as follows: an object possesses P_t iff in ten seconds from t its position will be 10 feet from the position at t. A sufficient ground for P_t will be any part of the trajectory that contains both the positions of the object at t and at $t + 10$ (given the assumption that $x(t + 10) = x(t) + 10$), while the ground for P_t will consist of just the positions at t and at $t + 10$. No smaller set than this set of properties can ensure that P_t will be possessed by an object, hence this set is indeed not only a sufficient ground but the ground simpliciter. We should further observe that the actual ground for any given property P need not be a necessary condition for the instantiation of P. In our example there is an infinite number of possible grounds of the considered property of moving ten feet away in ten seconds from now, differing from one another in their absolute values of $x(t)$, and only one of them is actually realized.

In the next step we should give a rigorous definition of a limit property. Surprisingly, the definition is going to be very simple:

(10) P is a limit property iff P has no ground but has sufficient grounds.

Given the definitions of grounds and sufficient grounds, we may derive the following consequences of def. 10. First of all, no sufficient ground for a limit property can consist of a finite number of properties. If we had a finite set of properties Π forming a sufficient ground for a groundless property P, then by sequentially eliminating particular properties from Π we could create a descending chain of sufficient conditions $\Pi_n, \Pi_{n-1}, \dots$ which inevitably terminates in a one-element set Π_1. But a one-element set of properties cannot be a sufficient ground for P without being a ground *simpliciter*, hence we have proven that P is not a limit property, contrary to the assumption.

Another fact regarding limit properties is that each of their sufficient grounds can be the first element in an infinite sequence of sufficient grounds such that each element in the sequence is properly included in the previous element. We can call such sequences "infinite descending chains of sufficient grounds":

(11) An infinite descending chain of sufficient grounds for property P is an infinite sequence $SG_1(P)$, $SG_2(P)$, ..., $SG_i(P)$, ... such that each $SG_i(P)$ is a sufficient ground for P and $SG_i(P) \subsetneq SG_j(P)$ if $i > j$.

Of particular interest to us are infinite descending chains of sufficient grounds such that all their lower bounds are themselves not sufficient ground. Such chains can be called "terminal":

(12) An infinite descending chain Γ of sufficient grounds for property P is terminal iff for every set of properties α, if $\alpha \subsetneq \beta$ for all $\beta \in \Gamma$, then α is not a sufficient ground for P.

It can be easily verified that derivative-based properties, including instantaneous velocities, are limit properties in the sense of def. 10. No set of values of the function $x(t)$ satisfies the definition of being a ground for the derivative of $x(t)$ taken at point t_0 (due to the inevitable violation of clause (b) of def. 8), hence the first condition of def. 10 is satisfied.[11] On the other hand, derivatives

---

11   At this point someone could object that by rejecting the existence of grounds for limit properties I am effectively abandoning the reductive view regarding the nature of instantaneous velocities. After all, what else can a reductionist claim if not that instantaneous velocities are grounded in facts regarding the positions of moving bodies? However, a broader understanding of reductionism is still applicable here. Instantaneous velocities can be claimed to be reducible to positions in the sense that the former supervene on the latter. That is, there can be no difference in the instantaneous velocities of a body without

clearly possess sufficient grounds in the form of any fragments of function $x(t)$ on an interval containing point t_0. An example of a terminal descending chain for the derivative of $x(t)$ at t_0 can be the sequence consisting of the trajectories defined on the intervals $\left(t_0 - \frac{1}{i}, t_0 + \frac{1}{i} \right)$, where $i \in \mathrm{N}$. Note that this sequence has the infimum (the greatest lower bound)[12] in the form of the one-element set $\{x(t_0)\}$, which is obviously not a sufficient ground for the derivative at t_0.

Not all limit properties are simple derivative properties taken at a point. Consider for example a moving body which came to a rest precisely at time t_1 and started moving again at a later time t_2. Let us consider the property P of the body whose possession is exhibited in the fact that its *entire* period of uninterrupted rest is identical with the closed interval $[t_1, t_2]$. This property is a limit property. First of all, no combination of positions forms a ground of this property. The positions of the body in the interval $[t_1, t_2]$ are not sufficient (fixing them does not exclude the possibility that the body might have been at rest a bit longer than the duration of the interval). On the other hand, any interval of the form $(t_1 - \Delta_1, t_2 + \Delta_2)$ is too large in the sense that we can select a smaller interval $(t_1 - \delta_1, t_2 + \delta_2)$, where $0 < \delta_i < \Delta_i$, and the positions in the smaller interval will also fix property P. The sequence of intervals $\left\{ \left(t_1 - \frac{1}{i}, t_2 + \frac{1}{i} \right) \right\}_{i \in N}$ defines a terminal descending sequence for P whose infimum is precisely the trajectory of the body within the interval $[t_1, t_2]$.

The infimum of a terminal descending chain of sufficient conditions is the closest we can get to the full-fledged ground for a given limit property. For that reason we may call it "a limit ground":

(13)   The set of properties Π is a limit ground for a limit property P iff Π is the infimum for all terminal descending chains of sufficient grounds for P.

Even though Π itself is not a sufficient ground of P, it is 'infinitesimally close' to P's sufficient grounds. Thus, a limit ground is an approximation of a sufficient ground which also does not possess any redundant elements (eliminating

---

some differences in its trajectory. Or, to put it differently, the complete trajectory of a body entirely determines its velocities. The lack of grounds in the case of limit properties only signifies that the trajectories 'overdetermine' velocities in that they contain more information than is necessary to fix the velocities.

12   The infimum (greatest lower bound) of a set Π ordered by a relation $\leq$ is an object α such that $\alpha \leq \beta$ for all $\beta \in \Pi$, and for all γ satisfying this condition, $\gamma \leq \alpha$ (α is the greatest of all the elements 'lower' than the elements in Π). If the infimum exists, it is unique.

any property from it will take us even further from the sufficient grounds). By introducing the concept of a limit ground, we can approach the problem of a correct temporal characteristic of limit properties. The derivative property taken at a particular point t_0 (for instance the instantaneous velocity $v(t_0)$) is typically assumed to be a property possessed by an object precisely at moment t_0. But an immediate objection is that this can't be true, since velocity $v(t_0)$ cannot be grounded in the fundamental properties of the object at t_0. If velocities are reducible to the positions of an object, and the position at t_0 is not a sufficient ground for the velocity at t_0, this is taken to imply that instantaneous velocities cannot be genuinely instantaneous properties (that is, they can't be possessed precisely at one moment). But this argument presupposes that if a property P is reducible to a particular type of fundamental property, and if P is attributed to an object at a given moment t, P has to be grounded in the fundamental properties possessed precisely at t. However, this assumption does not seem to be appropriate in the case of limit properties which do not possess grounds but merely sufficient grounds forming descending chains. In that case the temporal attribution of the non-fundamental properties should arguably be associated not with grounds (which are not available) but limit grounds. Thus, the following criterion seems to be a reasonable choice:

(14) A limit property P is attributable to an object at a moment t iff there is a fundamental property Q within P's limit ground which is possessed by the object at t.

Given this criterion, we may conclude that derivatives are properties possessed at single instants of time, even though they are not strictly reducible to the fundamental properties at these instants.[13]

5 Limit Properties as Causes

We can now return to the central problem of this article which is the question whether limit properties can participate in causal relations. As we recall, the main reason for answering this question in the negative is the self-causation argument.

---

13 It may be objected that my criterion of temporal attributions for limit properties is arbitrary and therefore solves the problem merely by fiat. To that I can only reply that one is free to reject my proposal, but in consequence one has to accept that limit properties do not have any well-defined temporal locations. Any suggestions that instantaneous velocities are possessed at specific non-zero temporal intervals are bound to be inadequate, since these intervals, no matter how small, will always possess elements that are irrelevant to the value of velocity at a point.

The argument alleges that because derivative properties cannot be reduced to fundamental properties at a given temporal point t_0, they must involve some fundamental facts that occur right before and right after t_0. And if this is the case, then the assumption that the considered derivative property of a body at t_0 is a cause of all the subsequent instantiations of the fundamental properties by this body leads to the conclusion that some of these instantiations are their own causes. Now we can see that this argument is fatally flawed due to the falsity of its main premise. As we have already stressed, the derivative at t_0 is not grounded in any non-zero interval surrounding t_0. The only concept of a ground applicable to limit properties is that of a limit ground as introduced in def. 13. And according to criterion (14), the limit ground for the derivative at t_0 is located precisely at t_0, so there is no *prima facie* reason to believe that derivatives involve any *specific* facts regarding possession of the fundamental properties after or before t_0.

This last conclusion can be argued for directly even without reference to the possibly controversial concept of a limit ground. Consider any moment t after t_0. If we take any terminal descending sequence of sufficient grounds for the derivative $\dfrac{dx(t)}{dt}$ taken at t_0 – for instance the sequence of trajectories defined on intervals $\left(t_0 - \dfrac{1}{i}, t_0 + \dfrac{1}{i} \right)$ – then it is easy to observe that no elements of this sequence except a finite number will contain the moment t. Thus, the value $x(t)$ is irrelevant to the value of the derivative at t_0, since it can be discarded from an infinite number of sufficient grounds without affecting their ability to necessitate the value of $\dfrac{dx(t)}{dt}$ at t_0. And the rebuttal of this argument based on the common cause objection, as proposed by Lange (see sec. 3), should be viewed now as completely misguided. Take two moments t_1 and t_2 such that $t_0 < t_1 < t_2$. On what ground can we defend the curious claim that the instantaneous velocity $v(t_0)$ that causes $x(t_1)$ is distinct from the instantaneous velocity that causes $x(t_2)$?

The only reason I can think of for such a bizarre claim is that there exists a terminal descending chain Π of sufficient grounds for $v(t_0)$ such that no element of Π contains the value $x(t_2)$, while some elements of Π contain the value $x(t_1)$. But in that case we can 'cut off' the initial elements of the original sequence at a point where no further elements will contain $x(t_1)$. This is easy – all we have to do is choose any number j for which it is true that $t_0 + \dfrac{1}{j} < t_1$. All elements SG_i of the original chain Π for which $i > j$ will be such that they will exclude both $x(t_1)$ and $x(t_2)$. And clearly this 'truncated' chain has the exact same infimum as the original one, hence it corresponds to precisely the same limit property at t_0. Thus, it can be safely concluded that the instantaneous velocity $v(t_0)$ causes both $x(t_1)$ and $x(t_2)$ without implying that any of these positions causes itself.

The same argument can be repeated *mutatis mutandis* for any finite number of positions $x(t_1)$, ..., $x(t_n)$. That is, we can find a terminal descending chain of sufficient grounds for $v(t_0)$ such that no element in this chain will contain any of the positions $x(t_i)$. But what if the number of the considered positions is infinite? In particular, can we claim that the instantaneous velocity $v(t_0)$ is a common cause for *every* single position $x(t)$, where $t > t_0$? In that case there is no single terminal descending chain that would be appropriate for all positions $x(t)$ in the sense that its elements would not contain any position $x(t)$. But this is not a problem. We are not identifying the instantaneous velocity $v(t_0)$ with any *particular* terminal chain. All terminal chains of sufficient grounds for $v(t_0)$ that have the same infimum represent the same limit property, even if they don't have a single element in common. Thus, for every position $x(t)$ where $t > t_0$ we can select a terminal descending chain Π_t whose elements do not contain $x(t)$, thus avoiding the charge of self-causation, and then we can argue that all chains Π_t have the same infimum, which makes them represent one and the same property. Hence, contrary to what Lange seems to suggest, the instantaneous velocity at t_0 is a common cause of *all* subsequent positions.[14]

One may still insist that the problem of self-causation returns when we consider not the individual positions of the body at separate moments after t_0 but whole continuous segments of its trajectory. Take for instance the trajectory of the body in an open interval (t_0, t_1). It seems natural to assume that the instantaneous velocity $v(t_0)$ is a cause not only for each individual position $x(t)$, where $t \in (t_0, t_1)$, but also for the entire trajectory understood as the set of positions $\{x(t): t \in (t_0, t_1)\}$. However, this trajectory is a sufficient ground for $v(t_0)$.[15] Doesn't this imply that the trajectory is its own cause? Not at all. Being a sufficient ground is not enough, as sufficient grounds may contain elements that are irrelevant for the derivative property $v(t_0)$. We cannot pinpoint any

---

14   Lee [2013] gives a very similar argument for the same claim. However, he refuses to admit that instantaneous velocities are intrinsic to the moments they are taken at.

15   At least when we define the instantaneous velocity as the right-side derivative. If the velocity is defined as the two-side derivative, then the trajectory in (t_0, t_1) is a sufficient ground for $v(t_0)$, provided that the left- and right-side derivatives exist and are equal to each other.

part of the trajectory in the interval (t_0, t_1) as the ground *simpliciter* for the instantaneous velocity at t_0. Hence, we can't appeal to the intuitive principle similar to that adopted by Lange that any part of the ground of a cause is itself a cause (obviously it would be erroneous to claim that any part of a merely *sufficient* ground of a cause is also a cause). Actually, we can give a very simple reason why all the arguments from self-causation are bound to fail: since limit properties do not possess grounds, we cannot make use of the aforementioned principle which is required in order to derive the conclusion that a particular element of the ground is its own cause.

So limit properties can be used in causal explanations in physics, after all. But I believe that a stronger claim can be made – the use of limit properties in causal explanations is not only possible but essential in order to account for the dynamical aspects of the temporal evolution of physical systems. Many authors point out that it is not a coincidence that virtually all physical laws use derivatives of various orders.[16] One possible explanation of this fact may be found in the peculiar character of derivative-based properties which, even though defined at and limited to a temporal point, in some sense transcend the temporal confines of a zero-dimensional point and reach toward the past and the future, thereby connecting past processes with future ones. In order to delve deeper into this problem, let us focus first on the types of nomic connections that can be captured with the help of 'ordinary', non-limit properties defined at temporal points. Essentially there are two options here: either a fundamental law of physics connects the values of two properties at the same temporal moment, or it connects their values at different moments. In the first, synchronic scenario it can be claimed that such a law does not offer a genuine causal explanation of why a particular property of a system evolves in time in such and such way. All we can say is that at each temporal instant the two properties are correlated, so that if we knew the temporal evolution of one property, we could infer the temporal evolution of the other one. But it remains inexplicable why the first property evolves in the particular way it does. The whole picture is reminiscent of the position of parallelism in the philosophy of mind, according to which physical and mental processes evolve side by side without actually causally influencing one another. By analogy, it can be

---

16   This is an observation made by Easwaran [2014]. In addition to that, he produces an argu-
      ment to the effect that all fundamental causal equations of a given physical theory have
      to use derivatives of the same order for a given fundamental quantity. But his argument
      presupposes the modified two-property view that we reject in the current approach. See
      also [Smith 2000] for an extensive analysis of various causal interpretations of differen-
      tial equations in physics.

claimed that the synchronic correlation between two momentary properties is not genuinely causal but merely represents an inexplicable parallelism of the two.

The alternative option is a diachronic law connecting the values of two properties at different moments. This looks more like a genuine causal connection between present (or past) events and future events. However, there is one crucial problem with this causal picture: namely, that it involves action at a temporal distance (temporal non-locality). Some people object to the idea that two events which are not in contact with one another could directly influence each other. For instance David Hume famously insisted that the cause and effect have to be contiguous in space and time. The existence of a temporal gap between the cause and effect without any intermediary connecting elements raises the question of how to explain the fact that the system 'remembers' (i.e. retains some information of) the past cause in the intervening moments before the effect comes into existence. Another way to express this concern is to observe that processes which admit causal links at temporal distances seem to violate the so-called Markov condition – the well-known statistical condition that the complete state of a system at any moment should probabilistically 'screen off' all the earlier states. And given the continuous character of time, there can be no two distinct moments that are located next to each other, hence the temporal gaps between causes and effects seem inevitable.

It may be argued that limit properties in general, and derivative properties in particular, can help us mitigate the above-mentioned difficulties. As we have stressed, derivative properties can function both as effects and as causes. Suppose that a particular derivative property is synchronically connected via a law of nature with some other fundamental property. A ready-made example of such a situation is provided by the second law of dynamics, where the value of force at a given moment determines the derivative property of acceleration at the very same moment. Given that acceleration is equal to the rate of change of a body's velocity, the value of acceleration at a particular moment contains some information about the future behavior of the system. This information does not include specific future values of any fundamental properties – as we already know this would lead to trouble with self-causation if accelerations were to play the role of causes – nevertheless it tells us something about the trajectory of the body that transcends a particular point in time. In the case of acceleration this information is about the curvature of the spatio-temporal trajectory at a point, and fixing the curvature of a body's trajectory definitely puts some constraints on its future evolution. Thus, synchronic laws that involve derivative properties can actually underlie genuine causal processes that extend towards the future.

The 'infinitesimal' character of derivative properties helps avoid the difficulty with temporal gaps between causes and effects. The value of a given derivative property at t_0 does not cause directly and across a non-zero temporal gap the occurrence of a value of a given property at a later time t. Rather, the causal influence goes through the moments that are infinitesimally close to t_0.[17] We can illustrate this with the help of the case of instantaneous velocity. At a moment t_0 a body has the initial position $x(t_0)$ and velocity $v(t_0)$. Velocity $v(t_0)$ as a derivative property characterizes the momentary rate of change of position, which together with the actual value $x(t_0)$ causally determines the values $x(t)$ in the infinitesimal neighborhood of t_0 (mathematically this is often represented by the equation $x(t_0 + dt) = x(t_0) + v(t_0)dt$, where dt stands for an infinitesimal increase in time). At the same time the value of instantaneous acceleration $a(t_0)$, determined by the force according to the second law, causes (together with the initial value $v(t_0)$) a new value for velocity at $t_0 + dt$ to replace the old one: $v(t_0 + dt) = v(t_0) + a(t_0)dt$. This process gets repeated infinitely many times, until we reach a non-infinitesimal temporal distance between t and t_0. Thanks to the fact that instantaneous velocities and accelerations act at infinitesimal temporal distances dt, it is possible to evade the problem of action at a temporal distance.

6   Concluding Remarks

We can now state the main conclusion of the analysis given above. We have argued that there are no fundamental obstacles to limit properties playing a causal role in physical processes. In particular, instantaneous velocities can be assumed to cause future positions and trajectories of bodies without implying that these positions and trajectories cause their own occurrences, or that the instantaneous velocity of a body cannot be a common cause for all subsequent positions the body occupies. And in order to defend the causal role of limit properties we don't have to resort to any non-standard interpretations of derivative-based properties, such as the two-property view or the dispositional view. We have also argued that derivative properties, insofar as they can be assumed to possess any well-defined temporal characteristics at all, are properties that are exemplified by objects at temporal instants. Thus we side with

---

17   We have already mentioned this feature of derivative properties in Sec. 2.1.

those who, like Smith (2003), believe that instantaneous velocities are genuinely instantaneous. The instantaneous character of the time-derivatives of positions does not threaten the reductionist view, since we do not assume that instantaneous velocities should be grounded in specific positions or trajectories, but only that the former supervene on the latter (instantaneous velocities are nothing 'over and above' complete trajectories). The key observation that we have used time and again in our arguments is that limit properties by their very nature do not possess grounds but only sufficient grounds. Failure to properly acknowledge this fact is responsible for the incorrect and misleading arguments used in the debates on the nature and role of limit properties.

Acknowledgments

I would like to thank Naftali Weinberger and Chungyoung Lee for numerous discussions that helped me develop the ideas presented in this paper. The work on this paper was supported by grant No. 2017/25/B/HS1/00620 from the National Science Center, Poland.

Bibliography

Ajdukiewicz, Kazimierz (1948). Change and Contradiction. [In:] [Ajdukiewicz 1978], pp. 192–208.
Ajdukiewicz, Kazimierz (1978). *"The Scientific World-Perspective" and Other Essays (1931–1961)*. Dordrecht 1978: Reidel.
Arntzenius, Frank (2000). Are There Really Instantaneous Velocities? *The Monist* vol. 83, No. 2, pp. 187–208.
Arntzenius, Frank (2003). An Arbitrarily Short Reply to Sheldon Smith on Instantaneous Velocities. *Studies in History and Philosophy of Modern Physics* 34, pp. 281–282.
Bigelow, John & Pargetter, Robert (1990). *Science and Necessity*. Cambridge: Cambridge University Press.
Carroll, John W. (2002). Instantaneous Motion. *Philosophical Studies* vol. 110, pp. 49–67.
Easwaran, Kenny (2014). Why Physics Uses Second Derivatives. *The British Journal for the Philosophy of Science* vol. 65, pp. 845–862.
Iwasaki, Yumi & Simon, Herbert Alexander (1994). Causality and Model Abstraction. *Artificial Intelligence* vol. 67, No. 1, pp.143–194.
Lange, Marc (2005). How Can Instantaneous Velocity Fulfill Its Causal Role? *The Philosophical Review* vol. 114, No. 4, pp. 433–468.

Lee, Chungyoung (2013). Instantaneous Velocity and the Causal Explanation Problem. 과학철학 16–1, pp. 133–160.

Mackie, John Leslie (1965). Causes and Conditions. *American Philosophical Quarterly* vol. 2, No. 4, pp. 245–264.

Russell, Bertrand (1903). *Principles of Mathematics*. London: G. Allen & Unwin.

Smith, Sheldon R. (2000). Resolving Russell's Anti-Realism About Causation: the Connection Between Causation and the Functional Dependencies of Mathematical Physics. *The Monist* vol. 83, No. 2, pp. 274–295.

Smith, Sheldon R. (2003a). Are Instantaneous Velocities Real and Really Instantaneous? An Argument for the Affirmative. *Studies in History and Philosophy of Modern Physics* vol. 34, pp. 261–280.

Smith, Sheldon R. (2003b). Author's Response. *Studies in History and Philosophy of Modern Physics* vol. 34, p. 283.

Tooley, Michael (1988). In Defense of the Existence of States of Motion. *Philosophical Topics* vol. 16, pp. 225–54.

Weinberger, Naftali (2019). Near-Decomposability and the Time-Scale Relativity of Causal Representations. Preprint.

CHAPTER 8

Causality in the Law

Bartosz Brożek and Bartłomiej Kucharzyk

1 Introduction

Causality matters to the law. Legal textbooks, monographs, and court decisions are filled with discussions pertaining to causal chains linking human actions with harmful (or, more generally, legally relevant) outcomes. Causality matters because it is an essential element of ascribing criminal responsibility or civil liability to people.

However, a philosopher perusing legal texts may be surprised by what kind of causality matters in the law. It has little to do with the complex theories and painstaking conceptual analysis featuring so prominently in thick philosophical volumes. The reason for that is very simple: while philosophers concerned with causality are mainly preoccupied with perplexing aspects of physics and other natural sciences, lawyers are focused on human behavior. Moreover, a theory of causality developed against the background of the empirical sciences has little bearing on the practice of physics. On the other hand, the understanding of causal chains adopted by the lawyers may substantially shape legal practice and directly influence human life.

In this chapter we would like to delve into some problems surrounding the legal approach to causality. In the course of our analysis, we will be defending two claims:

(1) That the law embraces two interconnected concepts of causality, physical and mental (intentionality).

(2) That the legal conceptual scheme capturing human agency is deeply rooted in folk psychology, while being largely silent about the theories of behavior and causation developed in science and philosophy.

These claims pinpoint the most intriguing aspects of the legal understanding of causality. On the one hand, legal causal links do not "inhabit" exclusively physical reality: mental factors, as well as normative considerations, even if conceptually differentiated, play an essential role in establishing causal relations. On the other hand, the legal conceptual scheme is in a constant "dialogue" with two other perspectives: the scientific and the folk psychological. This triangle is a source of numerous theoretical and practical problems, but

© BARTOSZ BROŻEK AND BARTŁOMIEJ KUCHARZYK, 2022 | DOI:10.1163/9789004522244_010 at the same time constitutes a constant source of deep reflection on human action.

We will begin by analyzing the legal conceptual apparatus pertaining to causality and intentional action. In order to provide a general overview of the issue, we will take into account both the continental and common law traditions. To illustrate the first approach, we will present and analyze some relevant aspects of the Polish legal system, while to get a grasp of the second we will delve into the complexities of American law. The next section will be devoted to folk psychology: its definition and the understanding of human behavior and causality it embodies. This section will serve to establish the claim that the legal conceptual scheme is firmly based on the folk psychological rendering of some key concepts such as intention, awareness, or causal link. Finally, we will provide a very broad picture of the scientific theories pertaining to human action and the philosophical conceptions of causality, in order to assess whether they have any significance for the law.

2   Legal Abstractions

Let us begin with a reconstruction of the view of causality as encapsulated in Polish law, which belongs to the family of the so-called continental legal systems.

In the field of Polish criminal law, the concept of causality is closely related to the concept of the structure of crime.[1] According to this concept, a human behavior may be recognized as a crime only if it is an (1) unlawful, (2) punishable, (3) reprehensible, and (4) culpable (5) action. Those five factors (elements of the crime structure) are necessary conditions of criminal responsibility.[2]

First, in order to be considered criminal a behavior must count as an action. This means that a behavior in which "a man was only a passive link in causation" [Wróbel & Zoll 2013: 157] cannot constitute a crime. Action requires decisiveness – mental and physical control over one's behavior. A behavior is

---

1   See [Zoll 2016]. Section 2. "Struktura przestępstwa" [The Structure of the Crime].
2   See article 1 of the Polish Criminal Code:
    § 1. Only a person who commits an act prohibited under a penalty by a statute in force at the time of its commission is subject to criminal liability.
    § 2. A prohibited act of negligible social harmfulness does not constitute a crime.
    § 3. The perpetrator of a prohibited act does not commit a crime if fault cannot be attributed to him at the time of the act.

not an action – and hence cannot be a crime – in the case of, for example, *vis absoluta* (an irresistible physical force applied to one's muscles).

An action entails criminal responsibility if it is: unlawful – "it violates the sanctioned norm, in the absence of circumstances justifying such violation" [Zoll 2016]; punishable – the law establishes a criminal sanction for such a violation; reprehensible – it is (in the particular case) socially harmful to a degree higher than negligible; and culpable – fault can be attributed to the actor.

Within this framework causality matters in at least two ways. First, the law recognizes an action as a particular type of material crime[3] (punishable accordingly) only if it caused a particular effect: the causal link between the action and the effect must be established (proven). Shooting someone who two days later dies in the hospital due to food poisoning is homicide no more (and sometimes less) than trying to kill someone who then lives long and prospers.[4]

In the doctrine of Polish criminal law and in the decisions of Polish courts, at least three different theories (methods) of establishing causation (ascribing effect) may be found [Góralski 2009]. The equivalence theory utilizes the *condicio sine qua non* test – if without action A there would be no effect E (or the "effect" would be substantially different) then action A should be considered the cause of effect E. According to the adequate causation theory only the typical aftermaths of the action should be recognized as its effects. The adequate causation theory is dominant in Polish civil law (see below). The objective attribution theory supplements the empirical link[5] with a normative element – from the criminal law perspective only those actions violating the rules of conduct designed to prevent harmful effects should be considered causes.

It is worth observing that Polish criminal law has a very specific understanding of causation. While the equivalence theory, based on the *condicio sine qua non* test, is close to what a philosopher would consider a sound definition of causation (or, at the very least, as a starting point of a philosophical analysis of the problem), the two remaining theories considerably deviate from the mainstream approach to causation. The adequate causation theory introduces the concept of "typical aftermaths" of the action; moreover, it should be stressed that "typical" in this formulation is not a statistical, but rather psychological concept. In other words, only those events count as caused by an action which might have been anticipated by the actor. The objective attribution theory goes

---

3 And not another type with a less serious effect or some kind of formal (inchoate) offense.
4 Instead it may be recognized – depending on the actual effect and other circumstances – as, e.g., infliction of grievous bodily harm or attempted murder.
5 Established, desirably with a probability bordering on certainty, on the basis of scientific laws and statistical regularities (the proper condition test).

even further in deviating from the more traditional accounts of causation and adds a normative element: the pool of potential causes is restricted by the content of the legal norms.

In its second role causality is understood as intentionality. Responsibility for some types of crime (especially the most serious[6]) may be ascribed only if the actor acted with intent. Article 9 § 1 of the Polish Criminal Code states that "A prohibited act is committed intentionally if the perpetrator intends its commission, i.e., wants to commit it or, foreseeing the possibility of its commission, accepts it". Therefore, scholars of Polish criminal law distinguish direct intent ("wants to commit it") and resultant intent. Within Polish law some crimes may be committed only with direct intent.[7]

The above considerations must be supplemented with the following three observations. First, the concept of intent as utilized in Polish criminal law involves the actors' awareness of their behavior. This awareness is not present in acts committed unintentionally ("when the perpetrator, not having the intent to commit it, nevertheless does so because he is not careful in the manner required under the circumstances, although he should or could have foreseen the possibility of committing the prohibited act"[8]). Clearly, committing a crime "without intent" is an exception, while "a model crime" involves intentionality, and hence awareness. Second, Polish criminal law, at the conceptual level, distinguishes between physical causation and mental causation (intentionality). They constitute two different aspects in the conceptual structure of crime. However, they are interconnected since criminal law is interested only in actions, i.e., such behaviors in which an individual is not only a passive link in causation. Third, and finally, the doctrine of Polish criminal law does not associate intent (and awareness) with the concept of fault (guilt). Intent is a part of prohibited action, fault is a part of crime. Fault occurs if an actor takes a prohibited action which would not be taken by a normative ("good") citizen under the same circumstances.

In the field of Polish civil law the relationship between causality and liability is defined in article 361 of the Civil Code:

> § 1. A person obliged to pay damages shall only be liable for the ordinary effects of an action or omission which the damage resulted from.

---

6   See article 8 of the Polish Criminal Code:
    A felony may be committed only intentionally; a misdemeanour may also be committed unintentionally if a statute provides so.
7   See articles 16, 18, 207 and 278 of the Polish Criminal Code.
8   Article 9§2 of the Polish Criminal Code.

§ 2. Within the above-mentioned limits, in the absence of a different statutory or contractual provision, the redress of damage shall involve losses which the injured party has suffered as well as profits which it could have obtained if no damage had been inflicted.

Hence, the concept of civil liability includes "ordinary" causal relationships between an action (or omission) and damage (harm) [Wiśniewski 2018]. In this context, the doctrine of Polish civil law is based on the adequate causation theory. From this theoretical perspective causation (and, in consequence, liability) may be ascribed for the standard (normal, typical, usual, average, common, expected) consequences of actions (omissions) only. The occurrence of objective causal relationship ("proven", e.g., with the *condicio sine qua non* test) is necessary but insufficient. Liability is limited to the effects considered ordinary in light of life experience and scientific knowledge.[9] This means that the scope of compensation is determined by the "typical" outcomes of an action. A person found liable only has to compensate for the damages which are considered standard effects of her behavior.

However, there are exceptions to the principle of an "ordinary" causal relationship. Specific regulations of the Civil Code may ascribe liability on the basis of a "normative" relationship (e.g., articles 422, 846 § 1 and 876 § 1) or extend its scope beyond "ordinary" causation (e.g., articles 478 and 714). Exceptions may also be contracted between particular parties. It follows, however, that a "model" understanding of action in Polish civil law involves causal relationships which are defined by taking into account the "typical" or "average" consequences of human behavior.

Moreover, Polish civil law strictly separates issues of causation and culpability. A causal relationship is objective, fault is subjective (personal). In contrast to criminal law however, here fault is related to awareness and intent. It is identified with a "person's reprehensible decision regarding her unlawful action" [Radwański 1997: 172]. The decision process includes two vital factors: prediction and will.[10] These factors intersect with the distinction of intentional and unintentional fault. The former should be ascribed if the actor is aware of the deleterious effect of her behavior, predicts that the effect will occur, and deliberately aims for it (direct intent) or at least agrees to its occurrence (resultant intent).[11] The fault is unintentional when the actor predicts the possibility of

---

9   See the ruling of the Polish Supreme Court of June 2, 1956 (3 CR 515/56).
10   See articles 425 and 426 of the Polish Civil Code.
11   See articles 777, 801, 849 and 852 of the Polish Civil Code.

the harmful effect but believes (without warrant) that she will avoid it, or when the actor should and is able to predict it but fails to do so. In Polish tort law any kind and degree of fault implies liability.[12] Within contract law the parties are entitled to set the threshold (for example "gross negligence").

It transpires that, save for some conceptual differences concerning the relationship between fault (guilt) and intent, the general approach to causation in Polish civil law is quite similar to that found in criminal law. Particularly, physical and mental causation are conceptually distinguished: they represent two different aspects of the evaluated action. Moreover, physical causation is not taken in its "pure" form (as based solely on the *condicio sine qua non* rule), but is "colored" by the concept of "typical outcomes" of behavior. Finally, intentionality – in its "model version" – includes acting with intent and being aware of what one is doing.

Let us now move to the question of how causation is understood in the common law systems (and, more specifically, American law). As in the continental systems, causation (in many instances[13]) is considered a necessary condition of legal liability. Causation may be a part of a set of prerequisites of such liability (e.g., in addition to the duty of care) or effectively the only requirement (e.g., strict product liability). Common law scholars, more clearly than their "continental" colleagues, distinguish "factual" causation (causation-in-fact) and "legal" causation [Stapleton 2008]. The former should be established before the latter. The standard method for this is the *sine qua non* test (also-called the but-for test by the Anglo-Saxon scholars).[14] Since the but-for test fails in situations where each of several acts alone is sufficient to cause harm, the common law courts support it with intuition ("common sense") and assume that causation should be understood "as the man in the street" understands it.[15]

"Legal" causation, on the other hand, is understood in light of the doctrine of proximate cause – some harms are found to be too remote from the action

---

12   See the verdict of the Polish Supreme Court of October 10, 1975 (I CR 656/75) and article
      415 of the Polish Civil Code: "A person who has inflicted damage to another person by his
      own fault shall be obliged to redress it."
13   Exceptions include, for example, contracts of indemnity insurance and inchoate offenses.
14   See New South Wales Civil Liability Act 2002, Section 5D and Adeels Palace Pty Ltd v
      Moubarak; Adeels Palace Pty Ltd v Bou Najem [2009] HCA 48 (10 November 2009).
15   See e.g. Yorkshire Dale Steamship Co v Minister of War Transport [1942] AC 691 (HL);
      March v Stramare (E & MH) Pty Ltd [1993] HCA 12, (1991) 171 CLR 506 (24 April 1991), High
      Court (Australia); State v. Tally, 15 So 722, 738 (Ala. 1894): "The assistance given ... need not
      contribute to criminal result in the sense that but for it the result would not have ensued.
      It is quite sufficient if it facilitated a result that would have transpired without it".

to entail liability [Witt 2018: 333]. The most common tests of proximate cause are based on the factor of (objective) foreseeability, i.e., courts usually determine if the harm resulting from an action could reasonably have been predicted (the "extraordinary in hindsight" rule).[16] For example, Justice Cardozo suggested utilizing two questions in this context:

1. Is the plaintiff's injury a reasonably foreseeable consequence of the defendant's breach of duty?
2. Is the plaintiff a reasonably foreseeable victim of the defendant's breach of duty?

The doctrine of proximate cause has been adopted in the Model Penal Code[17] which states that the actual result cannot be "too remote or accidental in its occurrence to have a [just] bearing on the actor's liability".[18] The Model Penal Code also specifies the foreseeability requirement (depending on whether the defendant acted purposely, knowingly, recklessly or negligently – see below).

The issue of intention depends on the branch of law. In tort law negligence (the failure to take sufficient care in fulfilling a duty owed) is usually sufficient. Moreover, in the case of strict liability torts the actor is liable for injuries regardless of precautions taken. However, if harm results from an intentional action there appears a possibility of punitive (above and beyond compensatory) damages. This suggests that an action involving intent constitutes a "model" object of legal evaluation, while unintentional behavior may lead to liability as an exception.

In criminal law, intent (*mens rea*) is an essential element of most crimes. Criminal intent is a premise of fault and a factor in grading punishment.[19] Common law criminal intent may be ranked in order of culpability: malice aforethought, specific intent, and general intent. Malice aforethought ("intent to kill") applies to the crime of murder only. Specific intent typically means that "the defendant acts with a more sophisticated level of awareness".[20] Specific intent is required in case of crimes including intention to cause a certain harmful result (e.g., mayhem defined as "physical contact with another, inflicted with the intent to maim, disfigure, or scar"), crimes including intention to exceed the criminal act (e.g., theft defined as "a permanent taking of

---

16   See e.g. California Criminal Jury Instructions No. 520, 2011.
17   MPC was published in 1962 by the American Law Institute to motivate and help the state legislatures to modernize and unify the criminal law of the U.S. See [Dubber 21015].
18   Model Penal Code § 2.03 (2) (b).
19   See e.g. New York Penal Law 125.27.
20   Connecticut Jury Instructions No. 2.3–1, 2011.

property belonging to another") or crimes with scienter (defendant's knowledge that his or her conduct is illegal, e.g., crime defined as "willfully filing a
false tax return").[21] General intent is simply the intent to perform the criminal
act (*actus reus*, e.g., battery defined as "intentional harmful or offensive physical contact with another") without the additional desire to exceed it or cause
a certain result.

A different division of criminal intent has been adopted in the Model Penal
Code which lists four states of mind in order of culpability:

- purposely – "A person acts purposely with respect to a material element of
  an offense [...] if the element involves the nature of her conduct or a result
  thereof, it is her conscious object to engage in conduct of that nature or to
  cause such a result";[22]
- knowingly – "A person acts knowingly with respect to a material element of
  an offense when [...] she is aware that her conduct is of that nature [...] i.e.,
  if the element involves a result of her conduct, she is aware that it is practically certain that her conduct will cause such a result";[23]
- recklessly – "The risk must be of such a nature and degree that ... its disregard involves a gross deviation from the standard of conduct that a law-
  abiding person would observe in the actor's situation";[24]
- negligently – "A person acts negligently ... when she should be aware of a
  substantial and unjustifiable risk that the material element exists or will
  result from her conduct".[25]

It is easy to observe that the conceptualization of human action in the common law systems is quite similar to that in the continental systems, despite the
utilization of different vocabulary. The main tenet on which both conceptual
schemes rest is a distinction between physical causation and mental causation
(intentionality). In the model view, an action is legally relevant (i.e., it may be
the basis for legal responsibility) if it is (a) intentional (e.g., an actor aims at
doing something and is aware of it), and (b) there is a (physical) causal link
between her intentional action and the harmful outcome. In other words,
the intentional action constitutes an element of the causal link leading to the
undesirable outcome.

This model view may be modified in various ways to account for the specific
features of some kinds of behavior. First, intention does not have to be direct

---

21   See U.S. v. Pomponio, 2010.
22   Model Penal Code § 2.02 (2) (a).
23   Model Penal Code in § 2.02(2) (b).
24   Model Penal Code § 2.02(2) (c).
25   Model Penal Code § 2.02(2) (d).

(*dolus directus*) but may take the form of an indirect intent (*dolus indirectus, dolus eventualis*). Also, some types of unintentional action may be subject to legal liability (i.e., in the case of negligence when one unintentionally causes injury to someone in a situation where one should have known one's action could cause harm). It must be stressed that both the "weaker" version of intentional action (*dolus indirectus, dolus eventualis*) as well as unintentional action may become the foundation of legal liability against the backdrop of some normative criteria (e.g., one has not foreseen the outcomes of one's behavior even though one *should have* done so; or one has foreseen the possibility of a harmful outcome but *baselessly* believed that one would avoid it).

Second, (physical) causation in law is not understood in a "pure" way (i.e., as the existence of an actual physical causal link between one's actions and the harmful outcomes), but with modifications. In particular, the causal link in question is usually considered as limited to "typical" or "average" aftermaths of the given kind of behavior. Also, in some instances these modifications involve normative criteria, as when the causal link is restricted only to those actions which are directly prohibited by the existing law.

Having described the general picture of physical and mental causation in the law, we would like to move on to the justification of our first claim: that this picture ultimately rests on a folk psychological understanding of human behavior.

3   The Wisdom of the Folk

Folk psychology is the ability of mindreading, i.e., of ascribing mental states to other people.[26] A more detailed characterization – albeit not an incontestable one – has it that folk psychology is a set of the fundamental capacities which enable us to *describe* our behavior and the behavior of others, to *explain* the behavior of others, to *predict* and *anticipate* their behavior, and to produce *generalizations* pertaining to human behavior [Stich & Ravenscroft 1994]. Those abilities manifest themselves in what may be called *the phenomenological level* of folk psychology.

> [This folk psychology is] a rich conceptual repertoire which [normal human adults] deploy to explain, predict and describe the actions of one another and, perhaps, members of closely related species also. [...] The

---

26   The next three paragraphs are taken from [Brożek 2017].

conceptual repertoire constituting folk psychology includes, predominantly, the concepts of belief and desire and their kin – intention, hope, fear, and the rest – the so-called propositional attitudes.

DAVIES & STONE 1995: 2

One can also speak of *the architectural level* of folk psychology which consists of the neuronal and/or cognitive mechanisms which enable ascribing mental states to others. Importantly, this level is not fully transparent or directly accessible to our minds – while we are able to easily describe the conceptual categories we use to account for other people's behavior (at the phenomenological level), we usually have no direct insight into the mechanisms behind mindreading. In psychological and philosophical literature two kinds of theories emerged pertaining to the architectural level of folk psychology: the theory of mind (TOM) and simulation theory (ST). According to the proponents of TOM, folk psychology is based on often unconscious and automatic inferences about the target's mental states. These inferences take advantage of a tacit theory about the relations between mental states as well as between mental states and behavior. Until the late 1980s, TOM was the leading theory of the architectural level of folk psychology. However, in 1986 Robert Gordon proposed a very different theory [Gordon 1986]. According to his radical simulationism, there is no need to propose an internally represented knowledge structure to explain the phenomenological manifestation of folk psychology. Instead of taking advantage of such a knowledge structure, the mind reader imagines the world from the perspective of her explanatory target, or, in other words, she "puts herself in their shoes". When simulating another person's behavior, the decision-making mechanism of the one who simulates works off-line, and the generated decision does not lead her to behave accordingly, but instead it is ascribed to the explanatory target.

There is little controversy regarding the biologically hard-wired nature of the architectural level of folk psychology. However, the question of how it generates the phenomenological level, and what exactly the extent of culture's influence is on the way we understand and explain the behavior of others, is a matter of fierce controversies. There is substantial evidence which seems to put into doubt the claim that the phenomenological level of folk psychology is culture-independent and hence universal. The capacity to mindread seems to be realized differently in different cultures, and the standard understanding of the phenomenological level of folk psychology assumed by many philosophers and psychologists is an artefact of Western culture.

Let us illustrate this point with an example. According to a much-discussed study by Michael Morris and Kaiping Peng, Asians tend to explain behavior by

citing situational factors, whereas Westerners explain it by focusing on personal causes such as beliefs and desires [Morris & Peng 1994]. The study in
question concerned, *inter alia*, the explanation of a mass murderer's behavior.
In the *World Journal*, the Chinese reporters focused on the situational causes
influencing the behavior of the mass murderer, and mentioned that the "gun-
man had been recently fired", "the post office supervisor was his enemy", and
that he "followed the example of a recent mass slaying in Texas". On the other
hand, in *The New York Times* the American reporters focused on the dispositions of the mass murderer, noting that he "repeatedly threatened violence",
"had a short fuse", "was a martial arts enthusiast", and was "mentally unstable".

This example strongly suggests that the folk psychological conceptualization of action may significantly differ between cultures. However, since our
interest lies in the question of how Western legal cultures understand causality
(and related concepts), we will focus our attention on the Western folk psychology and the understanding of action it embraces. The key concept in this
respect is intentionality [Knobe 2006b]. There is a long tradition of psychological research into this issue.[27] However, recent empirical studies and theoretical constructs have done much to reconcile differing approaches and remove
inconsistencies among the existing accounts.

According to a popular model developed by Knobe and Malle on the basis
of extensive empirical studies:

> In people's folk concept of intentionality, performing an action inten-
> tionally requires the presence of five components: a desire for an out-
> come; beliefs about an action that leads to that outcome; an intention
> to perform the action; the skill to perform the action; and awareness of
> fulfilling the intention while performing the action.
>
> MALLE & KNOBE 1997: 111

The first two elements – desire and belief – are self-explanatory. Together,
they represent a precondition for intention to be formed. However, an action
which involves intention is not, *eo ipso*, an intentional action. What is additionally needed is, on the one hand, the skill required to accomplish the
action, and, on the other, the awareness that one is doing something in order
to fulfill the intention. In order to realize that both these elements constitute
essential ingredients of intentionality, it is useful to consider some "abnormal"

---

27   See e.g. [Heider 1958], [Jones & Davis 1965], [Mascelli & Altrocchi 1969], [Shaver 1985],
      [Fiske 1989], [Fleming & Darley 1989].

scenarios. For instance, let us imagine that Peter, through relevant desires and beliefs, forms an intention to shoot a deer. He lacks skill with the rifle but hits the animal's heart by pure chance. People have a tendency to see such actions as not (fully) intentional. Or else let us assume that Peter has the intention and the skill, but at the moment of firing the rifle he is not aware what he is doing: his behavior does not deserve the label of a (fully) intentional action either [Knobe 2006b].

These considerations enable us to paint a picture of a "model intentional action", brought about by intentional actors, who act on the basis of individual choices, preferences and beliefs. Indeed, it should be underscored that it is a "model" or a "prototype"; this means that particular actions may resemble it to a lesser or greater degree. In other words, actions cannot be divided into two disconnected sets of intentional and unintentional. Rather, we have a kind of continuum, where one extreme is occupied by fully intentional actions, while the other – by fully unintentional actions. Also, it is important to note that the level of intentionality involved in an action is positively correlated with the intensity of blame: the more intentional an action is, the more blameworthy it is considered.

It has also been demonstrated in a series of ingenious experiments that moral emotions and consideration may modify the "standard" understanding of human action. Let us come back to our example with unskilled Peter shooting the dear by accident. The opinion of whether his action was intentional – and to what extent – depends, as it turns out, also on whether one considers Peter's behavior morally good, bad, or neutral. If one believes that killing animals is wrong, then Peter's action will be regarded as "more intentional" than in the case when the person passing judgment has a different view on hunting [Knobe 2006b].

This is an intriguing aspect of the folk psychological concept of intentionality and agency. Painting with a broad brush, one may say that in the traditional approach such concepts were understood as means for explaining and predicting human behavior; in this sense, they were seen as descriptive rather than normative. Meanwhile, the moral "coloration" of intentionality as illustrated by the above example suggests that the folk psychological concept in question also performs an evaluative task: we do not merely *describe* someone's action as intentional but – to an extent at least – ascribe or impute it to them.[28] This shows that, at the level of folk psychology, there is no clear distinction between descriptive and normative concepts.

---

28   Cf. [Knobe 2006b]. See also [Hart 1948–1949].

This conclusion may be reinforced when one considers the concept of causality involved in the folk psychological understanding of action. The first point to note is that people seem to think that holding someone responsible for their actions requires a causal link between one's (more or less) intentional action and its outcome [Roxborough 2009]. However, as the above analysis suggests, the causal link in question involves both physical *and* mental events. This mixture is highly characteristic of folk psychology. It follows that theoretical conceptions of causation as developed by philosophers of science are, in a sense, artificial: they do not "cohere" with the understanding of causation by a philosophically untrained mind. (The same holds for the theories of causation developed in legal doctrine described in the previous section).

One more observation should be added in this context. Let us consider the following example:

> Lauren and Jane work for the same company. They each need to use a computer for work sometimes. Unfortunately, the computer isn't very powerful. If two people are logged on at the same time, it usually crashes. So the company decided to institute an official policy. It declared that Lauren would be the only one permitted to use the computer in the mornings and that Jane would be the only one permitted to use the computer in the afternoons. As expected, Lauren logged on the computer the next day at 9:00 am. But Jane decided to disobey the official policy. She also logged on at 9:00 am. The computer crashed immediately.
>
> ROXBOROUGH & CUMBY 2009: 206

When asked who *caused* the computer to crash, people have a strong tendency to say that Jane did, although both her and Lauren's behavior were necessary for the event to occur. The reason for this surprising outcome is probably that Jane's behavior was immoral, while Lauren acted according to the rules set by the company. But if so, then:

> Causal attributions are not purely descriptive judgments. Rather, people's willingness to say that a given behavior caused a given outcome depends in part on whether they regard the behavior as morally wrong.
>
> KNOBE 2006a: 62

It is further evidence that the folk psychological concept of intentional action, as well as concepts associated with it such as causation, are not purely descriptive, but also normative.

The above considerations suggest the following general picture of human behavior as assumed in the folk psychological conceptual scheme. First, a model action is intentional. This means that it involves beliefs and desires, which serve to form intention; if intention is accompanied by skill and awareness, an action is called intentional. Moreover, if an intentional action is the first link in a causal chain leading to a harmful outcome, there is a foundation to blame an actor for the outcome. This description coincides with the legal understanding of the "model" action described in the previous paragraph.

Second, the model account is modified in various ways. In particular, intentionality is not understood as a discreet, but rather a "continuous" feature: there are phenomena that lie in between the "purely intentional" and "purely unintentional" behavior. Also, the causal link between an intentional action and the harmful outcome is not understood in purely physical terms, but rather by virtue of "typical" consequences. Thus, e.g., the link is "weaker" if an unskilled person succeeds in doing something "by luck". This corresponds to the legal understanding of action and causation, where different forms of intentionality (*dolus directus*, *dolus indirectus*, negligence) as well as restrictions on the causal chain ("typical outcomes") serve to modify the "model action".

Third and finally, it transpires that both "intentional action" and "causal link" are not fully descriptive conceptual devices. They are not only applied in normative contexts but also involve normative factors: an action which deserves moral condemnation becomes "more intentional" than a morally neutral, but in all other respects similar, behavior. Also, this aspect of the problem finds its reflection in the legal conceptual scheme, where normative criteria may feature in the definitions of both intentionality and causation.

This demonstrates that the legal conceptual scheme is largely based on folk psychology. This should come as no surprise. For the law to operate efficiently, it must be understandable to its addressees; following legal rules should come to them "naturally". If the law were based on a completely different conceptualization of behavior, it would be unable to perform its function of regulating social interactions. Of course, legal definitions are much more precise and abstract than the corresponding folk psychological concepts. However, at the core, they are – and must be – the same.

4 Science Enters the Stage

The view of human action presented above – i.e., as depicted by both folk psychology and the law – is quite different from what science has to say about the issue. To see that this is the case, let us consider again – but from the scientific perspective – the problems of intentionality and physical causation.

There is no unique view of human agency arising from the contemporary sciences (experimental psychology, neuroscience, etc.). However, one can identify certain tendencies in the theories developed therein, which seem to converge – to a lesser or greater extent – on two theses. The first reads:

(Thesis 1) Human behavior is in large part unconscious.

The last 40 years have witnessed the rise of conceptions which put emphasis on the unconscious mechanisms that guide our actions. It transpires that most of the decisions we make are intuition-driven, where intuition is understood as an emotion-based, relatively fast mechanism, which works in an effortless way outside our awareness and conscious control.[29] Intuition leads to judgment (emerging "as if from nowhere") and action (with no prior consideration or the formation of intent). Importantly, it is not a capricious device which guides us in unpredictable directions; rather, it is trained from birth in our countless interactions with the environment [Damásio 1994]. Moreover, the view described here does not preclude the possibility of deliberative, conscious action. However, it emphasizes that such an action is relatively rare.

If this picture of the role of the unconscious mechanisms in human behavior is true, then the folk psychological (and, in consequence, legal) view of agency is substantially flawed. We are not usually capable of consciously forming intention on the basis of beliefs and desires; and we are often unaware of executing an action (or, at least, of all the relevant aspects of doing so). What in fact happens is far from what we think is happening – the real forces behind our actions are not transparent to us.

The second thesis describing human action from the perspective of the contemporary cognitive sciences reads:

(Thesis 2) Human behavior is often justified *ex post factum*.

The need to justify our actions has deep evolutionary roots. Such justifications help to manage one's social status, cement group identity, ease intragroup tensions, and disseminate knowledge on what is – and what isn't – socially acceptable behavior [Haidt 2001]. It is speculated that these factors have provided evolutionary fuel for the development of language [Mercier &

---

29   Cf. [Haidt 2001], [Brożek 2020].

Sperber 2017]. Importantly, to justify action we utilize the vocabulary of folk psychology. We speak of beliefs, desires, and reasons, explain our intentions, and suggest that our decisions have been made in a fully conscious way. And when we want to play down our responsibility for our deeds, we try to persuade other members of the social group that we acted on "auto-pilot", with no conscious control of our actions. In reality, our behavior may be largely determined by the unconscious, with only occasional exceptions; however, our narrative about our behavior completely reverses the accents: we tell others (and believe in it, too) that whatever we do, is usually done with due consideration and in full awareness.

Let us turn now to the problem of (physical) causality. The contemporary debate over this issue has been prompted, particularly, by the modern development of physics. The problems surrounding fundamental physical theories, including – but not limited to – quantum mechanics, have generated a conceptual environment in which the problem of causation has featured prominently. This does not mean, however, that there is much agreement on how to understand causality. In fact, there are several competing theories of causation which provide quite different definitions of the phenomenon and face differentiated objections. For example, the regularity theory of causation explores causal chains in terms of invariable patterns of succession of (types of) events; the probabilistic theory is based on the claim that causes raise the probability of their effects; the counterfactual theory explains the meaning of causal claims in terms of counterfactual conditionals ("If X had not occurred, Y would not have occurred"); according to the interventionist theory, X is a cause of Y if and only if there is a possible intervention on X that changes Y; the mechanistic theory holds that causes and effects are connected by an underlying physical mechanism; and the complex-systems theory speaks of a causal connection between X and Y just in case X and Y both feature in the same complex-systems mechanism.[30]

As we can see, there is an abundance of theoretical ways of understanding causation, all requiring the use of highly abstract terminology. It is also clearly visible that these approaches have little to do with the folk psychological rendering of the concept. In particular, all the theories presented above provide us with purely descriptive criteria for establishing causal connections; in folk psychology, on the other hand, causal links are firmly embedded in normative conceptual schemes.

---

30   Cf. [Baumgartner 2020], [Tooley 1987], [Suppes 1970], [Suppes 1970], [Davidson 1967],
      [Dowe 2000].

It is clear, therefore, that the theoretical accounts of both intentional action and causality are quite different from the folk psychological and legal understanding of both concepts. This leads to interesting questions: what exactly is the relationship between law, folk psychology, and science? Are scientific theories pertaining to human behavior and philosophical conceptions (such as that of causality) completely useless from the perspective of a lawyer?

A straightforward answer to this question seems to be "Yes". Courts and legislators cannot simply replace the folk psychological understanding of agency with the one emerging from the cognitive sciences. Such a maneuver would be very confusing for the addressees of the law. However, straightforward answers are not always the best ones. A more nuanced position regarding the relationship between the legal, the folk psychological, and the scientific conceptual schemes is called for. It may be encapsulated in the following three observations.

First, although the "scientific" conceptual scheme pertaining to human behavior is so different from the folk psychological (and legal) one, it provides some insights as to the structure of the latter. In particular, the fact that – in reality – most of our actions are driven by unconscious processes explains why folk psychology (and law) cannot stick to the "model intentional action" but have to modify it with respect to certain types of behavior (e.g., by introducing negligence as the unintentional mode of violating moral or legal rules). Also, the scientific theories provide explanation for the development, stability, and durability of the folk psychological conceptual scheme: it has emerged and is used as a means to justify one's action to the other members of one's community.

Second, knowledge does not come in strictly divided and isolated chunks. It is a complex network of interacting elements, various perspectives, and competing answers to more or less pressing questions. Therefore, the scientific view of human agency is not, and cannot be, completely irrelevant for lawyers. At the very least, it constitutes a much welcome background for developing new doctrinal interpretations and theoretical accounts of legally relevant aspects of human behavior. It may be a source of inspiration or contrast, and of better and more profound understanding. The fact that it is "out there" makes the lawyer's work easier [Brożek 2020].

Third and finally, folk psychology – and, in consequence, the legal conceptual scheme based on it – is not an unchangeable and unchanging thing. The theories we construct in science and philosophy do influence our folk psychological understanding of phenomena. However, this does not happen instantly, but over a period of time. If we compared the understanding of human agency or causation characteristic of, say, a late medieval man (and we can do so by perusing the literature from that period [Lewis 2012]), we would find a significantly different picture from the one assumed by contemporary people.

5   Conclusion

In this chapter we have attempted to provide a general picture of how intentional action and causation are seen from a legal perspective. It has transpired that the legal conceptual scheme – in the considered context – is deeply rooted in folk psychology. The way in which we spontaneously grasp the factors influencing human behavior, or understand causal links, constitutes the point of reference for the legal evaluation of one's actions. Moreover, the concepts involved in the evaluation are not purely descriptive; rather, they involve modifying conditions and normative criteria. From the legal perspective, human behavior and its outcomes are not "out there" in the world, ready to be discovered and objectively labelled. One can say, following in the footsteps of H.L.A. Hart, that they are ascribed or imputed to the agents [Hart 1948–1949].

Science and philosophy, on the other hand, strive to provide us with objective, value neutral and descriptive models of intentional action and causality. The theories developed under such assumptions are not – and cannot be – directly relevant for the law. This is far from saying, however, that they are completely irrelevant. To the contrary: the constant growth of knowledge of the actual mechanisms behind human behavior as well as reconceptualization of key concepts such as causality, contribute to the development of a broad theoretical framework, which serves as an important source of inspiration for legal thinking, and – over time – reshapes our folk psychological conceptual scheme.

Bibliography

Baumgartner, Michael (2020). Causation. [In:] [Berg-Schlosser & Badie & Morlino (eds.) 2020], pp. 305–321.

Berg-Schlosser, Dirk & Badie, Bernard & Morlino, Leonardo A. (eds.) (2020). *The Sage Handbook of Political Science*. London: Sage.

Berkowitz, Leonard (ed.) (1965). *Advances in Experimental Social Psychology*. Vol. II. New York: Academic Press.

Brożek, Bartosz (2013). *Rule-Following. From Imitation to the Normative Mind.* Kraków: Copernicus Center Press.

Brożek, Bartosz (2017). The Troublesome Person. [In:] [Kurki & Pietrzykowski (eds.) 2017], pp. 3–13.

Brożek, Bartosz (2020). *The Legal Mind. A New Introduction to Legal Epistemology.* Cambridge: Cambridge University Press.

Damásio, António (1994). *Descartes' Error: Emotion, Reason, and the Human Brain.* New York: Grosset/Putnam.

Davidson, Donald (1967). Causal Relations. *Journal of Philosophy* vol. LXIV, No. 21, pp. 691–703.

Davies, Martin & Stone, Tony (eds.) (1995). *Folk Psychology: The Theory of Mind Debate.* Oxford: Blackwell Publishers.

Dowe, Phil (2000). *Physical Causation.* Cambridge: Cambridge University Press.

Dubber, Markus D. (2015). *An Introduction to the Model Penal Code.* Oxford: Oxford University Press.

Fiske, Susan T. (1989). *Examining the Role of Intent: Towards Understanding Its Role in Stereotyping and Prejudice.* [In:] [Uleman & Bargh ed. 1989], pp. 253–283.

Fleming, John H. & Darley, John M. (1989). Perceiving Choice and Constraint: The Effects of Contextual and Behavioral Cues on Attitude Attribution. *Journal of Personality and Social Psychology* vol. LVI, 27–40.

Góralski, Piotr (2009). Związek przyczynowy w prawie karnym na tle orzecznictwa sądowego [The Causal Relationship in Criminal Law against the Background of Judicial Decisions]. *Prokuratura i Prawo* vol. VI, pp. 26–45.

Gordon, Robert M. (1986). Folk Psychology as Simulation. *Mind & Language* vol. I, pp. 158–171.

Gudowski, Jacek (ed.) (2018). *Kodeks cywilny. Komentarz. Tom III. Zobowiązania. Część ogólna* [Commentary on Civil Code. Part III. Obligations], 2nd ed., Warszawa 2018, https://sip.lex.pl/#/commentary/587754664/552104/gudowski-jacek-red-kodeks-cywilny-komentarz-tom-iii-zobowiazania-czesc-ogolna-wyd-ii?cm=URELATI ONS (retrieved: 2021–06-22, 3:28).

Haidt, Jonathan (2001). The Emotional Dog and Its Rational Tail: A Social Intuitionist Approach to Moral Judgement. *Psychological Review* vol. CVIII, No. 4, pp. 814–834.

Hart, Herbert Lionel Adolphus (1948–1949). The Ascription of Responsibility and Rights. *Proceedings of the Aristotelian Society.* New Series vol. XL, pp. 171–194.

Heider, Fritz (1958). *The Psychology of Interpersonal Relations.* New York: Wiley.

Jones, Edward E. & Davis, Keith E. (1965). From Acts to Dispositions: The Attribution Process in Person Perception. [In:] [Berkowitz (ed.) 1965], pp. 219–266.

Knobe, Joshua (2006a). *Folk Psychology, Folk Morality.* Unpublished doctoral dissertation.

Knobe, Joshua (2006b). The Concept of Intentional Action: A Case study in the Uses of Folk Psychology. *Philosophial Studies* vol. CXXX, pp. 203–231.

Kurki, Visa A.J. & Pietrzykowski, Tomasz (eds.) (2017). *Legal Personhood – Animals, Artificial Intelligence and the Unborn.* Dordrecht: Springer.

Lewis, Clive Staples (2012). *The Discarded Image.* Cambridge: Cambridge University Press.

Malle, Bertram F. & Knobe, Joshua (1997). The Folk Concept of Intentionality. *Journal of Experimental Social Psychology* vol. XXXIII, pp. 101–121.

Maselli, Mary D. & Altrocchi, John (1969). Attribution of Intent. *Psychological Bulletin* vol. LXXI, pp. 445–454.

Mercier, Hugo & Sperber, Dan (2017). *The Enigma of Reason.* Cambridge (MA): Harvard University Press.

Morris, Michael W. & Peng, Kaiping (1994). Culture and Cause: American and Chinese Attributions for Social and Physical Events. *Journal of Personality and Social Psychology* vol. LXVII, pp. 949–971.

Radwański, Zbigniew (1997). *Zobowiązania.* Część ogólna [*Commitments. General Part*]. Warszawa: C.H. Beck.

Roxborough, Craig & Cumby, Jill (2009). Folk Psychological Concepts: Causation. *Philosophical Psychology* vol. XXII, No. 2, pp. 205–213.

Shaver, Kelly (1985). *The Attribution of Blame: Causality, Responsibility, and Blameworthiness.* New York: Springer-Verlag.

Stapleton, Jane (2008). Choosing What we Mean by "Causation" in the Law. *Missouri Law Review* vol. LXXIII, pp. 433–480.

Stich, Stephen & Ravenscroft, Ian, (1994). What is Folk Psychology? *Cognition* vol. L, pp. 447–468.

Suppes, Patrick (1970). *A Probabilistic Theory of Causality.* Amsterdam: North Holland.

Tooley, Michael (1987). *Causation: A Realist Approach.* Oxford: Clarendon Press.

Uleman, James S. & Bargh, John A. (eds.) (1989). *Unintended Though.* New York: Guilford Press.

Wiśniewski, Tadeusz (2018). Komentarz do art. 361 *Kodeksu cywilnego* [Commentary on Art. 361 of the *Civil Code*]. [In:] [Gudowski (ed.) 2018], https://sip.lex.pl/#/com mentary/587754664/552104/gudowski-jacek-red-kodeks-cywilny-komentarz-tom -iii-zobowiazania-czesc-ogolna-wyd-ii?cm=URELATIONS (retrieved: 2021–06-22, 13:28).

Witt, John Fabian (2018). *Torts: Cases, Principles, and Institutions.* CALI eLangdell® Press. Third edition.

Wróbel, Włodzimierz & Zoll, Andrzej (2013). *Polskie prawo karne.* Część ogólna [*Polish Criminal Law.* General Part]. Kraków: Znak.

Wróbel, Włodzimierz & Zoll, Andrzej (eds.) (2016). *Kodeks karny.* Część ogólna. Tom I. Część I. Komentarz do art. 1–52 [Criminal Code. General Part. Volume I. Commentary on Articles 1–52], 5th edition, Warszawa 2016, https://sip.lex.pl/ #/commentary/587276754/510465/wrobel-wlodzimierz-red-zoll-andrzej-red-kod eks-karny-czesc-ogolna-tom-i-czesc-i-komentarz-do-art...?cm=URELATIONS (retrieved: 2021-06-22, 13:31).

Zoll, Andrzej (2016). Komentarz do art. 1 *Kodeksu karnego* [Commentary on Art. 1 of *The Criminal Code*]. [In:] [Wróbel & Zoll (eds.) 2016], [Wróbel & Zoll (eds.) 2016], https://sip.lex.pl/#/commentary/587276754/510465/wrobel-wlodzimierz-red-zoll -andrzej-red-kodeks-karny-czesc-ogolna-tom-i-czesc-i-komentarz-do-art...?cm =URELATIONS (retrieved: 2021-06-22, 13:31).

CHAPTER 9

Cause and Effect Relationships in Theology

Marcin Tkaczyk

The concept of cause and effect belongs in the inner circle of the method-ologically most important concepts of theology and knowledge in general. According to an ancient skeptic philosopher, Aenesidemus, the possibility of science and knowledge rests entirely on three ideas: truth, causality, and deduction. Hence, skeptics tend to criticize those ideas. This pertains particu-larly to theology, where the concept of cause and effect is ubiquitous and serves to define a wide variety of concepts. In the absence of the concept of causality any genuine theology turns out to be infeasible, whereas, given a good theory of causality, key parts of theology can be reconstructed. The common failure to recognize that is a source of the general failure of contemporary theology.

It should be clear that theology is here to be identified as classical Catholic theology, originated by the Church Fathers, and further developed by the school-men. Such a definition is justified historically, as it is the only kind of theology to have been debated in the Lvov-Warsaw School by Jan Łukasiewicz, Józef M. Bocheński, Jan F. Drewnowski, Jan Salamucha, and Bolesław Sobociński, that is, the Cracow Circle. Hence, the term "theology" is to be understood in the way it was understood in the Cracow Circle ([Bocheński 1937], [Bocheński 1949], [Drewnowski 1937], [Salamucha 1946a], [Salamucha 1946b], [Tkaczyk 2017]). It is also justified systematically, for theology in this sense has its own subject matter, research tradition, objectives, and, first of all, characteristic methods known as the *scholastic method*. Therefore, it is methodologically unique and distinct from other kinds of theories covered by the umbrella term "theology".

1 Epistemic Ambitions of Theology

The methodological distinctiveness and peculiarity of classical Catholic the-ology has its source in the preconceived manifesto of its founding fathers, particularly the early Church Fathers. According to this manifesto, theology is somehow both knowledge and faith at the same time. To be more specific, theology makes a claim to possess simultaneously two qualities:

theology is entirely a body of knowledge (a science), (1a)

theology essentially surpasses the whole range of human knowledge. (1b)

Hence, *knowing* and *believing* at the same time is essential in theology, which at face value seems to constitute a contradiction. As many authors, such as Étienne Gilson ([1936], [1939]), have struggled with the problem of the coincidence in one mind of the psychological attitudes of knowledge and faith, it should be said that no such question is here under consideration. Rather, a methodological problem is dealt with here, the problem of justification: theorems of theology allegedly *can* as well as *cannot* be justified in a way acceptable in science or philosophy.

On the one hand, according to claim (1a), all theorems of theology are not only a matter of belief or even merely a matter of truth, but are also *demonstrably* true. Demonstrability means any adequate justification accepted within the confines of scientific knowledge in a broad sense or even human reason in general, with no presumption of its being deductive, or empirical, etc. In other words, theorems of theology lay claim to the assent of every rational human mind, regardless of faith. On the other hand, according to claim (1b) some theorems of theology could never be demonstrated by means of human reason, unless they have been supernaturally revealed by God.

Bocheński [1937] mentions Alexandria as the starting point of thesis (1a). In fact, it has been documented that as early as in the 2nd century the dean of the Catechetic School of Alexandria at that time, Pantaenus, was openly adopting such a stance, linking theology to Greco-Roman philosophy. It is likely that the view arose in Alexandria even earlier. Similar views also existed in other centers, with Justin's school in Rome as a prominent example. Thesis (1a) was viewed with suspicion by some Church Fathers, like Tertullian and Cyprian of Carthage, as well as some schoolmen, like Durandus and Vásquez, who rather emphasized the differences between philosophy and the content of faith, and adopted thesis (1b). Among the Church Fathers theology was thought of both as a science and as a supernatural initiation ([Malaty 1995], [Olson 1999]).

It is presumably this very methodological split in theology which reverberated in Salamucha's characterization of Thomism: maximalism regarding both scope and method. Typically, maximalism regarding method, i.e., high demands on precision and justification, coincides with a narrow scope of problems to be solved, and *vice versa*. The higher standard one sets for methodology, the fewer theses one is ready to accept that meet the standard. In

Thomism, Salamucha observes, bold theories promise high standards of justification [Salamucha 1946b]. It is likely that high methodological standards mirror thesis (1a), whereas the maximalist scope of theories mirrors thesis (1b). The Church Fathers as well as the schoolmen sought to secure both ambitions (1). The solution they delivered is known as the scholastic method, which consists, among other ideas, of

a characteristic partition of the set of theorems, in particular the   (2a)
division of *articles of faith* into *mysteries of faith* and *revelabilia*, (2a)
the structure of the system of theology as a combination of three   (2b)
subsystems, i.e. *dogmatics, metaphysics,* and *apologetics.*

This leads to grounding theology on a special argument from authority: some theorems are justified by an authority, but there are also other theorems to demonstrate the reliability of the authority. The whole construction rests to a high degree on the concept of a cause-and-effect relationship.

2   Distribution of Dogmas

To be considered orthodox, any system (theory) of theology must contain the entire set of the *articles of faith* (*dogmas*) as a subset of the content of the system. The articles of faith are derived from the *deposit of faith*, which is believed to have been revealed by God between the call of Abraham and the death of the last of the Twelve Apostles, and which is therefore both binding and invariant. Apart from the dogmas other theorems are allowed and even necessary, such as the logical consequences of the dogmas as well as theologians' own assumptions and hypotheses that serve as explanation of the dogmas and enable the construction of a well-built theory. In any case, the articles of faith are indispensable.

The entire collection of the *articles of faith* (*dogmas*) is strictly divided into *mysteries of faith* and *revelabilia*. Mysteries of faith defy the abilities of human reason to the effect that they can never be demonstrated unless by divine revelation. On the contrary, *revelabilia* can be grasped, discovered, and sufficiently demonstrated by natural human means. Hence, *revelabilia* are achievable for human reason and failure to accept them is an error in cognition in the same way as failure to accept the Pythagorean theorem. Some dogmas are certainly classified as mysteries of faith, e.g., that God is one in three Divine Persons.

Some other dogmas are certainly classified as *revelabilia*, e.g., that God exists. There are, however, some articles of faith which are classified differently by different theologians, e.g., that the universe had origin in time is a revealed truth according to Bonaventure but a mystery of faith according to Aquinas. Every article of faith belongs to one and only one of the two subsets – it is either a mystery of faith or a revealed truth, but never both – with no subset being empty. Aside from articles of faith, all theorems are to be justified and evaluated in the same way as in other sciences, hence, no mystery is permissible outside the collection of the dogmas ([Gilson 1936], [Gilson 1939], [Scheeben 1873–1887]).

It is worth noting that only essential indemonstrability is an element of the concept of mystery by virtue of the method of theology itself; for there are some stances in theology which involve a stronger concept of mystery. Besides the concept of mystery as an essentially indemonstrable sentence, Bocheński [1965] speaks of a sentence whose meaning may not be grasped and of a sentence of unknown logical relations to other sentences classified as a mystery of faith by some theologians. Hence, clearly there are at least three different meanings of the phrase "mystery of faith" in logical analyses of theology:

mystery of meaning,	(3a)
mystery of consequence,	(3b)
mystery of demonstration (justification).	(3c)

Only the mildest concept of mystery (3c) is strictly required in any proper system of theology. In fact, many Church Fathers and prominent schoolmen take the radical concept of mystery (3a) out of the equation, for it is difficult to understand how a theory could be regarded as a body of knowledge in case its important expressions are practically meaningless. Intermediate concepts of mystery are also allowed [Scheeben 1873–1887]. All in all, by mystery of faith one should understand such a sentence φ, that (a) φ is an article of faith (dogma), and therefore a theorem of every admissible system of theology, and (b) φ cannot be demonstrated by a human agent unless φ has been revealed to the agent by God.

As described the difference between mysteries of faith and *revelabilia* lies in cognitive abilities. Like all legitimate pieces of knowledge, *revelabilia* are demonstrable such that a human agent can see that they are true provided the agent is endowed with sufficient cognitive abilities. The agent can see them directly or only indirectly. In the latter case, the agent can see that every step in a demonstration is justified. On the contrary, every mystery of faith is essentially indemonstrable such that no human agent can ever see – even indirectly – that the mystery sentence is true, unless God has revealed it to this agent. This incapability of demonstration is essential for mysteries of faith, but more radical versions of mystery should not be involved in theology as a science. Furthermore, no human agent could ever correctly demonstrate the negation of a mystery of faith, hence, mysteries of faith are in principle neither provable nor disprovable.

3   Subsystems of Theology

Theology is supposed to be not only a body of knowledge, as stated in the claim (1a), but furthermore a system of knowledge (theory). That means, *inter alia*, that theorems are interrelated logically and closed under the logical consequence. The tendency to deliver a system was predominant among Catholic thinkers from the very beginning. This tendency matured in Anselm of Canterbury, Pierre Abélard, and especially Thomas Aquinas, but originated among the early Church Fathers.

It is a commonly accepted and recurring view that the system of theology consists merely of the articles of faith serving as axioms and their consequences (e.g. [Scheeben 1873–1887]). This view has been held even by an author as logically sophisticated as Salamucha [1946a]. Although it is widely treated as obvious, this view is certainly false and in fact quite naive. Firstly, no serious system of theology could ever spring to life simply as the set of consequences of the dogmas. Secondly, there are clearly several acceptable systems of theology, whereas by definition there is exactly one set of consequences of the set of dogmas. Thirdly, even some superficial knowledge of classic works in theology is sufficient to realize that what great theologians actually do is much more than simply deducing consequences of dogmas. And fourthly, to lay down the set of dogmas is in itself a cognitive challenge, for dogmas – like facts in physics – are not given ready to use but often rather hidden in the unwritten deposit of faith entrusted to the Twelve Apostles' safekeeping. Hence, theology is admittedly a system, but a complex one, and its structure is more elaborate than it is usually said to be. Some use of the inductive method has been accepted in Bocheński's postwar works [1965]; however, the comprehensive structure of theological theory has yet to be described.

It seems fair to say that the entire system of theology consists of three subsystems: *dogmatics, metaphysics,* and *apologetics.* These are subsystems and not only subsets of theorems, for each is supposed to be a system (theory) in itself. Hence, although dogmatics, metaphysics, and apologetics come together to constitute a system of theology, they may be separated by logical filtration and treated individually. It is also worth mentioning that the subsystems of theology may and in fact do overlap, i.e., some theorems may belong to more than one subsystem. The distinction of the three subsystems is more profound than partitions into branches or subdisciplines, e.g., soteriology, eschatology, and the like, for the three subsystems are methodologically different and widely autonomous relative to one another.

The three subsystems of theology differ from one another in their objectives and methods. Pertaining to the method, mysteries of faith may appear only in dogmatics. The only articles of faith permissible in metaphysics or apologetics are *revelabilia*. This essential characteristic is presented in chart (4), with the sign "+" indicating a nonempty set and the sign "−" the empty set of theorems.

	articles of faith (dogmas) mysteries of faith *revelabilia*	(4)
dogmatics	+ +	
apologetics	− +	
metaphysics	− +	

Hence, there is a restriction put on the ability of the subsystems of theology to share theorems; namely, mysteries of faith cannot be shared and must be restricted to the confines of dogmatics.

It follows that neither metaphysics nor apologetics claims any special status among bodies of knowledge. Their theorems are demonstrable – at least according to the plan – in a perfectly appropriate way as in typical, say secular, sciences. And those theorems are to be analyzed, evaluated, and criticized accordingly. The incapability of demonstration must be restricted to dogmatics. In addition to standard ways of demonstration, in dogmatics and only in dogmatics, there is a peculiar assumption requiring that every sentence revealed by God be recognized as a theorem:

if sentence φ belongs to the deposit of faith, then sentence φ is a   (5)
theorem.

Rule (5) is an analogue of the heuristic rule and the basic dogma combined in Bocheński's account of religious discourse [Bocheński 1965]. The rule just mentioned (5) is the only way for a mystery of faith to be classified as a theorem (with its consequences); hence, no mystery of faith is a theorem except in the system of dogmatics. In the system of theology, the joint objective of metaphysics and apologetics is to justify the efficacy of rule (5). In that sense, metaphysics and apologetics may be called, in Thomistic terms, *preambula fidei*.

The objective of metaphysics *qua* subsystem of theology is to demonstrate that God exists and has attributes that render Him absolutely credible. The arrière-pensée in indicating the objective of metaphysics is vital, as metaphysics is a broad and autonomous discipline, and its different branches may have different objectives. So, its duty within theology is to demonstrate that

God exists,	(6a)
it is impossible for God to be mistaken (God's cognitive power),	(6b)
it is impossible for God to mislead those he speaks to (God's moral qualifications).	(6c)

Systems of metaphysics differ from one another, e.g., they tend to demonstrate that God exists with necessity rather than that he merely exists, and usually are quite comprehensive. And yet, theorems (6) outline the minimal content of metaphysics *qua* subsystem of theology, much as the minimal set theory within mathematics needs to allow reconstruction of natural numbers.

The objective of apologetics in turn is to establish a link between the God metaphysics speaks of and the deposit of faith, to the effect that the entire content of the deposit of faith has been revealed by God and therefore is grounded in God's authority. Hence, the minimal apologia within the system of theology is indicated by the theorems:

God delivered revelation within the course of history,	(7a)
sentence φ belongs to the deposit of faith if and only if φ is revealed by God.	(7b)

This practically requires at least two outcomes, namely, some justification of the heuristic description of the deposit of faith as well as demonstration that it is God's statement. Unlike in the religions of the Book, e.g., Judaism, Islam, and

Protestantism, in Catholic theology the description of the deposit of faith itself presents a challenge and a research program, for in Catholicism the deposit of faith is not to be identified with any existing book but rather with the authoritative teaching of the Twelve Apostles, which is called the Word of God, partially written in the Bible, and partially communicated in the oral Tradition (hence the authority of the ancient Church Fathers).

Metaphysics and apologetics together (i.e., *preambula fidei*) deliver the basis to accept the inference rule (5) as a means to discover the truth. By theorems (6) God exists and is reliable. It follows that anything would be true were it stated by God. No theorem of metaphysics secures that anything has actually been stated by God. Such a theorem belongs to apologetics. However, in metaphysics there is often an auxiliary theorem – based on divine omnipotence – to the effect that God's statement, namely divine revelation, is possible. By theorem (7a) God actually delivered a statement, and by theorem (7b) the content of this statement is identical with the deposit of faith established once and for all by the Twelve Apostles. It follows that the content of the deposit of faith is infallibly true. This is sufficient to secure the theorem:

if sentence φ belongs to the deposit of faith, then sentence φ is (8)
true.

Theorem (8) is a sound basis for theorem (5). By theorems (5) and (8) no false theorem may appear in the system of theology as an article of faith. Other theorems are to be demonstrated as in other branches of knowledge; hence, the system of theology consistently meets both conditions (1). Theorems that surpass the range of human knowledge may be introduced by means of authority, and yet, as the reliability of the authority in question has been justified independently, the whole system of theology presents a body of knowledge, for within the system of theology two subsystems are selected that (a) do not contain mysteries of faith and (b) jointly and directly demonstrate that every article of faith is true.

4 The Fulcrum and Lever of Theology

Archimedes' assertion, "give me a fulcrum and with a lever I will move the whole world", in demonstrating the principle of the lever has been quoted by Pappus of Alexandria and others. It seems fair to say that metaphysics and apologetics constitute a fulcrum, whereas rule (5) is the lever which enables moving the edifice of theology towards fulfillment of ambitious claims (1).

This is so important because the structure (2) of systems of theology is the sole means to classify theology as a body of knowledge, as claimed in statement (1a). To understand this, it is helpful to mention the distinction between assertive and neutral theories. Regardless of the logical relations between formulas, a system is assertive relative to a person if the person actually believes in the theorems of the system. A system is neutral relative to a person if the person takes no stance towards the theorems, neither accepting nor rejecting them [Ajdukiewicz 1960]. Now, for a theory to be classified as a body of knowledge, it is necessary that adequate reasons exist to accept the theorems of the theory as literally true. Otherwise, the theory in question should be considered a subject matter for knowledge rather than a piece of knowledge. For example, literary works or bodies of laws are not truly bodies of knowledge, they do not contain knowledge, but rather they are subjects for knowledge. There is certainly a science or knowledge about civil law or Shakespeare's plays, and one does not need to believe Shakespeare or lawmakers to possess that knowledge. Even in logic and mathematics, especially since alternative theories have been constructed, there is a considerable body of opinion that those theories should be considered subjects for knowledge rather than contents of knowledge. In empirical sciences, it is mostly observation and experiment that give ground to claims to truth. In theology, the structure (2) plays an analogical role, so, if theorem (8) has been demonstrated, the theologian can legitimately say, e.g.:

we have demonstrated, and we know, that God is triune.   (9a)

Otherwise, he can only say:

We have demonstrated, and we know, that Christians claim God   (9b)
is triune.

In a sound system based on principles (2) with theorem (8) demonstrated to be true, every article of faith (dogma) is also demonstrated to be true. Statements like God is triune, heaven and hell are eternal, the Last Judgment is coming, etc., are demonstrated scientific truths. If theorems like (9a) are legitimate, theology is a proper body of knowledge, a scientific theory, no less than physics or history. But if all legitimate theorems are of the kind (9b), sources of theology are not sources of knowledge, but rather – important and influential – literary works. Theology is a subject for knowledge, never knowledge itself, and theologians are similar to lawyers or philologists rather than physicists or historians. In such a case, articles of faith present great narratives, but no scientific truths. That is why the structure (2) of theological theories is vital. And this is exactly why the vast majority of scholastics insisted on the full methodological autonomy of metaphysics and apologetics within systems of theology. As Bocheński [1935] emphasized, since the turn of the 19th and 20th centuries this had been the unanimous stance of all factions within Neo-scholasticism.

For that reason, the uncontested method for laying the fundaments for theology as a body of knowledge consists in detecting cause and effect relationships. For these fundaments are only laid by providing adequate systems of metaphysics and apologetics, so that theorem (8) may be demonstrated. And metaphysics and apologetics qua subsystems of theology rest entirely on detecting cause and effect relationships. This does not have to apply to metaphysics or even apologetics in general, but to those *qua* subsystems of theology. It is important to understand that in metaphysics and apologetics *qua* subsystems of theology the concept of cause and effect is not merely a concept but rather *the* concept, just as detecting causal relationships is not a method but rather *the* method. Hence, the epistemic ambitions of theology depend on the cause and effect relationship as a cornerstone.

In particular, metaphysics *qua* subsystem of theology seeks to demonstrate theorems (6) by demonstrating the existence and attributes of a transcendent object. Technically to implement this a metaphysician seeks to (a) find in the knowable world properties which make it clear that the world is a creation, i.e., an effect of some unknown intelligent cause and (b) establish what properties such a cause should have to be able to create such a world. In other words, the content of the metaphysics *qua* subsystem of theology is the detection of some cause-and-effect relationship within the world we know by acquaintance as the effect and to describe the cause we cannot know by acquaintance. So, the whole of metaphysics is about a cause-and-effect relationship called *creation*.

Quite similarly, the whole of apologetics is about a cause-and-effect relationship called *revelation*. The objective of apologia is to show that the deposit of faith is an effect of some extraordinary activity of the same cause metaphysics qualified as the creator of the world. Apologists normally seek to demonstrate theorems (7) by concomitance of two kinds of events: *prophecies* and *miracles*. A prophecy consists in a very unlikely event being successfully foretold at a significant distance in time, like Cyrus the Great's conquering the Neo-Babylonian Empire foretold in the *Book of Isaiah*. A miracle is an event which to be enacted requires power over laws of nature, generally beyond human abilities, like the Israelites' Crossing of the Red Sea in the *Book of Exodus*. A prophecy and a miracle combined take place when the event to be successfully foretold actually itself counts as a miracle. Prophecies and miracles are considered manifestations of divine powers, specifically God's omniscience for prophecies and God's omnipotence for miracles. It is again all about a cause-and-effect relationship, for prophecies and miracles are to be recognized as effects of God's direct actions, and so, to demonstrate the deposit of faith, which has been signed and sealed with those effects, is itself an effect of God's similar deeds.

It should be clear that creation, prophecies, miracles, and revelation are strictly causal concepts. In metaphysics and apologetics, some states of affairs we know by acquaintance are to be recognized as creation, prophecies, miracles, revelation, i.e., generally effects of one cause we know by acquaintance, the cause to be called God. It is fair to say that metaphysics and apologetics constitute a fulcrum for theology. And it is equally justified that the concept of cause and effect is the lever of the fulcrum. In dogmatics, the situation is not the same, as it is based on theorem (5) and its objective is articulation, interpretation, and arrangement of the content of the deposit of faith. Hence, it is mostly humanistic work, based on sources. And yet, although the concept of cause and effect is not a cornerstone of the system of dogmatics itself, it is astoundingly ubiquitous in the system, even if it is often present in disguise.

5   Analysis and Construction of the Concept of Cause

As the number of theories as well as misunderstandings in the field is enormous, any account of cause-and-effect relationships in the three subsystems of theology must be preceded by an outline of the concept of cause and effect in general. This is due to a manifold peculiarity of the concept in question.

Firstly, it is received wisdom that the term "cause" is ambiguous. However, the key factor is the distinctive kind of its ambiguity. The term "cause" is ambiguous in a very special way, namely, its meaning presents a *concept family*. Basically, a univocal term has exactly one concept associated with it as its meaning and a definitely ambiguous or equivocal term has two or more meanings which are quite different and unrelated. Between the two extremes there are a number of circuitous semantic constructions, with analogical terms being the most famous case. Roughly, an analogical term is associated with two or more concepts which are partially different but related to each other in a particular way. Now, a concept family is something weaker than analogy, i.e., it

CAUSE AND EFFECT RELATIONSHIPS IN THEOLOGY

is closer to mere equivocity. A concept family term has two or more different meanings which are interconnected by the relation of resemblance. What is vital here is that the resemblance relation is not transitive. This means that, unlike the case of analogy or isomorphism, it is possible (and usually the case) that one meaning is related to some, but not to all, other meanings of such term. Let then α be a term of a concept family and $\sigma_1, \sigma_2, ..., \sigma_n$, be the concepts associated with α as its different meanings. As the concepts $\sigma_1, \sigma_2, ..., \sigma_n$ represent a concept family, it is permissible that σ_k bears a resemblance to σ_l in some respects, and σ_l bears a resemblance to σ_m in some other respects, but σ_k bears no resemblance to σ_m whatsoever or alternatively σ_k bears admittedly some resemblance to σ_m but only in yet another respect ($1 \leq k, l, m \leq n$). In other words, a plurality of standards is permissible in the case of terms of a concept family. Consequently, there is no single extension of a concept family term, but rather a family of extensions, and neither by union nor by intersection can one single comprehension of the term be achieved. So, an adequate account of a concept family term requires (a) identifying the initial concept (initial meaning), and then (b) step by step identifying derivative concepts, (c) each time determining the resemblance between an input and the output concept, i.e., between a concept already identified and the new concept. Concept families are often produced when a vernacular term has come into use in different domains of science or culture (a concise account of concept families has been provided by Pawłowski, 1986).

The term "religion" gives a simple example of a concept family. In somewhat simplified words, in ancient Greece and Rome worshipping the gods of one's community was included into the concept of religion. Then Christianity sprang into life and involved worship of the God of revelation. With hesitation and delay Christianity was eventually classified as a religion. Finally, Buddhism was also classified as a religion even though it involved no worship and no belief in God, and was actually a kind of skepticism. However, Buddhism is like Christianity in that they both involve a kind of personal salvation from a congenital accursed fate. The result is that there is the Greco-Roman concept of religion, including worship of a deity but not salvation, the Christian concept of religion, including worship of a deity as well as salvation, and the Buddhist concept of religion, including salvation but no worship of a deity. The Greco-Roman and Christian concepts of religion clearly bear some resemblance to each other and so do the Christian and Buddhist concepts of religion, but there seems to be no such clear resemblance between the Greco-Roman and Buddhist concepts. If "religion" is a concept family term, it would be erroneous to seek for one comprehension and extension of it. One should rather identify different comprehensions and extensions – as in the case of equivocal terms – and the web of resemblance between them.

Secondly, the initial concept of cause and effect has three features which make things even more complicated, namely (a) it is a merely intuitive concept, (b) it is explicated only by examples (ostensive definition), and (c) those examples involve essentially inner experience, not only sensory experience. A brief comment might be useful on the distinction between an articulate and a (merely) intuitive meaning. An articulate meaning (not to be confused with clear or exact) makes it possible to set down the comprehension (content), i.e., a collection of attributes shared by exactly all designata of the term, e.g., understanding the meaning of the term "square" gives the collection of three attributes: tetragonal, orthogonal, and equilateral as the comprehension of the concept of square. An intuitive concept gives one the ability to use properly the term without comprehending it, e.g., the terms "vegetable", "table" [Ajdukiewicz 1965].

The initial unit (member) in the concept family of cause and effect should be stipulated ostensively. So, imagine Gilbert. Suppose it is raining and Gilbert is walking in the rain with an unfurled umbrella. Gilbert may become aware of the following two states of affairs:

that it is raining, (10a)

that the umbrella is unfurled. (10b)

Next Gilbert may realize that state of affairs (10b) can be legitimately attributed to him in the sense that it was Gilbert who opened the umbrella, but state of affairs (10a) cannot be attributed to him in any similar sense. Gilbert chooses to use the term "cause and effect" to designate states of affairs legitimately attributed to him in a way similar to (10b). The effect is identified as that the umbrella is open, and the cause is identified as that Gilbert has opened the umbrella (by analogy, the cause may also be identified as Gilbert's decision to open the umbrella, or as Gilbert himself).

By way of recurring experience of this kind the initial concept of cause and effect arises. Enormous historical evidence confirms that it is quite a functional, efficacious, operational, and communicable concept, even though it has been characterized solely by means of examples, involves both sensory and inner experience together, and is merely intuitive. This may be termed the concept of *personal cause.*

The second member in the concept family of cause and effect, termed *natural cause,* is a descendant of the first. Come back to Gilbert who is continuing his walk in the rain. It is a matter of course for Gilbert that the state of affairs that it is raining may not be attributed to any personal cause Gilbert knows about. However, the relation between the clouds and state of affairs (10a) bears some resemblance to the relation between Gilbert and state of affairs (10b). State of affairs (10b) may be attributed to Gilbert in the sense of personal cause. Gilbert thinks that state of affairs (10a) may be attributed to the clouds in a different, but in some respect similar, sense. The construction of the concept of personal cause stems from Gilbert's inner experience of being able to see to some states of affairs by means of intentional action. Instead of that experience Gilbert comes up with a working hypothesis that objects have a *nature* which in certain circumstances makes those objects behave in a specific way. Gilbert allows that some objects in certain circumstances may literally be forced to see to specific states of affairs by nature instead of being able to do so by intentional action. Gilbert believes that the relation between the clouds and state of affairs (10a) is similar to the relation between himself and state of affairs (10b) with the reservation that intentional action is to be substituted with automatic action by the compulsion of nature. The concept of natural cause has been thereby constructed by means of resemblance to the concept of personal cause.

The concept of personal cause is the initial member and the concept of natural cause is the second member in the concept family of cause and effect (the distinction is somehow parallel to two kinds of explanation in [Swinburne 1974]). Other members of the family seem to arise – directly or not – from those two. For instance, in physics the concept of cause and effect is derived from the concept of natural cause, but it is also required by definition that a portion of energy be transmitted from the cause to the effect [Kiczuk 1995]. With the passing of time a concept family of a well-known term may happen to become a complicated network of concepts.

The concept of cause and effect has been criticized by skeptics since antiquity. The most famous, not necessarily the best, criticism of this concept was delivered by David Hume and developed by Immanuel Kant and John Stuart Mill. This originated a wide-scale search for a proper definition of causality. The definitions that have appeared can be roughly divided into four groups. Firstly, causality has been reduced to some purely empirical relations, like constant succession in time. That was the attitude of Hume and Mill. Secondly, it has been reduced to some logical concepts. The famous work by Jan Łukasiewicz [1906] and Bocheński's attempt [1948] to improve it are among this group, as well as a great variety of proposals in the field of non-classical logics with special emphasis on modal logics and logics of conditionals. However, since Hume it has been repeatedly shown that the existing concept of causality could not belong to either of those groups. Thirdly, metaphorical definitions of causality continue to appear, e.g., the cause "to provide existence" or "to really influence" the effect, as defined by Bocheński's in an early work [1935]. Fourthly, barefacedly circular definitions of causality are enormously widespread, with the term "cause" being simply replaced by its vernacular synonyms, e.g., a cause is something that brings on, brings about, creates, or sees to an effect. Definitions of the third and fourth groups are popular among representatives of Neo-scholasticism, Christian philosophy generally, common sense philosophy, phenomenology, and the like, as well as in academic textbooks. No such definition could easily be accepted on any scientific level.

For that reason, it should be accepted that the cause and effect relationship has a family-concept type of meaning with at least two initial members being stipulated ostensively, i.e., the concepts of personal and natural cause. Other options available for such primitive concepts would be a purely axiomatic characteristic or the lack of any characteristic altogether. However, in both such cases the concept of cause and effect would turn out to be purely mathematical, which is certainly not the case. As stipulated above, the concepts are not very exact, but they are flexible and open to regimentation according to the needs of different theories. It is also not foreign to scientific discourses to make use of intuitive concepts regimented in different ways, like those of planet or continent.

6   Cause and Effect in Metaphysics and Apologetics

The main objective of metaphysics and apologetics *qua* subsystems of theology (*preambula fidei*) is to demonstrate theorem (8), no dogmas having been assumed except *revelabilia*. And metaphysics itself aims toward a demonstration of theorems (6). This has been typically done by searching for the universal first cause of the knowable world and/or of human nature. From that causal point of view there are three general metaphysical stances regarding God's existence:

there exists the universal first cause and it is personal (theism),	(11a)
there exists the universal first cause and it is natural (pantheism),	(11b)
there exists no universal first cause (atheism).	(11c)

Hence, theologians trouble themselves to show that the knowable world is an effect of some personal first cause, and, furthermore, the universal first cause is reliable, namely, it presents qualities described in theorems (6). To accomplish this, it would not suffice to have at one's disposal even an elaborated concept of cause and effect. A theory of cause-and-effect relationships is also indispensable. Theologians thus developed a range of metaphysical theories which belong to metaphysics and their justifications are purely philosophical, but they are clearly inspired by the articles of faith. This certainly demonstrates that Christian beliefs have truly had an impact on philosophy. Those theories of cause and effect differ from one another, and yet most share a template.

The first step in the template is usually to demonstrate a version of the *principle of causation*, which is always to be distinguished from the concept of cause and effect. The schema of the principle of causation reads as follows:

for every member x of the set X there is such a member y of   (12a)
the set Y that
x is an effect of y (y is a cause of x).

And to move from the schema to a principle of causation it is necessary to stipulate two sets of states of affairs, i.e., a set X of effects and a set Y of possible causes, as well as a unit (or several units) of the concept family of cause and effect to come into play. For example, in classical physics $X=Y$ is the set of all empirically detectable events, and the concept of causality is a derivative of the concept of natural cause involving energy transmission, as described above. As the role of metaphysics in the system of theology has been clarified it is no longer strange that attempts to formulate and justify thesis (12a) were considered the main objective of the Catholic philosophers in the period of Neo-scholasticism, as reported by Bocheński [1935].

It is not an obvious question whether any given object is an effect of some cause or not, especially of an unknown cause. Hence, theologians seek to demonstrate that the knowable world is such an object or a collection of such objects that could not ever exist unless by operation of a certain cause. As part of such arguments two important ideas have been conceived and incorporated into the system of metaphysics, namely, the concepts and several theories of:

contingent being,   (12b)

existential cause,   (12c)

which were foreign to Greco-Roman philosophy. These concepts were invented
by the Persian Muslim thinkers, Al-Farabi and Avicenna, and developed by
schoolmen [Tkaczyk 2012]. A contingent being is one that cannot exist unless
caused to exist by another existing object, and the concept of existential cause,
a new member of the concept family of cause and effect, involves existence
transmission in either a personal or natural way. The third vital concept, that
of transcendent being, has been received from Platonism. In the most famous
version of the principle of causality in theology the existence of every knowable object belongs to the set X whereas the set Y includes all conceivable
states of affairs, likewise those which are transcendent. That is why theologians constantly seek to demonstrate that all knowable objects are contingent,
i.e., belong to the set X. However, there are other versions of the theological
principle of causality (see e.g., Bocheński 1935). And to demonstrate that a
given object is contingent seems to be much more problematic than many
theologians think. This seems to be the most sensitive point of metaphysics
within the system of theology.

It is not at all obvious that basing the system of metaphysics on concepts
(12) is inevitable. On the contrary, it is *prima facie* possible that a more modest
theory of God as the author of the order of nature would be already sufficient
to establish theorem (6) and consequently (8). This could be a theory similar to
that in Plato's *Timaeus*. Many Church Fathers and even some early schoolmen
followed such a cautious idea. The bold and audacious metaphysics based on
concepts (12) is certainly grounded in the Biblical narrative of God as the creator of all things and is inspired by articles of faith. In particular, application
of the concepts of contingent being and existential cause is inspired by the
dogma of *creatio ex nihilo*. Still, whether or not there is dogmatic inspiration,
as long as no mystery of faith has been invoked to demonstrate theorems of
the system of metaphysics, the system is to be qualified as philosophical and
usable for theorem (8), for it is the method of demonstration that is free of acts
of faith, and not necessarily the inspirations.

In the second step some properties of the causal relation are to be determined. Sometimes they may be derived from the concept of cause and effect.
However, this is possible only when an extremely artificial concept of causality
is in use. Such concepts could be a precise tool to conceptualize some ideas,
but they are not likely to improve the reliability of the premises. Anselm's

ontological proof is an extreme example of an argument based on intemperately artificial concepts. Therefore, key properties of the causal relationship should be presupposed and justified. The typical claims theologians have accepted regarding the cause-and-effect relationship are the following:

no effect contains its own cause,   (13a)

no chain of cause-and-effect relationships is infinite,   (13b)

with some claims pertaining to the content, such as that

the effect follows the cause in nature,   (14)

meaning that the nature of the effect is never greater than the nature of the cause, e.g., no unconscious object could produce consciousness. Interestingly, no temporal succession was ever considered crucial by the schoolmen. It was predominantly accepted that no effect could precede the cause in time, but simultaneous or timeless causes were typically permissible. Temporal aspects of causality have clearly been tailored for the transcendent and eternal cause. Generally, time seemed to be marginal for causality, although some order and some irreversibility belonged to the theory by means of such claims as (13).

It should be admitted that metaphysics based on the concept of cause and effect is not at all uncontested, even within systems of theology. At least two alternatives have been proposed. Since Clement of Alexandria many theologians have defended the view that theorems (6) are obvious, either a subject of some innate knowledge or concept analysis, with Anselm's ontological proof being the most famous example. However, those theories were considered so doubtful that even their proponents, including Anselm, typically issued some parallel causality related theories. The other major alternative to causality, originated by Immanuel Kant, was to base the entirety of metaphysics on practical postulates, i.e., requirements of operation of perfect justice. This is considered even less successful than the former alternative, as, of the three ideas underlying knowledge, i.e., truth, causality, and deduction, not only has causality but also truth been erased here. It is therefore rather impossible to secure theorems (6) on the grounds of such metaphysics. At most postulates, such as there should be a powerful and good God, may appear here instead. Hence, despite interesting attempts, no successful alternative exists

288

TKACZYK

for causality-based metaphysics within theology. Furthermore, the concept of cause and effect is vital for apologetics and dogmatics, including the description of God and creation, so it is there ready to use in metaphysics anyway.

Nevertheless, none of claims (12)-(14) is obvious. Some of them, like (14), are neither clear nor exact. Those claims and the like have been articulated for one purpose: to secure a sound deductive proof of theorems (6), as by claims (12) and (13) the existence of the knowable world has an occult, supersensible first cause, which requires no further cause to exist. In a much more obscure way theorem (14) hopes to lead to the conclusion that God is live, personal, sufficiently powerful, and perfectly good to be able to virtually deliver an infallible revelation. All in all, securing an adequate account of the cause-and-effect relationship remains the number one problem in theology.

In a sense apologetics is expected to methodologically bridge metaphysics with dogmatics, for the objective of apologetics is to attribute the deposit of faith – which is a source of dogmatics in the sense of the methodology of the humanities – to God, as accounted for in metaphysics. There is no exaggeration in saying that the objective of apologetics is to establish a causal relationship with God as the personal cause of the deposit of faith, delivered by action called revelation. In other words, apologetics moves from a virtual revelation of metaphysics to the revelation the Twelve Apostles pledged to have actually received directly from God.

No significant contribution to the concept of cause and effect has been made within apologetics, as the concept has been simply adopted from metaphysics. Instead, apologetics presents outstandingly interesting case studies of detecting causal relationships. For example, historically well-established events: (a) Jesus' execution and burial, (b) the empty tomb, (c) numerous eyewitness accounts of Jesus' being alive after the burial, have served to draw the conclusion that an exceptional empirical event occurred, called resurrection, which was an effect of the direct intervention of the creator of the world, i.e., the God of metaphysics.

In apologetics, methods of metaphysics and of history work together, for a certain event is always here to be stated (historically) to have occurred and identified (metaphysically) as an effect of God's direct supernatural action. In a sense, apologetics works analogically to finger-print technology or graphology; it aims to trace the cause of a given effect. It is important that apologetics is underlain by metaphysics. Hence, unlike in natural sciences, where only purely natural causes are permissible, God is available there in the universe of discourse as a prospective cause, ready to use. In some respects, apologetics presents an interesting case of idiosyncratic empirical philosophy.

7   Cause and Effect in Dogmatics

In dogmatics – unlike in metaphysics or apologetics – the concept of cause and effect is no methodological cornerstone on its own. The key method of dogmatics is humanistic interpretation of the existing sources, in particular the deposit of faith, in line with principle (5). And yet the concept of cause and effect turns out to be ubiquitous even in dogmatics due to its well-proven efficiency in articulating the deposit of faith, especially in defining theological concepts. It plays a similar role to the concept of integral and differential in mechanics – it does not stick out; at first glance it may even be imperceptible, and yet it defines key concepts like velocity and momentum. Borrowing expressions from literary studies, one could quite accurately say that in metaphysics and apologetics the concept of cause and effect is the focal character, whereas in dogmatics the concept of cause and effect is the viewpoint character, like Dr. John H. Watson in the Sherlock Holmes stories by Arthur Conan Doyle: you are not supposed to focus on him, but you see the focal character, Holmes, and even the whole story exclusively through his perspective. It is important to understand that the enormous efficacy of the concept of cause and effect in dogmatics additionally supports causality-based systems of metaphysics within theology. The main areas of dogmatics with an essential contribution by the cause-and-effect relationship would include

the Catholic version of theism,	(15a)
the science of grace,	(15b)
the sacramental worldview,	(15c)
the theory of biblical inspiration,	(15d)
the theory of moral action,	(15e)
mysticism.	(15f)

Although the cause-and-effect relationship is not a topic in any of those areas, no doctrine in set (15) could be easily articulated without exploitation of the concept of cause and effect. Of course, a theologian is at liberty to construct a theory to his liking to save the articles of faith. Therefore, it is in principle possible to reconstruct some of the doctrines (15) without exploiting the concept of cause and effect. And yet, no successful theory of the kind has been recorded for the last twenty centuries.

Regarding the Catholic version of theism, within the confines of metaphysics, God has already been identified as the universal first cause. Based on the mysteries of faith the theory of God has been further developed. God is considered the first cause of everything but himself. It follows that God is not absolutely omnipotent, for there is one and only one limitation of his power: his nature. On the one hand – unlike in Plotinus, the ancient Egyptian *Book of the Dead,* or in Islam – God does not create himself, and therefore God is not able to act contrary to his nature (which explains, among other things, why it is not possible for him to include falsehoods in the deposit of faith). On the other hand, no other limitation to God's power is permissible in Catholicism, such as the laws of logic, the scope of possible worlds of which one is the best, or the world of ideas enrapturing the Demiurge in a restrictive matter. To be clear, all possibilities are considered created, hence, God is the first cause of possibilities as well. God's inner self and inner life has also been described by means of causality. God has been described as the Holy Trinity: the Father, the Son, and the Holy Ghost. The three Divine Persons differ from one another in nothing except mutual relations, and these turn out to be – not a great surprise – causal. The Father is the cause of the Son, and the Father together with the Son are the cause of the Holy Ghost. Now, one of the most famous theological controversies of all times, involving Arianism, could be encapsulated in the question: since God the Father is the first cause of everything but himself, hence, is the first cause of the Son, the Holy Ghost, and the created world, how could the Son and the Holy Ghost possibly be considered divine and creating rather than created? The Catholic answer has been delivered in the *Nicene Creed*: "God of God, [...] begotten, not made, being of one substance with the Father", becoming a hallmark of the Catholic orthodoxy [Ayres 2006]. The very collocation "begotten, not made" indicates two different concepts of cause and effect, namely, within the Holy Trinity God the Father is the natural cause of his Son and Holy Ghost (therefore they are equally "uncreated, eternal and without beginning", as stated in the *Athanasian Creed*), whereas outside the Holy Trinity God is a personal cause of everything else that exists, namely creation. Those relations are both causal, but the generation of the Son of God is more like rain dropped by clouds or causing one's heartbeat, whereas the creation of the world is more like Gilbert opening an umbrella.

While in the Catholic theory of God it is mostly the metaphysical concepts of cause and effect which come into play or are adjusted, new members of the concept family happen to be created within theology as well. A good example is the theory of grace and the sacraments.

According to theology, human nature is created by God, i.e., it is an effect of God's causal activity. Mere possibilities are a part of creation as well. So, the nature of an object determines the abilities of the object to act as well as the limitations of its possible action. In particular, no objective may ever be accomplished by an object unless the objective is situated within the reach of that object, the reach being defined by its nature. For example, no human activity whatsoever would allow humans to fly, if flying exceeded the limitations of human nature. Now, it is an article of faith that salvation is situated beyond human reach. Therefore, no human activity could produce the effect of coming to know God, escaping final damnation, and entering heaven. According to another article of faith, this is, however, possible, by God's grace. To bring these dogmas together the schoolmen developed the theory of uncreated and created grace – uncreated grace being God's causal action and created grace being an effect of the action within a human soul, like a second nature allowing one to achieve supernatural objectives [Abárzuza 1956].

As uncreated grace is to be infused into an existing object, Thomas Aquinas developed a causal theory of sacraments. In his system of theology, sacraments are considered causes of God's grace. According to Catholicism, since the Incarnation of the Son of God, grace has been essentially connected with some elements of the material world; first and foremost, with the human nature of Christ, and consequently with some material signs Christ established, e.g., baptism. It is believed that Christ relied on his human nature to distribute grace. To conceptualize these dogmas Aquinas invented a new unit in the concept family of causality, namely the concept of *instrumental cause* (*Summa theologica*, 3.62.1–6). The concept of instrumental cause is a crossbreed of the concepts of personal and natural causality. An instrumental cause acts in the way of natural thatcausality but produces an effect within the user's reach, the user being a personal cause. Now, sacraments have been described as instrumental causes of grace with God playing the role of the user. The conceptual analysis and construction of instrumental causality is considered a true novelty that Aquinas elaborated and introduced into the existing metaphysics in order to improve the system of dogmatics.

Interestingly, the very concept of instrumental cause was later adjusted and applied to the theory of Biblical inspiration. God can be considered the author of the *Holy Scripture* because the human writers who produced the sacred texts are considered instrumental causes of their works. This is again a new concept, as the original concept of instrumental cause bears resemblance to natural causality. And yet, the new concept of instrumental cause can be stipulated, resembling the first one in some respects and that of personal causality in other respects, provided the cause-user knows the future contingent intentional actions of the personal cause-instrument, which God is said to do.

The concept of human action underlying Catholic moral doctrine is causal as well. As documented by Alasdair MacIntyre, in the ancient world, when moral philosophy sprang into life, the scope of responsibility was commonly identified with the scope of the effects of one's actions. Consequently, praise and rewards were automatically connected to success, and blame and penalties to failure. Whenever a man caused anything that violated the appropriate moral criteria, the man was considered to deserve punishment, whether or not he wanted to or could have behaved otherwise. So, when Homer's Odysseus comes back to Ithaca, he blames the suitors for wooing his wife, Penelope, and punishes them by death, although the suitors think quite sincerely that Odysseus is dead and Penelope is a widow. The suitors' false belief, their mistake, is qualified as their full-blooded guilt [MacIntyre 1966]. Similar pictures may easily be found across ancient literature. In accordance with this view, Socrates defined wrong or guilt as error in cognition regarding the good. To overcome this influential and then-consensual idea required enormous effort on the part of theologians. Only after centuries, did the schoolmen, especially Pierre Abélard, Aquinas, John Duns Scotus, and, Francisco Suárez, succeed in reconstructing the concept of moral responsibility. And the modification they proposed is causal even though this is usually passed over. The schoolmen proposed that a man be morally responsible only for his so-called human acts, distinguished from acts of man. This means that the scope of one's moral responsibility is to be identified with the scope of the effects of one's personally causal actions, and not of naturally causal actions.

The cause-and-effect relationships play a significant role in the Catholic theory of prayer. Prominent Catholic thinkers, like Theresa of Ávila, always insisted that absolutely no meditation techniques are permissible, for according to theologians lower levels of prayer consist in actions of the man, whereas higher levels involve direct and palpable actions of God. The prayer of lower levels is to be an activity of the intellect and the will (but never the emotions), whereas on higher levels infused prayer is supposed to take place, i.e., an effect of God's activity. Now, should any meditation technique be employed, the symptoms of infused prayer will likely be their effect rather than the effect of God's action. That is a significant difference between Catholic mysticism and mysticism in other religions, which among other reasons led Henri Bergson (1932) to the conclusion that Catholic mysticism is the only true one. As in apologetics, an analysis of certain states of affairs, prophecies, miracles, or infused prayer, leads to the conclusion that they could not have a cause within the created world.

8   Conclusion

Of Aenesidemus's three ideas underlying knowledge, a vast majority of research of the Cracow Circle concerns deduction with emphasis on mathematical logic; a few remarks concern truth, but hardly any consideration has been dedicated to causality. Despite the central role it plays in the system of theology the concept of cause and effect remains underdeveloped. It is likely that, on the one hand, skeptics' criticism of causality still presents some obstacle for those who are attempting to modernize theology. On the other hand, in the second half of the 20th century theology itself has changed profoundly, distancing itself from the scholastic method and classical philosophy, and mimicking philology or the social sciences. In such theology, the problem of finding grounds for theorem (8) does not even arise.

Nevertheless, if the manifesto of the Cracow Circle were to be continued and the methodological problems of theology as scientific knowledge were to be treated seriously, the search for a new comprehensive account of cause-and-effect relationships would certainly turn out to be indispensable. It is likely – and let this be the final hypothesis of this work – that it would have to be connected with rediscovery of induction, a method nearly completely foreign to theology. It is no accident that Hume jointly criticized the concepts of causality, miracles, and induction. And it is striking that, according to Bocheński [1935], representatives of Neo-scholasticism tried to apply a variety of methods, like deduction, concept analysis, and phenomenological method, but never induction. Presently, the inductive method is still absent in the circles of Christian philosophy and theology (except sociological questionnaires). And yet, induction is a method especially designed to discover causal relationships; perhaps it is the only way to deal with causality with the exception of the inner experience of one's own causal actions. Hence, apart from a new account of the concept of cause and effect, some proper and advanced inductive method must be accepted and mastered within the confines of theology, especially in metaphysics and apologetics.

Bibliography

Abárzuza, Xaverio de (1956). *Manuale theologiæ dogmaticæ*. Vol. I–IV. Madrid: Editiones Studium.

Ajdukiewicz, Kazimierz (1960). The Axiomatic Systems from the Methodological Point of View. [In:] [Ajdukiewicz 1979], p. 282–294.

Ajdukiewicz, Kazimierz (1965). *Pragmatic Logic*. Dordrecht &Warszawa 1974: D. Reidel Publishing Company & PWN.

Ajdukiewicz, Kazimierz (1979). *"The Scientific World-Perspective" and Other Essays. 1931–1963*. Dordrecht 1978: D. Reidel Publishing Company.

Ayres, Lewis (2006). *Nicea and Its Legacy: An Approach to Fourth-Century Trinitatian Theology*. Oxford: Oxford University Press.

Bergson, Henri (1932). *Les deux sources de la morale et de la religion*. Paris: Félix Alcan.

Bocheński, Józef M. (1935). The Problem of Causality in the Neo-scholastics. In this volume: 177–190.

Bocheński, Józef M. (1937). Tradycja myśli katolickiej a ścisłość [The Tradition of Catholic Thought and Precision]. *Studia Gnesnensia* vol. XV, pp. 27–34.

Bocheński, Józef M. (1948). Wstęp do teorii analogii [Introduction to the Theory of Analogy]. *Roczniki Filozoficzne* vol. I, pp. 64–82.

Bocheński, Józef M. (1949). O metodzie teologii w świetle logiki współczesnej [On the Method of Theology in the Light of Contemporary Logic]. *Collectanea Theologica* vol. XXI, No. 2–3, pp. 171–192.

Bocheński, Józef M. (1965). *The Logic of Religion*. New York: New York University Press.

Brożek, Anna & Stadler, Friedrich & Woleński, Jan (eds.) (2017). *The Significance of the Lvov-Warsaw School in the European Culture*. Wien: Springer.

Drewnowski, Jan Franciszek (1937). Neoscholastyka wobec nowoczesnych wymagań nauki [Neo-scholasticism in the Face of Modern Requirements of Science]. *Studia Gnesnensia* vol. XV, pp. 49–57.

Gilson, Étienne (1936). *Christianisme et philosophie*. Paris: Vrin.

Gilson, Étienne (1939). *Reason and Revelation in the Middle Ages*. New York: Scribner's Sons Ltd.

Kiczuk, Stanisław (1995). *Związek przyczynowy a logika przyczynowości* [The Causal Connection and the Logic of Causality]. Lublin: RW KUL.

Łukasiewicz, Jan (1906). Analysis and Construction of the Concept of Cause. In this volume: 3–66.

MacIntyre, Alasdair (1966). *A Short History of Ethics*. New York: The Macmillan Company.

Malaty, Tadros Y. (1995). *Lectures in Patrology: The School of Alexandria*. Book I: *Before Origen*. Jersey City: St. Mark's Coptic Orthodox Church.

Olson, Roger E. (1999). *The Story of Christian Theology*. Downers Grove, Ill.: Inter-Varsity Press.

Pawłowski, Tadeusz (1986). *Tworzenie pojęć w naukach humanistycznych* [Creating Concepts in the Humanities]. Warszawa: PWN.

Salamucha, Jan (1997). *Wiedza i wiara* [Knowledge and Faith]. Lublin: TN KUL.

Salamucha, Jan (1946a). Teologia i filozofia [Theology and Philosophy]. [In:] [Salamucha 1997], pp. 47–50.

Salamucha, Jan (1946b). Tomizm jako *philosophia parennis* [Thomism as *philosophia parennis*]. [In:] [Salamucha 1997], pp. 57–63.

Scheeben, Matthias Joseph (1873–1887). *Handbuch der katholischen Dogmatik*. Vol. 1–5. Freiburg im Brisgau: Herder.

Swinburne, Richard (1974). *The Existence of God*. Oxford 1991: Clarendon Press.

Szatkowski, Mirosław (ed.), (2012). *Ontological Proofs Today*. Frankfurt am Main: Ontos Verlag.

Tkaczyk, Marcin (2012). A Debate on God: Anselm, Aquinas and Scotus. [In:] [Szatkowski ed. 2012], pp. 113–141.

Tkaczyk, Marcin (2017). Cracow Circle. Theology in the Lvov-Warsaw School. [In:] [Brożek & Stadler & Woleński (eds.) 2017], pp. 173–188.

Conclusion

The Problem of Causality

Jacek J. Jadacki

Each consistent implementation of the unambiguity of certain terms must be combined with the violation of certain expressions of everyday speech

ZAWIRSKI 1912: 123

∴

1   The Omnipresence of the Term "Cause" in Life and Science

The term "cause" is omnipresent in life and science.

Here are a few not invented, but "living" examples taken from texts in various fields.

In the field of geology: The *cause* of the observed acceleration of the rising sea level lies in the increase in temperature, which works in two ways. First, it leads to the melting of glaciers; secondly – it increases the volume of water, which expands when heated.

In the field of biology: One of the most common *causes* of tomatoes and peppers fruiting poorly are bed growing conditions, leading to insufficient pollination of flowers.

In medicine: the *causes* of myocardial infarction are complex, including elevated level of cholesterol, excessive smoking, or obesity.

In the field of technology: The most common *cause* of the failure of air conditioning systems is the lack of professional technical handling and specialized service.

In the field of historiography: The *cause* of the collapse of the First Polish Commonwealth was the adoption of the *Constitution of May 3rd*.

In the field of legal-judicial matters: The most probable *cause* of the Notre Dame cathedral fire was a short circuit in the electrical installation.

As a certain *curiosum*, I shall quote a statement that I cannot accurately attribute to some particular field (out of pity, I will omit the author's name):

© JACEK J. JADACKI, 2022 | DOI:10.1163/9789004522244_012

Among the most frequently mentioned *causes* of hunger are, among others: extreme poverty, armed conflicts, authoritarian forms of exercising power, migration and refugee crises, fights for natural resources, climate changes, land appropriation and excessive concentration, weakness of state structures in supporting farmers and ensuring food security, discrimination in access to land between men and women and between members of various communities, speculation on food prices and commodification of food, international trade – trade agreements favoring highly industrialized countries and the institutions derived therefrom, lack of states' capacity to protect against natural disasters, and insufficient international humanitarian and development assistance.

What struck me was the almost complete absence of the term "cause" in newer statements in the field of physics as it is widely understood. The matter cleared up when I noticed that modern physicists – more than anyone else susceptible to philosophical indoctrination – to avoid the term "cause", which has been so cursed by the (neo)positivists, simply use its camouflaged synonyms. So instead of saying/writing: x is the cause of y, they say/write, among other things:

x brings about y; y is entailed by x; y occurs when x occurs; y occurs as a result of the occurrence of x; y arises thanks to x; y arises when x; y is the result of x.

I shall limit myself to an example illustrating the use of one of these intentional synonyms of "cause" – in the field of hypotheses or, as I would say, cosmological fantasies:

Matter compressed until it exceeds critical density collapses – *as the result* of gravitational attraction, until it becomes a singularity.

2   The Awkwardness of the Existing Definitions of "Cause"

It is surprising how generally awkward are the existing general-dictionary and even "professional" definitions of "cause" and its derivative terms. Here is an example from an English dictionary with an incorrect definitional "chain", typical for these dictionaries:

Cause – somebody or something that brings about an effect or result.
      (To) *bring about* – to cause (something), to take place, to effect (something).

(*To*) *cause* – to serve as the cause of (something).[1]

Thus, after appropriate substitutions, it turns out that the *cause* is somebody or something that serves as the cause.

It is no better with "professional" definitions. Here is an example taken from Father Józef M. Bocheński, after all a representative of the Lvov-Warsaw School to which I profess membership (I abbreviate the original definition):

> The relation [...] ["*x* is the cause of *y*"] means, first, that "if *x* occurs, *y* occurs", and, second, that "*x* exerts real influence on the existence of *y*". Thus, [...] [the effect] is not only a logical but also a real *result* of [...] [the cause], which "provides" [...] [the cause] with its existence.
>
> BOCHEŃSKI 1935: 127

Of what can we accuse this so-called dynamic definition?

(a)   It is uncertain whether or not the formulas given as "first" and "second" form conjunctive *definiens*.

(b)   Defining "being-cause-of" as influencing has a raison d'être only when it happens that the relation of influencing occurs, and the relation of being-cause-of does not occur; otherwise, we are dealing here with giving a non-analyzable synonym.[2]

(c)   It is not quite clear what is indicated (result?) by the functor "thus" connecting the two sentences that make up the quoted passage.

(d)   Lack of explication as to how "occurrence" and "existence" relate to each other, and what the literal meaning of "provide [existence]" is.

Such allegations could be multiplied.

3   A Word about Defining

If a definition is to play an explicative role, i.e., if it is to enable or at least make it easier for the recipient of the definition to understand the defined term, the expressions appearing in the *definiens* must be comprehensible to the

---

1   *The New Penguin English Dictionary*. London 2001: Penguin Books, pp. 172, 219.

2   Even Łukasiewicz did not avoid such a pseudo-definition, when in the recapitulation of his dissertation, "Analysis and Construction of the Concept of Cause", he gave the following explanation of the word "cause": "We use this word only for objects which [...] stand to an effect in a *necessary relation* such that an object that is a cause necessarily *brings about* an object that is an effect" [Łukasiewicz 1906: 55].

recipient. It is not easy to meet this condition and even to determine whether it has really been met in a given case. If, in any case, it is not met, then we fall into the trap of definitional *regressus*: we need to define *ignotum* using comprehensible expressions, and if it turns out that the latter are incomprehensible, you need ... etc. This *regressus* can be interrupted but probably always only partially: either by indicating (unfortunately usually using linguistic means) some *designatum* or some part of the denotation of a defining expression, or by constructing a "plastic" model of the situation to which the defining expression applies. Needless to say, none of these paths leads to complete success.

So, I have no illusions that my explications will be absolutely satisfactory.

Let's call all and only those expressions that appear in the definitional formula of a given term, except for the term itself, "definitional expressions". In the definition of "being the cause", which I will give below, the following expressions are definitional expressions:

(a)   functors of definitional equivalence ($\leftrightarrow_{\text{def}}$) and implication ($\rightarrow$);
(b)   generalizer ($\bigwedge$);
(c)   variables: x, y, t, t', m, m' and o, as well as $\mathbf{x}, \mathbf{y}, \mathbf{t}, \mathbf{t}', \mathbf{m}, \mathbf{m}'$ and $\mathbf{o}$;
(d)   the symbols: K and L;
(e)   the nominalizing word ("that");
(f)   unary functors: at-[period], on-[area],[3] under-[circumstances], in-[manner], (x) changes;
(g)   binary functors: and, acts-on.

It is easy to see that at least the functors (f) and (g) – and probably the functor (e) – are terms outside the language of classical logic; let's call them "ontological terms".

4   Definition of "Cause"

Here is my proposal for the definition of "cause".

Let the variables $x, y, \mathbf{x}$, and $\mathbf{y}$ represent any individuals, the variables o and $\mathbf{o}$ any circumstances, the variables $t, t', \mathbf{t}$, and $\mathbf{t}'$ any periods (of time), and the variables $m, m', \mathbf{m}$, and $\mathbf{m}'$ any areas (of space). Let the letters K and L symbolize specific types of (processes of) acting-on and changes respectively. We then have:

[1] $\bigwedge x \bigwedge y \bigwedge t \bigwedge t' \bigwedge m \bigwedge m' \bigwedge o$

---

3   I am aware that the correct form should be here "in [area]"; however, I wanted each parameter to be indicated by a different preposition and I reserved "in" for "in [manner]".

⟨(the fact) that x at period t on area m under circumstances o acts in way K on y is the *cause* of (the fact) that y at period t' on area m' changes in way L

$\overset{\leftrightarrow}{}_{\text{def}}$

$\{[(x$ at period t on area m under circumstances o acts in way K on $y \wedge y$ at period t' on area m' changes in way $L)$

$\wedge$

$\bigwedge x \bigwedge y \bigwedge t \bigwedge t' \bigwedge m \bigwedge m' \bigwedge o$ (x at period t on area m under circumstances o acts in way K on $y \to y$ at period t' on area m' changes in way $L)]\}\rangle$.

To make the structure of formula [1] more transparent, let's omit temporal-spatial parameters and assume that the matter here is about any circumstances and that there is one way of acting-on and one way of changing. This formula would then take the form:

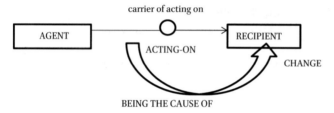

FIGURE 1   Model of the causal situation

[2] $\bigwedge x \bigwedge y$
⟨⟨⟨(the fact) that x acts on y is the *cause* of (the fact) that y changes

$\overset{\leftrightarrow}{}_{\text{def}}$

$\{[(x$ acts on $y \wedge y$ changes)

$\wedge$

$\bigwedge x \bigwedge y \, [(x$ acts on $y \to y$ changes)]\}\rangle$.

As we can see – formula [1] is an equivalent, contextual definition and it reflects the categorical – multi-parameter – structure of the cause-effect connection.

Some might suppose that formula [1] is a version of the so-called substantive concept of causality, criticized by Łukasiewicz in his dissertation, "Analysis and Construction of the Concept of Cause".[4] This assumption is incorrect. This

---

4   If we believe Czeżowski, such a substantive conception of causality is an invention of Hellenistic philosophy and was adopted by both the Stoics and the Epicureans. Czeżowski characterized this conception as follows: "Bodies, while acting on other bodies, bring about qualitative or quantitative changes in them; the effect is always some change or, generally speaking, some property of the other body. [...] The causal relation is [...] the relation of agency, that is, [...] the relation between bodies which consists of producing an effect. [...] [In this conception] there is clearly the moment of temporal succession between cause and effect" [Czeżowski 1933: 172].

is because the definition of "cause" in accordance with this conception should be reconstructed schematically as follows:

[3] $\bigwedge x \bigwedge y$ [x is the *reason* of (the fact) that y changes $\leftrightarrow_{def}$ (x acts on $y \to y$ changes)].

According to Łukasiewicz, formula [3] is unacceptable because, among other reasons, contrary to it, the cause of change is not substance x acting in a certain way, but the action of substance x. However, if we substitute "action of x" in [3] for "x", then the predecessor of the *definiens* will take the form: "the action of substance x acts on y"; meanwhile – as Łukasiewicz notes – no action acts (on something). Fortunately, the criticism carried out by Łukasiewicz on the basis of formula [1] cannot be reproduced.

Formula [3], criticized by Łukasiewicz, could, however, be transformed – something he did not notice – into formula [6], which will be discussed below; it is similar to formula [1] – but it is still not the same.

Another of Łukasiewicz's arguments against the substantive conception of causality, i.e., explaining the concept of cause through the concept of acting-on, is that – according to Łukasiewicz – substances that physically or mentally act in the strict sense can only be *living entities* (in particular: people), because "to act" means as much as "to make an effort in order to overcome resistance" [Łukasiewicz 1906: 116], and the concept of effort has a literal sense only in relation to living beings; meanwhile, a cause-effect connection also occurs in the field of inanimate nature.

I will come back below to the question of action – or more precisely: of acting-on; here I shall say only briefly that the *explicatum* for "acting-on" may not be an anthropomorphic concept of effort (as Łukasiewicz believed), but a concept of strength, neutral from this point of view.

Next, I will detail the semantic comments on the definitional expressions used and then introduce some important concepts from the semantic nest of "cause" with the aid of the term "cause" defined in [1].

Comments (necessarily short) will concern in turn:
- the logical constants specified in[1] and the concept of necessity;
- ontic categories of objects belonging to the ranges of variability of variables x, y, x and y;
- the functor of acting-on (of type K);
- the concept of the circumstances of acting-on forming the range of variability of variables o and o;
- the concept of change (of type L);
- relations between moments t and t';
- formal properties of the relation of being-cause-of;
- the problem of the complexity of cause and of effect.

By using the defined term "cause" – as the defining expression – the following related terms will be defined:
– "effect";
– "causal law";
– "causality principle";
– "cause-effect relation";
– "perpetrator";
– "God-Creator" and "(human) creator".
I will precede all these considerations with some short historical remarks and a kind of self-criticism.

5   Traditional Counterarguments Aimed at the Existence of Cause-
         Effect Relations

In the expositions of the problem of causality, some traditional arguments aimed at the very existence of cause-effect relations in the world are constantly repeated, even today. I shall mention three.

(1) Hume's argument based on the unobservability of the cause-effect connection.

It is true. This connection is not really visible, but acting-on and change are "visible" (or "visibility" is postulated and strives to implement this postulate), the occurrence of which is necessary for the cause-effect relation to occur. Let us add that based on definition [1], for phenomenon Z_1 to be allowed to be the cause of phenomenon Z_2, it is not enough to know that phenomenon Z_2 always follows phenomenon Z_1.

(2) The arguments of Comte from the *désintéressement* of scientists regarding cause-effect connection.

It is not true. Scientists study not only dependencies between any phenomena, but also – and sometimes with particular interest – dependencies between (processes of) acting-on and changes, and thus *de facto* cause-effect connections (even if for doctrinal reasons they avoid the terms "cause" and "effect").

(3) Heisenberg's argument based on the indeterminacy (or even indeterminability) of states of affairs in the micro-world.

Suppose it is true. However, this would not be an argument against the existence of cause-effect connections in the macro-world, but rather that they should be treated as statistical dependencies (dependencies such that our knowledge of them is a statistical hypothesis).

6 Self-Criticism

Definition [1] is the fruit of many years of my reflection. In the process of constructing it, I encountered various difficulties. I will indicate two of them here.[5]

The first difficulty is of the following sort. Suppose we define "being-husband" as follows:

[4] $\bigwedge x \bigwedge y$ (x is the husband of y) $\leftrightarrow_{def}$ (y is the wife of x).

Let us skip any reservations about the definitional nature of formulas stating the semantic identity of two simple words. On the basis of definition [4], we can say that:

[5] Socrates was the husband of Xanthippe $\leftrightarrow_{def}$ Xanthippe was the wife of Socrates.

And everything is alright.

Initially, I considered a definition much simpler than formula [1]. I shall present this finally rejected definition in the idealized version, following formula [2]:

[6] $\bigwedge x \bigwedge y$
[(the fact) that x acts on y is the cause of (the fact) that y changes
$\leftrightarrow_{def}$ (x acts on $y \to y$ changes).

Well, one would like to perform an operation similar to the one carried out on formula [4]. Suppose that Socrates drank hemlock and Socrates died. Now let's put forth the (simplified) hypothesis that:

[7] (The fact) that Socrates drank hemlock was the cause of Socrates' death.[6]

One would like to be able to say here that on the basis of formula [6], formula [7] means the same as:

[8] Socrates drank hemlock $\to$ Socrates died.

However, this cannot be said because formula [8], with the usual understanding of the implication, is true on the basis of our assumption, but it does not prejudge that between the facts to which this assumption applies there is a cause-effect connection whose occurrence in final formula [1] is guaranteed by the law explicitly included in the definition of this formula. By the way – we use a simplified understanding of "cause", which is indicated in formula [6],

---

5 This is, so to say, self-criticism "provoked" by my student, Professor Anna Brożek, who otherwise became acquainted with the original version of my entire text and pointed out other shortcomings. I thank her very much for this here, although I am not sure if I have dealt with them in a way that would satisfy her completely.
6 To be more precise – it should be said in formula [7] that the cause of Socrates's death was the hemlock he drank acting on him; for greater "intuitiveness" I give a brief formulation – but this is how it should be understood after explication.

when we formulate general sentences such as "Drinking hemlock is always the cause of the death of those who drink it" (and not individual sentences such as "Drinking this hemlock was the cause of Socrates' death").

The second difficulty, unfortunately, also concerns the final form of formula [1].

Suppose that types of agents, recipients and circumstances[7] are one-element sets. The law contained in the *definiens* of formula [1], then, essentially states only the coexistence of its predecessor and successor. I suspect that this is just the situation in which there are so-called historical laws – regarding unrepeatable facts in history. Perhaps this is why reflections on the causes of historical facts are so methodologically suspicious.

7   Logical Constants and Necessity

In definition [1], there are three logical constants: two functors from the language of propositional calculus ('$\leftrightarrow_{\text{def}}$' *and* '$\rightarrow$') and the generalizer from the language of predicate calculus ('$\bigwedge$'). They have their usual meanings here.

In connection with these constants – I add here a note regarding necessity. Necessity is treated persistently as a component of the connotation of the term "cause". I am a supporter (similarly to Łukasiewicz) of the nomothetic interpretation of necessity, i.e., the definitional reduction of the following type. Let variables x and y be of types X and Y respectively. Then:

[9] *It is necessary that* $[P(X) \rightarrow Q(Y)] \leftrightarrow_{\text{def}} \bigwedge x \bigwedge y\, [P(x) \rightarrow Q(y)]$.
Because (in short):

[10] It is necessary that $\alpha \leftrightarrow_{\text{def}}$ it is impossible that $\sim \alpha$.
or:

[11] It is possible that $\alpha \leftrightarrow_{\text{def}}$ it is not necessary that $\sim \alpha$.
so:

[12] It is possible that $[P(X) \rightarrow Q(Y)] \leftrightarrow_{\text{def}} \sim \bigwedge x \bigwedge y\, [P(x) \rightarrow Q(y)]$.
or more generally:

[13] It is possible that $[P(X) \rightarrow Q(Y)] \leftrightarrow_{\text{def}} \bigvee x \bigvee y\, [P(x) \wedge \sim Q(y)]$.

---

7   The same can be repeated for types of (processes of) acting-on and types of changes – as well as for situations in which time is identified with the mereological class of (all) periods, and space – with the mereological class of (all) areas.

I would like to point out that these functors do not precede simple sentences but rather complex implicational sentences. I honestly confess that I just don't understand formulas like:

[14] It is possible that *p*.

where '*p*' is a simple sentence.[8]

8 Ontic Categories of Objects in the Field of the Relation of Being-Cause-Of

It is interesting that despite the puzzle of causality "rolling on" for centuries, terms referring to the subjects of acting-on have not been coined (since the word "perpetrator" refers only to hominoid subjects), and neither have terms for the subjects of change which are the effect of acting-on.

I propose, for our use, to speak of agent and recipient, respectively.

Let us remind ourselves that, on the basis of formula [1] the domain of the being-cause-of relation is not identical with agents, and the counter-domain is not identical with recipients, but, respectively, with (processes of) acting-of-agents-on-recipients and changes-of-recipients.

What are agents and recipients? It seems that they can be any *objects*, in particular things or people. In any case, they must be not fictitious objects – but *real* ones: *mental* or *physical* (including physiological). To avoid misunderstandings, let us point out that the effect of a certain acting-on can be a change (including coming into existence) of someone's imagination of some fictitious object, but the very image of the recipient cannot be fiction.

If we now agree that the acting-of-*x*-on-*y* is a special *change*-of-*x*, then we may consider a certain subset of the class of changes as a certain subset of the field of changes. If we consider a change to be a special kind of *state of affairs*,[9] namely, an *event*, i.e., a temporal-spatial state, then we can consider a subset of the class of events as the field of the being-cause-of relation. If we identify the class of events of type *A* or *B* – after Ajdukiewicz [Ajdukiewicz 1965: 155] – with the *phenomenon* of *A* or *B*, respectively, then we can, like Bandrowski, say that "causal connections occur between phenomena" [Bandrowski 1903: 55].

---

8 In a text, written together with Professor Anna Brożek [Brożek & Jadacki 2008], we interpreted possibility as non-contradiction with a specific set of sentences.

9 Łukasiewicz believed that only some relations of being-cause-of occur between changes; more often the arguments of the relation of being-cause-of are features (including "hidden" features) or – as he said – relations of the type: *x*-has-feature-*c*. One can think that these are in fact some states of affairs.

9   Acting-On

I would be inclined to understand "acting-on" as follows (for simplicity, I omit generalizers and most of the parameters of acting-on):[10]

[15] x acts on y in way $K \leftrightarrow_{def} \bigvee z$ (z is the carrier of acting-on in way $K \land$ changes-of-recipients z moves from x to y)].

The carrier of acting-on can be the whole x, a piece of x, the energy contained in x, or a portion of this energy,[11] etc.

Kotarbiński treats the question differently. Let us fully quote his definition of "cause":

> Pressure N from the earlier moment A is the *cause* of event Z from the later moment B, and event Z is the *effect* of pressure N, always and only if N is an essential component of such a set of circumstances from the moment A, which is a sufficient condition for event Z from the later moment B due to some natural law of the succession of events (that is, after which, according to this law, event Z must occur at a certain later moment).
>
> KOTARBIŃSKI 1951: 404–405

If we compare this definition with my formula [1], it can be seen that in Kotarbiński:

(a)   he speaks of pressure instead of acting-on;

(b)   the circumstances of exerting pressure (in my case: acting-on) do not constitute parameterization of this acting-on, but are treated together as a sufficient condition for the effect, and the pressure itself is considered an essential condition of that sufficient condition;

(c)   that something is a sufficient condition for an effect is stated in "some natural law of the succession of events", according to which this condition must occur after the occurrence of that condition.

The disadvantages of Kotarbiński's formulation are obvious. According to (a), Kotarbiński does not specify what the cause-pressures would consist of (everything indicates that they are at most only one of the variations of causal acting-on) and what they should be exerted on. According to (b), no criterion which would allow us to isolate the underlying significant component from the components of the condition of sufficient effect is present in Kotarbiński.

---

10   I wrote about the concept of acting-on in [Jadacki 2003], p. 113 ff.

11   This is the case with physical interactions; cf. [Kiczuk 1977: 120, 126].

According to (c), the concept of cause is, in terms of Kotarbiński, explained using, among others, the meta-linguistic concept of causal law,[12] which, let us add, has already been pointed out as a mistake in this approach by Łukasiewicz.

Let us return to my formula [10], which is the definition of "acting-on". If someone were to find it unsatisfactory,[13] I could – as is often done (see above – § 4) – give examples of the subtype of acting-on that are discussed in individual scientific disciplines. Here are examples:

(a)   physical acting-on: direct (e.g., pulling, pushing, twisting, lifting, stretching, tearing, compressing, bending, crushing) or at a distance – basic (i.e., electromagnetic, gravitational, and nuclear: weak and strong) and intermolecular;

(b)   chemical acting-on (bonds): ionic and atomic;

(c)   biological-medical acting-on, e.g., pharmacodynamic and pharmacokinetic, and infectious (i.e., infection with pathogens, e.g., viruses, bacteria, parasites);

(d)   mental acting-on, e.g., intra-psychical and psychical-physical motivation, as well as physical-psychical activation;[14]

(e)   sociological (interpersonal) acting-on.

The philosopher would expect that individual modes (viz., subtypes) of acting-on will be subjected-to scientific analysis within the scientific disciplines dealing with them. In general, however, such intradisciplinary analysis is missing or is highly imperfect. Characteristic acting-on for a given scientific discipline is identified almost exclusively by the characteristics of the agent, recipient,

---

12   In other words: this explanation is nomological; cf. [Bigaj 1996: 218].

13   Ajdukiewicz spoke very critically about attempts to specify the concept of acting-on (or acting) – at least the attempts known to him. He wrote, among other things: "Many philosophers think [...] that the essence of the causal nexus, next to a constant sequence in time, includes a dynamic relationship which consist in the cause evoking the effect by its "action". [...] But – as far as the present writer knows – no one has ever succeeded in formulating precisely in what that dynamic relationship, that "action", which next to the regular succession in time is supposed to be an essential component of the causal nexus, would consist" [Ajdukiewicz 1965: 163–164]. Therefore, in his definition of "cause", he did not use the concept of action. This definition was namely: "When we say that a phenomenon of A is a cause of a phenomenon of B, then we mean that if phenomenon A occurs in any object x at any time t, then phenomenon B occurs in that object x at a time t+τ (where τ≠0)" [Ajdukiewicz 1965: 163]. In a slightly different formulation: "When we say that a given event α is the cause of a given event β, we mean to state that the fact that β has followed α at a certain time is a special case of a phenomenon B always following a phenomenon A, the given events β and α being materializations of B and A, respectively" [Ajdukiewicz 1965: 163].

14   Kotarbiński called this interaction "pressure [...] [of a] psychological nature" [Kotarbiński 1951: 406].

and effect, which is justified by the fact that different modes of interaction occur between different types of objects. Only gravitational acting-on has a wider field – namely, it covers all physical bodies. It is not ruled out, however, that some modes of acting-on are reducible to others; the tendency for such a reduction is seen, in any case, in relation to biological and medical acting-on.

10   Motivation

There is sometimes talk of a relation of being-cause-of occurring between mental objects, between physical (physiological) and psychical objects – and *vice versa*.

Generally speaking – in the case of intra-psychical motivation and physical-psychical activation, recipients are experiences (willingness, beliefs, mental images, but also feelings).[15] In practice, however, it is exceedingly difficult to reconstruct in a satisfactory way psychologists' statements about what they consider to be the agents and recipients of motivation.

The starting point of our reconstruction will be statements by Professor Janusz Reykowski contained in the chapter "Motivation" of a textbook of *General Psychology*:

> - By the concept of motivation [...] [we understand] the specific ability of the human psychical apparatus to form, in the mind, a design of a specific state of affairs that directs activities and acts on the amount of energy that a person uses to implement a given direction. In other words, motivation conditions the implementation of activities, i.e., goal-oriented behaviors.
>
> REYKOWSKI 1992: 62

> - We use the term "motive" [...] to refer to a specific internal state, which is characterized by a sense of non-fulfillment and readiness to take up activity, i.e., motivational tension.
>
> REYKOWSKI 1992: 74

---

15   Psychologists carry out different typologies of motives. Hilgard, for example, distinguishes: (a) motivational dispositions (impulses) and induced motives; (b) biological motives with physiological (hunger, thirst, pain) grounds and unidentified motives (dispositions for activity, manipulation or exploration); (c) social motives (maternity, sex, and disposition to dependence or affiliation, to dominance or submission, to aggression), and personal motives (e.g., striving for achievement). Hilgard himself is aware that these typologies are unsatisfactory in terms of methodology. Cf. [Hilgard 1953].

- *Motive* [is] the state of the subject characterized by a sense of non-fulfill-
ment or disruption and the readiness, associated with this sense, for activity that can reduce this state [...]; it is accompanied by increased affective
sensitivity to factors capable of increasing or reducing it. A motive may
have negative or positive affective characteristics (e.g., longing, anxiety,
pain or joyful excitement, appetite, curiosity, etc.). Sometimes the term
"need" is used with the same (or similar) meaning.

REYKOWSKI 1992: 113

- *Motivation* (or motivational process [...]) [is] a process of mental reg-
ulation that creates aspirations. The function of aspirations is to control
human activities in such a way that they lead to a specific effect in line
with the intention, or the goal. We can talk about pursuit or motivation
to achieve a [specific] goal.

REYKOWSKI 1992: 113

I would reconstruct these formulations as follows.[16] Let us extract the volitional
center from the psyche of the human individual, covering all his willingness
(viz., inclinations, aspirations), both "dormant" (i.e., in the form of dispositions),
and undertaken (i.e., in the actualized form) – with a certain strength (i.e.,
intensity) and a specific goal (i.e., intention). Let us further extract the human
manipulative apparatus (i.e., organs, or those parts of the body by which the
individual can perform specific physical activities) from the human body. For
simplicity, let's leave the emotional center aside. According to formula [1], omit-
ting the relevant generalizers, the correct formula using the concept of "cause"
in the context of psychical-physical motivation would be:

[16] (The fact) that the (excited) willingness of x with strength s_1 (from the
volitional center of x) aimed at achieving goal c, in conditions w (including,
among others, a belief or a sense of x about the reachability of goal c by x
through action d), acts on the handling apparatus of x: it is the *cause* of
the change in the handling apparatus of x, which consists in x performing
action d.[17]

16   I would like to thank Professor Reykowski for giving me comments on my reconstruction
      that allowed me to make it more adequate.
17   I have the impression that formula [15] can also be considered a reconstruction of the
      following formulations of psychologist-behaviorist Hilgard: "By a *motive* we mean some-
      thing that incites the organism to action or that sustains and gives direction to action
      once the organism has been aroused. [...] By *activation* we mean the change that occurs
      between sleeping and waking, between being relaxed and being tense, between "taking

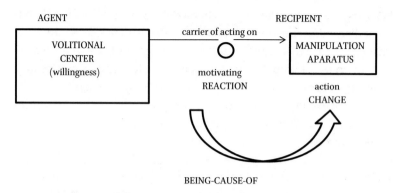

AGENT   RECIPIENT
                          carrier of acting on

VOLITIONAL   MANIPULATION
CENTER   ○   APARATUS
(willingness)   action
                          motivating   CHANGE
                          REACTION

                          BEING-CAUSE-OF

FIGURE 2   Model of the motivational situation

By the word "motivating", psychologists usually mean exactly the acting-on mentioned in formula [15]. The motive[18] of a given activity is identified by psychologists with a willingness which motivates a given physical activity.[19]

It is also said – let us skip generalizers again – that:

[17] x *aims* to achieve goal $c \leftrightarrow_{def} x$ performs an action motivated by x's willingness to achieve goal c.

Let us now consider, for example, a situation in which John wants/decides to poison his mother-in-law and gives her poison. Using the terminology introduced above, we will say that:

(a) the motive of John's act of giving poison to his mother-in-law is John's willingness/decision to poison his mother-in-law;

(b) the cause of (the fact) that John gives poison to his mother-in-law is that John's willingness/decision to poison his mother-in-law acts on John's manipulative apparatus so that John gives poison to his mother-in-law.

Of course, although the (intentional) goal of giving poison to John's mother-in-law is to poison her, the result of giving poison does not always lead to the realization of this goal, because, e.g., his mother-in-law was "fat Berta" and the dose of poison turned out to be too small.

---

it easy" and putting forth effort. Motivational activation produces a state of readiness for behavior" [Hilgard 1953: 118].

18   As Professor Reykowski pointed out to me, psychologists usually use the term "motive" to signify what I would call "simple motivating agent" and the term "motivation" to signify what I would call "complex motivating agent".

19   Professor Reykowski mentions *expressis verbis* that this action is to lead to "changes in the physical or social state of affairs" [Reykowski 1992: 71].

Let us remember that formula [16] applies to psychical-physical motivation. However, it can easily be transformed into a formula that reconstructs intra-psychical motivation, in which experiences are agent and recipient. An example of such intra-psychical motivation is the acting-on that causes arousal of specific willingness:

[18] (The fact) that x's sense of lack of c (the relevant internal resolution[20]) in conditions w acts on the volitional center of x: it is the cause of the change in the volitional center of x, consisting in stimulating the willingness of x oriented to achieve goal c.

Let us note that Ajdukiewicz had a different conception of motivation in which the presence of an appropriate sense plays an essential role. Let us give voice to him:

> *If in performing any act* (physical or mental), *we have the sense that we are inclined to perform this act by a certain psychical experience, then we say that this experience is a motive of this act.*
>
> *An act, the motive of which is a conscious pursuit of a certain goal, is called "an act aware of the goal" or "an action aware of the goal". The Goal of a purpose, which is the motive of action, is called "a conscious goal" or "a conscious intention of action".* So, when we want to find out what the conscious goal was of someone's action, we ask about the motive of that action, i.e., we ask what pursuit inclined the perpetrator of this action according to his own sense. When he tells us that he was motivated to the action by the intention to make this-and-this exist, then we will call this-and-this the "conscious goal of action".
>
> AJDUKIEWICZ 1938: 172

Ajdukiewicz, as we can see, believed that a given experience is considered be a motive only when we "have sense" that this experience "inclines" us to a specific act.

11   Circumstances of Acting-On

The circumstances referred to in the definition of "causes" [1] have either a positive form, i.e., such that some positive states of affairs occur, or a negative form, i.e., such that some positive states of affairs do not occur. The former are

---

20   Let us add that an external command can also be an agent here.

the factors favoring a given acting-on, and the latter are the lack of factors disturbing this acting; if disturbing factors were to occur, then a specific acting-on would not be the cause of the change.[21]

"Factor favoring something" (or "factor enabling something") can be defined as follows:

[19] (The fact) that q, due to (the fact) that p, is a *factor* favoring (the fact) that s $\leftrightarrow_{\text{def}} \{[(p \wedge q) \to s] \wedge \sim (p \to q) \wedge \sim (p \to \sim q) \wedge \sim (p \to s) \wedge \sim (q \to s)]\}$.

For example: Suppose that if a passer-by is hit by a car in some way and deprived of specific medical assistance, he will die. We are right to say that both the hitting and the lack of medical assistance are factors favoring the death of the passer-by. If the provision of medical assistance in the described accident was someone's legal obligation, the judge has the right to consider both the action of the driver of the car as well as the lack of action of someone who was obliged to take the action as the (co-)cause of the crime (here: death).

In turn:

[20] (The fact that) r is, due to (the fact that) p, a *factor disturbing* (the fact that) s $\leftrightarrow_{\text{def}} \{[(p \wedge \sim r) \to s] \wedge \sim (p \to r) \wedge \sim (p \to \sim r) \wedge \sim (p \to s) \wedge (\sim r \to s)\}$.

In our example – providing specific medical assistance may be a factor disturbing the death of a passer-by. NB. The non-occurrence of the disturbing factor is also a type of favorable factor.

In connection with the concept of the circumstances of acting-on, four reservations must be made.

First of all, *neutral factors*, i.e., those that are neither favorable nor disturbing, are not included in the set of circumstances of acting-on. Those who accept the doctrine of the interconnectedness of all phenomena (and consequently the view that there are no neutral factors) – and would not like to deprive formula [1][22] of operability – would have to assume that the *multum* of factors accompanying a given acting-on can be ignored, because they favor or disturb this acting-on to a degree, so to speak, imperceptibly.

Secondly, the operability of formula [1] requires that among *sensu lato* favoring factors (and thus also including the absence of disturbing factors), we should take into account factors which, in a given case (!), are necessary for

---

21   Pański [1933] was a firm opponent of introducing the term "disturbing factor" (or disturbing condition) into the definition of the "cause". However, his arguments do not convince me.

22   One consequence of this doctrine would be that the object is the reciprocate of all later interactions. Zawirski declares *expressis verbis* this doctrine to be unacceptable. "One can carve out for each phenomenon those with which it is causally related and those with which one certainly does not have any causal relationship" [Zawirski 1924: 406–407].

the acting-on – together with these factors – to be a sufficient condition of a respective change occurring. Sometimes it is possible to extract the necessary factors by proper "isolation" of the acting-on area so that this area becomes an isolated system.[23]

Thirdly, in some cases, the factors making up the circumstances of the acting-on themselves rely on the acting-on. Then one of the riddles of causality arises: What are the reasons for choosing this and not another acting on recipient as the cause of changing this recipient? It seems that we are guided by "professional" interests in general. The judge, e.g., from a series of (processes of) acting-on, which together form a sufficient condition of a change in the recipient recognized by the legislative norms as a crime (e.g., of the death of the recipient), is interested in those (processes of) acting-on whose potential agent is the alleged criminal – and treats only them as the causes of the crime, and not e.g., (the processes of) acting-up, whose agents are non-human objects, which he places among the circumstances of the cause-being-acting-on.

Fourthly, formula [1] should not be understood in such a way that the recipient, on which the agent acts in such a way that this acting-on is the cause of the change of recipient itself, apart this acting-on, is never subject to any other change during this period, and, in particular, does not resist the action of the agent or does not act on the agent in a similar or other way. As Zawirski wrote:

> The stone's movement [dropped to the ground] is influenced not only by the earth acting on it [or its attraction force], but also by the stone itself, i.e., the whole earth-stone system [...]. The mere presence of the earth is not enough, because [...] [the earth and its power of attraction] also exist when the stone is lying motionless on the ground.
>
> ZAWIRSKI 1912: 111

In a particular situation – the acting of object y, which from the point of view of the acting-on of agent x is the recipient, is the cause of the change of agent

---

23   See [Kotarbiński 1925], p. 380; [Kiczuk 1977], p. 126. Kotarbińska is pessimistic about this procedure. It is worth quoting her argument: "Natural laws [...] are formulated with reference to an isolated system in a stricter sense, i.e., one in which the resultant of all factors not taken into account in a given law is zero. The condition of the existence of such a system [...] is never met, which means that the predecessors of natural laws [...] are never checked, and therefore those natural laws are never false [...]. The applicability of such laws [...] would consist in the fact that in any case of occurrence of a phenomenon one can choose such a natural law whose predecessor will contain [...] – even as one of the factors – a description of a given phenomenon, [and] moreover ... true sentences [...], whose successor turns into a true sentence" [Kotarbińska 1931: 55–56].

x; thus, the latter becomes the recipient of the acting-up of its recipient y. In everyday life – if both (processes of) acting-on are of the same type but with clearly different strengths, we neglect the weaker of them and treat the whole situation as such, in which simply the acting of x on y is the cause of changes of y.

12   Change

The effect of the agent acting on the recipient is – generally speaking – a change in the recipient (or perhaps more smoothly: a change in the recipient's state). Regarding the concept of change, I share Łukasiewicz's semantic intuitions, which he expressed as follows:

> *A real change is a relation of difference that obtains between two features of the same concrete object which are inherent to it at two different moments of time, and which are species of the same kind.*
> ŁUKASIEWICZ 1906: 50

I would schematically reconstruct Łukasiewicz's – and my – intuitions as follows (I omit the method parameter).

[21] $\bigwedge x \bigwedge t \bigwedge m$ [x at period t on area m changes $\leftrightarrow_{def} \bigvee w_1 \bigvee w_2$ (x at period t on area m loses property w_1 in favor of property w_2)].

To avoid paradoxical consequences – formula [21] should be supplemented with the reservations that properties w_1 and w_2: (a) are of the same type (e.g., they are various colors) and (b) are positive properties (and not only the lack of some positive properties).

Due to the role of the concept of change in the definition of "cause", a comment is still needed regarding time of its occurrence. Formula [21] suggests that change is a momentary and punctual event, but – strictly speaking – one should also take into account the situation in which the loss of one property to another takes place in a certain non-instantaneous period, at the beginning of which the recipient has the first property and finally instead it has a second property – and on some non-point area. Taking these situations into account enables, among other things, different approaches to the temporal relations between the cause (acting-on) and effect (change). We will come back to this matter below. Let us add here only that – in the event of a change occurring in a non-instantaneous period – both the moment of beginning of the change and the moment taking-place of the change may be considered as the effect.

An important reservation – to avoid pointless controversies – is that:

(a)   the cause of the change can be not only acting-on but also interruption
       of acting-on;[24]
(b)   the effect of acting-on may also be interrupting (stopping) some ongo-
       ing change, and thus to some extent change of changing, and preventing
       a change, which without a given acting-on, would occur "naturally".[25]

To the question whether the complete destruction (disappearance) of recipient is its change, and whether the effect-change can be considered the total
arising of something, we will return to in § 19.

13   Temporal Relations Connected with the Relationship of
      Being-Cause-Of

From formula [1], it can be seen that the full characterization of the relationship of being-cause-of requires a determination in which temporal and spatial
relations of cause and effect remain. Here – for shortness – we shall limit ourselves to comments on temporal relations.[26]

    Initially, Łukasiewicz [1906] believed that all three temporal relations are
admissible *a priori*, and how things "actually" are must be checked *a posteriori*.
He wrote about it as follows:

> We cannot maintain that there are no future causes of present phenom-
> ena, because no one has ever sought such causes. And if we note that we
> do not perceive necessary connections in nature either, and that often
> it is only after arduous intellectual work that we can suppose what the

---

24   In this case, Kotarbiński speaks of negative pressure, and he comments on the situation
      as follows: "There can be positive pressure or negative pressure, consisting in releasing
      positive pressure. [...] Negative pressure always has a positive prior pressure as a condi-
      tion" [Kotarbiński 1951: 405].
25   Kotarbiński seems to be thinking about this situation when he writes that the effect
      "may [...] be [...] some kind of persistence, without change, of a certain state of affairs"
      [Kotarbiński 1951: 405].
26   The ancient skeptics attempted to demonstrate the impossibility of the relation of being-
      cause-of by assuming that "every activity takes place in space and that no body can act
      at a place where it is not found, or, in other words, there is no such thing as acting from
      a distance. Since the acting body and the body on which it acts are not in the same place
      but next to each other in space, the acting body would have to, so to speak, go out of itself
      to be able to act on another body, and that, in accordance with the assumption, is impos-
      sible" [Czeżowski 1933: 173]. Unlike the skeptics I do not accept this assumption, and
      thus I also do not accept the conclusions of the reasoning reconstructed by Czeżowski,
      because interaction at a distance is simply a fact.

cause is of a given phenomenon, then we should also admit that a merely general and superficial survey of the data of experience does not justify rejecting this logically possible view.

ŁUKASIEWICZ 1906: 44

Later [1922] Łukasiewicz changed his view on the question of the temporal succession of cause and effect. He expressed this new view as follows:

Fact F occurring at instant s is called the "cause" of fact G occurring at instant t, and fact G the "effect" of fact F, if instant s is earlier than instant t, and if facts F and G are so connected with each other that by means of known laws obtaining between the respective states of affairs it is possible to infer the statement of fact G from the statement of fact F.[27]

ŁUKASIEWICZ 1922: 118

I tend to interpret ... the cause of this change in Łukasiewicz's view as follows.[28] The formulation from the "Analysis and Construction of the Concept of Cause" indicates what the possible temporal relations are in this case; in the text "On determinism" the relation of being-earlier-than is considered as the one which is actually taken into account in (then) science.

In my opinion, whether we allow the being-earlier-than and simultaneity of cause in relation to effect depends solely on whether we consider the moment when the change starts or its occurrence as an effect, and whether we consider the moment when the acting-on begins or ends as a cause; this, of course, only makes sense if the influence of the agent and the change of recipient takes place in non-instantaneous periods.[29]

Because of the temporal relation involved in the relation of being-cause-of, there is a jumble about the so-called final cause. To explain what this jumble is, I need to make an excursion to – perhaps involuntarily – the perpetrator of this jumble, i.e., to Aristotle, or more precisely to his scholastic interpreters.

---

27   As we remember – Kotarbiński also incorporated the being-earlier-than of cause in rela-
      tion to effect into his definition of "cause", cited in § 9.

28   The actual motive for Łukasiewicz's abandonment of the admissibility that the cause is
      later than its effect was the criticism that Zawirski submitted to this view. The conclusion
      of this (justified) criticism appears firm: "The influence of future phenomena on the past,
      placed in the same row with the usual accepted understanding of causality, seems mysti-
      cal" [Zawirski 1912: 113].

29   Borowski puts this case much more radically: "If, in fact, [...] everything that is neces-
      sary and sufficient for the existence of this phenomenon, then past and present as well
      as future phenomena and circumstances should be included in this cause. There is no

As we know, Aristotle used the terms "αἰτία" and "τέλος", translated into English as "cause" and "end" respectively; but I noticed that he used neither the term "αἰτία τελική" nor "final cause"; it was the Latins who introduced the latter term, as *causa finalis*, in the philosophical dictionary. If we trust the English translations of John H. McMahon and Jonathan Barnes, in Aristotle we find two different concepts of – let's say in accordance with the scholastic tradition – a final cause.

Consider any change.

According to the first understanding, the final cause of this change is the final phase of this change.[30] One may wonder if it is best to call the final phase of the change the "cause"; however, it is obvious that the *real* end (goal) of some change in this approach is later than the *causa efficiens* of this change, as scholastics would say.

According to the second understanding – the final cause for a certain change, or more precisely a certain conscious action, is the *intentional* end of the acting person,[31] and this end is obviously prior to the possibly achieved real end.

Therefore, only a final cause understood in the first way could be an example of Łukasiewicz's "future cause of present phenomena". Surely, needless to say, the cause understood in this way has nothing to do with the cause in the sense of my formula [1].

---

avoiding one of these kinds of phenomena, and each type alone is not enough for the existence of a given phenomenon. One can, however, use the word "cause" in a narrower and improper scope, namely either with regard to the emergence of a given phenomenon one can take into account only the preceding phenomena; or with regard to its *duration*, one can take into account only contemporaneous phenomena; or finally with regard to its *ending*, one can take into account only the subsequent phenomena. But there is no real meaning here, because there are no phenomena given to us in experience that do not come forth, do not last for some time, and do not change" [Borowski 1907: 79–80]. I must honestly admit that this reasoning – because of its unclarity – does not convince me.

30 Here are the relevant contexts for Aristotle: "If a thing undergoes a continuous change toward some end, that last stage is actually that for the sake of that end [viz., final cause]" [Aristotle-iva: 331]. "Action for an end is present in things that come to be and are by nature. [...] Where there is an end, all the preceding steps are for the sake of that" [Aristotle -iva: 339–340]. "The final cause is an end; [...] other things [subsist] on account of that. [...] If there is no such thing – I mean that which is last – the final cause will have no existence" [Aristotle -ivb: 38].

31 Here are the relevant contexts for Aristotle: "Action is for the sake of an end. [...] Artificial products are for the sake of an end" [Aristotle -iva: 340]. "One who is possessed of mind always does a thing for some purpose or other (for this is a termination for it), for the end proposed is a termination" [Aristotle ivb: 38]. "The most natural act [of the nutritive soul] is the production of another like itself. [...] That is the goal towards which all things strive,

14   Formal Properties of the Relation of Being-Cause-Of

There is almost universal agreement that the relation of being-cause-of is an irreflexive, asymmetric, and inconsistent relation in the class of phenomena. To avoid misunderstandings, let us point out that: (a) irreflexibility does not, of course, exclude the situation when a certain object is composed, e.g., of two parts and the acting-on of one of them on the other is the cause for the change of the other, and the acting-on (different one!) of the other on the first is the cause of the change of the former; (b) anti-reversibility is a simple consequence of the assumption that the cause is prior to effect; this assumption would not entail the reversibility of the relation of being-cause-of only if we allowed the reversibility of the temporal order; (c) the inconsistency would have to be questioned in the aforementioned doctrine of the interconnectedness of all phenomena; incidentally – the adoption of this doctrine is the background for emerging tendencies to "blur" responsibility for evil done to someone (on the basis of ethics) and for the committing of a crime (on the basis of legislation).

As for the characteristics of the relation of being-cause-of in terms of transitivity and functionality – there is no longer such agreement as in relation to the irreflexibility, anti-reversibility, and inconsistency of this relation.

It is generally believed that the relation of being-cause-of is transitive. In fact, however, this property is possessed only by the relations of being-cause-of which occur in exactly the same circumstances. Let's suppose that some influence a is in circumstances b the cause of change c, consisting in acting-on, while change-acting-on c is in circumstances d the cause of change e. If circumstances b are identical with circumstances d, it can probably be said that the acting-on of a is the *indirect* cause – and therefore briefly: is the cause – of changes e. Most often, however – or maybe just so – circumstances b are not the same as circumstances d; consequently, the acting-on of a – without this identity – cannot be the cause of change e.[32]

---

that for the sake of which they do whatsoever their nature renders possible. The phrase "for the sake of which" is ambiguous; it may mean either (a) the end which to achieve, or (b) the being in whose interest the act is done" [Aristotle -IVc: 661]. Let us add that some of Aristotle's examples of purposeful causes can be interpreted as both real and intentional goals. See, e.g.: "In the sense of the end or that for the sake of which a thing is done, e.g., health is the cause of walking about" [Aristotle -IVa: 332]. This can be both about the fact that strengthening health is the final stage of the walk-filled process, and about the fact that the walk has been taken to strengthen the health of the walker.

32   Therefore, I cannot agree with the statement that the relation of being-cause-of possesses the so-called space-time continuity, in any case understood as Bigaj describes it: "If there is a causal relation between event S_1 occurring in place m_1 and at time t_1 and event S_2

The answer to the question about the uniqueness of the relation of being-cause-of requires the prior introduction of the concept of effect and the settlement of the question of the complexity of both arguments of this relation.

15   Cause and Effect and the Problem of Their Complexity

The semantic connection between "cause" and "effect" can be presented simply if, instead of the formulas "that object x at the moment t and in place m and in circumstances o acts in way K on object y", and "that object y at moment t' and in place m' changes in way l", we give "that p" and "that q" respectively. Then we will have:

[22] ((The fact) that q is the *effect* of (the fact) that p) $\leftrightarrow_{\mathrm{def}}$ ((the fact) that p is the cause of (the fact) that q).

Let us remember that the relation of being-cause-of would be a functional (many-one) relation, if exactly one specific change as an effect was correlated with each specific acting-on; it would be an injective (one-many) relation, if exactly one specific acting-on as a cause was correlated with each specific change; of course, if our relation were a bijective (one-one) relation, it would have to be functional and injective.

If the acting-on of a given type were always simple (indecomposable) and would never require supplementation with additional circumstances to become the cause of a simple change of a given type, then it seems that the relation between being-cause-of would be a functional (many-one) relation, and maybe also an injective (one-many) relation. There are many indications that the idealization conditions mentioned above do not have real concretization: (a process of) acting-on always occurs in non-zero circumstances, with which it jointly becomes the cause of certain changes; these effects-changes are usually (if not exclusively) also plexuses of phenomena.[33]

---

occurring in place m_2 and at time t_2, then at the time interval determined by moments t_1 and t_2, certain intermediary events must occur (which are both the effects of event S_1 and the causes of event S_2), located on a certain path connecting m_1 and m_2" [Bigaj 1996: 218]. It is not known what these intermediary events would be if event S_1 were the acting of agent on recipient, whereas event S_2 would be the change of recipient.

33   Borowski, among others, emphasized the complexity of both causes and effects, believing that ignoring this fact is one of the sources of the difficulties of many conceptions of the cause [Borowski 1907: 72].

Therefore, I would be inclined to believe that the relation of being-cause-of is a mutually ambiguous (many-many) relation.[34]

16   Causal Law

I am inclined to consider the following member of the *definiens* of the definition of "cause" [1] as the *causal law*:

[23] $\bigwedge x \bigwedge y \bigwedge t \bigwedge t' \bigwedge m \bigwedge m'$ (*x* at period *t* on area *m* in circumstances *o* acts in a way *K* on *y* → *y* at period *t'* on area *m'* changes in a way *L*).

I distinguish causal law from *causal statement*. The latter is a sentence which claims that there is a cause-effect relation in a particular case. If – for the sake of simplicity – we omit the temporal parameters, we will have the following sentence as the actual statement:

[24] (The fact) that x_1 in circumstances o_1 acts in way *K* on y_1 is the cause of (the fact) that y_1 changes in way *L*.

Of course, we can state the sentence [24] with an assertion when the causal law of [23] applies, and it is at the same time that:

[25] x_1, y_1 and o_1 are in the range of variability of variables *x*, *y* and *o*.
and

[26] $[(x_1$ acts in circumstances o_1 in way *K* to $y_1) \wedge (y_1$ changes in way *L*$)]$.

17   The Principle of Causality

Does every change have a cause?

The principle of causality says: yes.

If that were the case, then any acting-on which would be the cause of any change would have a cause and *ad infinitum*. So, e.g., gravitational acting would also have a cause. As far as I know, physicists do not ask themselves whether this is the case. Maybe this is because they do not want to do so; but maybe it is because they reject the principle of causality believing, or at least allowing, that some changes (more broadly: states of affairs) have no cause.

---

34   In Kotarbiński, we find the statement that "every event has many causes at every earlier moment" [Kotarbiński 1951: 405]. However, he can only deal with a multitude of factors of favourable circumstances.

18   The Cause-Effect Relation

With similar – not difficult to explicate – simplifications, made in the case of reducing the concept of effect to the concept of cause, the concept of causal connection can be introduced as follows:

[27] (Between (the fact) that p and (the fact) that q, there is a *cause-effect connection*) $\leftrightarrow_{def}$ ((the fact) that p is the cause of (the fact) that q).

Sometimes, there has been a tendency to identify a cause-effect connection with logical (semantic etc.) conditioning. In particular, consideration was given to identifying the cause with a sufficient condition,[35] a necessary condition, or with a sufficient and necessary condition understood as follows:

[28] (The fact) that p is a sufficient condition of (the fact) that q $\leftrightarrow_{def}$ ($p \rightarrow q$).[36]

[29] (The fact) that p is a necessary condition of (the fact) that q $\leftrightarrow_{def}$ ($\sim p \rightarrow \sim q$).

[30] (The fact) that p is both a sufficient and necessary condition of (the fact) that q $\leftrightarrow_{def}$ ($p \leftrightarrow q$).[37]

According to the so-called counterfactual conception of causality, considered by Łukasiewicz and other thinkers, identification of the cause with the necessary condition is expressed by the formula:

[31] (The fact) that p is the cause (the fact) that q $\leftrightarrow_{def}$ if $\sim p$, then it would be that $\sim q$.

I believe that the *definiens* of formula [31] differs from the *definiens* of formula [29] only in the fact that in formula [31], the statement of the occurrence of (the fact) that p is added to the *definiens* of formula [29].

I also think that, on the basis of definition [1], it is clear that none of the above identifications is justified, although it is so that the antecedent of the causal law is a sufficient condition for the successor of this law. Therefore, the statement of the occurrence of such a conditioning between acting-on and change is sometimes used as a criterion for the occurrence of an appropriate causal connection,[38] and the statement of the absence of such conditioning

---

35   I suppose that this (wrong!) identification has led, in some areas of discourse, to the elimination the concept of causality in favour of the concept of determination. This is the case, for example, given to me by Fr. Professor Andrzej Bronk's book [Sławianowski 1969: 31–34]. It is significant that this book is titled *Causality in Quantum Mechanics*, and causality is mentioned only in the indicated short passage; the whole is devoted to the problems of determination in the context of the determinism-indeterminism controversy.
36   Bandrowski, for example, took this solution into account.
37   A detailed analysis of these three concepts is contained in the text [Jadacki 2005].
38   Hempoliński wrote *expressis verbis* about such a criterion [Hempoliński 1989: 263–265].

between any phenomena – as a criterion for the absence of any causal connection between them.

19   The Perpetrator

We will now introduce the concept of perpetrator. It is interesting that it did not appear in English (or in Polish), neither the term for the designation of acting x, nor the term for the designation of x, whose acting on y is the cause of the change of y. Only for x-s that are thinking beings, we have:

[32] $\bigwedge x \bigwedge y \bigwedge o$ [x is in the circumstances o a *perpetrator* of (the fact) that y changes in way $L \leftrightarrow_{def}$ ((the fact) that x in the circumstances o acts in way K on y is the cause (the fact) that y changes in way L)].

It is important – e.g., within legislation – to distinguish between conscious and unconscious, intentional and unintentional perpetration.

On the basis of definition [32], and assuming that in it the matter is about a perpetrator who is a thinking being:

[33] x is a *conscious* perpetrator $\leftrightarrow_{def} x$ is aware that x is the perpetrator.

[34] x is an *unconscious* perpetrator $\leftrightarrow_{def} x$ is unaware that x is the perpetrator.

[35] x is an *intentional* perpetrator of the change of $y \leftrightarrow_{def}$ achieving the change of y is the conscious goal of the conscious acting-on undertaken (consciously?) by x.[39]

[36] x is an *unintentional* perpetrator of the change of $y \leftrightarrow_{def}$ achieving the change of y is not the conscious goal of the conscious acting-on undertaken (consciously?) by x.

It is clear that the perpetrator may be intentional or unintentional, while the unconscious perpetrator is always unintentional.

As we know, in many legislative systems the unintentionality of a crime is a mitigating circumstance, and the unawareness (insanity) even excludes the perpetrator's legal liability.[40]

---

39   It was intentionality that Kotarbiński meant when he emphasized that "the perpetrator of a given event is this and only this person whose free pressure is the cause of this event. [...] This is always about cases in which someone has exerted pressure, so that we can rightly say that he pressed, not that that his body simply pressed due to inertia or gravity, etc." [Kotarbiński 1951: 405].

40   See Kotarbiński's comment: "*The law punishes*, in principle, [...] only *in cases of perpetration or negligence*. However, the perpetrator is not always responsible. In principle, only if he is sane [i.e., such that he has the ability] [...] to understand that he becomes the perpetrator of a forbidden thing or that he neglects to do a commanded thing. From the point

Lawyers are particularly interested in the situation when the change, resulting from the acting-on of the perpetrator, is a crime that deserves punishment. And when does a crime deserve punishment? This is decided by the provisions of the codes (i.e., legal regulations) of the form:

[37] x is a perpetrator of a crime of type $P \to x$ *should* be punished in a manner of type U.[41]

In connection with the concept of perpetration in the area of the law, as a kind of *curiosum*, I will remind you of the distinction between two conceptions of perpetration in this area, at least in one time: subjective and so-called present:

> According to subjective theory, the perpetrator is considered the one who is the author of the crime (he acts *cum animo auctoris* [with perpetrator's will]), [...] even if he did not directly perform the criminal activity related to the features of the crime [...].
>
> The perpetrator in [...] the approach [of subject theory] will be the one whose action corresponds to the verb characterizing the essence of a criminal act (e.g., in the case of murder, the one who commits the act corresponding to "killing").
>
> KUROWSKI (ed.) 1960: 486

In this second conception, it is curious that a linguistic criterion of agency is provided. In a slightly caricatured form, this conception would say that the perpetrator of an act is the one who can be said to have been the perpetrator of that act.

20   God-Creator and Creator

As we know, in three situations, God's actions – at least in terms of *Catholicism* – clash with perpetration: in the act of creation of the world, in the acts of

---

of view of the theory of causal relation, applied to human actions, it remains a question whether negligence cannot be reduced by a roundabout way to cases of perpetration. If this cannot not be done, the unremoved paradox would be that the law considers it appropriate to sometimes punish for what has not been done" [Kotarbiński 1951: 407].

41   Sometimes the legal regulations take the form of declaratives of the kind "Whosoever is the perpetrator of a crime of type P, is subject to a penalty of type U"; however, such sentences are always reducible to formulas of type [36].

creating human souls, and in acts of intervention into the ordinary cause of the history of the world.

The acts of intervention can be successfully described in terms of agency and – ultimately – in terms of cause. Acts of creation can be described in such a way only if they are *not creatio ex nihilo*. In the event that God created the world and souls "out of nothingness", then on the basis of my definitions [1] and [32] the Creator could not be regarded as the perpetrator, because such an act requires an acting on something that already exists before this acting. The act of *creatio ex nihilo* would not have to be about acting-on but about some kind of emergence (emanation) or explosion (as in the Big Bang hypothesis).

It is worth noting that human creators[42] do not create works of which they are perpetrators *ex nihilo* either. An exhaustive description of the creative situation in terms of ordinary perpetration must be put aside for another occasion. Let it suffice here that even a work of art understood as a so-called artistic idea is the result of the artist's psychical acting on his own already existing experience-ideas – acting-on modifying those initial experiences.

It is interesting that there is no conceptual symmetry between the rise and the complete destruction (disappearance) of something. The occurrence of the latter would not, *a priori*, be incompatible with a case where the total destruction of something was caused by some kind of acting on something. The hypothesis already quoted that:

> Matter compressed so that it exceeds critical density collapses – in the result of gravitational attraction, until it becomes a singularity.

This can be interpreted in such a way. This singularity, if I understand this hypothesis correctly, is a so-called black hole, *ergo* nothingness. If someone shows me my mistake, I shall be happy to withdraw this interpretation and agree that there simply is no such thing as complete destruction of something.[43]

---

42   It is an interesting linguistic fact that although the description of the activity of the perpetrator and creator in terms of acting-on is not fundamentally different, the perpetrator is spoken of in a case where the effect of this acting-on is something negative (cf. e.g., the perpetrator of death – and not the creator of death), but about the creator – when this results in something positive (cf. e.g. creator of the novel – not the perpetrator of the novel). Perhaps, moreover, that the "creator" is called someone not because of the change of which he is the perpetrator, but because of the recipients, changed by the acting-on of that perpetrator.

43   Bandrowski, it seems, was of a different opinion. He wrote *expressis verbis*: "We can only talk about causation where something arises, perishes, or changes" [Bandrowski 1903: 54].

By the way, the fact is that *creatio ex nihilo*, or at least creation of the world out of nothingness, is one of the dogmas of Catholicism, and as dogma has been confirmed by the Fourth Lateran Council and the Second Vatican Council. This dogma is justified *ad auctoritate* and the authority in this case is Saint Theophilus of Antioch. Let me remind his statement on the subject, usually quoted in the context of this dogma:

> What marvel had it been if God had made the world out of subject matter? For an artist, if he receives materials from anyone, he makes of it what he pleases; but the power of God is manifested in this, that out of nothing He makes what He chooses.
>
> THEOPHILUS -II: 22

I leave out that it is not the case what St. Theophilus claims, that a man "if he receives materials from anyone, he makes of it what he pleases". Does marvelness have to be granted to everything done by the God of Catholicism? Well, I do not think that if God had not created the world *ex nihilo*, Catholic ethics would lose its binding force.

I may be wrong, but it is Catholic ethics that is the quintessence of Catholicism.

Bibliography

Ajdukiewicz, Kazimierz (1938). *Propedeutyka filozofii* [Introduction to Philosophy]. Wrocław-Warszawa 1948: Książnica-Atlas.

Ajdukiewicz, Kazimierz (1965). *Pragmatic Logic*. Warszawa: PWN.

Aristotle -IVa. *Physics*. [In:] [Aristotle 1984], pp. 315–446.

Aristotle -IVb. *The Metaphysics*. Mineola 2007: Dover Publications, Inc.

Aristotle -IVc. *On the Soul*. [In:] [Aristotle 1984], pp. 641–692.

Aristotle (1984). *Complete Works*. Vol. I. Princeton 1995: Princeton University Press.

Bandrowski, Bronisław (1903). O metodach badania indukcyjnego [About Methods of Inductive Research]. [In:] [Bandrowski], pp. 29–63.

Bandrowski, Bronisław (2015). *Logika, analiza mowy, psychologia. Pisma zebrane* [Logic, Analysis of Speech, Psychology. Collected Writings]. Warszawa: Wydawnictwo Naukowe *Semper*.

Bigaj, Tomasz (1996). Związek przyczynowy [Causal Connection]. [In:] [Krajewski (ed.) 1996], p. 218.

Bocheński, Józef M. (1935). The Problem of Causality in Neo-scholastics. In this volume: pp. 177–190.

Borowski, Marian (1907). The Criticism of the Concept of Causation. In this volume: pp. 67–81.

Brożek, Anna & Jadacki, Jacek (2006). *Ethica: terra ubi leones.* Skąd się biorą rozbieżności w naszych ocenach etycznych [Where Do the Differences in Our Ethical Assessments Come from?]. *Przegląd Humanistyczny* t. L, nr 5–6, s. 163–169.

Brożek, Anna & Jadacki, Jacek (2008). Intuicje modalne [Modal Intuitions]. *Roczniki Filozoficzne* t. LVI (2008), nr 1, s. 39–59.

Czeżowski, Tadeusz (1933). *How Did the Problem of Causality Arise?* In this volume: pp. 139–176.

Hempoliński, Michał (1989). *Filozofia współczesna. Wprowadzenie do zagadnień i kierunków* [Contemporary Philosophy. Introduction to Problems and Directions]. Warszawa: PWN.

Hilgard, Ernest Ropiequet (1953). *Introduction to Psychology.* New York 1967: Harcourt, Brace & World.

Ingarden, Roman (1974). *Spór o istnienie świata.* T. III. *O strukturze przyczynowej realnego świata* [The Controversy over the Existence of the World. Vol. III. On the Causal Structure of the Real World]. Warszawa 1981: PWN.

Jadacki, Jacek (2003). *Człowiek i jego świat. Propedeutyka filozofii* [Man and His World. Introduction to Philosophy]. Warszawa: Wydawnictwo SWPS *Academica.*

Jadacki, Jacek (2005). O relacjach kauzalnych [On Causal Relations]. [In:] [Jadacki 2010], pp. 25–29.

Jadacki, Jacek (2010). *Metodologia i semiotyka. Idee – metody – problemy* [Methodology and Semiotics. Ideas – Methods - Problems]. Warszawa: Wydawnictwo Naukowe *Semper.*

Jadacki, Jacek & Markiewicz, Barbara (red.) (1993). *... A mądrości zło nie przemoże* [And Evil Cannot Prevail over Wisdom]. Warszawa: Wydawnictwo PTF.

Kiczuk, Stanisław (1977). Związek przyczynowy w fizyce współczesnej a logika przyczynowości [Causal Connection in Contemporary Physics and the Logic of Causality]. *Roczniki Filozoficzne* t. XXV, z. 3, s. 119–134.

Kotarbińska, Janina (1931). O tzw. konieczności związków przyczynowych [On the So-Called Necessity of Causal Connections]. [In:] [Kotarbińska 1990], pp. 19–58.

Kotarbińska, Janina (1990). *Z zagadnień teorii nauki i teorii języka* [From the Questions of the Theory of Science and the Theory of Language]. Warszawa: PWN.

Kotarbiński, Tadeusz (1925). O stosunku sprawstwa [On the Relation of Perpetration]. [In:] [Kotarbiński 1957], pp. 365–386.

Kotarbiński, Tadeusz (1951). Przyczynowość w myśleniu prawniczym [Causality in Legal Thought]. [In:] [Kotarbiński 1993], pp. 403–407.

Kotarbiński, Tadeusz (1957). *Wybór pism.* T. I. *Myśli o działaniu* [Selected Writings. Vol. I. Thoughts about acting]. Warszawa: PWN.

Kotarbiński, Tadeusz (1993). *Dzieła wszystkie. Ontologia, teoria poznania i metodologia nauk* [Collected Writings. Ontology, the Theory of Cognition, and the Methodology of Science]. Wrocław: Ossolineum.

Krajewski, Władysław (ed.) (1998). *Słownik pojęć filozoficznych* [Dictionary of Philosophical Concepts]. Warszawa: Wydawnictwo Naukowe *Scholar*.

Kurowski, Leon (ed.) (1960). *Mała encyklopedia prawa* [A Small Encyclopedia of Law]. Warszawa: PWN.

Łukasiewicz, Jan (1906). Analysis and Construction of the Concept of Cause. In this volume, pp. 3–66.

Łukasiewicz, Jan (1922). On Determinism [In:] [Łukasiewicz 1970], pp. 110–128.

Łukasiewicz, Jan (1970). *Selected Works*. Amsterdam-London & Warszawa: North-Holland Publishing Company & PWN.

Pański, Antoni (1934). Uwagi o zagadnieniu definicji "związku przyczynowego" [Remarks on the Problem of the Definition of "Causal Connection"]. [In:] [Jadacki & Markiewicz (eds.) 1993], pp. 127–135.

Reykowski, Janusz (1992). Motywacja [Motivation]. [In:] [Tomaszewski (ed.) 1992], pp. 59–188.

Sławianowski, Jan Jerzy (1969). *Przyczynowość w mechanice kwantowej* [Causality in Quantum Mechanics]. Warszawa: *Wiedza Powszechna*.

Tkaczyk, Marcin (2015). *Futura contingentia*. Lublin: Wydawnictwo KUL.

Theophilus -II. *The Three Books* [...] *to Autolycus on the Christian Religion*. London 1860: Joseph Maters and Co.

Tomaszewski, Tadeusz (ed.) (1992). *Psychologia ogólna* [General Psychology]. Warszawa: Wydawnictwo Naukowe PWN.

Zawirski, Zygmunt (1912). Causality and Functional Relation. A Study in the Theory of Cognition. In this volume: pp. 82–138.

Zawirski, Zygmunt (1924). Związek zasady przyczynowości z zasadą względności [Connection of the Principle of Causality and the Principle of Relativity]. *Kwartalnik Filozoficzny* vol. ii, No. 4, pp. 397–419.

Index of Names

Printed in the United States
by Baker & Taylor Publisher Services